Greetings in the Lord

Early Christians and the Oxyrhynchus Papyri

HARVARD THEOLOGICAL STUDIES
60

CAMBRIDGE, MASSACHUSETTS

Greetings in the Lord

Early Christians and the Oxyrhynchus Papyri

AnneMarie Luijendijk

DISTRIBUTED BY

HARVARD UNIVERSITY PRESS

FOR

HARVARD THEOLOGICAL STUDIES

HARVARD DIVINITY SCHOOL

Greetings in the Lord
Early Christians and the Oxyrhynchus Papyri

Harvard Theological Studies 60

The foreign language fonts (New Jerusalem, Symbol GreekII, and Coptic LS) and transliteration fonts used in this book are available from Linguist's Software, Inc., PO Box 580, Edmonds, WA 98020-0580; tel: (425) 775-1130. Website: www.linguistsoftware.com

Luijendijk, AnneMarie.
Greetings in the Lord : early Christians and the Oxyrhynchus papyri / AnneMarie Luijendijk.
p. cm. -- (Harvard theological studies ; 60)
Includes bibliographical references and index.
Summary: "Investigates private letters and official documents found at the ancient Egyptian city of Oxyrhynchus pertaining to Christians in the pre-Constantinian era, taking the reader to the marketplace, church, and court room. Analyzes scribal habits, discovers the city's first known bishop and examines his work, and finds evidence of Christian resistance during times of persecution"--Provided by publisher.
ISBN 978-0-674-02595-0 (alk. paper)
1. Bahnasa (Egypt)--Church history. 2. Church history--Primitive and early church, ca. 30-600. 3. Oxyrhynchus papyri. 4. Manuscripts, Greek (Papyri)--Egypt--Bahnasa. I. Title.
BR1380.L85 2008
276.2'201--dc22

2008046584

To Jan Willem van der Werff

with love

Table of Contents

Part Two: Papa Sotas, Bishop of Oxyrhynchus

Part Three: Legal Matters and Government Dealings

Acknowledgments

This book chronicles, figuratively speaking, my journey to the ancient Egyptian city of Oxyrhynchus. On my travels I encountered many different practices of early Christians and others, such as extending hospitality, networking, name-giving, scribal practices, resistance against persecution, church financing, government bureaucracy and book-production. I also had amazing travel companions—colleagues, friends and family members—who helped me navigate the ancient and modern world and whom I am pleased to thank here.

Tjitze Baarda accompanied me during the first stretch and has remained my "hooggeleerde vriend." As my advisor at the Vrije Universiteit in Amsterdam, he suggested that I write my ThM thesis on an Oxyrhynchus fragment with the beginning of the Gospel of Thomas in Greek (P.Oxy. 4.654). Working on that piece, I became fascinated with the inhabitants of Oxyrhynchus.

At Harvard Divinity School, I chose the early Christians in the Oxyrhynchus papyri as the subject of my dissertation (May 2005), of which this book is a revised and expanded version. On the long road to Oxyrhynchus, the conversations with my advisor Karen King were oases of wonderful academic exchange. Every time we met to discuss my research, I continued my journey inspired and with a clearer vision. An eminent guide on this road, Roger Bagnall shared his phenomenal knowledge of the field of papyrology and contributed generously to many topics discussed in this book. I also enjoyed his hospitality during my visits to the papyrology seminar in New York City. With François Bovon I could share a passion for manuscripts. He has been an unfailing reader and interlocutor on ideas of my work as they developed.

Several people read the manuscript of this book. Laura Nasrallah generously gave her time and made valuable suggestions for improvement. Her guidance sustains me in countless ways. Margot Stevenson offered many important and concrete suggestions that helped me turn my dissertation into a book. Charles Watkinson provided helpful editorial insights. With his sharp eye for language and consistency, Eduard Iricinschi was a meticulous proofreader. Peter Brown read chapters 4 and 5 about bishop Sotas and generously shares his vast knowledge of the world of late antiquity. Graeme Clarke offered helpful feedback on chapter 7.

On actual travels through Greece and Turkey, Helmut Koester taught me much about the material remains of the ancient Mediterranean and early Christian texts. Ann Hanson and Hélène Cuvigny, together with Adam Bülow-Jacobsen and Ruth Duttenhöfer, guided me deeper into the fascinating world of papyrology during the first papyrological summer school at Yale University in the summer of 2003.

Mark Kurtz consistently helped out with good advice and active support. I remember with fondness our conversations on the topics discussed in this book. Laura Beth Bugg and Elizabeth Penland were delightful partners in our dissertation group and I benefited much from their intellectual and creative input. Melanie Johnson-DeBaufre has generously advised and encouraged me from the start of this project and through the stages of academic life.

At Princeton University, I have found a stimulating and wonderful interdisciplinary intellectual environment. I thank everyone in the Department of Religion for their collegiality and support, especially my colleagues in Religions of Late Antiquity, Martha Himmelfarb, Elaine Pagels and Peter Schäfer, and our staff Lorraine Fuhrmann, Kerry Smith, Patricia Bogdziewicz, and Mary Kay Bodnar. I also gratefully acknowledge the encouragement of my colleagues in Judaic Studies and Hellenic Studies, notably Dimitri Gondicas.

Many others helped and encouraged me along the way in innumerable ways. I mention here gratefully Ellen Aitken, Marianne Bonz, Denise Buell, Raffaella Cribiore, Eldon Epp, Ken Fisher, Annewies van den Hoek, Amy Hustad, Nicole Kelley, Beverly Kienzle, Maria Mavroudi, Elisabeth Schüssler Fiorenza, Sasha and Chris Wyckoff and the members of the advanced New Testament seminar at Harvard Divinity School.

For the *amicitia papyrologorum*, I thank Bart van Beek, Malcolm Choat, Nikolaos Gonis, Dirk Obbink, Peter Parsons, Patricia Spencer, and the members of the papyrology seminar in New York City. Guido Bastianini, Jean-Luc Fournet, Rosario Pintaudi, and Mervet Seif el-Din kindly sent me images of papyri and allowed me to reproduce them in this book.

I am deeply thankful for the financial support of fellowships that allowed me to complete this research, especially the Charlotte W. Newcombe Doctoral Dissertation Fellowship, the Clarence G. Campbell Scholarship and the

Dean's Dissertation Fellowship at Harvard Divinity School. The Dean of the Faculty of Princeton University funded a trip to London and Oxford, where I could examine in person many of the papyri discussed here.

At Harvard Theological Studies, I thank Richard Jude Thompson for making my writing stronger, Anne Browder for her accuracy in editing, and Dr. Margaret Studier, managing editor, for her perseverance and patience in seeing this project through. Michael Ferreira prepared the index.

In the end mistakes and shortcomings remain mine.

My parents, Gerie and Ary Luijendijk-Hordijk have supported me every step of the way and I treasure the time we spend together. I thank my sister Erica Luijendijk for the generosity of her time and love. Kees and Erik, my sons, have tolerated their mother spending her time with the Oxyrhynchites. Their sweetness and abundant happiness give me great joy every day. My sweetest, funniest, and most faithful travel companion has been my husband, Jan Willem van der Werff. I look forward to many more wonderful adventures together and dedicate this book to him with all my love!

Chapter 7 appeared in a different version as "Papyri from the Great Persecution: Roman and Christian perspectives" in the *Journal of Early Christian Studies* 16 (2008) 341–69, with thanks to the John Hopkins University Press for permission to incorporate the chapter in this book.

Abbreviations

Abbreviations for editions of papyri, ostraca, and tablets follow John F. Oates et al., eds. *Checklist of Editions of Greek and Latin Papyri, Ostraca and Tablets*. 5th ed. BASP Supplement 9, 2001. The online and expanded edition is available at http://scriptorium.lib.duke.edu/papyrus/texts/clist.html. Papyrological editions are listed with abbreviation, then the volume number, followed by a stop and the papyrus number. The page number in the edition follows after a comma. Thus P.Oxy. 12.1492, 249 indicates The Oxyrhynchus Papyri, volume 12, number 1492, page 249. Journals and standard works follow the abbreviations of Patrick H. Alexander et al., eds. *The SBL Handbook of Style*. Peabody, Mass: Hendrickson, 1999.

Aeg	*Aegyptus*
ABD	*Anchor Bible Dictionary*. Edited by D. N. Freedman. 6 vols. New York, 1992
ABRL	Anchor Bible Reference Library
AJP	*American Journal of Philology*
AnBib	Analecta biblica
AnBoll	Analecta Bollandiana
ANRW	*Aufstieg und Niedergang der römischen Welt: Geschichte und Kultur Roms im Spiegel der neueren Forschung*. Edited by H. Temporini and W. Haase. Berlin, 1972–
APF	*Archiv für Papyrusforschung*
ASP	American Studies in Papryology
BALAC	Bulletin d'ancienne littérature et d'archéologie chrétienne
BASP	*Bulletin of the American Society of Papyrologists*

BASPSup	*Bulletin of the American Society of Papyrologists: Supplement*
BETL	Bibliotheca ephemeridum theologicarum lovaniensium
BHT	Beiträge zur historischen Theologie
BIFAO	*Bulletin de l'Institut français d'archéologie orientale*
BSAA	*Bulletin de la Société archéologique d' Alexandrie*
CClCr	*Civiltà classica e cristiana*
CCSL	Corpus Christianorum series latina
ChrEg	*Chronique d'Égypte*
CP	*Classical Philology*
CPJ	*Corpus papyrorum judaicorum*. Edited by V. Tcherikover. 3 vols. Cambridge, 1957–1964
Cribiore	Raffaella Cribiore. *Writing, Teachers, and Students in Graeco-Roman Egypt*. ASP 36. Atlanta, Ga: Scholars, 1996
DACL	*Dictionnaire d'archéologie chrétienne et de liturgie*. Edited by F. Cabrol. 15 vols. Paris, 1907–1953
DDBDP	Duke Databank of Documentary Papyri http://www.perseus.tufts.edu/Texts/papyri.html
EMC	Echos du Monde classique / Classical Views
GCS	Die griechische christliche Schriftsteller der ersten Jahrhunderte
HGV	Hauptregister of the Heidelberger Gesamtverzeichnis der griechischen Papyrusurkunden Ägyptens http://www.rzuser.uni-heidelberg.de/~gv0/gvz.html
HSCP	*Harvard Studies in Classical Philology*
HTR	*Harvard Theological Review*
JAC	*Jahrbuch für Antike und Christentum*
JBL	*Journal of Biblical Literature*
JdI	*Jahrbuch des deutschen archäologischen Instituts*
JEA	*Journal of Egyptian Archaeology*
JJP	*Journal of Juristic Papyrology*
JJS	*Journal of Jewish Studies*

JRA	*Journal of Roman Archaeology*
JRS	*Journal of Roman Studies*
JTS	*Journal of Theological Studies*
Lampe	G. W. H. Lampe. *A Patristic Greek Lexicon*. Oxford: Clarendon, 1961–1968
LEC	Library of Early Christianity
LCL	Loeb Classical Library
LDAB	Leuven Database of Ancient Books http://www.trismegistos.org/ldab/
MPER	Mitteilungen aus der Papyrussammlung der Nationalbibliothek in Wien. Papyrus Erzherzog Rainer
NewDocs	*New Documents Illustrating Early Christianity*
NovTSup	Novum Testamentum Supplements
NTS	*New Testament Studies*
NPNF2	*The Nicene and Post-Nicene Fathers. Series 2*
PBR	*Patristic and Byzantine Revue*
PTS	Patristische Texte und Studien
REA	*Revue des études anciennes*
RGRW	Religions in the Graeco-Roman World
SAOC	Studies in Ancient Oriental Civilization
SBLDS	Society of Biblical Literature Dissertation Series
SBLSBS	Society of Biblical Literature Sources for Biblical Study
SC	Sources chrétiennes
SFMA	Studien zu Fundmünzen der Antike
SPap	*Studia Papyrologica*
TAPA	Transactions of the American Philological Association
TSAJ	Texte und Studien zum antiken Judentum
TU	Texte und Untersuchungen
van Haelst	Joseph van Haelst. *Catalogue des papyrus littéraires juifs et chrétiens*. Papyrologie 1. Paris: Publications de la Sorbonne, 1976

VC	*Vigiliae christianae*
VT	*Vetus Testamentum*
WO	*Die Welt des Orients*
WS	*Wiener Studien*
ZNTW	*Zeitschrift für die neutestamentliche Wissenschaft und die Kunde der älteren Kirche*
ZPE	*Zeitschrift für Papyrologie und Epigraphik*

A Note on Translations

Translations are mine, unless indicated otherwise.

In the transcription of the papyri the following sigla from the so-called Leiden system occur:[*]

[ ]	lacuna in the papyrus
[αβγδ]	text in lacuna reconstructed by the editor
< >	omission in the original
[[ ]]	deletion in the original
( )	resolution of a symbol or abbreviation
{ }	cancellation by the editor of the text
` ´	cancellation by the editor of the text
α̣β̣γ̣δ̣	uncertain letters
....	illegible letters
vac.	*vacat*: empty space in the papyrus

[*] Adapted from Pestman, *New Papyrological Primer*, 319, see also 14–15.

CHAPTER 1

Destination Oxyrhynchus: Historical Detective Work in the Footsteps of Monks and Papyrologists

Greetings in the Lord! Early Christians penned this salutation at the opening of their letters to family and fellow Christians. These letters and other documents pertaining to Christians and Christianity from the site of the ancient Egyptian city Oxyrhynchus form the topic of this book.

My fascination with this subject began some years ago while working on a Greek fragment of the *Gospel of Thomas* (P.Oxy. 4.654) from Oxyrhynchus. Upon checking the first edition of that manuscript, I discovered—and fell in love with—the grey volumes entitled *The Oxyrhynchus Papyri*. These volumes overflow with the literary and documentary textual remains from the inhabitants of this city. Browsing through the volumes, I became curious about the people who had owned and read these papyri and whose lives constitute their subject matter. The papyri from Oxyrhynchus opened up for me the religious and cultural horizon of Christians of a distant time and distinct place. This book details my quest to identify Christians in the papyrus documents from Oxyrhynchus of the pre-Constantinian era. Detecting those Christians can at times make for tedious work, but the resulting encounters have proved refreshing and worthwhile. In order to find early Christians, we embark on a tour through Oxyrhynchus. We linger at the marketplace, visit a church, and eavesdrop at the courthouse.

In the study of documentary papyri, we take on an inherently indiscreet task.[1]

[1] Verbeeck, for instance, calls the scholarly discipline of papyrology "de indiskrete papyrologische wetenschap" ("Dioskoros," in *Familiearchieven* [ed. Pestman] 151).

Throughout this book we shall read texts that no one originally intended for our eyes: a private letter from a husband to his wife, a letter from a woman to a clergy member, a fundraising letter from a bishop to a potential donor, and an official summons for a Christian man. The documents pertaining to early Christians and Christianity that I have selected for this study represent several documentary genres and a range of social locations. Collectively, these documents nuance our perspective on early Christianity and, sometimes, tickle our imagination. As historical detective work, this book investigates the situations and business of people from different walks of life and specifically questions their identity as Christians.[2] This study provides glimpses of life for Christians in three spheres: 1) in the public sphere through forms of address and scribal habits; 2) in the sphere of the emerging church, which by this time, as we shall see, has developed strong networks and a somewhat centralized administration; and 3) in the political sphere, where hints of persecution are felt.

In order to conduct a thorough investigation and to draw a multidimensioned picture of the persons of interest, our historical detective work entails making exhaustive and ample use of all relevant sources. We scrutinize the content of the papyrological documents by means of literary and textual analysis. We discuss philological and exegetical puzzles alongside questions concerning the genre of the document and its social setting. We examine the material culture of these documents as well because characteristics such as writing material and features of handwriting yield historical information. Having analyzed the papyrological documents in their literary-textual and material dimensions, we then propose hypotheses and historical reconstructions about individual situations that these documents reflect. Our detective work, at this stage, involves comparisons and contrasts, as we put the documentary papyri into dialogue with other literary and historical sources pertaining to the subject

[2] I agree with Wipszycka that this is a tough task for such an early period, which does not always lead to grand vistas in comparison with literary texts. She wrote: "Je suis . . . obligée d'avouer mélancoliquement que, contrairement à ce qu'on pourrait imaginer, les renseignements fournis par les papyrus documentaires au sujet de l'Église du IIIe siècle et des premières décennies du IVe ne sont pas assez nombreux ni assez détaillés pour constituer une contrepartie adéquate par rapport aux témoignages des textes littéraires" ("Les papyrus documentaires," in *Atti del XXII Congresso* [ed. Andorlini] 2:1307). Nevertheless, I value especially the glimpses that the papyri offer against the backdrop of our knowledge of the period from literary texts, and the opportunity to meet otherwise unknown individuals, if only in passing.

matter and period. Bridging two disciplines, papyrology and early Christian historiography, our investigations aim to bring to the forefront previously unheard voices of early Christian women and men.

Just as literary texts have their biases, so do papyri. In general the activities of the propertied classes make up the written record, and specifically, they constitute the kinds of documents and social transactions that we study here. Property registration, acquisition of land, and marriage presuppose a certain level of material well-being, which excluded many people in antiquity (if not the majority).[3] Private letters also often belong to wealthier people because they had more access to education. Moreover, travel itself, the very reason that generated the writing of letters to one's family and relations, required money. People who engaged in travels had more occasion to write letters. Papyrus documents, moreover, record matters that necessitate writing; people do not write down everyday conversations and activities in mundane situations, such as during a meal or at a shop, and consequently such everyday activities leave little trace in the papyrological record.

The *Historia Monachorum in Aegypto*

We begin our travels to Oxyrhynchus in the company of a small group of Palestinian monks, who were traveling through Egypt at the end of the fourth century in order to meet their Egyptian counterparts.[4] In their travelogue, now known as the *Historia monachorum in Aegypto*,[5] the author describes their stay at Oxyrhynchus as follows:

[3] See also Bagnall, *Reading Papyri*, 13–16.

[4] According to Ward in 394–395 C.E. (*Lives of the Desert Fathers*, 5).

[5] Edition: Festugière, *Historia monachorum in Aegypto*. See also Schulz-Flügel, *Tyrannius Rufinus, Historia monachorum*. Recent discussions of this work are, e.g., Bammel, "Problems of the Historia Monachorum," *JTS* 47 (1996) 92–104; Baumeister, "Historia Monachorum in Aegypto," in *Coptic Studies on the Threshold* (ed. Immerzeel and van der Vliet) 1:269–80; Frank, "Miracles, Monks, and Monuments," in *Pilgrimage and Holy Space* (ed. Frankfurter) 483–505. The author of this work is unknown. The Prologue informs us that he was a member of the Mount of Olives Monastery in Jerusalem. Rufinus or Palladius have been mentioned as possible authors. Rufinus may have translated the work into Latin; as such it gained a large popularity. The association with Palladius is through his *Lausiac History*. See Frank, "Miracles, Monks, and Monuments," 484–85 n. 9; and Bammel on Rufinus and the Greek and Latin text of the work ("Problems of the Historia Monachorum," 96–97).

> 1) We also went to Oxyrhynchus, a city in the Thebaid. It is impossible to do justice to the marvels which we saw there. For the city is so full of monasteries that the very walls resound with the voices of monks. Other monasteries encircle it outside, so that the outer city forms another town alongside the inner. 2) The temples and capitols of the city were bursting with monks; every quarter of the city was inhabited by them. 3) Indeed, since the city is large, it has twelve churches where the people assemble. As for the monks, they have their own oratories in each monastery. The monks were almost in a majority over the secular inhabitants. 4) In fact there are said to be five thousand monks within the walls and as many again outside, and there is no hour of the day or night when they do not offer acts of worship to God. Moreover, not one of the city's inhabitants is a heretic or a pagan. On the contrary, all the citizens as a body are believers and catechumens, so that the bishop is able to bless the people publicly in the street. 5) The chief officials and magistrates of the city, who distributed largesse to the common people, had watchmen posted at the gates and entrances, so that if some needy stranger should appear, he would be taken to them and receive victuals for his sustenance. And what can one say about the piety of the common people, who when they saw us strangers crossing the agora approached us as if we were angels? How can one convey an adequate idea of the throngs of monks and nuns past counting? 6) However, as far as we could ascertain from the holy bishop of that place, we would say that he had under his jurisdiction ten thousand monks and twenty thousand nuns. It is beyond my power to describe their hospitality and their love for us. In fact each of us had our cloaks rent apart by people pulling us to make us go and stay with them. 7) We saw there many great fathers who possessed various charisms, some in their speech, some in their manner of life, and others in the wonders and signs which they performed.[6]

This account describes Oxyrhynchus as a thoroughly Christian city—and an exclusively orthodox one at that, for it has "no heretics and pagans," and the

[6] 1) Παρεγενόμεθα δὲ καὶ εἰς Ὀξύρυγχον πόλιν τινὰ τῆς Θηβαΐδος, ἧς οὐκ ἔστιν εἰπεῖν κατ' ἀξίαν τὰ θαύματα. γέμει γὰρ οὕτως ἔνδοθεν μοναστηρίων, ὡς τά τείχη ἐξηχεῖσθαι ὑπ' αὐτῶν τῶν μοναχῶν, περιέχεται δὲ ἔξωθεν μοναστηρίοις ἑτέροις, ὡς ἄλλην εἶναι παρ' αὐτὴν τὴν ἔξω πόλιν. 2) ἔγεμον δὲ τῆς πόλεως οἱ ναοὶ καὶ τὰ καπετώλια τῶν μοναχῶν καὶ κατὰ πᾶν μέρος τῆς πόλεως οἱ μοναχοὶ ᾤκουν. 3) δεκαδύο γάρ εἰσιν ἐν αὐτῇ ἐκκλησίαι μεγίστης οὔσης τῆς πόλεως, ἐν αἷς οἱ ὄχλοι συνάγονται· τὰ γὰρ τῶν μοναχῶν εὐκτήρια καθ' ἕκαστον ἦν μοναστήριον. καὶ σχεδὸν πλείους ἦσαν οἱ μοναχοὶ ὑπὲρ τοὺς κοσμικοὺς πολίτας κατὰ τὰς εἰσόδους τῆς πόλεως καὶ ἐν τοῖς πύργοις τῶν πυλῶν καταμένοντες. 4) πεντακισχίλιοι γὰρ μοναχοὶ ἐλέγοντο εἶναι ἔνδοθεν, τοσοῦτοι δ' ἄλλοι ἔξωθεν αὐτὴν

narrative does not even mention Jews.[7] According to its author, the inhabitants consist for the largest part of nuns and monks; the city's monasteries overflow, and many monastics do "signs and wonders" (section 7) in an allusion to the work of the apostles. The virtue of the common people becomes evident from their great hospitality to strangers. Despite this ideal situation in Oxyrhynchus, the travelers from the *Historia monachorum* decided to continue their journey through Egypt and declined to enjoy the hospitality so generously offered to them.[8] I suggest, however, that we accept the invitation and stay to explore the city.[9]

If not for the papyri that we will examine below, this short chapter in the *Historia monachorum* would constitute our main impression of Christianity

περιέχοντες, καὶ οὐκ ἦν ὥρα ἡμερινὴ οὐδὲ νυκτερινὴ ἐν ᾗ τὰς λατρείας οὐκ ἐπετέλουν θεῷ· ἀλλὰ γὰρ οὐδεὶς ἦν οἰκήτωρ αἱρετικὸς οὐδὲ ἐθνικὸς ἐν τῇ πόλει, ἀλλὰ πάντες ὁμοῦ οἱ πολῖται πιστοὶ καὶ κατηχούμενοι, ὡς δύνασθαι δοῦναι τὸν ἐπίσκοπον ἐν τῇ πλατείᾳ εἰρήνην τῷ λαῷ. 5) οἱ δὲ στρατηγοὶ αὐτῶν καὶ οἱ ἄρχοντες οἱ τὰς φιλοτιμίας τοῖς δήμοις παρέχοντες κατὰ τὰς πύλας καὶ τὰς εἰσόδους σκοποὺς ἔστησαν πρὸς τὸ εἰ ξένος που πενόμενος φανείη ἀχθῆναι πρὸς αὐτοὺς ληψόμενον πρὸς παραμυθίαν ἀναλώματα. καὶ τί ἄν τις εἴποι τὴν εὐλάβειαν τῶν δήμων ὁρώντων ἡμᾶς τοὺς ξένους διὰ τῆς ἀγορᾶς παριόντας καὶ ὥσπερ ἀγγέλοις ἡμῖν προσιόντων; τί δὲ τὸ πλῆθος ἐξείποι τις τῶν μοναχῶν καὶ παρθένων ἀναριθμήτου ὄντος; 6) πλὴν ὅσον παρὰ τοῦ ἐκεῖ ἁγίου ἐπισκόπου ἠκριβευσάμεθα ἐδηλώσαμεν, μυρίους μὲν μοναχοὺς ὑπ' αὐτόν, δισμυρίας δὲ παρθένους ἔχοντος. τὴν δὲ φιλοξενίαν αὐτῶν καὶ τὴν ἀγάπην οἵαν καὶ εἶχον, ἐμὲ οὐχ οἷόν τε ἐξειπεῖν· διεσπᾶτο γὰρ ἡμῶν τὰ πάλλια ἑκατέρων ἡμᾶς πρὸς ἑαυτοὺς ἀνθελκόντων· 7) Καὶ εἴδομεν ἐκεῖ πολλοὺς καὶ μεγάλους πατέρας διάφορα χαρίσματα ἔχοντας, τοὺς μὲν ἐν λόγῳ, τοὺς δὲ ἐν πολιτείᾳ, τοὺς δὲ ἐν δυνάμεσι καὶ σημείοις. Greek text: Festugière, *Historia monachorum in Aegypto* 5.1–7, 41–43; translated by Norman Russell, "V On Oxyrhynchus," in *The Lives of the Desert Fathers*, 67.

[7] See below for a discussion of Jews at Oxyrhynchus.

[8] Leaving behind city life, they visited a father called Theon in the desert not far from Oxyrhynchus on their next stop. Geographically, the order of the travels does not always make sense, as scholars such as Butler have pointed out (Palladius, *Lausiac History* [ed. Butler] 1.201–2). However, as Frank observes: "If one accepts that the *History of the Monks* contains descriptions of an actual journey, there is little to be gained from the critics who point to geographical or other errors. This anthology is a travel book and not a travel guide. . . . One doubts, then, that readers of the *History of the Monks* would have been perturbed to discover that Oxyrhynchus is improperly placed in the geographical sequence of chapters" (Frank, "Miracles, Monks, and Monuments," 489).

[9] The story in the *Historia monachorum* stands in contrast to a hagiographical story about a monk from the region called Apa Aphou (ca. 400 C.E.). Aphou visits Oxyrhynchus city once a year to hear the Easter letter read in church. But since he dresses as a farmer, no one pays attention to him; no guards at the city gate offer help or hospitality. See Drioton, "La discussion d'un moine," *ROC* 20 (1915–1917) 92–100 and 113–28.

in Oxyrhynchus.[10] The picture of Oxyrhynchus painted in the *Historia monachorum*, however, appears highly idealized, and the numbers are of only rhetorical significance.[11] Yet, as we shall see, scholars have read the Christian texts found at the site of Oxyrhynchus through the lens of the *Historia monachorum*[12] rather than apply an optical corrective to its idealized perspective.

"The Kind of Papyri Which We Most Desired to Find"[13]

On 20 December 1896, some fifteen hundred years after the monks of the *Historia monachorum* departed Oxyrhynchus, two young British classicists, Bernard P. Grenfell and Arthur S. Hunt, arrived at Al-Bahnasa, a hamlet on the edge of Egypt's western desert and site of the ancient city of Oxyrhynchus.[14] Little did they know that they would discover on the city's garbage heaps one of the richest repositories of manuscript finds relating to Greco-Roman Egypt.[15] The explorers had traveled to Oxyrhynchus in search of papyrus

[10] Oxyrhynchus is mentioned often in later hagiographic literature, as Timm noted: "In der koptisch-arabischen hagiographischen Literatur ist Oxyrhynchos//Pemdje//al-Bahnasa für die byzantinische Zeit als Heimat manches Heiligen oder als Ort, wo Christen (in der diokletianischen Zeit) ihr Martyrium erlangten, oft genannt" ("Al-Bahnasa," in *Das christlich-koptische Ägypten*, 3:283).

[11] Bagnall also noted: "J'espère que personne ne considère l'Historia Monachorum . . . comme historiquement sobre" ("Combat ou vide," *Ktema* 13 [1988] 293). See also Frank, "Miracles, Monks, and Monuments," 486. Earlier scholars took the numbers more literally; for example, Pfeilschifter wrote: "Auch wenn die Zahlen von 10 000 Mönchen und 20 000 Nonnen reichlich übertrieben sein werde, die Zahl zwölf bei Nennung der Weltkirchen (ich nenne sie so im Unterschiede von den nicht aufgezählten Klosterkirchen) tritt mit einer solchen Bestimmtheit auf, daß man an der Richtigkeit derselben nicht zweifeln kann" ("Oxyrhynchos," in *Festgabe Alois Knöpfler* [ed. Gietl and Pfeilschifter] 251). However, the number twelve is a highly symbolic number, and I would therefore be more cautious here.

[12] So, e.g., Pfeilschifter: "Oxyrhynchos ist typisch für ähnliche Städte zum mindesten in Ägypten, vielleicht aber über Ägypten hinaus" ("Oxyrhynchos," 251); and Timm: "Sein (Palladius's) Bericht über Oxyrhynchos darf als typisches Zeugnis für das christliche Leben in einer ägyptischen Gauhauptstadt gelten" ("Al–Bahnasa," 3:297 n. 10).

[13] Grenfell, "A.–Oxyrhynchus and Its Papyri," in *Egypt Exploration Fund* (ed. Griffith) 6; reprinted in *Oxyrhynchus: A City and Its Texts* (ed. Bowman) 345–52.

[14] Turner, "Graeco-Roman Branch," in James, *Excavating in Egypt*, 161–62.

[15] Also Rowlandson, 6.2.d "Oxyrhynchos (el-Behnesa)," in *Egypt from Alexander* (ed. Bagnall and Rathbone) 159.

manuscripts, as Grenfell wrote in his report of that first journey alluding to the description of the city in the *Historia monachorum*:

> I had for some time felt that one of the most promising sites in Egypt for finding Greek manuscripts was the city of Oxyrhynchus . . . Being the capital of the Nome, it must have been the abode of many rich persons who could afford to possess a library of literary texts. . . . Above all, Oxyrhynchus seemed to be a site where fragments of Christian literature might be expected of an earlier date than the fourth century, to which our oldest manuscripts of the New Testament belong; for the place was renowned in the fourth and fifth centuries on account of the number of its churches and monasteries, and the rapid spread of Christianity about Oxyrhynchus, as soon as the new religion was officially recognized, implied that it had already taken a strong hold during the preceding centuries of persecution.[16]

The find of papyri surpassed all expectations and confirmed Grenfell's intuition as to the fortune that he expected to find at Oxyrhynchus. Thus he could already write in this first report that "the total find of papyri was . . . enormous."[17]

According to the British papyrologist, the expedition to Oxyrhynchus had sought to find manuscripts of Christian texts. In fact, Grenfell commented with reference to the "Logia" (published as P.Oxy. 1.1, now known as part of the *Gospel of Thomas*) and a fragment containing the beginning of the *Gospel of Matthew* (P.Oxy. 1.2) that "by a happy freak of fortune we had thus within a week of excavating in the town lit upon two examples of the kind of papyri which we most desired to find."[18] They found many more fragments, both

[16] Grenfell, "Oxyrhynchus and Its Papyri," 1. The allusion to the *Historia monachorum* is in the last sentence of this quotation. It seems from this report that the passage about Oxyrhynchus in the *Historia monachorum* formed an incentive for the two Brittons to excavate there.

[17] Ibid., 3.

[18] Ibid., 6. Indeed, the first fragment from Oxyrhynchus that Grenfell and Hunt published was a Christian text, the *ΛΟΓΙΑ ΙΗΣΟΥ*, *Sayings of Our Lord* in 1897. This was later republished as the first text in the first volume of the *Oxyrhynchus Papyri* and thus received the prime position of P.Oxy. 1.1. This by itself already proves that Christian literature was a central goal of the expedition, or at least its most spectacular result in the eyes of the excavators. In addition, I suspect that the discovery of early manuscripts of Christian literary works, and even of previously unknown Christian texts, was attractive to donors to the Egypt Exploration Society, who were indispensable for funding new expeditions. Turner lays bare the fact that securing finances presented a persistent challenge for the society ("Graeco-Roman Branch," 163, 169–71). Therefore, Grenfell may have had more than a strictly academic interest in

literary and documentary, at Oxyrhynchus. Grenfell and Hunt excavated at Oxyrhynchus for six seasons.[19] The Italian *Società per la ricerca dei papyri greci e latini in Egitto*[20] and recently Kuwaiti[21] and a group of Catalan and Egyptian scholars have continued their efforts.[22]

The papyrus find at Oxyrhynchus and its first excavators, Grenfell and Hunt, have attained so much fame that Tony Harrison has featured them as the subject of a theatrical play: *The Trackers of Oxyrhynchus*. The play's opening scene features Grenfell handing Hunt a papyrus roll and declaiming:

> Here at Oxyrhynchus where there's never been much rain
> are rubbish heaps of riches. All these mounds contain
> preserved papyri from the distant past.
> These mounds need excavating fast . . . fast . . . fast.
> Rubbish heaps of riches! Quite a paradox
> there are priceless papyri in every crate and box.[23]

---

publishing them first. In this respect, "theological" texts are consistently, down to the present, given first place in the volumes of the *Oxyrhynchus Papyri*. On the media attention for Grenfell and Hunt's expeditions, see Montserrat, "News Reports," in *Oxyrhynchus: A City and Its Texts*, 28–39.

[19] In the winter of 1896–1897 and each year in 1903–1907. For each excavation season, they published a report.

[20] Excavations conducted in 1910 and 1913–1914 under Pistelli, and in 1927–1928, 1932, and 1934 under Breccia. See Turner, "Roman Oxyrhynchus," *JEA* 38 (1952) 80, and Pintaudi, "The Italian Excavations," in *Oxyrhynchus: A City and Its Texts*, 104–8. Papyri are published in the PSI series (*Papiri greci e latini*). Pruneti has published a list of reeditions of the documentary papyri in the series: "Papiri della Società Italiana" in *Miscellanea papyrologica*.

[21] See Fehérvári, "The Kuwaiti Excavations, 1985–7," in *Oxyrhynchus: A City and Its Texts*, 109–28.

[22] The team has worked on the site since 1992, see Padró, "Recent Archaeological Work," in *Oxyrhynchus: A City and Its Texts*, 129–38 and idem, "Excavaciones en Oxirrinco (1992–2002)" in *Españoles en el Nilo* 1 (ed. López Hervás et al., 2004) 119–45 (available online in PDF format at http://www.munimadrid.es/UnidadWeb/Contenidos/EspecialInformativo/TemaCulturaYOcio/Cultura/MuseosMuni/TemploDebod/Actividades/PDFsNilo/oxirrinco.pdf). See also Subías Pascual, *La corona immarcescible*. The second part of *La corona immarcescible* has the French translation of the articles: Guitart i Duran, "La couronne immarcescible," 43–44; Padró i Parcerisa, Mascort, Amer, "La nécropole haute d'Oxyrhynchos: Situation et premiers travaux archéologiques," 44–47; and Subías Pascual, "Les peintures de l'antiquité tardive," 48–58. According to Subías Pascual, some of the Oxyrhynchite frescoes are "d'une extraordinaire beauté, essentiels pour l'histoire de l'iconographie des premiers temps chrétiens" (ibid., 48). The book contains multiple color reproductions of the frescoes.

[23] Harrison, *Trackers*, 9–10.

Indeed, rubbish heaps of riches! Grenfell describes that during the first season, "the flow of papyri became a torrent which it was difficult to cope with." The team dealt with this abundance of material by employing 110 local workers; two additional workers made tin boxes to store the papyri.[24] Back at home, Grenfell and Hunt started the series *The Oxyrhynchus Papyri*, in which they published their finds.[25] So many texts were found at Oxyrhynchus that, as Roger S. Bagnall has remarked, "the quantity of material edited to date is large enough to make of Oxyrhynchus something of a papyrological standard."[26] Currently, more than eight thousand fragments of both literary and documentary texts from Oxyrhynchus have been published.[27] The large majority of these manuscripts is written in Greek.[28]

Compared to the large amount of papyri discovered there, excavators have found disappointingly few other archaeological remains from the site of ancient Oxyrhynchus.[29] "It is ironic," John Whitehorne observed, "that

[24] According to Grenfell, "for the next ten weeks they could hardly keep pace with us" ("Oxyrhynchus and Its Papyri," 7). In their fifth season at Oxyrhynchus (winter 1905–1906), Grenfell and Hunt employed "for the greater part of fourteen weeks 200 men and boys," this compared to the no-less-than 120 they normally employed! That season, they sent home "131 boxes, compared with 91 and 117 boxes filled in the two preceding seasons" ("Excavations at Oxyrhynchus," *Archaeological Report* 14 [1904–1905] 9). Pictures taken by Hunt during several excavation seasons, preserved in the archive of the Egypt Exploration Society in London, show these workmen, barefoot, excavating the rubbish mounds with their hands and shovels.

[25] Published by the Egypt Exploration Society in Graeco-Roman Memoirs, London, under different editors. Papyri from Oxyrhynchus are published in numerous other publications as well, for instance, in the Italian series *Papiri greci e latini* under different editors.

[26] Bagnall, *Reading Papyri*, 27.

[27] In total 5,476 documentary texts and 2,918 fragments of literary manuscripts from Oxyrhynchus have been published. This comes down to 9.7 percent of the 56,188 documents listed on the Hauptregister of the Heidelberger Gesamtverzeichnis der griechischen Papyrusurkunden Ägyptens (HGV), and almost a quarter (22.4 percent) of the 13,037 literary manuscripts on the Leuven Database of Ancient Books (LDAB) (as of June 2008).

[28] Texts in other languages, such as Coptic, Latin, Demotic, Hebrew, Syriac, and—from a later time—Arabic, have also been found at the site. The number of Coptic fragments discovered at the site is comparatively low and most of them have not been published. On Coptic Oxyrhynchus, see Clackson, "Coptic Oxyrhynchus," in *Oxyrhynchus: A City and Its Texts*, 332–41.

[29] In recent decades archaeologists have fruitfully dug in the upper necropolis of the ancient city (see footnote 22 above). However, these archaeological finds cannot compare to the finds in other Greco-Roman cities and towns, such as Alexandria and Kellis in Egypt, or Pergamon and Ephesus in Asia Minor, to mention just a few.

what is one of the best documented town sites of Roman Egypt if not of the entire Roman empire, should have left so few traces of its existence in the archaeological record."[30] Whereas the Napoleonic exploration team in the early-nineteenth century still mentions one Corinthian column standing, nowadays the site appears almost completely stripped of archaeological remains.[31] I should hurry to say that we cannot blame Grenfell and Hunt for that destruction, although their archaeological methods could not compare to our sophisticated modern standards. They arrived at an already barren site, as Grenfell describes it in his first archaeological report: "My first impressions on examining the site were not very favorable . . . a thousand years' use as a quarry for limestone and bricks had clearly reduced the buildings and houses to utter ruin."[32] When in 1922 the famous archaeologist Flinders Petrie came to Oxyrhynchus, he noted that daily one hundred or more tons of soil were transported from the site for *sebbakh* (fertilizer).[33]

Despite the lack of major archaeological remains from Oxyrhynchus, the city's papyrological record provides fertile grounds for research. Several monographs and numerous articles have delved into various facets of life.[34] In this book I investigate early Christians in the documentary papyri from Oxyrhynchus.[35] Studying one place over a discrete period of time allows me

[30] Whitehorne, "Pagan Cults," *ANRW* 2.18.5 (1995) 3051.

[31] Turner, "Roman Oxyrhynchus," 81.

[32] Grenfell, "Oxyrhynchus and Its Papyri," 2.

[33] See Petrie, "Oxyrhynkhos," in his *Tombs of the Courtiers and Oxyrhynkhos*, 13, reprinted in *Oxyrhynchus: A City and Its Texts*, 50–69, at 51.

[34] See, for instance, the articles in *Oxyrhynchus: A City and Its Texts*; Rink, *Straßen- und Viertelnamen von Oxyrhynchus*; MacLennan, *Oxyrhynchus: An Economic and Social Study*; Jones and Whitehorne, *Register of Oxyrhynchites, 30 B.C.–A.D. 96*; Kutzner, *Untersuchungen zur Stellung der Frau im römischen Oxyrhynchos*; Krüger, *Oxyrhynchos in der Kaiserzeit*; Rowlandson, *Landowners and Tenants in Roman Egypt*; Sarris, *Economy and Society in the Age of Justinian*; for a larger audience: Parsons, *City of the Sharp-Nosed Fish*. Frankfurter characterized Oxyrhynchus as "that well-scrutinized crucible for generalizations" (*Religion in Roman Egypt*, 62).

[35] My approach to examine Christians in one geographical location is influenced by Bauer's groundbreaking work *Rechtgläubigkeit und Ketzerei im ältesten Christentum*. Previous scholarship on Christian documentary texts from Oxyrhynchus includes the work of Modena and especially Epp. Modena's articles treat fifth- and sixth-century Christianity in Oxyrhynchus when the city was an important Christian center; see his "Il Cristianesimo ad Ossirinco secondo i papiri," *BSAA* 31 (1927) 254–69; and idem, "Il Cristianesimo ad Ossirinco," *BSAA* 33 (1939) 293–310. Most relevant for my study, Epp's contributions focus on the social milieu of the New Testament literary texts: "Oxyrhynchus New Testament Papyri," *JBL* 123 (2004)

to view a particular segment and specimen of early Christianity as an integral part of its broader socio-economic, cultural, ethnic, and religious context.[36] As we shall see, our examination of specific Oxyrhynchus documents reveals ambiguity over how to define "Christian" identity. Nevertheless, the earliest documentary papyri from Oxyrhynchus in which we certainly encounter Christians date from the mid-third century.[37] As the cutoff date for my investigations, I take the year 324 C.E., when Constantine defeated Licinius and became the sole ruler of the Roman empire. A decade earlier, after a period of persecution, the so-called Edict of Milan of 313 had granted freedom of worship to Christians.[38] Having specified the chronological boundaries, we now explore the geographical backdrop of this study, which

---

5–55; idem, "Codex and Literacy," *CRBR* 10 (1997) 15–37; idem, "New Testament Papyri at Oxyrhynchus," in *Sayings of Jesus* (ed. Petersen et al.) 47–68; and idem, "New Testament Papyri and the Transmission of the New Testament," in *Oxyrhynchus: A City and Its Texts*, 315–31. Epp's articles are reprinted in his *Perspectives on New Testament Textual Criticism: Collected Essays, 1962–2004*.

[36] I agree here with Castelli and Taussig when they observe that theological presuppositions in the field of Christian origins "have . . . drawn an indelible line around 'Christianity' as a subject matter. The result is that the rich diversity of the ancient Mediterranean is reduced to what scholars most often name 'backgrounds.' Such a practice has also characterized the vast majority of studies of Christian origins, portraying Christian beliefs or social formations or religious practices in singular counterpoint to ancient Judaism or various Greco-Roman religions." The effect of such an approach is that "it flattens out enormous social and cultural complexity into a unidimensional background" and "makes the implicit argument of Christianity's uniqueness on the cultural horizon of ancient Mediterranean life" ("Introduction," in *Reimagining Christian Origins* [ed. Castelli and Taussig] 11–12).

[37] Christian literary manuscripts found at Oxyrhynchus predate the documents; see below.

[38] Wipszycka also focused on the pre-Constantinian period. She explained her cutoff date as follows: "je m'arrêterai au début du tournant constantinien en Égypte, c'est-à-dire en 325, car l'un de mes buts, c'est de contribuer à l'étude de la condition de l'Église avant les grands changements qu'entraîna le règne de Constantin" ("Papyrus documentaires," 1307). Of course, any periodization of history has elements of arbitrariness; in the daily lives of most people there was probably not a sharp distinction between the years 324 and 325. Also, delimiting a timeframe is especially challenging when dealing with texts that do not contain a date—such as most of the papyrus letters, the date of which is determined often solely based on handwriting. In the course of the fourth century, Egypt became more and more Christian. Wipszycka, for instance, observes: "Nous savons que la conversion de l'Égypte a été rapide et que la religion chrétienne y est devenue la religion dominante au cours du IVe siècle. À partir du milieu du IVe siècle, les conditions dans lesquelles vivaient les chrétiens en Égypte étaient complètement différentes de celles de l'époque antérieure" ("Remarques sur les lettres," *JJP* 18 [1974] 204–5).

suggests both the economic and political importance of Oxyrhynchus and its religious character.

"The Glorious and Most Glorious City of the Oxyrhynchites"

Strategically located in Middle Egypt on the border of the western desert, Oxyrhynchus owed its significance to waterways and land routes. The city had a harbor on the west bank of the Tomis River, presently called the Bar Yusuf Canal.[39] Accessible over land by a military road on the west bank of the Nile,[40] roads and caravan routes connected Oxyrhynchus to the Small Oasis, the Fayum Oasis, and beyond that to Libya.

Because of its advantageous location, already in the Ptolemaic period Oxyrhynchus (called *Permedjed* in Egyptian) functioned as an important center and a major city in Egypt.[41] Not founded as a Greek *polis*, Oxyrhynchus had the designation of a city by the time of Hadrian (early-second cent.).[42] By the end of the third century, the city proudly displayed its honorific title "glorious and most glorious."[43] Coptic texts call the city *Pemdje* (ⲡⲉⲙϫⲉ). Nowadays, a small village named Al-Bahnasa occupies the site.

Oxyrhynchus City, the metropolis of the homonymous county or *nome*, occupied some 780 km^2 in the fertile stroke of land between the Nile valley and the Bar Yusuf canal.[44] The closest city and capital of a like-named *nome*,

[39] This is actually not a canal, but a branch of the Nile River ending in the Lake Moeris in the Fayum Oasis in the western desert. In antiquity, the Oxyrhynchites referred to this river as the Tomis River (Τῶμις ποταμός). See, e.g., P.Grenf. 2.116; P.Oxy. 10.1259; P.Oxy. 22.2341; and P.Oxy. 51.3638. In P.Oxy. 22.2341 the river is called both Tomis River and "our river" (ὁ ποταμὸς ὁ ἡμέτερος, i.4–5). The Nile was called ὁ μέγας ποταμός "the great river" (e.g., P.Oxy. 17.2125). See also Krüger, *Oxyrhynchos in der Kaiserzeit*, 58.

[40] Turner, "Roman Oxyrhynchus," 79; Krüger, *Oxyrhynchos in der Kaiserzeit*, 7.

[41] Turner noted: "Because the contrary is so often asserted I begin by emphasizing that Oxyrhynchus was an important place" ("Roman Oxyrhynchus," 78).

[42] P.Oxy. 43.3088, lines 7–8, a letter (dated probably 21 March 128 C.E.) of a prefect "to the city of the Oxyrhynchites" (Ὀξυρυγχειτῶν τῇ πόλει). See also Turner, "Oxyrhynchus and Rome," *HSCP* 79 (1975) 15 n. 45.

[43] λαμπρὰ καὶ λαμπροτάτη, see also Hagedorn, "Ὀξυρύγχων πόλις," *ZPE* 12 (1973) 288–89.

[44] So Bagnall, *Egypt in Late Antiquity*, 335. Bagnall explains: "The Oxyrhynchite nome had at one point in the fourth cent. 202,534 *arouras* of arable land taxable in grain . . . that would represent about 72 percent of the estimated total area" (ibid., 335 n. 4). According to Krüger, the land area was slightly more, 900 km^2 (*Oxyrhynchos in der Kaiserzeit*, 37). The area

Cynopolis, lies at a distance of about twenty km to the East. To the North, the Oxyrhynchite *nome* borders the Heracleopolite *nome*, and to the South, the Hermopolite. Alexandria, Egypt's main city and seat of government, lies about 300 km north of Oxyrhynchus.

Some 5,300 m of city wall surrounded Oxyrhynchus; at least five gates provided entrance to the city.[45] Grenfell measured the site of the ancient city as "1 ¼ miles long, and in most parts ½ mile broad."[46] Some 20,000 people crowded into this small area.[47] We shall try to spot the Christians among them.

"A Veritable Supermarket of Gods and Goddesses"[48]

Before focusing on the early Christians in Oxyrhynchus, I should sketch the broader religious milieu in this city. In an important article entitled "The Pagan Cults of Roman Oxyrhynchus," John Whitehorne contributed to the understanding of "pagan"[49] religion in Oxyrhynchus in the Roman period by describing cults and listing festivals. Whitehorne observed that "the inhabitants of the city were faced with a veritable supermarket of gods and goddesses," both Egyptian and Roman.[50]

---

of the nome changed as land was moved between the Oxyrhynchite and neighboring nomes (Cynopolite, Heracleopolite, and Hermopolite).

45 Turner, "Roman Oxyrhynchus," 81; with reference for the calculation of the walls to Jomard, *Description de l'Égypte*. The five city gates are mentioned in P.Oxy. 1.43*v*.

46 Grenfell, "Oxyrhynchus and Its Papyri," 2.

47 I follow here Obbink's estimate in "Imaging Oxyrhynchus," *EA* 22 (2003) 3. According to Obbink, "the metropolis . . . was populated by perhaps 20,000 inhabitants of the Greek-speaking settler class, Egyptian Greeks, and their later Roman counterparts" (ibid.). Others have proposed higher numbers: Fichman computed the population of the metropolis as ca. 30,000 ("Bevölkerungszahl," *APF* 21 [1971] 116) and according to Coles, "the population may have exceeded 30,000" ("Oxyrhynchus: A City and Its Texts," in *Oxyrhynchus: A City and Its Texts*, 8). For the late Roman period, Fichman comes to 15,000–20,000 people, although it is not exactly clear to me which centuries he has in mind for that number ("Bevölkerungszahl," 120). According to Krüger, ca. 300,000 people inhabited the Oxyrhynchite nome in the Roman period, although this number seems much too high. Krüger based this on the accounts of Diodorus and Flavius Josephus, and on calculations of the arable land and population of Egypt at the end of the nineteenth century (*Oxyrhynchos in der Kaiserzeit*, 37–38).

48 Whitehorne, "Pagan Cults," 3055.

49 Despite its polemical connotations, I use the term "pagan" for worshippers of Greco-Roman and Egyptian deities.

50 Whitehorne, "Pagan Cults," 3050–91. Whitehorne formulates the object of his article as "to present in a summary form an overview of the various pagan cults known from the city of

The city's Greek name already implies religion. Oxyrhynchus[51] owes its name to the sharp-nosed (ὀξύρυγχος) or Elephant-snout fish (*Mormyrus kannume*).[52] The "sharp-nosed fish" roamed the local waterways, yet the Oxyrhynchites' appreciation for this fish did not come, as one might think, from eating it![53] Instead it constituted an object of reverence for the inhabitants. Votives of the sacred fish have turned up in the archaeological record of Egypt.[54] Consumption of the Oxyrhynchus fish did become an issue, however, with the neighbors from Cynopolis. According to an account in Plutarch's *Isis and Osiris*, the Oxyrhynchites' reverence for the sacred sharp-snouted fish even led to hostile encounters with the Cynopolites, who honored the jackal-god Anubis. As Plutarch writes:

> And in our days the Oxyrhynchites, because the Cynopolites were eating the sharp-snouted fish, caught a dog and sacrificed it and ate it as if it had been sacrificial meat. As a result of this they became involved in war and inflicted much harm upon each other; and later they were both brought to order through chastisement by the Romans.[55]

Oxyrhynchus in the Roman period" (ibid., 3050). On later pagans see Zucker, "Priester und Tempel," in *Akten des VIII. internationalen Kongresses für Papyrologie*, 167–74.

[51] In Greek the city is referred to as Ὀξυρύγχων πόλις or ἡ Ὀξυρυγχιτῶν πόλις.

[52] Whitehorne, "Pagan Cults," 3052. Additional literature mentioned in Krüger, *Oxyrhynchos in der Kaiserzeit*, 7 nn. 4–5.

[53] Other fish were of course used for consumption, some of them even exported, as Bowman observes: "The rivers and lakes also harboured many varieties of fish . . . the silurus, sufficiently prized to be exported to Rome as a delicacy" (*Egypt after the Pharaohs*, 15). According to Plutarch, however, whereas certain people would abstain from eating a certain kind of fish, Egyptian priests abstained from eating all fish (Plutarch, *Isis and Osiris* 7 [353], in *Moralia* 5 [ed. and trans. Babbitt] 18–21).

[54] A tomb with depictions of the Oxyrhynchus fish was discovered during recent excavations, mentioned in Rowlandson, "Oxyrhynchos (el-Behnesa)," 161. Kessler published two Roman grave steles with depictions of the Oxyrhynchus fish that probably came from the site ("Zwei Grabstelen," *WO* 14 [1983] 176–88). Kessler also discusses the symbolism of the fish (ibid., 180–83). Pictures of Oxyrhynchus fish votives are available online at: http://www.papyrology.ox.ac.uk/POxy/oxyrhynchus/parsons1.html.

[55] οἱ δ' Ὀξυρυγχῖται καθ' ἡμᾶς, τῶν Κυνοπολιτῶν τὸν ὀξύρυγχον ἰχθὺν ἐσθιόντων, κύνα συλλαβόντες καὶ θύσαντες ὡς ἱερεῖον κατέφαγον. ἐκ δὲ τούτου καταστάντες εἰς πόλεμον ἀλλήλους τε διέθηκαν κακῶς καὶ ὕστερον ὑπὸ Ῥωμαίων κολαζόμενοι διετέθησαν. Text and translation (slightly modified) from Plutarch, *Isis and Osiris* 72 (380), in *Moralia* 5 (ed. and trans. Babbitt) 168–69.

Historically accurate or not, this account illustrates deep feelings of reverence for both Anubis and the Oxyrhynchus fish.[56]

The sharp-nosed fish did not constitute the only object of worship for the Oxyrhynchites. A wealth of temples and shrines to Egyptian and Greco-Roman deities appear in the papyri.[57] Thoeris, the hippopotamus goddess of fertility and childbirth, enjoyed great popularity at Oxyrhynchus. At least three temples were dedicated to her in Oxyrhynchus, and her cult and cult officers show up repeatedly in the papyri.[58] Archaeological and papyrological remains testify to the importance of the god Sarapis in Oxyrhynchus.[59] The Serapeum, one of the city's larger temples, apparently provided a good spot for hosting dinner parties because several papyri invite guests for festivities there.[60] It served as the main financial area and formed—in Whitehorne's description—"the focus of business life in Oxyrhynchus."[61] The Oxyrhynchites also practiced the imperial cult. Augustus and Hadrian had temples named after them in the city. The Hadrianeum functioned not only as cultic center, but in the fourth century appeared as a place for court

[56] Whitehorne comments on this passage that "it should be emphasized that there has been little trace to date in the papyri of the religious strife between different nomes which Greek and Roman writers made into such a rhetorical commonplace" ("Pagan Cults," 3059–60). The first-century-C.E. geographer Strabo mentions also that the Oxyrhynchites worship the sharp-nosed fish, and in this context informs us of a temple for the Oxyrhynchus fish. The Oxyrhynchites are not unique in their reverence for the fish, for Strabo notes that "other Egyptians in common also honor the oxyrhynchus" (τιμῶσι δὲ τὸν ὀξύρυγχον καὶ ἔστιν αὐτοῖς ἱερὸν ὀξυρύγχου, καίτοι καὶ τῶν ἄλλων Αἰγυπτίων κοινῇ τιμώντων τὸν ὀξύρυγχον. *Geography* 17.1.40, in *The Geography of Strabo* 8 [ed. and trans. Jones] 108–9). Strabo and other people of his time were quite fascinated with the Egyptian animal worship and expanded on this practice in the preceding and following paragraphs as he discussed towns along the Nile.

[57] I mention here only a few and refer for fuller treatment to Whitehorne, "Pagan Cults." Turner's brief report also draws a lively picture of the Egyptian and Roman cults ("Roman Oxyrhynchus," 82–83).

[58] Whitehorne, "Pagan Cults," 3080–82.

[59] Parlasca suggests that architectural elements and a larger than life-sized head of Sarapis, bought on the antiquities market from illegal excavations arguably conducted at Oxyrhynchus, attest to a small ante temple and cult statue dedicated to Sarapis ("Sarapistempel," *ChrEg* 81 [2006] 253–75). The cult head was published by Kraus, "Sarapiskopf aus Oxyrhynchos," *JAC* 75 (1960) 88–99. The god frequently features in papyrus documents from the site.

[60] For example, P.Oxy. 14.1755; P.Oxy. 62.4339 and P.Oxy. 66.4540. The Serapeum is also mentioned in a list of street guards (P.Oxy. 1.43). There are no remains of this temple.

[61] Whitehorne, "Pagan Cults," 3078.

proceedings and also as a prison.[62] Other emperors had statues set up for them and their relatives in different local temples and shrines.[63] Several of these temples and shrines still appear in fourth-century documents, but we do not know whether, besides a civic function, they still had a cultic function by then.[64]

Literary and documentary texts attest to a Jewish community in Oxyrhynchus.[65] Fragments of Septuagint manuscripts feature among the literary texts.[66] A late-first-century C.E. documentary papyrus mentions the sale of part of a house, specifies its location as the Jewish Quarter at Oxyrhynchus,[67] and that Jews had previously owned the house.[68] The Jewish Revolt under Trajan in 115–117 C.E. greatly impacted Jewish life in Egypt and dramatically reduced the Jewish population.[69] Oxyrhynchus papyri testify to this. One document mentions "open lots, in which there are buildings burnt by the Jews" (P.Oxy. 4.707*r*, early-second cent.); it suggests a city embroiled by the revolt.[70] By the year 199/200, the Oxyrhynchites still celebrated yearly their victory over the Jews, as they bragged in a petition to the emperor.[71] Only at the end of the third century do we learn of a Jewish community at

[62] Ibid., 3067.

[63] Ibid., 3067–68.

[64] See Bagnall, "Combat ou vide," 290.

[65] For scholarship on this topic see Epp, "Jews and the Jewish Community," in *New Testament Manuscripts* (ed. Kraus and Nicklas) 13–52; Kasher, "Jewish Community," *JJS* 32 (1981) 151–57; and sections in *Corpus papyrorum judaicarum* [*CPJ*] (e.g., vol. 1.5, 94, 101, and discussions of individual texts).

[66] The oldest Jewish Septuagint manuscript from Oxyrhynchus is P.Oxy. 50.3522, a first-cent.-C.E. fragment of a roll containing Job 42:11–12. Other Septuagint fragments are e.g., P.Oxy. 4.656 (second/third cent., van Haelst 13; no *nomina sacra*, and κύριος is added by a different hand) and P.Oxy. 7.1007 (end of the third cent., van Haelst 5; κύριος is written with two *jods* in the shape of a Z). For Christian Septuagint manuscripts, see footnote 95 below.

[67] ἐπ' ἀμφόδου Ἰουδα(ι)κ(οῦ). The house is "bought by Νικαίᾳ Σιλ[βα]νῷ Ψουβίου τῶν ἀπ' Ὀξ(υρύγχων) πόλ(εως) Ἰου[δ]αίων from Παῦλος" (P.Oxy. 2.335, dated "about 85 CE" = *CPJ* 2.423). The text is not published in full. Jewish quarters are known in other cities as well (see *CPJ* 1.5 n. 14). The Jewish quarter of Oxyrhynchus was not the only neighborhood with an ethnic name; there was, for example, also a Cretan quarter.

[68] So Kasher, "Jewish Community," 151.

[69] Tcherikover, *CPJ* 1.93; see 94: "The general impression is that of a complete breakdown of Jewish life in Egypt, at any rate at the beginning of this period."

[70] = *CPJ* 2.457 (translation Tcherikover).

[71] P.Oxy. 4.705 (= *CPJ* 2.450) lines 31–35: The petitioner, Horon, reminds the emperor of "the goodwill, faithfulness, and friendship [of the Oxyrhynchites] to the Romans which they

Oxyrhynchus again. A "Manumission *inter amicos*" dated 14 April 291 C.E. attests that the synagogue (συναγωγή), the Jewish community,[72] presumably of Oxyrhynchus, bought free a forty-year-old Jewish slave woman called Paramone and two or three of her children for the substantial sum of fourteen talents of silver (P.Oxy. 9.1205).[73] A Greek text documents the lease of a room and a cellar that a Jew called Aurelius Jose, son of Judas, rented from two nuns (P.Oxy. 44.3203, June–July 400 C.E.).[74] From the end-of-the-fourth or early-fifth century come several fragments written in Hebrew.[75] These documents show the presence of Jews and a Jewish community in Oxyrhynchus.

From the late-third century on, one could also encounter Manichaeans in Oxyrhynchus. Snippets of Manichaean literary manuscripts in Syriac, recognizable by their characteristic Estrangela script, occur among the Oxyrhychus find.[76] In addition to these, a letter of recommendation from a certain Paul—composed in a literary style and written in *ditto* handwriting—testifies to

exhibited in the war against the Jews, giving aid then and even now keeping the day of victory as a festival every year" (*CPJ* 2.450, 260).

[72] παρὰ τῆς συνα[γ]ωγῆς τῶν Ἰουδαίων (line 7): "The Jewish community of Oxyrhynchus is meant, not the 'synagogue' in the narrow sense of the word. The synagogue in Egypt is always called προσευχή" (*CPJ* 3.473, 35).

[73] = *CPJ* 3.473, 33–36. "The fact that the Jewish community paid the ransom implies that it possessed public funds and authority to use them, a right reserved exclusively for legal bodies" (Kasher, "Jewish Community," 153). See most recently Scholl, "Freilassung unter Freunden," in *Fünfzig Jahre Forschungen* (ed. Bellen und Heinen) 159–69; also Rowlandson, *Women and Society*, 193–94. The papyrus does not explicitly state that this was the Jewish community of Oxyrhynchus. One of the intermediaries, Justus, is a *bouleutes* from Oneitonpolis in Palestine. We only know that the papyrus was found at Oxyrhynchus.

[74] This document is interesting in comparison with the account of the *Historia monachorum*, dating from the same time, that does not even mention Jews at Oxyrhynchus.

[75] Cowley, "Notes on Hebrew Papyrus Fragments," *JEA* 2 (1915) 209–13; *CPJ* 1.101–2; and Harding, "Hebrew Congregational Prayer," *NewDocs* 8:145–47; a prayer dated "prior to the fifth century A.D." (ibid., 145).

[76] For their publication, see Margoliouth, "Notes on Syriac Papyrus Fragments," *JEA* 2 (1915) 214–16. Burkitt first identified these as Manichaean and republished them in Appendix 3: "Manichee Fragments in Syriac," in idem, *Religion of the Manichees*, 114–19. Recently, see Lieu, "5.1 Fragments in Syriac," in idem, *Manichaeism in Mesopotamia*, 62–64. One of the pieces contains a quotation of 2 Cor 5:21. Biblical quotations or allusions, even New Testament ones, are therefore not enough to give papyri a Christian identification. Recently, Choat has incorporated the study of Manichaean documents in his analysis of religion in Egypt. He brings up Manichaeans throughout the book (see Choat, *Belief and Cult*, 131–32, 137–39).

a Manichaean community at Oxyrhynchus (P.Oxy. 31.2603).[77] Until recently scholars classified this as a Christian letter,[78] which demonstrates that one can at times hardly distinguish Manichaeans from Christians.[79]

Finally, in the aisles of the "religious supermarket" at Oxyrhynchus, we also find Christians. We cannot determine the exact date at which Christians began to assemble at Oxyrhynchus. "It is conceivable that a letter from a Christian could have been received by a Christian community in Egypt by the late-first or early-second century," Stanton has noted. He refers to a letter found at Oxyrhynchus (P.Oxy. 42.3057) that has generated much discussion regarding its authorship, Christian or not.[80] The earliest definitely Christian texts found at Oxyrhynchus comprise fragments of Christian literary manuscripts dating to the second century.[81] Even the so-claimed earliest known fragment of a New Testament text, a small piece of the *Gospel of John*, may have come from Oxyrhynchus.[82] Someone might have copied these

[77] Editio princeps, Harrop, "Christian Letter," *JEA* 48 (1962) 132–40. For identification as Manichaean, see Lieu, *Manichaeism in Mesopotamia*, 98 n. 316; and Gardner, Nobbs, and Choat, "*P.Harr.* 107," *ZPE* 131 (2000) 118 n. 1. Harrop concluded that "the literary style of the letter . . . makes it likely that Paul was a man of considerable learning" ("Christian Letter," 137). The letter is not only literary in pretension, as Harrop mentioned; it is also written in a bookhand, an exceptional feature for private letters.

[78] For instance, Naldini, C*ristianesimo,* 212–15, and 442–43 (no. 47); Epp, "Oxyrhynchus NT Papyri," 45.

[79] On the issue of distinguishing Christians and Manichaeans, see especially Choat, *Belief and Cult*, 137–39. However, as Choat noted, "perspective should not be lost. . . . As nothing suggests the Manichaean community in Egypt was any more than a small fraction of the Christian community, marking every letter featuring traits shared by both Manichaeans and Christians as 'uncertain' seems extreme" (ibid., 138).

[80] Stanton, "Proposed Earliest Christian Letter," *ZPE* 54 (1984) 62. Stanton thought that the letter in question was not written by a Christian. For a brief discussion of this papyrus (P.Oxy. 42.3057), see ch. 2.

[81] *Gospel of Matthew*, P.Oxy. 64.4404 (late-second cent.); *Gospel of Peter*, P.Oxy. 60.4009 (second cent.); *Gospel of John*, P.Oxy. 50.3523 (second cent.).

[82] P.Ryl. 3.457 (= 𝔓[52]). Both provenance and date of this fragment are not certain. Colin H. Roberts, the first editor of the papyrus, noted that the fragment came from a batch containing papyri from the Fayum or Oxyrhynchus. In two publications, he seems to lean more toward Oxyrhynchus, but with all due caution: Roberts, *Unpublished Fragment*, 24; and idem, P.Ryl. 3.457, 2: "it is possible that the provenance of both texts is Oxyrhynchus—the parcel in which 457 was included was marked 'from the Fayum or Oxyrhynchus.'" Based on palaeography, Roberts argued that "on the whole we may accept with some confidence the first half of the second century as the period in which P. Ryl. Gk. 457 was most probably written" (Roberts, *Unpublished Fragment*, 16). This claim made the papyrus the earliest known manuscript

manuscripts at Oxyrhynchus or brought them there at a later time.[83] Only in the third century do records of individual Christians appear with certainty in the papyrological record. By this time, traces of characteristic Christian roles (e.g., bishop), forms of address (e.g., kinship language), and scribal practices (e.g., *nomina sacra*) appear in the papryi with some regularity.

Evidence for church buildings at Oxyrhynchus surfaces in papyri from the beginning of the fourth century. The earliest datable mention of a church building comes from a "Declaration of Church Property" from the year 304 (P.Oxy. 33.2673).[84] Another papyrus mentions two churches in Oxyrhynchus (P.Oxy. 1.43*v*).[85] This document, which probably dates to the first quarter of the fourth century, contains a list of streets and buildings in Oxyrhynchus City followed by the names of the men responsible for guarding them.[86] The papyrus mentions a North Church Street and a South Church Street.[87] Thus,

---

of a New Testament text. For a critical evaluation of the dating of this papyrus on solely paleographical grounds, see Brent Nongbri, "The Use and Abuse of 𝔓[52]: Papyrological Pitfalls in the Dating of the Fourth Gospel," *HTR* 98 (2005) 23–48.

[83] A mid-second-century manuscript found at Oxyrhynchus does not mean that there was a Christian community (no matter how small) at Oxyrhynchus at that time; the manuscripts may predate the founding of the community. Tov has argued that the Qumran manuscripts were not all copied *in loco* but that persons joining the Qumran community brought their own manuscripts with them. The date range of the manuscripts clearly shows that the earliest manuscripts predate the founding of the community and hence must have been contributed by persons joining the community (Tov, *Scribal Practices*, 5–6, 14–16). See also Epp, "Significance of the Papyri," in *Studies in the Theory and Method of New Testament Textual Criticism* (ed. Epp and Fee) 279.

[84] I discuss this text in ch. 7.

[85] "Military Accounts," ed. Grenfell and Hunt, dated after 295 C.E.

[86] The papyrus is quite large, measuring 25 x 90 cm (so large, that for the purpose of conserving it under glass, it is split in two parts at the British Library, inv. BM 748.1 and 2). The text is incomplete, for once not because of damage of the papyrus, but because it was not finished. Blanks occur in several places, where the name of the guard still had to be written. It is recorded on the *verso* of another official document, an account of supplies to the military dated 295 C.E. According to Grenfell and Hunt, the list of watchmen "was written not long afterwards" (P.Oxy. 1.43*v*, 95); according to Bagnall "perhaps as late as the 320s" (*Egypt in Late Antiquity,* 164 n. 83). On rewritten documents, see Rea's comments in P.Oxy. 58.3927, "List of Names," written about twenty-five years later than the text on the front, P.Oxy. 58.3926, 35: "A delay of about twenty-five years before the reuse of a document is within the attested limits" (with reference to Turner, "Recto and Verso," *JEA* 40 [1954] 102–6).

[87] ῥ(ύμη) τῇ βοριν[ῇ] ἐκκλησίᾳ (col. 1, line 10); and καὶ ῥ(ύμη) τῇ νοτινῇ ἐκκλησία (col. 3, line 19). I should note that the guards are assigned to the streets, not specifically to the churches.

not only do we see two churches in different parts of the city at this time, but the papyrus even indicates the streets by the presence of these churches and thus attests to their visibility and importance.[88] Papyri from a later date also mention the Southern Church.[89] Among the archaeological remains from the site appear "the remnants of a large Christian building" with a crypt.[90] Later papyri evoke a skyline crowded with churches, *martyria*, chapels, and monasteries.[91]

Papyrological finds make clear that the Oxyrhynchites had a large and diverse literary appetite.[92] The menu contained rare works such as Julius Africanus's *Kestoi*,[93] but most dishes served came adorned with the customary style of Homeric epic.[94] For those ordering *à la carte*, we find a large choice of early Christian manuscripts from Oxyrhynchus for our time period including fragments of multiple copies of Septuagint books,[95] the gospel of John,[96] the

[88] Later churches and shrines often bear the names of biblical personalities, saints, and martyrs. The generic, geographical names of North and South Church could suggest therefore a date before the end of the Great Persecution.

[89] See P.Oxy. 67.4617, a fifth-century "List of Festival Payments"; and P.Oxy. 11.1357, a "Calendar of Church Services," dated to the year 535–536 C.E. This papyrus "contains a list of συνάξεις at various churches on Sundays, festivals, and (apparently) other days through a period of five months" (P.Oxy. 11.1357, 19). This list, much later than our time period, mentions the Southern [Church] in col. 2, line 37 (see also line 61). For a reedition and recent discussion of this papyrus, see: Papaconstantinou, "La liturgie stationnale," *Revue des études byzantines* 54 (1996) 147, on line 37.

[90] For a full description of these remains, see Breccia, "Fouilles d'Oxyrhynchos," in *Le Musée Gréco-Romain 1931–1932*, 36.

[91] See P.Oxy. 67.4617 and P.Oxy. 11.1357.

[92] I do not claim that Oxyrhynchus was unique in this respect; it is just that these texts were preserved here.

[93] P.Oxy. 3.412 (third cent.).

[94] For classical literature from Oxyrhynchus, see Krüger, *Oxyrhynchos in der Kaiserzeit*; and earlier Kenyon, "Library of a Greek," *JEA* 8 (1922) 129–38.

[95] The following papyri were probably copied by Christian scribes: Genesis: P.Oxy. 9.1166 (third cent.); Exodus: P.Oxy. 8.1074 (third cent.); P.Oxy. 8.1075 (third cent.); and P.Oxy. 65.4442 (third cent.); Leviticus: P.Oxy. 11.1351 (third/fourth cent.); Judges: PSI 2.127 (third/fourth cent.); Tobias: P.Oxy. 13.1594 (third/fourth cent.); Esther: P.Oxy. 65.4443 (first/second cent.); Psalms: P.Oxy. 15.1779 (third cent.) and P.Oxy. 10.1226 (third/fourth cent.). For Septuagint manuscripts that were likely copied by Jewish scribes, see above, footnote 66.

[96] P.Oxy. 50.3523 (second cent.); P.Oxy. 10.1228 (third cent.); P.Oxy. 2.208 (third cent.); P.Oxy. 65.4445 (third cent.); P.Oxy. 65.4446 (third cent.); P.Oxy. 65.4447 (third cent.); P.Oxy. 65.4448 (third cent.). Perhaps also P.Ryl. 3.457 (second cent.).

Gospel of Thomas,[97] the *Gospel of Mary*,[98] the gospel of Matthew,[99] the *Gospel of Peter*,[100] Pauline letters,[101] and *Hermas*.[102] Single copies of, for example, Irenaeus's *Adversus haereses*, unidentified fragments containing sayings of Jesus, a hortatory text (sermon or letter), and the letters of James and Judas appear also among the Oxyrhynchus papyri.[103]

Can we catch glimpses of the people who worshipped in the churches and read these literary manuscripts in the papyrus documents from Oxyrhynchus? We will begin our historical detective work in search for Christians at Oxyrhynchus by going to the city's marketplace.

[97] P.Oxy. 1.1 (early-third cent.); P.Oxy. 4.654 (second-half third cent.); and P.Oxy. 4.655 (first-half third cent., before 250).

[98] P.Oxy. 50.3525 (third cent.); P.Ryl 3.463 (early-third cent.).

[99] P.Oxy. 64.4404 (late-second cent.); P.Oxy. 34.2683 + P.Oxy. 64.4405 (second/third cent.); P.Oxy. 64.4403 (second/third); P.Oxy. 64.4401 (third cent.); P.Oxy. 1.2 (third cent.); P.Oxy. 24.2384 (third/fourth cent.); and P.Oxy. 64.4402 (third/fourth cent.).

[100] P.Oxy. 41.2949 (late-second/early-third cent.); P.Oxy. 60.4009 (second cent.).

[101] Romans: P.Oxy. 11.1355 (third cent.); P.Oxy 66.4497 (third cent.); 1 Corinthians and Philippians: P.Oxy. 7.1008 (third/fourth cent.); 1 and 2 Thessalonians: P.Oxy. 13.1598 (third/fourth cent.); Hebrews: P.Oxy. 4.675; PSI 12.1292 (third/fourth cent.); and P.Oxy. 66.4498 (third cent.).

[102] P.Oxy. 3.404 (late-third/early-fourth cent.); P.Oxy. 15.1783 (early-fourth cent.); P.Oxy. 15.1828 (third cent.); P.Oxy. 50.3527 (late-third/early-fourth cent.); P.Oxy. 50.3528 (late-second/early-third cent.); P.Oxy. 69.4705 (third cent.); P.Oxy. 69.4706 (second/third cent.); and P.Oxy. 69.4707 (third cent.).

[103] Irenaeus: P.Oxy. 3.405 (second/third cent.); Christian sermon or hortatory text: P.Mich. 18.764 (second/third cent.); James: P.Oxy. 9.1171 (third cent.); and Jude: P.Oxy. 24.2684.

Part One: Meeting Christians at the Marketplace

CHAPTER 2

How Do You Know a Christian When You See One? God, Christians, and Personal Names

I would like to invite you to the marketplace in ancient Oxyrhynchus to sit down in a shady exedra to observe and meet some Oxyrhynchites. Overlooking the bustling crowd of shoppers and vendors, I wonder who among them are Christians. How can we tell? Can we even know? In this chapter I use the image of the agora as a metaphor for documentary papyri.[1] These letters and documents on papyrus allow us to spot Christians other than those known from literary texts.

In exploring questions of Christian identity an article by Shaye Cohen on Jewish identity offers helpful parallels and images.[2] Indeed, as we will see, many of the questions and insights Cohen brings up regarding Jewish identity are applicable for Christian identity also. Cohen's main interests lay "in the social dynamics of 'Jewishness' in the Roman diaspora in the last century BCE and the first centuries CE."[3] He started with an observation from silence and noted, "not a single ancient author says that Jews are distinctive

[1] See Gamble's observation: "All aspects of the production, distribution, and use of texts presuppose social functions and forces" (*Books and Readers,* 43). Like the agora, writing serves as a site of social and economic interchange. Thus I shall try to picture the "market-place" of Oxyrhynchus as it is constituted by the remains of its writings.

[2] Cohen, " 'Those Who Say They Are Jews,' " 1–45, in *Diasporas in Antiquity* (ed. Cohen and Frerichs). See also Cohen's *Beginnings of Jewishness.*

[3] Cohen asked, "How was Jewishness expressed? What did a Jew do (or not do) in order to demonstrate that s/he was not a gentile? If someone claimed to be a Jew, how could you ascertain whether the claim was true? In sum, how did you know a Jew in antiquity when you saw one?" ("Those Who Say They Are Jews," 3).

because of their look, clothing, speech, names, or occupations."[4] On the contrary, as Cohen wrote:

> The diaspora Jews of antiquity were not easily recognizable, if, indeed, they were recognizable at all. Jews looked like everyone else, dressed like everyone else, spoke like everyone else, had names and occupations like those of everyone else, and, in general, closely resembled their gentile neighbors. Even circumcision did not always make (male) Jews distinctive, and as long as they kept their pants on, it certainly did not make them recognizable.[5]

How, then, can you recognize a Jew as such? Cohen answers this question as follows:

> The Tosafot . . . deduce . . . that if an unknown person comes before us and claims to be a Jew, he is to be believed. This principle . . . seems to have been the norm in antiquity not only in the land of Israel but also in the diaspora. . . . In antiquity you did not know a Jew when you saw one, but if someone said he or she was a Jew, that statement alone apparently sufficed to establish the fact. A Jew is anyone who declares himself/herself to be one.[6]

Thus, according to this scholar, Jews cannot be recognized by their appearance, clothing, hairdo, or even circumcision, but only when they introduce them-selves as such. In sum, there are no unequivocal exterior markers of Jewish identity.

I have brought up Cohen's exploration of Jewish identity because much of what he says is also relevant for the question of Christian identity. According to the early Christian author of the *Epistle to Diognetus* (late-second century), one would not recognize Christians, for they share the same country, language, and customs with their neighbors. Christians are the same as everyone else, only better, as he writes:

> For Christians are no different from other people in terms of their country, language, or customs. Nowhere do they inhabit cities of their own, use a strange dialect, or live life out of the ordinary. . . . They

[4] Ibid., 10.

[5] Ibid., 39. Cohen's assertion about names is of course not entirely true, since some Jews did have distinctive names. I shall discuss scriptural names below, 46–54.

[6] Ibid., 41.

> inhabit both Greek and barbarian cities, according to the lot assigned to each. And they show forth the character of their own citizenship in a marvelous and admittedly paradoxical way by following local customs in what they wear and what they eat and in the rest of their lives (τῆς ἑαυτῶν πολιτείας).[7]

In the *Epistle to Diognetus*, the author negotiates difference and similarity and portrays Christians as the same as other people yet different; they display the same trusted brand but now improved.[8] As Karen King observes:

> Christians were integrally a part of ancient Mediterranean culture and necessarily shaped their identity within it. Their challenge was determining how to distinguish themselves clearly from others and yet at the same time not appear to be a "new" group lacking an ancient and therefore respectable genealogy.[9]

On a local level, for the people of Oxyrhynchus, this shared identity included inhabiting the same space—not only on the city level but also in neighborhoods and houses or apartments—belonging to a certain class (e.g., the gymnasium or a guild), shopping for food at the local markets, paying with the same coinage, wearing similar style clothing and having similar hairstyles that showed social status or profession, commissioning grave sculpture,[10] speaking

[7] *Epistle to Diognetus* 5. 1–2, 4 in *Apostolic Fathers* 2:139–41. The word πολιτεία in this context indicates a "way of life, conduct, behavior" (Lampe, 113 sub F).

[8] We perceive here, as Lieu comments, "the voice of an apologist, seeking both to deny any subversive potential in difference, and at the same time affirming its positive value" (*Christian Identity*, 235). Lieu also comments that "some authors even acknowledge their participation in the shared values of pagan society, while also trying to differentiate themselves from them. . . . This, clearly, is not a stark either/or: some accommodation is necessary in order to be able also to recognize differentness; a delicate negotiation is demanded between asserting an independent identity. Further, in these cases this is the stuff of apologetics, directed to the outsider" (ibid., 175).

[9] King, *What is Gnosticism?*, 39–40. King also states: "if we want to understand how any particular group or self-identity is produced, we have to ask whether and how various social constructions (such as political roles, economic conditions, social status, ethnicity, spheres of activity, division of space and time, or ritual activity) intersect in forming, defining, and bounding the religious self" (ibid., 286 n. 61).

[10] On iconography, see, e.g., Wipszycka, "La christianisation de l'Égypte," 63–105, especially 63–64, in *Études sur le Christianisme*; and Thomas's study on the archaeological remains from the Oxyrhynchite and Heracleopolite cemeteries in her *Late Antique Egyptian Funerary Sculpture*.

the same language—whether Greek or Egyptian—having an economic interest in the rise of the river, appreciating the neighborhood gossip, laughing at the same jokes, and fearing disease. It also meant writing letters appropriately with stereotyped language in opening and closing statements and naming children in a certain way.

In the end, for all groups the sameness is much larger than the distinctiveness,[11] and this sameness necessitates the rhetorical construction of discrete identities.[12] This means that considerable effort is needed to show distinction.[13] An impression of deep distinction—morally, socially, theologically—between Christians, Jews, and pagans appears sharpest in ancient Christian polemics.[14] Were these distinctions otherwise so clearly apparent? Thus from our perch

[11] Here I draw on French sociologist Bourdieu's notion of *habitus*, which he describes as "the durably installed generative principle of regulated improvisations" (*Outline*, 78). *Habitus* consists of aspects and behavioral patterns that people in a society share, mostly unconsciously, and that inform their actions. Reading Oxyrhynchus fragments through the lens of *habitus* enables me to see them not as isolated individual texts but as connected to a larger social framework.

[12] According to Lieu, identity "involves ideas of boundedness, of sameness and difference, of continuity, perhaps of a degree of homogeneity, and of recognition by self and others" (*Christian Identity*, 12). Contrary to common perception, identity is not "an absolute and irreducible 'given'," but "there has developed in recent decades a widespread consensus that it can better be understood and analysed as socially constructed" (ibid., 13).

[13] In King's words, "the problem for Christian self-definition was not difference but similarity; not distance but proximity" (*What is Gnosticism?*, 52). Thus sameness is the main challenge in polemical writings. Further, King writes, "The primary challenge for Christian self-definition was sameness, whether distinguishing the orthodox from heretics or Christians from non-Christians. Although the goal was to minimize actual differences within the group while maximizing the differences with outsiders, ironically the strategies were more or less the same, because in order to exclude Christian views the polemicists opposed, they needed to make their competitors look like outsiders, not insiders. Real differences had to be fully exploited and even exaggerated, while similarities were best overlooked altogether or portrayed as malicious or superficial imitation. The polemicists succeeded so well that for us the terms 'orthodoxy' and 'heresy' imply only difference, not similarity" (ibid., 22–23).

[14] Ancient polemics were so effective that—as King shows—they are still espoused by scholars today: "A . . . powerful, largely unrecognized tool [in the Christian discourse on identity formation] was the rhetorical consolidation of manifold ancient religious practices into three mutually exclusive groups: Jews, Christians, and pagans. These categories became further reified in later centuries and continue to operate almost automatically in contemporary historiography, reinscribing and naturalizing the rhetoric of fourth- and fifth-century orthodoxy into a seemingly common-sense division of ancient religious life. Their tenacity demonstrates the success of Christian rhetoric in dominating the politics of religious identity up to our own day" (ibid., 22).

on the Oxyrhynchite marketplace I ask: Do Christians appear to be distinctive in the papyri found in that city, and if so, how and where?

Papyrologists have confronted this question in the study of private letters. This has resulted in scholarly debate around establishing criteria for determining which letters had a Christian author.[15] Mario Naldini's *Il Cristianesimo in Egitto* presents a thorough—but by no means undisputed—discussion of criteria for Christian authorship.[16] With this book Naldini provides a useful collection of ninety-seven letters that he considered Christian, ranging up to and including the fourth century. In addition, Peter Parsons's 1974 publication of a first- or second-century private letter (P.Oxy. 42.3057) that may contain a suggestion of Christianity sparked a debate about what constitutes Christian authorship.[17] Most recently, Malcolm Choat has addressed the question with a focus on the fourth century.[18] In these and other discussions, scholars evaluate papyrus letters using the following criteria to determine whether the persons involved are Christians: a) God in the singular, b) the word "Christian," c) biblical quotations or allusions, d) *nomina sacra*

[15] As Choat noted, "Collections of Christian documents necessarily require designations of factors indicative of Christianity. The definition of 'Christian text' itself depends on the specific project. . . . The type of discussion dictates the selection criteria" (*Belief and Cult*, 11). See also the scholarship on "Papyri from the Rise of Christianity in Egypt," conducted at Macquarie University's Ancient History Documentary Research Centre.

[16] First published in 1968, an enlarged and improved edition appeared in 1998 but did not include letters published after the first edition. Naldini wrote about them elsewhere: "Nuove testimonianze cristiane," in *Studi sul cristianesimo antico e moderno* (ed. Simonetti and Siniscalco) 831–46; and idem, "Nuovi contributi," in *Atti del XXII Congresso Internazionale*, 23–29 (ed. Andorlini et al.) 1017–24. In his *Cristianesimo*, each letter is given in Greek edition and Italian translation and accompanied by a short bibliography and commentary. Wipszycka has addressed fundamental criticisms on Naldini's book in her article, "Remarques sur les lettres privées," *JJP* 18 (1974) 203–32. See also Naldini's reply, "In margine," *Civiltà classica e cristiana* 2 (1981) 167–76; and idem, "In margine" *JJP* 19 (1983) 163–68.

[17] See discussions by Llewelyn, "§25 Ammonios to Apollonios," *NewDocs* 6:172–77 (especially "Determining Christian Authorship"); Stanton, "Proposed Earliest Christian Letter," *ZPE* 54 (1984) 49–63; Naldini, "Nuovi contributi," 1017–24 (esp. 1022–23); Ramelli, "Una delle più antiche lettere cristiane extracanoniche?" *Aeg* 80 (2000) 169–85; Montevecchi, "ΤΗΝ ΕΠΙΣΤΟΛΗΝ ΚΕΧΙΑΣΜΕΝΗΝ," *Aeg* 80 (2000) 187–94 (plates on 187–88); Parsons, "The Earliest Christian Letter?" in *Miscellanea Papyrologica* (Pap. Flor. VII) (ed. Pintaudi) 289 (plate 12); Hemer, "Ammonius to Apollonius, Greeting," *Buried History* 12 (1976) 84–91; and Wipszycka, "Les papyrus documentaires," *Atti del XXII Congresso* (ed. Andorlini et al.) 1310–12.

[18] Choat defines his time-frame as "late antiquity," "from the late-third to the mid-fifth century AD" (*Belief and Cult*, 2).

and other Christian symbols, e) specific vocabulary, such as "beloved" (ἀγαπητός) and other words, and f) mention of church or clerical titles.[19]

These are indeed important elements to research—I shall examine most of them myself below. However, my own approach differs conceptually in that instead of looking for *criteria*, I interpret these signs in the texts as *markers of identity*. I contend that weighing texts against *criteria* runs the risk of reifying and essentializing Christianity.[20] In contrast, I argue that examining texts for markers of identity acknowledges factors that Christians themselves used to denote their identity, factors which nonetheless left room for multiple and shifting dynamics of identity.

[19] Not all scholars mention all these criteria. In her thorough review of Naldini's collection, Wipszycka describes her position as follows: "La difficulté essentielle que doit résoudre l'éditeur d'un recueil de ce genre consiste à distinguer les lettres écrites par des chrétiens des celles qui ont été écrites par des non-chrétiens. Il y a peu de critères sûrs: à mon avis, il n'y a que les mentions du culte chrétien ou de ses ministres, les citations ou échos du Nouveau Testament, les «*nomina sacra*», des expressions telles que ἐν θεῷ, ἐν κυρίῳ, les monogrammes chrétiens." But Wipszycka also points to the fact that "la publication de plusieurs nouveaux textes papyrologiques et les recherches sur la religiosité païenne ont montré que, surtout à partir du IIIe siècle, des changements de la mentalité religieuse non-chrétienne et en particulier une forte tendance au monothéisme ont fait naître un langage religieux commun aux païens et aux chrétiens" ("Remarques," 205). For Stanton, "criteria which are usually accepted for Christian attribution of the later letters" are as follows: "While we can scarcely expect to find self-identification of the author as 'Christian,' or an explicit expression of adherence to Christ, we would need to find specifically Christian nomina sacra . . . or symbols . . . , use of the Bible, reference to the Christian community or its officials . . . or language used primarily or exclusively by Christians (such as ἀγάπη)." He adds that "to take just one of these [criteria], the potential reference to a Christian community is quite uncertain" ("Proposed Earliest Christian Letter," 56–57). Llewelyn adopts these criteria from Stanton ("Ammonios to Apollonios," 175). See also Naldini, *Cristianesimo*, 7–32 and Tibiletti, *Lettere private*, 29–30 and 107–25. Choat has provided the most extensive treatment, but his book centers on the fourth century and therefore on texts from a later date than the period that I discuss.

[20] As King phrased it, "The very process of classification tends to reify its own categories, often at the expense of understanding how individual works cross and blur definitional categories. . . . The variety of ways that texts can be categorized reflects the variety of interests and perspectives of those doing the classifying. . . . The point is that though categories and categorization are useful for particular ends, any classification system is provisional and positional" (*What is Gnosticism?*, 164).

Finding God at Oxyrhynchus

As his first criterion to discern Christian letters, Naldini mentioned the use of the word god (θεός) in the singular.[21] Naldini associated Christian identity with the orthodox Christian theological claim of monotheism. He is, however, quick to nuance his statement and notes that god in the singular does not provide a guaranteed indication for Christianity;[22] the occurrence of god in the singular in a letter can also be indicative of other religions, whether Jewish or pagan.[23] Where do we encounter monotheistic expressions in Oxyrhynchus papyri?

In some documents from Oxyrhynchus, the god in the singular is mentioned explicitly, such as "the lord god Sarapis," or "the great god Ammon." This leaves no doubt as to who is meant.[24] Many occurrences of the word god (in singular and plural) in the papyri, indicating a Roman emperor, appear in dating formulae and official documents, but the emperor's name is always included. Of course, the cases where a deity is not further specified cause us trouble. One papyrus from the third century invites its recipient to god's party: "(the) god invites you to a dinner party in the Thoereion."[25] The location of this meal in the temple of Thoeris, the hippopotamus-shaped goddess of childbirth, discourages us from imagining a Christian meeting. In another invitation a man, Petosiris, urges a woman, Serenia, to attend god's birthday party.[26] Strictly speaking, nothing suggests which god is having a birthday celebration, but similar invitations mentioning Egyptian deities suggest that this again was not a Christian feast. In these cases we can safely assume that the recipients were not confused but knew for what sort of party they were showing up! These examples are not what Naldini meant with god in the singular, but they picture the milieu to which Christians belonged; this is

[21] "Il primo elemento indicativo della fede religiosa cristiana delle lettere è, *naturalmente*, l'uso di θεός al singolare" (Naldini, *Cristianesimo,* 7 [emphasis mine]).

[22] "Ma la presenza di questo vocabolo non ci offre, di per sé, un indizio del tutto sicuro in senso affermativo" (ibid.).

[23] Ibid., 8–9. Naldini refers to: "Il sincretismo filosofico-religioso nel mondo ellenistico-romano dell'Egitto" (ibid., 9). Naldini questions, for instance, any distinction between θεός with and without article.

[24] E.g., τὸ προσκύνημά σου ποιῶ καθ' ἡμέραν παρὰ τῷ κυρίῳ θεῷ Σαράπιδι (P.Oxy. 14.1670, third/fourth cent.) or θεὸς μέγας Ἄμμων (P.Oxy. 52.3694, 218–225 C.E.?).

[25] καλεῖ σε ὁ θεὸς | εἰς κλείνην γεινο(μένην) | ἐν τῷ Θοηρείῳ, P.Köln 1.57.

[26] τοῖς γενεθλείοις τοῦ θεο̣[ῦ, (P.Oxy. 1.112, late-third/early-fourth cent.).

how their neighbors identified themselves, how they celebrated their meals, and how in general texts were dated.

Letter to Apollo (P.Oxy. 14.1680)[27]

So far, the use of god in the singular has not led us to identify any Christians, but these examples have alerted us to the complexity of this marker of identity. Significant for our discussion on recognizing Christians by reference to god in the singular is a private letter that a concerned son penned to his father Apollo at the end of the third or beginning of the fourth century.[28]

Unfortunately, it is impossible to provide a description of this papyrus since it is lost.[29] I find it ironic that this papyrus that expresses anxiety about losing someone has now vanished itself.

The letter reads:

> [Χαίροις Ἀπόλλων, ἀγαπη-][τέ μου κύριε καὶ γλυκύ]τατε πάτερ, κα̣ὶ̣ ε̣[ὔχομ]α̣ι̣ τῷ̣ θεῷ̣ ὁλοκλη-ρεῖν σε καὶ εὐ̣ο̣δ̣ο̣[ῦ]σ̣θαι καὶ ὑγιαίνον-τί σε ἀπολαβεῖν ἐν τοῖς ἰδίοις. καὶ γὰρ πρὸ τούτου σοι ἐδήλωσα λυπού-μενος ἐπὶ τῇ ἐν ἡμῖν σου ἀπουσίᾳ, μήπως ὃ μὴ εἴοι σοι γένοιτο καὶ μὴ εὕρωμέν σου τὸ σῶμα. κα[ὶ γὰρ πολλάκις σοι δηλῶσαι{σοι} βού̣[λομαι ὅτι βλέπων εἰς τὸ ἀσύστατ̣ον σ̣ῆ̣[μα ἠ-[30] θέλησα ἐνχαράξαι σοι. καὶ νῦν γὰρ ἀκού-ω ὅτι σφόδρα Ἡράκλειος ὁ νῦν ἐπίτρο-πος ζητεῖ σε, καὶ ὑπονοοῦμαι ὅτι πάν-τως πάλιν τί ποτε ἔχει πρὸς σέ.

[27] I have adopted the reconstruction of the first two lines from Farid, "The Prescript of *P. Oxy* 1680," *Anagennesis* 1 (1981) 11–18, at 18.

[28] Ed. princ. Grenfell and Hunt, "Letter to Apollo from his son," P.Oxy. 14.1680 (1920) 140–41. See also Ghedini, *Lettere cristiane,* 134–37 (no. 15); Naldini, *Cristianesimo*, 161–63 (no. 32); Winter, *Life and Letters,* 62–63.

[29] This papyrus belonged to the Library of the Westminster School in London. The school's archivist has informed me that the papyrus has been lost.

[30] Naldini reconstructs the end of line 11 as σ̣ῆ̣[μά τι ἠ]||θέλησα (*Cristianesimo*, 162).

[εἴ τ]ί ποτε αὐτῷ χρεωστεῖς, καὶ τοῦτό
[γε βο]ύλομαί σοι γνῶναι ὅτι ἐκόμισα
[πρ]ὸς Γάειν σίτου ἀρτάβας δύο καὶ
. . . .
(On the verso)
τῷ κυρίῳ] καὶ ἀγαπητῷ πατρὶ Ἀπόλλωνι

4. υγιαινο̄τι, *l.* ὑγιαίνοντα, 5. ϊδιοις, 8. *l.* εἴη 12. *l.* ἐγχαράξαι, α of ακουω rewritten, 14. πᾱν, the ν being only partially formed owing to lack of space, 17. *l.* σε, 18. *l.* Γάιον.

Translation

> (May you be well, Apollo, my beloved lord and sweetest) father, and I pray to god that you are in good health and have a prosperous journey and that I receive you healthy among your relatives. For also before this I have informed you that I am sad about your absence from among us, lest happens to you what should not be and we do not find your body. For also I often want to inform you that in view of you being without recommendation, I wished that I had engraved (a sign?) upon you. For also now I hear that Heraclius, the current steward, seeks you intensively and I suppose that evidently he has something against you again. If you owe him something, I also want you to know this, that I have brought to Gaius two *artabas* of grain and . . .
>
> (Addressed) (To my lord) and beloved father Apollo.

This letter is typical of many papyrus letters in the sense that lack of context prevents us from fully understanding the content—whereas it is clear that the recipient must have comprehended the message. It also exemplifies our challenge to know the religious identity of the correspondents.

The recipient of the letter, Apollo, is away from home and his son tries to contact him.[31] Why this Apollo was absent or why Heraclius was searching for him does not become clear. Some have suggested that Apollo was away

[31] Given his worries about retrieving his father in case something happens to him, it is interesting to note that the son still sends him a letter. Apparently, he found someone who knew his father's whereabouts, and he expected his father to receive the epistle. Naldini thinks the son is still young ("un giovane"), too young to bother about fiscal matters (*Cristianesimo*, 161), but Wipszycka rightly comments that this assumption is unfounded: "C'est une lettre qu'un fils écrit à son père. Je ne comprends pas sur quoi se fonde M. Naldini

on business.[32] Or, in light of the remark that Heraclius is searching for him, that he had fled. In any case, the son worries that his father Apollo may die and that the family will be unable to retrieve his body. The reason for his worry is difficult to grasp. It centers on the meaning of the words βλέπων εἰς τὸ ἀσύστατον (line 11). Grenfell and Hunt rendered it as "having regard to the insecurity." It can also be translated as "in view of your undetermined legal status,"[33] or "in view of the lack of safety."[34] In Ghedini's interpretation it relates to the father's traveling lifestyle. For him, Apollo, a traveling businessman, leads a life on the road, away from home, making it hard to find him in case of an emergency.[35] However, the word ἀσύστατον probably indicates here that Apollo traveled without an ἐπιστολὴ συστατική (letter of recommendation).[36] As we shall see later, travelers in antiquity relied on such documents to receive shelter and various other necessities of life. Without a letter of recommendation, Apollo would have no social network on which to rely during his travels, which could cause his son's anxiety.[37] With his father away on a potentially perilous trip, the son writes that he wished he had stamped a mark on his father.[38] One can interpret this enigmatic statement figuratively, but also more literally.[39] Unfortunately, the lack of direct clues

pour penser que ce fils a l'âge où normalement on ne se soucie pas de charges fiscales" ("Remarques," 213).

[32] "Apollo è forse un negoziante in granaglie su lontani mercati" (Ghedini, *Lettere cristiane*, 134); "probabilmente per ragioni di commercio" (Naldini, *Cristianesimo*, 161).

[33] LSJ 265 give that meaning referring only to this text ("8. of legal status, *not determined*, *POxy*. 1680.11"). Other translations are the following: not solidified, not cohesive, unformed, incurable, incapable of subsistence, irregular, inadmissible, chaotic, confused, incapable of proof (ibid.).

[34] So Winter, *Life and Letters*, 63; and Naldini, *Cristianesimo*, 162: "considerando la mancanza di sicurezza."

[35] Ghedini writes: "pensando che Apollo, uomo d'affari, conduce una vita in viaggi continui, non sempre noti al figlio, impossibilitato a ritrovarlo in caso di una disgrazia. Il pensiero che segue, dei rapporti cioè del procuratore Eraclio verso Apollo, credo non sia affatto in relazione con τὸ ἀσύστατον" (*Lettere cristiane,* 136, note to line 11).

[36] See the section on Letters of Recommendation in ch. 4.

[37] This seems to be the case with a certain Judas, who writes to his family in Oxyrhynchus after getting stuck in Babylon due to a riding accident (P.Oxy. 46.3314, "Letter of Judas," fourth cent.). See also footnote 116 below.

[38] σῆ[μα ἠ]|θέλησα ἐνχαράξαι σοι (P.Oxy. 14.1680, lines 11–12). The verb is clear, but the noun is an uncertain reading.

[39] Winter comments on this line, "A like solicitude for his father's safety prompted one son to propose a mark of identification, a measure sometimes employed now by the natives

in the letter providing a context for the dangers Apollo faces prohibits us from grasping the full extent of this family's problems.[40]

In the opening greetings the son cites the common formula, "I pray to (the) god that you are well," with reference to god in the singular. For Naldini, this, together with the adjective "beloved" (ἀγαπητός), indicated that the correspondents probably were Christians.[41] However, which god is meant? Is it indeed the Christian god, or the Jewish god, the god Sarapis, or another deity?[42]

The occurrence of the word "god" in this letter does not inevitably mark the writer as Christian. The letter, however, contains another possible marker of Christian identity: the adjective "beloved" (ἀγαπητός).[43] Does, as Naldini argues, the use of this adjective tip the scale in favor of a Christian

---

of the Fayum" (*Life and Letters*, 62). A papyrus documenting the return of a loan mentions a veteran "who is engraved" (οὐετραν[οῦ] ἐνκεχαραγμένου̣), P.Oxy. 55.3798, line 4, 144 C.E.). This veteran is, however, not physically marked, but rather his name is engraved on a bronze stele in Rome (P.Oxy. 55.3798, lines 8–9).

[40] Winter cites P.Tebt. 2.333, a petition from Tebtynis dated 216 C.E., in which a woman, Aurelia Tisais, fears for the lives of her father and brother, who had gone on a hare hunting trip and not returned (*Life and Letters*, 62).

[41] "La formula del r. 3 costituisce un probabile indizio cristiano, cui si aggiunge, più decisivo, l'uso di ἀγαπητός nell'indirizzo" (Naldini, *Cristianesimo,* 161).

[42] With regard to this question of determining the religion of the correspondents in the *Abinnaeus Archive*, V. Martin worded his doubts on the feasibility of using the word θεός as indicator for religion as follows: "It is not easy to distinguish the pagans from the Christians . . . since the more or less conventional formulas of these references are not always in themselves easy to distinguish as pagan or Christian. Allusions to 'God' in the singular and to 'Providence' are found: yet there is never a mention of any particular divinity of the Greco-Roman pantheon by name, any more than Christ is named. But the general terms just enunciated are not reliable criteria on the basis of which to assign those who employ them to one or the other religion, for they were current on both sides. . . . In view of this it is embarrassing to determine the religion of the writers of letters in which the word θεός figures in one or other set phrase" ("IV Abinnaeus and his Correspondents," in *The Abinnaeus Archive: Papers of a Roman Officer in the Reign of Constantius II* [ed. H. I. Bell; Oxford: Clarendon, 1962] 30–31). I should note here that the Abinnaeus Archive does not come from Oxyrhynchus. Abinnaeus was a cavalry officer in Dionysias in the Fayum; his archive was probably found at Philadelphia (see Martin, "Introduction," 1–5). As to religion, the archive is dated to the mid-fourth century, a time when a large part of the population of Egypt was probably Christian. The absence in some letters of specific markers of religion should not surprise one: religion is either irrelevant or understood for the writers.

[43] Although, as Matthews observes, "for all the use they made of it," Christians did not have "a monopoly of the term *agapitos*" (*The Journey of Theophanes,* 30).

correspondence? Wipszycka refutes this hypothesis on the ground that "pagan" correspondents equally address each other as "beloved brother."[44] Indeed, she emphasizes that neither the prayer to god in the singular nor the adjective "beloved" in the address provide a definite answer as to the religion of this family.[45] Therefore, the use of the adjective "beloved" as title of address in letters needs further examination. In New Testament texts, the word appears some sixty times, especially in the letters addressed to Christian communities. The apostle Paul, for example, addresses the community in Rome as "beloved of God" (Rom 1:7) and at the end of that letter he calls three men and one woman "beloved": Epaenetus, Ampliatus, Stachys, and Persis (Rom 16:5, 8, 9, 12). Also, the author of 1 John uses the word in the plural six times for his audience.

Turning now to papyri found at Oxyrhychus: the word "beloved" (ἀγαπητός) occurs in nine documents, all letters, found at the site (including P.Oxy. 14.1680) for a total of fourteen times. These nine Oxyrhynchite letters fall in the time span of the late-third and fourth century, with one from the fifth

[44] With regard to the word ἀγαπητός, Wipszycka notes, "je doute à plus forte raison de la légitimité de la présence, dans ce recueil, de deux autres lettres, les nos. 32 [= our text under discussion, P.Oxy. 14.1680] et 46 [= PSI 7.830, provenance unknown, fourth cent.], que M. Naldini a considérées comme chrétiennes à cause de l'emploi de l'adjectif ἀγαπη-τός" ("Remarques," 215). See also Judge and Pickering: "not . . . a clear signal" ("Papyrus Documentation," *JAC* 20 [1977] 47–71, at 69). The famous *casus* is the letter from John and Leon in the Theophanes archive (P.Herm. 4, Hermopolis, ca. 317–323 C.E.), who address Theophanes as ἀγαπητὸς ἀδελφός. Among his correspondents are "pagans worshipping Hermes Trismegistus" (Rees, P.Herm., 2). For Bagnall, John and Leon are Christians (*Egypt in Late Antiquity*, 271–72 and notes); for Wipszycka and others they are pagans. The fact that some of Theophanes's correspondents were worshippers of Hermes Trismegistus, however, does not mean that all his correspondents were of the same mind with respect to religion. Considering his name, John must have been either a Jew or a Christian. John and Leon address Theophanes, probably a pagan, with this same adjective.

[45] Wipszycka writes, "Pour G. Ghedini et les autres savants de sa génération, il n'y avait pas de doute qu'on pouvait reconnaître dans les lettres un langage spécifiquement chrétien, par exemple l'emploi du mot θεός au singulier dans les formules de salutation initiales ou finales, ou des expressions telles que σὺν θεῷ, θεῷ χάρις, θεοῦ θέλοντος." She points to a shared monotheistic language used by Christians and pagans, and concludes, "Pratiquement, il ne s'est servi de ce critère [i.e., du monothéisme] que dans les cas de l'expression εὔχομα . . . παρὰ τῷ κυρίῳ θεῷ et de l'adjectif ἀγαπητός. Mais je crois que l'analyse des textes présentant ces expressions montre jusqu'à quel point ce critère est fragile" ("Remarques," 205).

century.[46] Addressed are beloved brother(s),[47] a beloved papa,[48] a "beloved one and father,"[49] and beloved Tithoes.[50] None of the letters are distinctly pagan. On the contrary, apart from the fifth-century letter and the letter under discussion here, seven of the nine letters contain *nomina sacra*, a strong marker of Christian identity.[51] It is therefore possible that the son addressed his father Apollo with a Christian greeting as beloved father.[52] This letter differs from the clearly Christian ones in that it uses the adjective to address a father, whereas most letters combine it with "brother."

This letter illustrates well the challenge of discerning markers of Christian identity in the documentary record.[53] Since nothing else in the letter hints

[46] P.Oxy. 8.1162, l.3 (fourth cent.), P.Oxy. 14.1680, l.19 (third/fourth cent.), P.Oxy. 16.1870, l.1, 27 (fifth cent.), P.Oxy. 36.2785, l.1, 13 (second half of the third cent.), P.Oxy. 56.3857, l.2, 16 (fourth cent.), P.Oxy. 56.3858, l.1 (fourth cent.), P.Oxy. 61.4127.3, l.37 (first half of the fourth cent.), PSI 3.208, l.1 (second half of the third cent.), and PSI 9.1041, l.1, 17 (second half of the third cent.); based on a search of the DDBDP for ἀγαπητός with Oxyrhynchus as provenance. A DDBDP search without specification of provenance resulted in 128 hits. In most instances, the correspondents were Christians by other markers of identity. A clear exception to this use of the adjective is PSI 6.577, a document from the Zenon Archive dated 248/247 B.C.E. See also the discussion in Choat, *Belief and Cult*, 90–94. Choat observed: "that ἀγαπητός ἀδελφός begins to appear in documentary papyri only when Christians become more numerous in the third century is suggestive of a connection. The lack of subsequent documentary employment of the phrase securely outside of the Judeo-Christian tradition forbids any certainty as to how widely (if at all) it penetrated into the general vocabulary of letter writing" (ibid., 93).

[47] P.Oxy. 8.1162, P.Oxy. 16.1870, P.Oxy. 56.3857, P.Oxy. 61.4127, PSI 3.208 and PSI 9.1041.

[48] P.Oxy. 36.2785 (see discussion in ch. 4).

[49] P.Oxy. 56.3858.

[50] P.Oxy. 61.4127.

[51] On *nomina sacra*, see chapter 3 below. I concur here in large measure with Naldini, who found no instances where this adjective is clearly pagan but numerous examples where it is used in a definitely Christian context. "Numerose invece sono le lettere private sicuramente cristiane in cui ricorre l'attributo ἀγαπητός" (*Cristianesimo*, 19). In his collection Naldini rightly remains cautious in assigning letters to Christian authors solely on the basis of this adjective.

[52] Choat concludes: "On the basis of the evidence as it stands, it will be imprudent to exclude ἀγαπητός ἀδελφός, and instances where the adjective qualifies other nouns, from a list of criteria indicative of Christianity: we may classify . . . *P.Oxy*. XIV 1680 . . . as uncertainly Christian, but to mark [it] as 'possibly non-Christian' goes too far" (*Belief and Cult*, 93).

[53] Wipszycka classifies this letter among a group of letters that are "à des degrés divers, suspectes; elles peuvent être chrétiennes, mais aussi bien païennes ou juives" ("Remarques," 221).

at religious or cultic interests, we join the son in wishing for a stamp of identity.

The Use of the Word "Christian"

Since the word "god" in the singular alone proved ambiguous, and "beloved father" could not fully convince us that Apollo and his son were Christians, we have to look for different markers of Christian identity. The (seemingly) easy cases occur when people are identified explicitly by the word "Christian."[54] The name "Christian":

> originated in the first century as an outsider's term for the believers and, due particularly to its association with official questioning, was not fully domesticated amongst them for three or four centuries.[55]

While literary Christian authors employ the word "Christian" as self-reference, it occurs only infrequently in the papyri in general.[56] No more than three Oxyrhynchite papyri within our time frame contain this word:

- P.Oxy. 42.3035 "Order to Arrest" (256 C.E.)
- P.Oxy. 43.3119 "Official Correspondence" (ca. 260 C.E.)
- SB 12.10772 Letter from Sarapammon to his mother and sister (late-third cent.)

[54] See also Choat, *Belief and Cult*, 43: "The clearest indicator of membership of a belief system or cult one could hope for is explicit self-identification by a writer, or the designation of a person by another, as a member of a particular social group." In most papyrus documents and in several literary manuscripts the word "Christian," χριστιανός, -ή, is written as χρηστιανός, -ή, with *eta* instead of *iota*; see also a fuller discussion and examples in ch. 5 (140–41, especially 140 n. 56). This way of writing associates χριστιανός with the adjective χρηστός (useful, righteous, honest); both words would of course be pronounced the same—"christianos" and "christos." Justin Martyr, for instance, elaborates on the relation between these terms (*Apol.* 4.5; 46.4; see Lieu, *Christian Identity*, 258–59).

[55] Judge and Pickering, "Papyrus Documentation," 67. On the word Christian, see also Townsend, "Who Were the First Christians? Jews, Gentiles and the *Christianoi*," in *Heresy and Identity in Late Antiquity* (ed. Iricinschi and Zellentin) 212–30, and De Kruif, "The Name Christians," *Bijdragen* 59 (1998) 3–19.

[56] SB 16.12497 (Ptolemais Euergetis, first half of the third cent.); P.Dubl. 31 (Panopolis, 355 C.E.); P.Lips 43 (= M.*Chr.* 98, Hermoupolis Magna, fourth cent.)—here the adjective modifies the noun βιβλίων (it concerns a nun called Thaesis, who wants to inherit Christian books), P.Lond. 6.1919 (330–340 C.E.).

A woman called Atheas, living at the end of the fourth and beginning of the fifth century—the time of the *Historia monachorum*—is the next person explicitly described as Christian from Oxyrhynchus (P.Laur. 2.42).[57]

The two earliest texts from Oxyrhynchus identifying Christians are both documents issued by government officials. One asks for a "Petosorapis, son of Horus, Christian" (P.Oxy. 42.3035), and the other, a fragmentary piece in the true meaning of the word, mentions the plural "Christians" twice in a context that seems to suggest inquiries about property (P.Oxy. 43.3119). I shall discuss them in chapter 6. The third text, a third-century private letter that Sarapammon wrote to his mother and sister, informs them that a certain "Sotas, the Christian" would bring them money (SB 12.10772). I shall treat this letter in chapter 5. For now I note that in none of these cases do people introduce themselves as Christian,[58] rather, the epithet is applied to them

[57] This is a late-fourth/early-fifth century letter from the Oxyrhynchite nome (Bagnall dates the *recto* between 366/7 and 368/9; this is the date *post quem* for the verso). The letter reads:

πάνυ ἐλυπήθην καὶ λοιπούμεθα πάνυ σφόδρα διότι [[τὸ κακὸν]]
ἐτόλμησας ποιήσῃς πρᾶγμα τοιοῦτο Ἀθηᾶτι χρηστιανὴ οὖσα, διότι
καὶ λαẹικὴ οὖσα καὶ μηδέποτε εὑρέθη πράγματα τοῦ κόσμου.
(2 centimeters empty space)
γνῶστι ὅτι σπεχουλάτωρα γέγονεν Θεόδωρος ὁ Τηείτης.
ἦλθεν μετὰ Θέωνος τοῦ ἀδελφοῦ μου.

PLaur. 2.42, edited by Rosario Pintaudi (1977), 50–52, plate II/14.
Translation: "I was very grieved and we are exceedingly grieved that you dared to do such a thing to Atheas, who is a Christian woman, because she also is a laywoman, and she has never been discovered (doing) worldly business." (translation adapted from Horsley, "102. χρηστιανή in a Christian letter" in idem, *NewDocs* 2:172–74, at 173). The participle in line 2, χρηστιανὴ οὖσα, needs interpretation. Does it refer to Atheas, or to the addressee of the letter? As Bagnall rightly comments, "The editor appears to take the phrase to refer to the addressee rather than the woman under discussion, but that seems surely wrong" (*Egypt in Late Antiquity*, 282 n. 126). Thus Atheas is a Christian. The case here seems to have to do with the behavior of a drunken sailor (see also *NewDocs* 2:173; Tibiletti, *Lettere private*, no. 34, 196–97). The message is clear: the reference to Atheas being a Christian has to do with behavior; Christians are supposed to treat each other differently. The way a Christian should be treated is a matter that is understood, although perhaps the emphasis here is on how a Christian *woman* should be treated. Again, the writer does not identify her or himself as Christian, but places this epithet upon someone else. However, from the context it is clear that this letter was written by a Christian.

[58] The first instance of self-referential use in the papyri is P.Kellis 1.48 (from Kellis, dated 355 C.E.), where a manumission of a female slave is "on account of excess of Christianity" (δι' ὑπερβ̣ολὴν χ[ρι]στιανότ̣ητ̣ο̣ς, P.Kellis 1.48, l.4). This strong profession of Christianity is followed by the conventional pagan phrase "under Zeus, Earth and Sun" (ὑ̣π̣ὸ Δία Γῆν

by others, in the first two instances clearly by outsiders.[59] Thus in these documentary papyrus texts, the term "Christian" is an external marker.

What's in a Name? Nomenclature as Marker of Christian Identity

Only a few people that we spotted in the marketplace were called "Christian," and no one self-identified as a Christian. In this section we will explore names as markers of identity. When people introduce themselves to someone, they mention their name, both verbally and in writing.[60] Personal names abound in papyrus documents, but—as Deborah Hobson observes—papyrologists have conducted mainly lexical and prosopographical research into these names. Important as that is, "only a very few studies have attempted to extrapolate from the evidence provided by names some insights into social or historical problems."[61] Since names often carry information about their bearers, we now take up the issue of personal names as potential markers of Christian identity.

In Roman Egypt, as in our Western society today, people received their names as infants from their parents. The giving of a name is not only meant to tell people apart; it is also an inherently social practice, as Richard Alford lays out in his anthropological study on *Naming and Identity*:

> An economical theory of naming might suggest that names are bestowed upon children as a direct and pragmatic means of distinguishing one individual from another. But naming typically does much more than this. Often the naming of a child is given significant social meaning. . . . Naming the child often symbolically brings him or her into the social sphere, and naming is often accompanied by other acts with similar symbolic significance.[62]

Ἥλιον, l.5). Even for the fourth century, as Choat concluded, "self-identification as 'Christian' occurs only rarely in fourth century documents" (*Belief and Cult*, 47).

[59] See Judge and Pickering, who also point out that the word does not occur in any of Naldini's letters ("Papyrus Documentation," 66). Lieu notes a similar situation among Manichaeans. Referring to the finds from Kellis in the Dakleh Oasis, Lieu states: "The private letters of the community . . . give the impression that its followers [the Manichaeans] were well integrated into normal village-life and they never referred to themselves as 'Manichaeans'—a term of opprobrium coined by their opponents" (*Manichaeism in Mesopotamia,* 98).

[60] If not by name, then sometimes people are identified by family relationship, profession, ethnic nickname, etc.

[61] Hobson, "Naming Practices," *BASP* 26 (1989) 157–74, at 158.

[62] Alford, *Naming and Identity,* 30.

In other words, the study of personal names can provide social information.[63]

In my view, names can be markers of several aspects of identity, although we often lack the information to recognize these in papyri. The following five elements may play a role in the practice of naming a child: 1) gender (i.e., names are recognizably female or male);[64] 2) family—that is, naming after a family member (e.g., paponymy); 3) social status or cultural influence; 4) ethnicity; and 5) religion or cultic identity (names often have a religious connotation). I shall focus on this last aspect of names as markers of religious or cultic identity. The Greco-Egyptian onomasticon contains a rich variety of theophoric names, and in the marketplace one can meet people such as Taisis (Ταΐσις, "she-who-belongs-to-Isis") and Philosarapis (Φιλοσαρᾶπις, "lover-of-Sarapis"). According to Bagnall,

> People in antiquity took much more seriously than we do the religious connotations of the names they gave their children, and we may be sure that the disappearance of Petechonsis, meaning "the one who has given him is Khonsu" (a name not found after the third century) and the appearance and flourishing of Papnouthios, "the (servant) of God," are not accidents of fashion in the sense that the popularity of names tends to be in modern society.[65]

Indeed, a passage by Dionysius, bishop of Alexandria (247–264), quoted by Eusebius, confirms that he considered nomenclature important. Dionysius noted in his treatise *On Promises* (*apud* Eusebius) that Christian parents often called their boys Paul or Peter.[66] Thus for Dionysius and people in his

[63] For a bibliography, see Bagnall, "Religious Conversion and Onomastic Change," *BASP* 19 (1982) 105–24; Harnack, *Mission und Ausbreitung* 1:438; Hornblower and Matthews, eds., *Greek Personal Names*; Colin, "Onomastique et société," in *Noms, identités culturelles et romanisation* (ed. Dondin-Payre and Raepsaet-Charlier) 3–15; Choat, *Belief and Cult*, 51–56; Fikhman, "On Onomastics," in *Classical Studies in Honor of David Sohlberg* (ed. Katzoff) 403–14; and the website of the Lexicon of Greek Personal Names (LGPN): http://www.lgpn.ox.ac.uk/index.html.

[64] Names unmarked for gender are, e.g., Herieus and Stotoetis.

[65] Bagnall, "Religious Conversion and Onomastic Change," 108.

[66] According to Dionysius, ὥσπερ καὶ ὁ Παῦλος πολὺς καὶ δὴ καὶ ὁ Πέτρος ἐν τοῖς τῶν πιστῶν παισὶν ὀνομάζεται (*Hist. eccl.* 7.25.14). See also Harnack, *Mission und Ausbreitung* 1:441, and Bagnall: "The proclivity of Christian parents to give specifically Christian names to their offspring was noted already in antiquity" ("Religious Conversion and Onomastic Change," 108).

congregation, these children stood out as Christians because they were named after those apostles. In other words, association with the figures Paul and Peter marked in part the identity of these children as Christian.

The names that we would pick up among the noises of Egyptian agoras in the middle of the fourth century and later, as Egypt became more and more a Christian country, would differ greatly from those used in the earlier Greek and Roman times. Instead of Thaesis and Philosarapis, we would encounter Maria and Papnuthis and a whole range of other people with biblical names, Egyptian Christian names, and names of saints.[67] Pertinent here is the question of whether Christian names are noticeable in the papyrus documents dating to the period before the year 325. In the Greek-Egyptian onomasticon for this period, we can distinguish three categories of names: theophoric pagan names, biblical names (Jewish, Christian, or Manichaean[68]), and "names not assignable with certainty to one or the other."[69]

If, however, certain names, at least for scholars today, are markers of Christian identity, why did not all Christians in antiquity have such names? This is a complex matter. In the first place, as Bagnall reminds us, children receive names from their parents at birth.[70] For children born to non-Christian parents, this would exclude a Christian name. Upon conversion to Christianity as adults, these people in general did not change their names.[71] Second, in the pre-Constantinian period, Christians may have been afraid to give their children clearly Christian names.[72] Although, as Bagnall observed:

[67] Bagnall, "Religious Conversion and Onomastic Change," 109; Clarysse, "The Coptic Martyr Cult," in *Martyrium in Multidisciplinary Perspective* (ed. Lamberigts and van Deun) 384–85; Wipszycka, "Christianisation de l'Égypte," 66–67. See also O'Callaghan, "I nomi propri nelle lettere cristiane," *Aeg* 41 (1961) 17–25 for an inventory of names.

[68] Choat rightly pointed out that Manichaeans need to be included in the discussion of biblical names (*Belief and Cult*, 53–54).

[69] Bagnall, "Religious Conversion and Onomastic Change," 109. I have slightly modified Bagnall's criteria.

[70] This also means that "to the extent that names are evidence for religion, they are evidence for the religion of the parents at the time of the children's birth, not of the children" (Bagnall, "Religious Conversion and Onomastic Change," 109).

[71] Ibid. But for examples of name change see Horsley, "Name Change as an Indication," *Numen* 34 (1987) 1–17.

[72] Bagnall cautions, "the conditions of certain periods in the third century and the beginning of the fourth, when official persecutions of Christians were carried out, would have discouraged some parents from giving children patently Christian names. It is possible, therefore,

> There is no direct evidence that this is so, and one must suppose that a Christian who was willing to die for the faith would not hesitate to name a child in a patently Christian manner. On the other hand, the majority of any population consists not of martyrs but of ordinary people for whom social pressure is important.[73]

If, however, some people indeed were cautious about nomenclature in view of persecution, that in itself would testify to the importance of names as markers of Christian identity. Thirdly, apparently not all Christians considered their personal names to be of great importance. For some, names were but "empty and invented."[74]

So are Christians distinguished from the non-Christian population in the pre-Constantinian period by their names?[75] Nomenclature is a complex marker of identification and a part of the answer is a simple "no." For various reasons, many Christians in this period could not be recognized as such by their names. In a section entitled "The First Names of Christians,"[76] Adolf von Harnack addressed the question of Christian personal names and wondered whether the practice of giving biblical names goes back to the pre-Constantinian period.[77] Harnack's most striking example that this was not the case are the Acts of the North African synod of 256, as detailed by Cyprian. He found that most of the 87 bishops listed there have Latin names, some have Greek names, none have names from the Hebrew Bible, and only two have a New

---

that any figures relating to naming before 313 reflect fear and are insufficiently representative of the Christian population" ("Religious Conversion and Onomastic Change," 113).

[73] Ibid., 113–14.

[74] Tertullian, *Idolatry* 15.5: inania atque conficta. See also *Idolatry* 20.2: Neque enim Saturnum honoro, si ita uocauero eum suo nomine; tam non honoro, quam Marcum, si uocauero Marcum ("For I do not honor Saturnus, if I call him thus by his name; I do not honor him more than Marcus, if I call someone Marcus) and *Apology* 3.5, and Athenagoras, *Plea for the Christians* 2.

[75] For his research on fourth-century papyri, Choat asked: "To what extent can naming practices disclose affiliation to a specific tradition?" (*Belief and Cult*, 51). He sees "a clear but frequently overlooked disjunction between onomastic analysis on a large scale (capable of charting general trends, for instance) and specific application to an given individual. . . . Every person with a 'Christian' name need not be a Christian" (ibid., 53). For Choat, "onomastics will only provide a reliable indicator if a social group has defined an observable pattern of onomastic usage, and if a substantial portion of their names are not shared with other social groups" (ibid.).

[76] Harnack, "Die Rufnamen der Christen," *Mission und Ausbreitung* 1:436–45.

[77] Ibid., 436.

Testament name, namely Petrus and Paulus. From this Harnack concluded that North African Christians in the middle of the third century used pagan names without inhibition and hardly saw the need to give Christian names, adding that this practice was typical for all areas where Christians lived.[78] Harnack also pointed out that Christians often bore names referring to pagan deities, which led to a certain irony considering the times of persecution in which they lived. He noted aptly, "the martyrs died, because they refused to sacrifice to the gods whose name they bore."[79]

In documentary texts from Oxyrhynchus, we observe the same situation that Harnack outlined: some evidently Christian letters or documents do not contain any Christian names at all. For instance, a man called Petosorapis, bearing the name of the Graeco-Egyptian deity Sarapis, whose father Horus was named after the falcon-headed god of the same name, does not immediately strike one as Christian. Yet in an arrest order, Petosorapis is

[78] "Man brauchte also in der Mitte des 3. Jahrhunderts in Nordafrika noch ganz unbefangen die alten heidnischen Namen; das Bedürfnis, sich christliche Namen zu geben, regte sich kaum noch" (ibid., 437).

[79] "Die Märtyrer starben, weil sie sich weigerten, den Göttern zu opfern, deren Namen sie trugen" (ibid., 437). Von Harnack's observations are true not only for the third century. Many of the bishops of the post-Constantinian era (ca. 325 until the mid-eighth cent.) still bear pagan theophoric names, as Worp concluded at the end of his comprehensive list of Egyptian bishops: "quite a few of the Egyptian bishops . . . bore distinctly pagan names which supposedly might have been offensive to Christian ears. It is now evident that there was, after all, no absolute need for a bishop to bear a 100% 'Christian' name like Abraham, Petros, Paulos, etc." ("A Checklist of Bishops," *ZPE* 100 [1994] 283–318, at 318). See also Morris, "Bishops in the Papyri," in *Proceedings of the 20th International Congress of Papyrologists* (ed. Bülow-Jacobsen) 582–87; and Martin, "Aux origines de l'église copte," *REA* 83 (1981) 35–56, at 48. Martin counted 253 bishops by name from the mid-third-century episcopate of Dionysius to the death of Athanasius; 90% of them occurred after the year 325. Of these bishops, 115 had Greek names, 60 Egyptian or Greco-Egyptian names, 34 Latin names, 30 had biblical—mostly Old Testament—names, and some 15 could not be classified. Out of these 253, 104 had theophoric names. Martin concludes the following: "On constate que les chrétiens ne se distinguent pas des païens par leur nom, ce qui revient à dire que celui-ci continu d'être un signe d'appartenance sociale et non un témoignage de conversion à la nouvelle religion" (ibid.). However, in this later period, nomenclature has a different complexity for, as Bagnall observed, the people bearing pagan names may in fact be named after Christian martyrs: "Christians frequently named children after saints and martyrs who themselves bore pagan theophoric names, having been born pagans or perhaps in a time when it was not safe to be too obvious about one's Christian faith; and so such pagan names survived in Christian use even to the present day' ("Religious Conversion and Onomastic Change," 109); see also Clarysse, "Martyr Cult," 384–85.

labeled as "Christian" (P.Oxy. 42.3035).[80] We shall also meet other Christians with distinctly pagan names such as Taion and Heracles.[81]

What, then, are Christian names? Presumably some of them were names from the Scriptures. But if biblical names mark Christian identity, what then about Jews bearing these same names? In order to address this question of biblical names, we have to take into consideration Jewish names. For the collection of Jewish texts in the *Corpus papyrorum judaicarum* (*CPJ*), Victor Tcherikover gave onomastics great weight as selection criterion. In the "Introduction" he enumerated the following criteria that he used for adoption in the series

> As "Jewish" are considered
> 1. Papyri in which the word Ἰουδαῖος, or Ἑβραῖος, appears.
> 2. Papyri which mention events or technical terms that point to Jews or Judaism. . . .
> 3. Documents originating from what are known to have been places of exclusively Jewish settlement.
> 4. Papyri containing Jewish names.[82]

Yet whereas Tcherikover does not explain the first three criteria, he adds that the criterion of the Jewish names "requires further elaboration." He admits that this is a difficult matter because Jews often bore common Greek names and later, Christians adopted Old Testament names. He concludes that until the death of Constantine, biblical names refer to Jews and after that to Christians. Bagnall rightly critiques Tcherikover's approach to nomenclature as criterion for distinguishing Jews only within this given period:

> That criterion, as usually applied, has been that persons with biblical names found in papyri dating before 337, the death of Constantine, may be taken to be Jewish, while persons with biblical names after that date may be considered Christian. Quite apart from the fact that such a principle prejudges the complex problem of the pace of Christianization of Egypt . . . it is patently illogical and certainly leads to false results. Given the fact that such names rise steadily in numbers from the late third century on, application of this principle leads to a paradoxical conclusion that Jews increased steadily in number until 337, after which they disappear and—all of a sudden—Egypt

[80] The text reads: Πετοσορᾶπιν Ὥρου χρησιανόν, see discussion in ch. 6.

[81] Respectively in P.Oxy. 36.2785 and PSI 3.208, see ch. 4.

[82] Tcherikover and Fuks, *Corpus papyrorum judaicarum* 1:xvii.

> is populated with large numbers of Christians. This absurdity is in itself sufficient to show that this principle does not work.[83]

Although Tcherikover considered onomastics an important marker of Jewish identity (or at least a topic worthy of investigation), this issue has received relatively little attention in collections of Christian papyri. For instance, the possibility of names as markers of Christianity does not come up in most studies of private letters.[84] Bagnall's article on the relationship between nomenclature and conversion rates has put the issue of the possible role of onomastics as a marker of identity on the scholarly agenda.[85]

Biblical Names: Jacob and Maria

Biblical names make good examples to illustrate the challenge of onomastics as a marker of identity. We find a man called Jacob, son of Achilleus, assigned as night guard to the temple of Sarapis in Oxyrhynchus together with five other men.[86] Jacob, a Jewish name but also a biblical name, turns up in Christian use as well.[87] Thus the question becomes: is this Jacob or James, Jew or Christian, or—as one scholar suggested—a former Jew and pagan convert?[88] For Tcherikover, the answer was evident: "Jacob, son of

[83] Bagnall, *Egypt in Late Antiquity,* 276. For an example of the application of Tcherikover's principle in a papyrus, see P.Oxy. 31.2599 (third/fourth cent.), which contains two letters from a woman Tauris mentioning a Susanna and an Esther.

[84] So Naldini, *Cristianesimo*; Stanton, "Earliest Christian Letter;" Tibiletti, *Lettere private.* See also Horsley's comment on Tibiletti's work: "Though some names are given attention, the onomastic criterion, as a way of helping to establish whether certain texts may be referring to Christians, is not sufficiently explored" (*NewDocs* 4:60). Exceptions are Bagnall, "Charite's Christianity," *BSAP* 32 (1995) 37–40 and Horsley throughout his articles in *NewDocs.*

[85] Bagnall, "Religious Conversion and Onomastic Change," 105–24; a response by Wipszycka, "La valeur de l'onomastique," *ZPE* 62 (1986) 173–81; Bagnall's reply, "Conversion and Onomastics," *ZPE* 69 (1987) 243–50; and Wipszycka's "Post-Scriptum I, "La Christianisation de l'Égypte," in eadem, *Études sur le Christianisme,* 103–4.

[86] P.Oxy. 1.43. ii.13: Ἰακὼβ Ἀχιλλέως (*post* 295 C.E.). For the date see Bagnall, *Egypt in Late Antiquity,* 164 n. 83.

[87] The case is clear in a much later text, P.Oxy. 44.3203 "Lease of Exedra and Cellar" (June–July 400 C.E.), where the person is explicitly described as Jew: "Aurelius Jose, son of Judas, Jew" (παρὰ Αὐρηλίου Ἰωσὴ Ἰούδα Ἰουδαῖως [*l.* Ἰουδαίου], line 7), involved in a business transaction with two nuns.

[88] Tcherikover refers to Neppi Modona, "La vita pubblica e privata degli Ebrei in Egitto," *Aeg.* 3 (1922) 40.

Achilleus—*obviously a Jew*, in spite of the fact that he performs his duty as a guard in the temple of Sarapis."[89] Tcherikover added that the idea that this Jacob had converted to paganism seemed "perhaps a too far-fetched supposition."[90] He put that politely, for the function of guard does not indicate religious affiliation to the building or temple.[91] The name Jacob may well have indicated a Jew, but according to Bagnall, "it is . . . much more likely that biblical names in post-Hadrianic documents are a sign of Christianity."[92] Perhaps then it indicated a Christian. Put less abstractly: Would this Jacob have attended church services in the north or south church of Oxyrhynchus mentioned in that same papyrus (P.Oxy. 1.43) or did he perhaps, as part of the Jewish community, contribute to the manumission of a Jewish slave woman and her children, as attested in a papyrus dated 291 (P.Oxy. 9.1205)?[93] This woman's four-year-old son is actually called Jacob (line 5), which proves that Jews used the name at this time.[94] Or, to make matters more complex, did Jacob fit in among those people that Origen or John Chrysostom famously fulminate about, who attended both synagogue and church?[95] If a Christian, he would be one of the earliest Christians in the papyrological record bearing

[89] *CPJ* 3.475 "From a list of night guards" (= P.Oxy. 1.43, ii.7–13), quote from pages 38–39 [emphasis mine].

[90] *CPJ* 3.475, quote from page 39.

[91] We do not even know, as Bagnall points out, whether the Sarapeum was still in use as a cult center at this time: "Les autres références aux temples ne fournissent beaucoup d'indications sur ce qui se passait à l'intérieur. . . . On ne peut donc pas dire si les temples de Sarapis et de Thoéris [mentioned in P.Oxy. 1.43] étaient vraiment encore des centres de culte" ("Combat ou vide," 290). In the same way, we cannot say that the guards for the two churches mentioned in this same document were Christians. The guard for the church in north street is Apphous, son of Theon (i.11), and for the one in south street it is Ammois, son of Parammon (iii.20). One has no way of telling their religious affiliation.

[92] Bagnall notes: "real Jewish communities of the Roman world had onomastic repertories in which biblical names played only a small role. Unless one can identify other contemporary Semitic names in the same matrix as the biblical ones, the latter have no claim to help identify Jews" (*Egypt in Late Antiquity*, 276). Also Cohen concluded: "Jews . . . had names and occupations like those of everyone else, and, in general, closely resembled their gentile neighbors" ("How Do You Know a Jew?" 39).

[93] "Manumission *inter amicos*." The woman's name is Paramone; two children are mentioned. See brief discussion and bibliography above in the Introduction, 17 and 17 n. 73.

[94] I see no value in speculating on whether this four-year-old Jacob from P.Oxy. 9.1205 could be identical with the night guard from P.Oxy. 1.43.

[95] Origen, *Hom. Lev.* 5.8 and Chrysostom, *Adv. Jud.* 1.5. See also Lieu, *Christian Identity*, 144–45 and 145 n. 130.

this name.[96] Thus without further context—his father's name does not help either—it is impossible to decide one way or the other. No matter where or how he spent his worship time, this man's name still was a marker of identity given to him by his parents[97] and perhaps also functioned that way for the people who met him. However, his name does not allow us to go beyond identifying him as son of a Jew or Christian at this point.

An example of a biblical female name is Maria (Hebrew: Miriam), a widely given Jewish name[98] and later also a popular Christian name. This name occurs only three times in pre-Constantinian papyri from Oxyrhynchus.[99] Can this name give us an indication of whether we are meeting Jewish, as Tcherikover would argue, or Christian, or even "pagan" women?[100] In P.Oxy. 44.3184,

[96] Based on a DDBDP search, most Jacobs appear only later in the papyrological record. Other fourth-century examples are the following: P.Oxy. 17.2124 (316 C.E.); P.Kellis 32, l.20 (364 C.E.; this Jacob is a reader in the Catholic Church); P.Flor. 1.66, l.2 (398 C.E.); and P.Neph. 12 (fourth cent.).

[97] Or perhaps his mother alone gave him the name. In this case and all others, the name may not be intended as marker of religious identity; Jacob may have been named after one of his grandfathers or received this name for any other reason.

[98] Ilan noted that "the name Mary (Miriam) was extremely popular in Palestine at the time of Jesus. It was by far the most popular name available and was born by over 25 per cent of the female population" ("In the Footsteps of Jesus," in *Transformative Encounters: Jesus and Women Re-Viewed* [ed. Kitzberger] 115–36 at 122). Maria (מרים/Μαριάμη), Salome, and Shelamzion were the names most used for women in Greco-Roman Palestine (330 B.C.E.–200 C.E.), as Ilan has demonstrated in her "telephone book" of that period. Ilan calculates that they "constitute roughly 48% of the female population" (*Lexicon of Jewish Names,* 9 [quote] and 242–48 [prosopography]).

[99] P.Oxy. 44.3184 (297 C.E.); P.Oxy. 36.2770 (304 C.E.); and P.Oxy. 55.3787 (ca. 313–320 C.E.). For the date of the latter, the editio princeps dated the document to 301/302; for a revision of the date of P.Oxy. 55.3787 to the years 313–320, see Bagnall, "Notes on Roman and Byzantine Documents," *ChrEg* 66 (1991) 282–96, "6. The Date of *P.Oxy.* LV 3787," 293–96. Cf. Wipszycka, who arrives at the earlier date: "après 288/9" ("Les papyrus documentaires," 1308–9, quote from 1308 n. 4). Two general observations are in place here: 1) Women appear much less in papyri than men. In two of these three examples, a Maria is mentioned as mother of a man in order to indicate his lineage. 2) Again, names are given upon birth, therefore a post-Constantinian document may still be evidence of the Christianity of the parents of those people in a much earlier time. A good example is the Maria in the "Archive of Papnouthis and Dorotheus" (published in P.Oxy. 48). Maria, the mother of the two protagonists, may have been born in the early decades of the fourth century by which time her parents were already Christians (unless she or they were Jewish).

[100] Horsley wondered: "Is this name sufficiently distinctive ethnically to allow us to identify its bearers always as Jews, or in the late Imperial period as Christians since it was

a "List of Village Liturgists," dated 9 January 297,[101] we meet a field-guard in the village of Talao named Aurelius Sarmates with his parents Theodorus and Maria.[102] Was this a Jewish or a Christian family? Tcherikover mentions three Jewish Marias, one of whom he notes is probably not Jewish. The dates of texts he cites are early in comparison with our text (not after 116 C.E.).[103] He also lists twelve Jewish men called Theodorus, none of whom fall into the period of our text however (75 C.E. is the latest one).[104] Examining the occurrences of the name Theodorus in Rome, Horsley concludes: "This name appears to be in the process of being appropriated by the Christians, but in the period of interest to us it has not yet become monopolized by them."[105]

For Egypt, the situation is different, because repression of the Jewish revolt under Trajan in 115–117 C.E. had devastated the Jewish communities in Egypt and the extent of their recovery in the later centuries is debated.[106] Thus all instances of these two names, which Tcherikover collected, occur in texts that are much earlier than our papyrus, which dates from the end of the third century. Maria and Theodorus therefore probably formed a Christian couple, but we should keep open the possibility that they were Jews. We do not know how old they were when this document was drawn up in 297 (if they were still alive), but with an adult son they must have been at least in

taken over as a Biblical name from Jews in the NT?" no. 115. ". . . a problem like Maria," in *NewDocs* 4:229. He gives examples of all three categories, the "pagan" Marias from the *gens* Maria: "Vibia Maria Maxima," and "Accia Maria Tulliana" (ibid., 230).

[101] Bowman, ed., P.Oxy. 44.3184 (1976) 140–44.

[102] Πεδιοφύλακ̣ες· Σα̣ρ̣μάτης Θεο̣δ̣ώ̣ρου μη(τρὸς) Μαρίας, b 17.

[103] The two certain texts are ostraca from Edfu, dated 114 and 116 C.E. Both Marias paid the Jewish tax. The third example is an undated epitaph from Antinoopolis, reading (in translation): "Maria, daughter of Phamsothis. 35 years old. May your rest be in peace." The editors commented that "the Jewish nature of this inscription cannot be said to be certain" (*CPJ* 3; "Appendix II: Prosopography of the Jews in Egypt," 184).

[104] Ibid., 177.

[105] But see Horsley: "Solin, *GPR* I.74–76 lists ca. 90 attestations of Theodoros from Rome, ranging from the beginning of the Principate to VII/VIII. From the third and fourth centuries (i.e., including those Solin marks as III/V, IV/V and IV/VI) there are 35 instances of which 17 are certainly Christian" (*NewDocs* 4:62). In this respect it is interesting to note a much later Greek grave inscription from Oxyrhynchus for a Theodorus, "slave of God" (written with a *nomen sacrum*), dated probably to 511 or 513 C.E. (see Petrie, "Oxyrhynkhos Revisited," reprinted in *Oxyrhynchus: A City and Its Texts*, 56 and 69, plate 5.13).

[106] See Modrzejewski, "ΙΟΥΔΑΙΟΙ ΑΦΗΙΡΗΜΕΝΟΙ," in *Symposion 1985* (ed. Thür) 337–61. By the end of third century, as we have seen, a Jewish community resurfaces at Oxyrhynchus; also late-fourth/early-fifth-century Hebrew texts have been found at Oxyrhynchus.

their thirties and forties. This means that their respective parents in the fifties and sixties of the third century or even earlier were Christians or Jews. Either way, these names are historically significant: either for the Jewish or for the Christian community in Egypt. In the end, the fact that we cannot decide positively whether some of these people bearing biblical names are Jews or Christians is, if anything, perhaps another indication of "the ways that never parted."[107]

The second Maria from Oxyrhynchus appears in a deed of divorce from 26 January 304 (P.Oxy. 36.2770).[108] Her ex-husband's name is Heracles. I quote here lines 4–9 of the document, the section of the deed containing the names of the former couple:

> [4]Ạὐ̣ρ̣ή̣λιοι Ἡρακλῆς Σ̣εραπίωṿọς μη(τρὸς)
> Ọ.....διṿας ἀπὸ τῆς λαμ(πρᾶς) καὶ λαμ(προτάτης)
> Ὀ̣ξυρυγχ̣ε̣ιτῶν π̣όλεως καὶ ἡ γενομένη
> καὶ ἀπηλλαγμένη μου γυναικὶ Αὐρηλία
> [8]Μαρία Ἡρακλεί̣δου μη(τρὸς) Ταυώνιος ἀπὸ τῆς
> αὐτῆς π̣όλεως χαίρειν·

4. *l.* Αὐρήλιος, 7. *l.* γυνή

Translation

> Aurelius Heracles, son of Serapion, his mother being O . . . , of the glorious and most glorious city of the Oxyrhynchites, and my former and divorced wife Aurelia Maria, daughter of Heracleides, her mother being Tauonis, of the same city, greetings.

David Rokeah, the text's editor, noted rightly: "The wife's name Maria raises the question whether she was Jewish or Christian." Referring to Tcherikover, he noted that the woman "should be considered as Jewish." But his own interpretation goes in a different direction:

> Since her family and her husband's family bear Graeco-Egyptian names, and the document itself offers no other indication of her religion, it is

[107] See the volume by Becker and Reed, *The Ways That Never Parted.* See also Boyarin, *Dying for God.*

[108] Ed. princ. David Rokeah, "Deed of Divorce," P.Oxy. 36.2770 (1970).

> possible to accept her as a pagan, believing her name to be a reflection of Jewish or Christian influence.[109]

Thus Rokeah does not seriously consider the possibility that this Maria was a Christian woman, but is sooner inclined to think of her as pagan—a far-fetched position in my view.[110] Indeed, as Bagnall suggests "in a fourth-century context a Christian identity is more likely."[111] Instead of concluding that the woman adopted the religion of her husband, I consider it quite possible that this text attests a mixed marriage, with Maria being Christian or Jewish and her husband a pagan. Again, Maria's name brings us a generation earlier, to her parents Heracleides and Tauonis in the seventies or eighties of the third century.

The deed specifies that Maria and Heracles did not have children.[112] It would have been interesting to learn what names they had given their offspring. Also, we do not know why they divorced. Two later texts from Oxyrhynchus (both fourth or fifth cent.) detail the unpleasant marital problems of the couples involved in separation,[113] but this official deed of divorce from Maria and Heracles does not satisfy our indiscreet, but of course academically motivated, interests.

The third pre-Constantinian text featuring a Maria introduces a "Plutarchus son of Maria" at the village of Ophis.[114] This tax list includes many other possibly Christian names, such as Stephanus, Pinution, Theodorus, Paulus, Sara, and Petrus, as well as a deacon and a reader. Rea, the editor, commented that "in view of the deacon and reader . . . there seems good reason to suppose

[109] P.Oxy. 36.2770, 60.

[110] I agree with Bagnall's position: "I think it is very unlikely that pagans gave their children Christian names" ("Religious Conversion and Onomastic Change," 112).

[111] Bagnall, *Egypt in Late Antiquity* 193, n. 72; see also his section on "Sex, Marriage, Divorce," 188–99.

[112] P.Oxy. 36.2770, lines 19–20.

[113] P.Oxy. 6.903 and P.Oxy. 50.3581. See e.g., Bagnall, *Egypt in Late Antiquity,* 194–95; Rowlandson, *Women & Society*, nos. 153 and 154, 207–9. In both instances, Christian clergy (bishop and priests) officiate. On divorce in papyri, see Arnaoutoglou, "Marital Disputes in Greco-Roman Egypt," *JJP* 25 (1995) 11–28; Bagnall, "Church, State and Divorce," in *Florilegium Columbianum,* 41–61; repr. in *Later Roman Egypt: Society, Religion, Economy and Administration* IV; and Yiftach-Firanko, *Marriage and Marital Arrangements*.

[114] Ὦφ[ε]ω̣ς (vac.) Π[λο]ύ̣ταρχος υ[ἱὸ]ς Μαρίας, P.Oxy. 55.3787, lines 54–55 (313–320 C.E.).

that the name here is that of a Christian."[115] Although this can become a circular argument, doing away with potential diversity, the context suggests that this Maria was a Christian woman.[116] Again, however, she may have been Jewish.

Not all Christian parents picked names for their children from the Scriptures or gave them existing pagan names. This leads to the question of whether we can detect newly formed Christian names in the onomasticon.[117] Which names qualify as such? According to Iiro Kajanto, "to be accepted as «Christian», a name should not be found at all in pagan material or at least be much less frequent."[118] Bagnall points out that these new names are either "based on abstract nouns and adjectives of theological content" or names derived from

[115] P.Oxy. 55.3787, note to line 55. See also references to this document in Part Three, 183–84 n. 121 and 198 n. 28.

[116] The challenge of determining whether the name Maria lets us meet a Jewish or a Christian woman is brought out strongly by a fourth-century letter found at Oxyrhynchus (Rea, P.Oxy. 46.3314 [1978] "Letter of Judas," 103–5). In this letter a man called Judas, away in Babylon, addresses his father Joses and his wife Maria in Oxyrhynchus and urges them to help him after he became injured due to a horseback riding accident. Judas also tells Maria that if she needs money, she can get it from a neighbor called Isaac. Rea concluded on the basis of the nomenclature, "that the letter originated from a Jewish family and circle," but he also pointed to possible Christian elements in the letter (103). All the people in the letter have biblical names. Judas is not a likely name for a Christian because of the unfavorable role that he played in the gospels as the betrayer of Jesus. However, several Christian Judases are known: Eusebius refers to a Christian called Judas (*Hist. eccl.* 6.7.1). Another Christian Judas (ⲛ̄ⲛ̄ⲓⲟⲩⲇⲁⲥ) can be found in Crum, "Fragment of a Church Calendar," *ZNTW* 37 (1938) 27, frg. A recto, line 4. See no. 100 "Divine Providence in a letter of Judas," *NewDocs* 3:141–48 with other examples of the name Judas. I note here also the positive connotations with the figure of Judas in the recently discovered Gospel of Judas. After ample consideration, Horsley is inclined to think that "the letter of Judas may after all emanate from a Christian milieu" (*NewDocs* 3:148). See discussions in the editio princeps, Tibiletti, "Appunti su una lettera di Ioudas (P.Oxy. XLVI, 3314)," in *Scritti in onore di Orsolina Montevecchi* (ed. Bresciane et al.) 407–11; Bagnall, *Egypt in Late Antiquity*, 276 n. 102; most recently Epp, "Jews and the Jewish Community," in *New Testament Manuscripts* (ed. Kraus and Nicklas). This letter falls beyond the time frame of this research.

[117] See also Bagnall on the name Adelphius. After examining papyrological, epigraphical, and literary sources, Bagnall concludes: "It seems to me therefore reasonable at least to adopt the working hypothesis that Adelphios was a name put into currency by Christians in the middle of the third century, which enjoyed some popularity in the fourth and fifth centuries before becoming uncommon" ("Charite's Christianity," 40). So far, this name has not occurred in papyri from Oxyrhynchus.

[118] Kajanto, "On the Problem of «Names of Humility»," *Arctos* 3 (1962) 45–59, at 46.

the Egyptian word for god (*ntr*, ⲛⲟⲩⲧⲉ).[119] In chapter 7 we will examine an example of the former—the name Athanasius. As for the latter, Bagnall explains: "Pagan names in Egyptian used the name or epithet of a specific god or cluster of gods, not the general or abstract word for god."[120] Among these names are Papnoutius (Παπνούτιος or Παπνούθιος and other spellings)[121] and Pinoution (Πινουτίων).[122] The name Papnoutius (ⲡⲁ-ⲡ-ⲛⲟⲩⲧⲉ, meaning "he-who-belongs-to-god") is a common name in the post-Constantinian era. The pre-Constantinian occurrences are difficult to interpret. Since the name Papnoutius already appears in two mid-first-century papyri, it cannot be a new Christian name. This name occurs, however, probably infrequently enough to allow it to pass at a later time as Christian. In later instances the name does not occur in contexts that give even the slightest hint at Christianity.[123] Therefore, we cannot classify it as a newly coined Christian name.

The situation is slightly different with the name Pinoution. This name never gained much popularity at Oxyrhynchus—it occurs only five times in papyri from Oxyrhynchus. The texts are comparatively early: three third-century

[119] Bagnall, "Religious Conversion and Onomastic Change," 111.

[120] Ibid., 110.

[121] E.g., Παπνούθης, Παπνοῦθις, Παπνούτε, Παπνούτ, Παπνοῦτις (see Preisigke, *Namenbuch*, 276–77; Foraboschi, *Onomasticon*, 234, and Hagedorn, *WörterListen*, http://www.zaw.uni-heidelberg.de/hps/pap/WL/WL.pdf (accessed September 19, 2008) 83.

[122] Bagnall, "Religious Conversion and Onomastic Change," 110.

[123] The chronological distribution of this name is as follows: The two earliest appearances are in mid-first-century C.E. papyri from Philadephia: Ἀτρῆς Παπ̣νούτ(ιος) in a census list (P.Princ. 1.14, dated 48–49 or 62–63 C.E.) and Παπνοῦτις Πνεφερῶτος μη(τρὸς) Τεμβίου in a tax register (P.Harr. 1.72, dated 40–68 C.E.). In view of the first-century date, these Philadelphian men are certainly not Christians. The first Papnoution in a text found at Oxyrhynchus appears in official correspondence dated 161 C.E., as the father of Diogenes, a run-away guard, however, from Memphis: Διογένης Παπ̣ν̣ο̣υτί̣ω̣(νος) (P.Oxy. 60.4060; the text is mutilated at this point and the reading is not certain). It is highly unlikely that this man was a Christian. Only at the end of the third or beginning of the fourth century do we meet another Papnoution in an Oxyrhynchus papyrus, in the patronym of a Sotas from the village of Taampitei, Σωτᾶς Παπνούτιος (P.Oxy. 14.1747). These people may be Christian—in chs. 4 and 5 of this book, a Christian bishop called Sotas is the focal point—but again, the onomastics alone make too fragile an argument for this period. Compared to these meager findings, the instances of this name in the fourth century, on the contrary, are striking: 21 men (52 hits in the DDBDP, but not counting the same man twice, *in casu* the Papnouthis from the "Archive of Papnouthis and Dorotheus" published in P.Oxy. 48). It is thus only in the fourth century, after Constantine, that this name became in fashion in Oxyrhynchus among Christians.

papyri, one early-fourth, and only one of post-Constantinian date (386 C.E.).[124] After this—as far as the preserved papyri reveal—the name Pinoution fell out of fashion in the Oxyrhynchite onomasticon. One of these Pinoutions, the son of Harachthus (Πινουτίων υἱὸς Ἀράχθου) shows up in the village of Mermertha in the tax list that included several women and men with Christian names, and among them appeared one of our Marias (P.Oxy. 55.3787). This Pinoution may therefore also be a Christian. Concerning the third-century occurrences of this and other names the lack of context prevents a decisive judgment. By themselves these names do not provide enough evidence to support the weight of an exclusive marker of Christian identity.

In view of our interest in naming practices in Christian families, we observe here that in two instances the presumably Christian parents give their child a non-Christian name: Maria and Theodorus named their son Sarmates (P.Oxy. 44.3184);[125] another Maria called her son Plutarch (P.Oxy. 55.3787; the text does not mention his father; perhaps not a Christian). Thus by no means do all Christians bestow Christian names upon their offspring. Jacob, on the other hand, bears a biblical name, whereas his father goes by name of the Homeric hero Achilleus. Whether the name Pinoution indicated a Christian or not, his father's name Harachthes did not represent a Christian. Although we do not know what motivated these people when selecting the names of their children, we do know that many factors other than religious ones come into play when choosing names.[126]

So far our observations on the marketplace have introduced us to three markers of Christian identity: god in the singular, the use of the word Christian, and nomenclature. Through these we could distinguish Christians in passing by. In the next chapter we turn our attention to a corner in the

[124] The name Pinoution occurs five times out of 315 total instances in papyri (from a DDBDP search): PSI 12.1248, Letter of Condolence, which mentions Pinoution (235 C.E.); P.Oxy. 12.1531 (before 258 C.E.); P.Oxy. 55.3811 "Business Letter" (third cent.); P.Oxy. 55.3787 (313–320 C.E., this document contains several Christian names, see above, section on Maria); and SB 18.13916 (386 C.E.).

[125] The name Sarmates does not occur in the *CPJ* texts, nor in Ilan's *Lexicon* (for Palestine).

[126] As Hobson noted: "it is more difficult to deal with the question of what kinds of names were chosen. Here there is a sharp divergence between the sources available to the anthropologist and those which the papyrologist has at hand. . . . [W]e . . . have to extrapolate the meaning simply from the words. This offers us only a limited understanding of the significance of names, since there is often a critical distinction to be made between the literal meaning of a name and its *real* significance" ("Naming Practices," 162–63).

marketplace where Christian scribes write letters and use a firmer marker of Christian identity: *nomina sacra*.

CHAPTER 3

What's in a *nomen*? Recognizing Christians through *nomina sacra*

The scribal practice of *nomina sacra* (sacred names) expresses visually the Christian identity of a writer. In this chapter I argue that the *nomina sacra* indicate a Christian education and/or familiarity with Christian manuscripts. They also constitute a link between literary manuscripts and documentary papyrus letters.

Colin H. Roberts provided a useful summary of this scribal practice:

> *Nomina sacra* as a term in Greek and Latin paleography denotes a strictly limited number of words, at most fifteen, the sacral character of which, intrinsic or contextual, is emphasized by abbreviating the word in question, normally by contraction, occasionally in the earliest period by suspension. A horizontal line is placed above the abbreviation as a warning that the word cannot be pronounced as written.[1]

New Testament scholars generally associate *nomina sacra* with literary manuscripts. Indeed, Gamble rightly describes these contractions as a "noticeable and extremely widespread peculiarity in the inscription of early Christian books."[2] *Nomina sacra* also occur in nonliterary texts, such as inscriptions and papyrus letters, and this phenomenon has not yet received adequate discussion.[3]

[1] Roberts, *Manuscript, Society and Belief*, 26.

[2] Gamble, *Books and Readers*, 74–75.

[3] An exception is Choat, "XII 'Nomina Sacra,'" *Belief and Cult*, 119–25 (for fourth-cent. documents). See also Epp, "Oxyrhynchus New Testament Papyri," *JBL* 123 (2004) 21–26.

The relatively modern term for this ancient practice, *nomina sacra,* comes from Ludwig Traube, who coined it in his 1907 book.[4] Since then, these Christian contractions have constituted a topic for textual critics and students of Christian literary manuscripts that competes in popularity only with the development of the codex. Scholars have debated their origins (whether Jewish or Christian) and studied their forms (regular and derivate) and their theological implications.[5] All scholars who have written about this practice agree that the reverence for the name of God is Jewish, but the debate persists about whether that has any explanatory significance.[6] My approach differs from previous scholarship on the topic in that I do not focus on their origins but rather view *nomina sacra* as evidence of teaching in Christian circles. I also show that in several instances the people using *nomina sacra* in their private letters also wrote and owned literary manuscripts. Thus my approach bridges, at least partly, the gap between literary and documentary texts.[7]

[4] Traube, *Nomina sacra.*

[5] For literature on this topic after Traube's *Nomina sacra*, see: Rudberg, *Neutestamentlicher Text*; Paap, *Nomina sacra*; O'Callaghan, *Nomina sacra in papyris graecis*; Brown, "Concerning the Origin," *Studia Papyrologica* 10 (1971) 7–19; Jankowski, "I 'nomina sacra' nei papiri," *Studia Papyrologica* 16 (1977) 81–116; Roberts, *Manuscript, Society and Belief,* 26–48; Gamble, *Books and Readers*, 74–78; Millard, "Ancient Abbreviations," in *The Unbroken Reed* (ed. Eyre, A. Leahy and L. Leahy) 221–26; Hurtado, "Origin of the *Nomina Sacra*," *JBL* 117 (1998) 655–73; idem, "Earliest Evidence," in *Text and Artifact* (ed. Wilson and Desjardins) 271–88; Tuckett, "P52 and Nomina Sacra," *NTS* 47 (2001) 544–48; Hill, "Did the Scribe of P[52] Use the Nomina Sacra?" *NTS* 48 (2002) 587–92; Hurtado, "Nomina Sacra," *Tyndale Bulletin* 54 (2003) 1–14; Tuckett, " 'Nomina sacra': Yes and No?" in *Biblical Canons* (ed. Auwers and de Jonge) 431–58; Hurtado, "The *Nomina Sacra*," in *Earliest Christian Artifacts*, 95–134; Choat, "Nomina Sacra," in *Belief and Cult*, 119–25.

[6] Gamble commented: "No theory of the origin and significance of the system of nomina sacra has yet commanded general assent. There is broad agreement that it has something to do with Jewish reverence for the Tetragram, the name of God, but it has proved difficult to say exactly what" (*Books and Readers*, 75).

[7] Clarysse, "Literary Papyri" in *Egypt and the Hellenistic World* (ed. Van 't Dack, Van Dessel, and Van Gucht) 43–61. In this article Clarysse, reflecting on the relationship between literary and documentary papyri, observes that they "usually . . . belong to different worlds: the literary texts become part of the slowly growing corpus of Greek literature, whereas the documents give us a vivid glimpse of the people in Egypt from 300 B.C. to 600 A.D. . . . [T]hey are often studied by different categories of scholars. Literary papyri . . . usually appear only as indicators of the cultural interests of Graeco-Roman times. Yet those hundreds of literary texts were all copied for, and read by, the very Greeks who lived in Egypt from Alexander to Mohammed. Each one was originally written with a specific purpose and used by a particular person or group of persons: books were kept in the libraries of gymnasia, temples or private individuals" (ibid., 43).

Although the origins of the writing of *nomina sacra* remain under discussion,[8] no one any longer disputes the Christian character of these contractions.[9] As a matter of fact, scholars always interpret the presence of *nomina sacra* in literary manuscripts as an indicator that a Christian scribe has copied the manuscript,[10] and apply this principle both for literary manuscripts and for epigraphical and papyrological sources. We have no indication yet suggesting that Jewish scribes used this system in their Septuagint copies.[11]

[8] See e.g., the works by Roberts, Brown, Gamble, and Hurtado in footnote 5 above.

[9] Traube located the origins of *nomina sacra* in the Alexandrian-Jewish community. This position cannot be maintained any longer due to a lack of manuscript evidence.

[10] As Hurtado noted: "so distinctive is the practice that palaeographers tend to consider the presence of *nomina sacra* in a manuscript as a strong indication that it comes from Christian hands" ("Earliest Evidence," 277; and a similar statement in his *Earliest Christian Artifacts*, 96). Roberts stated: "There are two stigmata of Christian texts, the most conspicuous and the most important . . . the early and consistent use of the codex and the *nomina sacra*" (*Manuscript, Society and Belief*, 19); see also Aland and Aland, *Der Text des Neuen Testaments*, 86.

[11] Future work may disturb the consensus that *nomina sacra* are exclusively Christian because the reasoning is at least in part circular. Kraft notes: "In most instances, such an identification [as Christian] is clear from the content, in which Jesus (abbreviated) is depicted as 'savior' (abbreviated) and the source of holy 'spirit' (abbreviated), etc. But there are a few instances in which the only such abbreviations refer to God and Lord (the normal Greek representation of the tetragrammaton). Might these be 'Jewish' materials, showing an extension of otherwise well attested treatments of the tetragrammaton? The question is seldom raised, but it deserves closer examination. And there are some suggestive examples, even if no 'smoking gun'—yet" ("Continuities and Discontinuities" [cited October 20, 2007]. Online: http://ccat.sas.upenn.edu/rs/rak/jewchrpap.html. Kraft provides examples at: http://ccat.sas.upenn.edu/rs/rak/lxxjewpap/kyrios.jpg). Roberts mentions a fifth- or sixth-century manuscript with the Tetragrammaton in paleo-Hebrew letters (= van Haelst 74) and "a single instance of κύριος contracted to $\overline{\kappa\upsilon}$ at the end of a line and three of Ἰσραήλ contracted to $\overline{\iota\sigma\lambda}$, again at the end of a line" (*Manuscript, Society and Belief*, 32–33, see 32 n. 6). Also, "Ἱερουσαλήμ appears once as Ιουσαλμ, again at the end of a line where space was short" (ibid., 33 n. 1). For a nonliterary context, see two Jewish inscriptions from Asia Minor, where "God" is contacted: no. 90 (after 380 C.E., from the Sardis synagogue) and no. 226 (fourth century or later, from Ikonion) in *Inscriptiones Judaicae Orientis* (ed. Ameling) 2.248, 261–63, and 485–88. Other examples of *nomina sacra* used in synagogue inscriptions are discussed in Horsley, "§69. Nomina sacra," *NewDocs* 1:107–12. Another example is "a bronze incense-burner from Egypt, (ca. 300–500) with a menorah and a dedication by a certain Auxanon (= Heb. Joseph). . . . The editor regards Auxanon as 'a semi-hellenized Jew'" (see *NewDocs* 5:138). Hurtado emphasizes the lack of evidence for Jewish use of *nomina sacra*: "There is no undisputably Jewish manuscript in which any of the *nomina sacra* are written as we find them in undeniably Christian manuscripts" ("Origin of the *Nomina Sacra*," 662). Roberts: "What is true is that the contracted form of κύριος is in the first three centuries the mark of a Christian manuscript" (*Manuscripts, Society and Belief*, 31 n. 1).

Pagans did not employ these contracted forms.[12] Manichaeans, on the contrary, did write *nomina sacra* in their literary and documentary texts.[13] A writing containing a *nomen sacrum* can thus derive from either a Christian or a Manichaean milieu. However, as Choat remarks, given the small size of the Manichaean community in Egypt we should classify the use as Christian, unless specific indicators of Manichaeism occur.[14]

Nomina sacra appear in all sorts of Christian manuscripts and cross the rhetorical territories of "orthodox" and "heretical" writings. Copyists wrote them, for instance, in the *Gospel of Thomas*, the gospel of Luke, and in magical texts.[15] As text critics rightly maintain, this lack of distinctiveness not only means that the practice of writing *nomina sacra* started at an early date in the

[12] An interesting case appears in a document on the condition of the Nile (P.Aberd. 18 = SB 14.11474, dated 15 September 292 C.E.), which mentions ὁ θε(ὸς) καὶ κύ(ριος) Νῖρ (i.e., Νεῖλος). This short note, with unknown provenance (Soknopaiou Nesos? Arsinoites?) immediately evokes questions: Can we really call these forms *nomina sacra*? Are they not better described as abbreviations? Choat notes that "the first two abbreviations are not signaled by a suprelinear stroke or otherwise" (*Belief and Cult*, 120). Or was the person writing this note perhaps a Christian? The river Nile kept having religious importance for Egyptian Christians, and prayers for its rise are still said today. Also, river deities are depicted in early Christian art.

[13] Choat complexified the picture by drawing attention to Manichaean use of *nomina sacra*: "As with many of the other criteria of Christian authorship . . . Manichaean usage again can be detected, in both literary and documentary context" (*Belief and Cult*, 122; see also ibid., 124–25). Examples of Manichaean usage of *nomina sacra* include the well-known Kölner Mani-codex. An interesting documentary case is P.Harr. 1.107, a letter from Besas to his mother Maria (probably from Oxyrhynchus; see Naldini, *Cristianesimo*, 76, and the discussion of provenance of P.Harr. 2.208). Powell, its editor, characterized it as "an illiterate letter written by a Christian to his mother in a boyish hand" and tentatively assigned the papyrus to the third century (P.Harr. 1.107, 89). Other scholars have even postulated a date in the early third century, making it one of the earliest Christian letters known: so, e.g., Roberts, "Early Christianity in Egypt," 95; Naldini, *Cristianesimo*, 76 (no. 5); Epp, "Oxyrhynchus NT Papyri," 25. See, however, the new appreciation by Choat, Gardner, and Nobbs, "*P.Harr.* 107," *ZPE* 131 (2000) 118–24. These scholars argue that the letter comes from a Manichaean milieu (ibid., 121–22), and should be dated based on the handwriting "in the late third or early fourth century" (ibid., 120).

[14] Choat, *Belief and Cult*, 138–39.

[15] P.Oxy. 6.924: "Gnostic Charm" (fourth century) with the *nomina sacra* for Jesus, Christ, and spirit. Grenfell and Hunt write about this papyrus: "A charm for warding off fever . . . but Christian instead of pagan. . . . The Deity is not addressed under any particular name at the beginning, but the essentially Gnostic character of the charm is shown at the end by the mystical symbols and the occurrence of the title Abrasax, a common Gnostic name of the Supreme Being" (P.Oxy. 6.924, 289). Without making it explicit, the *nomina sacra* determine the Christian character for the papyrologists.

transmission of Christian manuscripts. It also indicates that the boundaries between Christian groups were not so distinct as polemics lead us to believe. Groups with different theologies or christologies shared certain practices, one being the use of *nomina sacra* in the inscription of manuscripts. In light of the importance of writings in their group self-definitions, this common scribal practice is significant.

The distinctly Christian character of this scribal system has two relevant implications: First, *nomina sacra*, as an in-group language in written form constitute a Christian sociolect. Gamble pointed this out clearly in his discussion on Christian book production: "the system of *nomina sacra*, though not an esoteric code, stands out as an in-group convention that expressed a community consciousness and presumed a particular readership."[16] Although Gamble referred to *nomina sacra* in literary manuscripts, I contend that the statement holds true for documentary texts as well. The people who wrote these *nomina sacra* in their letters used them to express their identity as part of a social group. Second, *nomina sacra*, unlike spoken language, represent a visual expression of in-group language. Hurtado has drawn attention to this aspect: "The *nomina sacra* were a strictly visual phenomenon, and functioned to register Christian piety visually. . . . [T]he *nomina sacra* manifest early Christian reverence for what the words represent."[17] This visual quality stands out just as clearly in documentary texts as it does in Christian literary manuscripts.[18]

The visual aspect of *nomina sacra* gives them a symbolic quality. For Roberts, *nomina sacra* are "a unique device that in the minimum of space provides a summary outline of theology."[19] Their symbolism does not need words, for, as Lieu has noted, symbols "evoke instant recognition and a sense of familiarity without waiting for a disquisition on their precise theological

[16] Gamble, *Books and Readers*, 78.

[17] Hurtado, "Earliest Evidence," 277. Hurtado returns to this aspect in his *Earliest Christian Artifacts*, 121, 132–33.

[18] Christians did not use *nomina sacra* consistently. Several correspondents in private letters who stand out as Christians through other markers of identity did not write *nomina sacra*. Likewise not all Christian literary manuscripts contain *nomina sacra*, as Traube already noted: "Die Papyrus- und Pergamentreste, deren ägyptische Herkunft sicher ist, . . . zeigen, daß seit dem 4., vielleicht schon seit dem 3. Jahrhundert folgende Formen geläufig waren: . . . [gives list]. *Es ist dabei immer so gewesen, daß statt einzelner Kurzformen auch die voll ausgeschriebenen Wörter gesetzt wurden*" (*Nomina sacra*, 44; emphasis mine).

[19] Roberts, *Manuscript, Society and Belief*, 47.

meaning."[20] *Nomina sacra* do just that. Therefore the "theology" (à la Roberts) does not need to be made explicit. This symbolic quality may explain the wide use of the *nomina sacra* in Christian manuscripts.

Nomina sacra in Letters from Oxyrhynchus

What then can we learn about early Christians in Oxyrhynchus who wrote *nomina sacra* in their letters? I provide an inventory of letters containing this scribal practice from Oxyrhynchus and dating to the pre-Constantinian period:[21]

1.	PSI 3.208	Sotas to Peter (second half of third cent.)*
		χαῖρε ἐν κ̅ω̅ (line 1)
		ἐρρῶσθαί σε ἐν θ̅ω̅ εὔχομαι (lines 11–12)
2.	PSI 9.1041	Sotas to Paul (second half of third cent.)
		χαῖρε ἐν κ̅ω̅ (line 1)
		ἐρρῶσθαί σε εὔχομαι ἐν κ̅ω̅ (lines 15–16)
3.	P.Oxy. 36.2785	priests of Heracleopolis to Sotas (second half of third cent.)
		χαῖρε ἐν κ̅ω̅ (line 1)
		ἐρρῶσθαί σε ἐν κ̅ω̅ εὐχόμεθα (lines 13–14)
4.	P.Alex. 29	[Sot?]as to Maximus (third cent.)
		ἐρρῶσθαί σε εὔχομαι ἀγαπητὲ ἀδελφὲ ἐν κ̅ω̅ (lines 12–15)

* Numbers 1–3 and possibly 4 belong to what I call "the correspondence of Sotas." I shall discuss these in detail in chapter 4. I do not provide a discussion of numbers 7, 8, 12, and 13 in this book.

[20] Lieu, *Christian Identity*, 155.

[21] These letters are all dated by palaeography and context. P.Oxy. 14.1774, a letter from Didyme and her sisters to Atienatia, was dated to the early-fourth century and contains the phrase, with *nomen sacrum*, ἐν κ̅ω̅ χαίρειν (line 3). I have not adopted this letter, however, following Wipszycka's new dating of this letter to ca. 340 C.E. ("Del buon uso," in "*Humana sapit*" [ed. Carrié and Testa] 469–73, esp. 470).

5. P.Oxy. 8.1162 — Leon, presbyter, to fellow presbyters and deacons (third/fourth cent.)[*]

ἐν κ̅ω̅ θ̅ω̅ χαρᾷ χα[ί]ρειν (lines 4–5)

προσαγορεύεσθαι κ̅ω̅ (line 12)

ἐρρῶσθαι ὑμᾶς [ε]ὔχομε ἐν κ̅ω̅ [θ̅]ω̅ ε̅μ̅μ̅λ̅ μ̅α̅ρ̅τ̅ (lines 13–14)

6. P.Oxy. 56.3857 — to brothers and fellow ministers (third/fourth cent.)[**]

ε̅μ̅λ̅ (line 13)

ἐρρῶσθαι ὑμᾶς ἐν κ̅ω̅ εὔχομαι (lines 14–15)

7. P.Congr. 15.20 — Colluthus to Ammonius (Oxyrhynchus?)[***] (late-third/early-fourth cent.)

ἐν κ̅ω̅ χαίρειν (line 2)

8. P.Oxy. 12.1493 — Thonis to Heracleus (late-third/early-fourth cent.)

παρὰ τῷ κ̅ω̅ θεῷ (lines 4–5)

9. P.Oxy. 12.1592 — woman to her Father (late-third/early-fourth cent.)

κ̅ε̅ μου π̅ρ̅ (line 3)

π̅η̅ρ̅ (line 5)

10. P.Oxy 31.2601 — Copres to Sarapias (early-fourth cent.)

εὔχομε ὑμᾶς ὁλοκληρῖν παρὰ τῷ κυρι̅ θ̅[ω̅] (lines 4–5)

[*] P.Oxy. 8.1162 and P.Oxy. 56.3857, two letters of recommendation, are dated fourth century on the basis of paleography. However, van Haelst is correct when he comments: "En raison de considérations paléographiques et stylistiques . . . il faut attribuer au denier tiers du IIIe siècle, et non au IVe siècle, une dizaine de lettres d'introduction et de recommandation" ("Sources papyrologiques," in *Proceedings of the Twelfth International Congress* [ed. Samuel] 497–503, at 498).

[**] See previous note.

[***] On the provenance of this papyrus, A. H. El-Mosallamy, the editor, comments: "Although I have been told that this papyrus almost (certainly) comes from Oxyrhynchus, and the names mentioned in it are not rare there, I can not assure that this is an Oxyrhynchite papyrus" (P.Congr. 15.20, 94). I should note here as well that the parallels for the handwriting El-Mosallamy mentions are "all late 3rd cent. A.D." (ibid.).

11. P.Oxy. 63.4365 Letter about Christian books (early-fourth cent.)[*]
ἐν κ̅ω̅ χαίρειν (line 1)
ἔρρωσο ἡμεῖν ἐν θ̅ω̅ (line 6)

Possibly pre-Constantinian:

12. P.Oxy. 61.4127 Ptolemaeus to Thonis (first half of fourth cent.)
ἐν κ̅ω̅ χαίρειν (lines 4–5)

13. P.Oxy. 56.3858 Barys to Diogenes[**] (fourth cent.)
ἐν κ̅ω̅ χαίριν (line 3)
ὁ θ̅ς̅ φυλάξε σε (line 25)

[*] The editor, Rea, suggests a pre-Constantinian date based on the absence of names in this document, noting also that the "parallels to the language of the petition are from the later third century, so that an early fourth century date for the letter is very possible" (P.Oxy. 63.4365, 44).

[**] The letter is written in a literary hand, dated to the fourth century. According to Sirivianou, its editor, it parallels documents (P.Herm. Rees 4 and 5, letters from the Theophanes archive, dated ca. 316–323 C.E.) and literary manuscripts from the first quarter of the fourth century. She concludes: "A date in the fourth century seems likely, not necessarily as early as Theophanes" (P.Oxy. 56.3858, 117). This letter is on the cutoff time for this project.

In these letters from Oxyrhynchus, *nomina sacra* occur for the following words: lord (κύριος), God (θεός), father (πατήρ), and Emmanuel (is my) witness (Ἐμμανουήλ μάρτυς). In comparison with contractions used in literary manuscripts, two matters stand out: 1) the absence of the words Jesus and Christ and 2) the presence of the name Emmanuel.

The *nomina sacra* for Jesus and Christ, so prominent in literary manuscripts of the third century (some scholars even argue that abbreviations for the name Jesus initiated the practice of writing *nomina sacra*),[22] do not occur at all in the papyrus letters of this period. The contracted form of the name Jesus Christ does not appear until an (early?) fourth-century letter.[23] A

[22] So Roberts: "as it looks probable enough, Ἰησοῦς was the first name to be treated as a *nomen sacrum*" (*Manuscript, Society and Belief*, 37). See also Hurtado, "Origin of the *Nomina Sacra*," 665–71, and *Earliest Christian Artifacts*, 112–20. Other scholars, such as Traube, took the *nomen sacrum* for Θεός as first one, interpreting the practice from the Jewish reverence for the name of God.

[23] Naldini describes this letter in his introduction as "una sola lettera contiene per esteso la denominazione del Salvatore, Ἰησοῦς Χριστός" (*Cristianesimo*, 22). Metzger edited that papyrus, P.Graec.Vindob. Inv. 39838, in his "Spätantik-byzantinische Papyri," *MusHelv* 18 (1961) 24–27 (provenance unknown).

mid-fourth-century letter between two monks and a fourth-century letter to a teacher called Philoxenus contain the earliest examples of the contracted form.[24] In the letters from Oxyrhynchus with *nomina sacra*, most people referred to the Lord, while some referred to God or the Lord God. The letters thus display a strong preference for the marker Lord. These writings, however, do not make explicit whom they meant by "Lord:" the Lord God as in the Septuagint or the Lord Jesus as in Christian writings.[25]

The occurrence of the *nomen sacrum* for Emmanuel in two private letters illustrates a striking difference in the usage of *nomina sacra* in private letters compared to that of literary manuscripts (P.Oxy. 8.1162 and P.Oxy. 56.3857).[26] Although contracting Emmanuel ("God-with-us") as an indication for a divine name makes perfect sense,[27] that *nomen sacrum* does not occur

[24] P.Lond 6.1927 (provenance Oxyrhynchites?) ι̅η̅υ̅ χ̅υ̅ (line 6) and SB 14.11532 (provenance unknown) ἡ χάρις τοῦ κ̅υ̅ ἡμῶν ι̅η̅ χ̅ρ̅ (line 11). I should note here that P.Heid. 1.6 (mid-fourth cent.) has the *nomen sacrum* for the Lord Christ: ἐν κ̅ω̅ χ̅ω̅ (line 24). The closing greeting of SB 14.11532, the letter to Philoxenus, is Pauline. An interesting aspect of this letter is that the sender wrote *nomina sacra* in addressing people, women and men (see also below). For discussion, see Eisen, "IV A. Ein Papyrusbrief," in *Amtsträgerinnen*, 87–93; Horsley, *NewDocs* 1:79, 121; idem, *NewDocs* 4:122, 240; Tibiletti, *Lettere private*, no. 32, 192–93.

[25] About the use of κύριος, Naldini remarks: "Non possiamo neppure tentare di stabilire in quali casi il termine κύριος si possa o si debba riferire a Cristo" (*Cristianesimo*, 22). Tibiletti comments on the almost complete absence of Jesus Christ and the Holy Spirit in private letters: "La scarsa frequenza della menzione di Gesù Cristo e dello Spirito Santo, rispetto a quella di Dio, può avere anche una giustificazione nel fatto che solo con Nicea si ha il completo Simbolo di fede e che a causa delle numerose controversie dogmatiche attorno alla figura del Cristo si preferisca citare solo Dio" (*Lettere private*, 114). Naldini says nothing of the significance of the use of *nomina sacra* in nonliterary texts, neither does Ghedini, although he provides a list of abbreviations (ibid., 327).

[26] Images of these papyri are online through APIS and the Oxyrhynchus website, respectively.

[27] The fifteen common *nomina sacra* are contractions of the words Jesus, Christ, Lord, God (Ἰησοῦς, Χριστός, κύριος, θεός)—these form the top four of oldest contracted words—and spirit, human, cross, father, son, savior, mother, heaven, Israel, David, and Jerusalem (πνεῦμα, ἄνθρωπος, σταυρός, πατήρ, υἱός, σωτήρ, μήτηρ, οὐρανός, Ἰσραήλ, Δαυείδ, and Ἰερουσαλήμ). See Roberts, *Manuscript, Society and Belief*, 27; Metzger, *Manuscripts of the Greek Bible*, 36 and 37 n. 85; and Hurtado, *Earliest Christian Artifacts*, 96–98. Traube mentions these fifteen *nomina sacra* in the context of the Egyptian school ("wir [sind] wirklich doch nur unterrichtet über den Gebrauch der christlichen Schreiber Ägyptens," *Nomina sacra*, 44).

elsewhere besides these two papyrus letters, as far as I know.[28] Roberts remarked that "in any period there are very occasional eccentric forms, most of which occur once only and then usually in a badly written manuscript, the result of the misunderstanding or vagaries of a particular scribe." He admits, however, that some forms "represent an experimental phase in the history of the system when its limits were not clearly established, though the basic words were. . . . By the end of the second century the list had been pruned and effectively closed."[29] Roberts thus interprets these additional *nomina sacra* with hindsight as uninformed or experimental uses. This, however, presupposes a fixed system that clearly did not exist.

I understand these different forms as evidence of a lively practice and creative application of *nomina sacra* that was meaningful for these writers. Notably, the correspondents (both senders and recipients) of the two letters containing the rare *nomen sacrum* for Emmanuel are clergy; people presumably used to seeing *nomina sacra* in early Christian texts. In my opinion this *nomen sacrum* at the end of these letters creates a powerful formula with layers of significance. It consists of a visible sign of Christian identity for the in-group members, a cryptic appeal to Emmanuel (as witness), and then the affirmation of God's presence (Emmanuel, "God-with-us").[30] This interpretation does not require knowledge of Hebrew, because we find this basic early Christian Messianic exegesis readily available, for instance, in the gospel according to Matthew.[31] This employment of a *nomen sacrum*

[28] Emmanuel occurs only twice in the Christian bible in Isa 7:14 and Matt 1:23. P.Oxy. 3.401, a fifth- or sixth- century vellum fragment of the gospel of Matthew with the passage, contains the word in full, whereas it uses several other *nomina sacra* (for Jesus, son). Emmanuel as *nomen sacrum* does not appear in Aland's Appendix of *nomina sacra* in early Christian manuscripts in his "4. Nomina Sacra," in *Repertorium*, 420–28. Other rare *nomina sacra* are for instance, μ̅ω̅ for Μωυσῆς and η̅[σ̅α̅ς̅ for Ἠσαΐας in P.Egerton 2 = *Fragments of an Unknown Gospel* (ed. Bell and Skeat), 2; P.Bod. 13 features α̅β̅ρ̅μ̅ for Ἀβραάμ (Hurtado, *Earliest Christian Artifacts*, 98 n. 12).

[29] Roberts, *Manuscript, Society and Belief*, 39. Metzger also wrote about "a certain amount of experimentation" and classified rare forms as "eccentricities" (*Manuscripts of the Greek Bible*, 37).

[30] Naldini comments on this in his introduction as follows: "l'autore, che pur nella concisione del testo rivela familiarità con i libri sacri, sigilla biblicamente il suo scritto col nome del Messia nell'A. T., Ἐμμ(ανουή)λ (*nobiscum est Deus*)" (*Cristianesimo*, 22).

[31] Matt 1:23 explains the Messianic prophecy in Isa 7:14 (καὶ καλέσουσιν τὸ ὄνομα αὐτοῦ Ἐμμανουήλ) as: ὅ ἐστιν μεθερμηνευόμενον *μεθ' ἡμῶν ὁ θεός* (see also Isa 8:8). In the gospel of Matthew, Matt 1:23 and Matt 28:20b ("I am with you always") form a "literary *inclusio*" (Hurtado, *Lord Jesus Christ*, 332). Many early Christian writers, from Ignatius and

fits exactly into the purpose of an in-group language; as a distinct, secret, creative, and powerful tool.

In the small corpus of letters from Oxyrhynchus, the *nomina sacra* appear fairly consistently in form, although some variation in spelling and use occurs. I consider Roberts's rather negative assessment of the scribal qualities of these writers as typical for scholars commenting on *nomina sacra* in documentary texts:

> the contractions occur in documents as well as in literary manuscripts and where exceptions to the rule—rare even in documents—are listed they will be found on examination to occur in private letters or prayers or in e.g. magical texts, often the work of an amateur or careless scribe.[32]

Indeed, we see differences in use where some documents have one word in abbreviated form, and the next word written in full.[33] I evaluate these differences more positively as a conscious effort to show reverence.[34] In my opinion, no matter how these writers executed the *nomen sacrum*, the message of shared Christian identity must have come across visually and symbolically.

Nomina sacra and Christian Education

Beyond visually communicating Christian in-group language, *nomina sacra* also, I argue, provide evidence of Christian education. Writing *nomina sacra*,

---

Justin Martyr to Origen, and especially Eusebius, commented on this name Emmanuel and the Matthean passage on the Isaiah prophecy. The church historian gives a lengthy exposé on the name Emmanuel in his *Demonstratio evangelica* (7.1) and in his *Commentarius in Isaiam* (1.44, 48–51, 54). Cyprian quotes Isa 7:14 when writing about persecution. See *Letters of St. Cyprian* (ed. Clarke) 1:73, letter 10.4.2.

[32] Roberts, *Manuscript, Society and Belief*, 27. See also Bell: "contracted forms of *nomina sacra*, though well established, were not yet completely understood by the less literate writers" (P.Lond. 6.1917, 80–81).

[33] For instance, a writer contracted "Lord" (κύριος) but twice wrote "God" (θεός) in full: παρὰ τῷ κ̅ω̅ θεῷ (lines 4–5) and ἐκ τούτου θεοῦ (line 13) (P.Oxy. 12.1493). In a much later fragment (P.Oxy. 17.2156, late fourth/fifth cent.), the opposite is the case: κύριος is written full, and θεός is contracted. Copres, whom we shall meet in ch. 7, penned παρὰ τῷ κυρι̅ θ̅[ω̅], as if he forgot to abbreviate the word κύριος but then at the last letter realized that he needed or wanted to use a *nomen sacrum* (P.Oxy. 31.2601).

[34] This way I also interpret the few *nomina sacra* used for humans: ordinary, or perhaps *extraordinary*, people (P.Oxy. 12.1592, discussed below).

not an exceedingly difficult skill to master, presumes a rather straightforward system: take the first and last letter of a word and then write a line above them[35]—this works for most words. Nevertheless, no matter how easy, one still had to know about the practice, and this must have happened at school or in church. The earliest Christian school exercises show that *nomina sacra* were taught at a basic educational level. For instance, a third-century papyrus fragment of unknown provenance preserves the opening lines of the first Psalm written in what Raffaella Cribiore classifies as a "proficient bookhand, an example of *Biblical Majuscule*." This piece probably served as example for students to copy (P.Laur. 4.140).[36] Psalms were popular in school exercises; an early-fourth-century notebook belonging to Aurelius Papnouthion, with handwriting of both pupil and teacher, contains Ps 146:1–11, together with passages from Menander.[37] In this Psalm text, the "*nomina sacra* are mostly abbreviated with carelessly drawn supralineations."[38] A third example of *nomina sacra* in a school exercise comes from an early-fourth-century

[35] Jerome described the system of Greek abbreviations thus in his *De monogramma* $\overline{XPI}$: In libris etenim Graecorum ubicumque per notam scribuntur nomina primae et novissimae notantur litterae et virgula superposita in dexteram aeque veniente a sinistra (Jerome, *Monogr.*, ed. Morin, 195, 1.10–12). ("For in the books of the Greeks, whenever names are written by means of short-hand characters, the first and last letters are indicated also by an accent mark (twig) placed above them to the right coming from the left"). See also Traube, *Nomina sacra*, 4. This sentence in a tractate on the monogram $\overline{\text{XPI}}$ shows that writing *nomina sacra* was a scribal practice that was reflected upon and indicates that this was a way of writing people were taught.

[36] What makes it a "school book" is that "the words are divided into syllables by middle dots and observe *scriptio plena*." So Cribiore, *Writing, Teachers, and Students*, no. 244, 295.

[37] Boyaval commented: "La présence d'un psaume (VII–VIII) et de chrismes (IV 1, VI 1) prouve l'origine chrétienne du cahier. 3 mains s'y sont succédées. La main 1 est celle d'un maître, la main 2 celle de l'élève, Aurelius Papnouthion, qui a signé en II 1, IV 1 et VI 1. . . . La main 2 . . . évoque les écritures du début du IV^{p}, date probable de tout le cahier." ("Le cahier scolaire," *ZPE* 17 (1975) 225–35 + plates 7–8, 227). See also LDAB 2746; Pack 1619; van Haelst 0239; Cribiore 396, and Boyaval, "La tablette scolaire Pack^{2} 1619," *ZPE* 14 (1974) 241–47, plate 12. I should add here that it is not just the psalm that makes Aurelios Papnouthion a Christian, but especially the *nomina sacra* (in lines 1 and 13—suggested also as reconstructions for the lacunae in lines 9 and 12) and his name Papnouthion. The provenance of this text is perhaps Memphis. Another example of a psalm text as school exercise is a third/fourth-century papyrus fragment containing Ps 11:7–14:4, also with contracted *nomina sacra* (P.Lond.Lit. 207 = Cribiore, *Writing, Teachers, and Students*, no. 297, 245; van Haelst 109). For the popularity of Psalms in Greek and Coptic school texts, see Cribiore, "Greek and Coptic Education," in *Ägypten und Nubien* (ed. Emmel) 2:279–86, esp. 282–83.

[38] Cribiore, *Writing, Teachers, and Students*, no. 396, 277–78. Cribiore wonders whether "the *Psalm* perhaps was written from memory."

fragment from Oxyrhynchus and features the opening verses of the letter to the Romans (Rom 1:1–7; P.Oxy. 2.209).[39] Cribiore characterizes the handwriting as " 'evolving,' with letters almost always separated" and having "difficulties of alignment."[40] This text contains the *nomina sacra* for Christ, Jesus, God, son, spirit, and father. These examples thus demonstrate that at the end of the third and beginning of the fourth century *nomina sacra* formed part of the curriculum of (at least some) Christian educational settings. Behind these Christian school exercises, we may witness a two generational arrangement with parents compensating someone, presumably a Christian, to teach their child(ren).

Outside of school, literate Christians-in-the-making will have learned of the practice of *nomina sacra* in the period of their catechumenate through the study of Christian manuscripts. In the educational setting of the catechumenate, an introduction to Christian manuscripts must have entailed an explanation of the contracted forms. In this context, I refer to Roberts's reflection that the "full meaning [of the *nomina sacra*] was only apparent to the faithful to whose attention it was brought whenever the sacred books, whether of the Old Testament or of those that became later the New, were read."[41] Once readers grasped the meaning of these *nomina sacra* as signifiers of sacrality, they would have wanted to demonstrate their reverence by writing these words in contracted form in their own documents as well.[42] We see this indeed in the two examples of private letters with *nomina sacra* that we will examine next. Both letters involve women.

[39] Grenfell and Hunt characterize this as a school text ("written in a large rude uncial—no doubt a schoolboy's exercise," 8), and so does Cribiore (see below). In cursive script beneath the quotation one reads the name Aurelius Paulus (line 15)—the name Paul also being indicative of a Christian milieu. Grenfell and Hunt comment in their edition that "the papyrus was found tied up with a contract dated in 316 A.D., and other documents of the same period." As I shall argue elsewhere, this document forms part of a known archive. According to Deissmann, P.Oxy. 2.209 was a Christian amulet, not a school exercise (*Licht vom Osten*, 203 n. 4 and plate on 204).

[40] Cribiore, *Writing, Teachers, and Students*, no. 302, 246–247, at 247 (= van Haelst 490). The student made several mistakes, such as omitting part of verse 6.

[41] *Manuscript, Society and Belief*, 48. See also Choat, *Belief and Cult*, 120.

[42] See also Teeter's comments on P.Col. 11.300: "The hands that produced P.Lond. 1917, P.Abinn. 6 (both from an ecclesiastical background and of about the same date) and **300** show knowledge of something, viz. *nomina sacra*, that probably came from studying a text, most likely the Bible. This fixation on a text, even to using an imperfectly understood principle from it in correspondence, raises again the question of an impetus to literacy provided by Christianity" (P.Col. 11.300, 58–59).

Nomina sacra in a Bookish Milieu (P.Oxy. 63.4365)[43]

A "Letter about Christian Books" takes us to a studious setting. As we have seen, students learned to write *nomina sacra* either at school by copying scriptural passages or else they learned about the practice when reading Christian texts. Both activities involve literary manuscripts. Therefore, the use of *nomina sacra* in private letters forms one of the closest links between Christian literary manuscripts and Christian documentary texts second only to direct quotations from scripture.[44] No wonder then that the sender of a note on exchanging manuscripts (one of the documents on our shortlist) wrote *nomina sacra* in both the opening and closing greetings.

For this letter the sender used the back of a petition (published as P.Oxy. 63.4364) and cut the original document down to a small sheet of 11.5 x 8 cm. The front contains a formal request from an otherwise unknown woman called Aurelia Soteira alias Hesychium (line 6). The petition's formulaic language has parallels in other documents from Oxyrhynchus dating to the second half of the third century,[45] which led the editor to date the petition to the "end of the third century or the beginning of the fourth." For the letter on the back side (P.Oxy. 63.4365), he considered "an early fourth century date . . . very possible."[46] The latter document, written with a fairly thin pen, has

[43] Ed. princ. Rea, "Letter about Christian Books," P.Oxy. 63.4365 (1996) 44–45. Image online at http://www.papyrology.ox.ac.uk/POxy/. See also Hagedorn, "Die 'Kleine Genesis'," ZPE 116 (1997) 147–48; Otranto, "Alia tempora, alii libri," *Aeg* 77 (1997) 101–24, esp. 106–8 (= eadem, *Libri su papiro*, 128–29); Franklin, "Note on the Pseudepigraphal Allusion," *VT* 48 (1998) 95–96; Kraus, "Bücherleihe im 4. Jh. n. Chr.," *Biblos* 50 (2001) 285–96; Epp, "Oxyrhynchus NT Papyri," 21–35. Translation also in Rowlandson, *Women & Society*, 78 (no. 59).

[44] In his discussion of *nomina sacra*, Gamble links this scribal practice with the in-house production of Christian literary manuscripts: "The use of nomina sacra may therefore be another pointer to the practical character of Christian texts. Further, the occurrence of this convention in Christian manuscripts is a clear indication that the transcription of early Christian books was not farmed out to the professional book trade but was done in-house by Christians themselves" (*Books and Readers*, 77–78).

[45] P.Oxy. 63.4365, note to line 7. The dates of the parallel documents vary from 241 to 298 C.E..

[46] Respectively P.Oxy. 63.4364, 42 and P.Oxy. 63.4365, 44. Rea noted: "The date range raises the possibility that the letter on the back dates from before about 325" (P.Oxy. 63.4364, 43). Also the word choice in the address in line 1 suggests a fourth-century date, as Gonis argued in "Notes on Two Epistolary Conventions," *ZPE* 119 (1997) 148–52. Gonis observes that "in no other private letter from the first three centuries of Roman rule in Egypt does φίλτατος qualify ἀδελφός" (ibid., 150).

clear, fluent, and largely uncial letters.[47]

The letter reads as follows:

τῇ κυρίᾳ μου φιλτάτῃ ἀδελφῇ ἐν κ(υρί)ῳ χαίρειν.
χρ̣ῆσον τὸ̣ν Ἔσδραν,
ἐ̣π̣εὶ ἐχρη̣σά σοι τὴν
Λεπτὴν Γένεσιν.
ἔρρωσο ἡμεῖν ἐν θ(ε)ῷ.

---

2. κ̅ω̅, 6. *l.* ἡμῖν, θ̅ω̅

Translation

> To my dearest lady sister in the Lord, greetings. Lend the Ezra, since I lent you the Little Genesis. Farewell from us in God.

The anonymous writer of this note addresses a likewise unnamed "dearest lady sister in the Lord." Despite the address as "sister," the correspondents are probably not siblings, because the use of kinship language in this context indicates Christian fellowship.[48] The adjective "dearest" indicates a more business-like relationship.[49] The first two sentences speak in the first person singular. In the greetings section, the sender changes to the first person plural, "farewell from us"; this allows a vague glimpse of a larger familial, or perhaps ecclesiastical, setting.

[47] Based on the handwriting, Rea proposed that the petitioner who signed her name on the front possibly also wrote the Christian letter on the back. However, from my own examination of the papyrus at Oxford and consultation with Bagnall and Cribiore, this cannot be maintained. Aurelia Soteira alias Hesychium has a precise and regular hand. It is not so much the thickness of the pen that makes the two different, but the letter forms and the small serifs on the letters of the verso.

[48] Dickey acknowledges the difficulty of interpreting family words without context ("Literal and Extended Use," *Mnemosyne* 47 [2004] 131–76, at 134). In a Christian context, the "extended kinship terms" frequently indicate fellow Christians (ibid., 165). In our letter, the sender addresses the addressee as "dearest" (φιλτάτη) and not as "beloved" (ἀγαπητή) sister; the adjective "beloved" is more common in a Christian letter. See discussion in ch. 2.

[49] See Gonis, "Notes," *ZPE* 119 (1997) 148–54, at 148, with reference to Koskenniemi.

The writer has lent the addressee a copy of "Little Genesis," *id est*, the book of *Jubilees*[50] and asks her to lend in return her copy of "Ezra," that is, perhaps *4 Ezra*.[51] If the language of this letter (Greek) indicates the language of these manuscripts—which I think it does—then this letter provides evidence of Greek copies of *Jubilees* and *4 Ezra*. As of yet, we have no Greek manuscript containing *Jubilees*, therefore I find the mention of the book here significant.[52] The correspondents' preference for Jewish apocryphal works does not necessarily make them Jews, although one has to consider it a possibility. The *nomina sacra* in this letter, however, in combination with the popularity of these works in Christian circles, point us more towards Christian readers.[53]

The note does not mention why these two are trading manuscripts—perhaps for reading but maybe also for copying or collating.[54] The possession of books and the ability to read situate the sender and recipient of this note

[50] Rea proposed that the "little" indicated a miniature codex of Genesis (ed. princ.; also Otranto, "Alia tempora," 107–8), but, as Hagedorn was quick to point out, "Little Genesis" is the title of the book of *Jubilees*, for instance in Epiphanius, *Panarion* 49.6.1 ("Die 'Kleine Genesis'," 147–48).

[51] As Rea noted in his edition, this is probably what is currently referred to as *4 Ezra*, but not necessarily so. The textual history of Ezra literature is complex. Besides being applied to the canonical books of Ezra and Nehemiah, there is a cluster of extracanonical writings that bear the name of Ezra, imaginatively numbered from 1 Ezra to 6 Ezra. The core text in the apocryphal Ezra literature is titled *4 Ezra*; 5 and 6 Ezra consist of Christian additions. Without specific information it remains uncertain which "Ezra" the correspondent is requesting. Metzger in his piece on "The Fourth Book of Ezra," provides a page long table on "the confused and confusing nomenclature of the diverse titles applied to the work" ("The Fourth Book of Ezra," in *Apocalyptic Literature* [ed. Charlesworth] 516). A leaf of a miniature codex containing 6 Ezra is among the papyri found at Oxyrhynchus (P.Oxy. 7.1010). The short passage of this fragment (16:57–59) contains no words that allow us to conclude whether or not its scribe wrote *nomina sacra*. A church inventory from the seventh or eighth century lists a new copy of the Apocalypse of Esdras among its property (P.L.Bat. 25.13, line 36).

[52] See also Hagedorn, "Die 'Kleine Genesis'," 148. On the Greek fragments of *Jubilees*, see Denis, "Fragments" in idem, *Introduction aux pseudépigraphes grecs*, 150–62.

[53] The reception history of these Jewish books is mainly Christian, see Kraft, "Pseudepigrapha in Christianity," in *Tracing the Threads* (ed. Reeves) 55–86.

[54] Several other letters mentioning books indicate that people were interested in copying or collating manuscripts. For collating manuscripts, see the well-known "Letter about Books," P.Oxy. 28.2192 (late second cent.), and discussion on the aim of this exchange in Kraus, "Bücherleihe," 289–94 (specifically on P.Oxy. 63.4365). I see no grounds to exclude the copying or collating of these manuscripts. See also Krüger, *Oxyrhynchos in der Kaiserzeit*, 201–4; Turner, *Greek Manuscripts*, 114; Haines-Eitzen, *Guardians of Letters*, 3.

among the more well-to-do.[55] This note addresses a woman, but we do not know the gender of the writer.[56] Literary references also illuminate Christian women's access to books. Jerome reports that Pamphilus of Caesarea (died 309 C.E.), a contemporary of the correspondents of this note, lent books from his library at Caesarea "not only to men, but also to women."[57]

Uncommon in correspondence, this letter identifies neither sender nor recipient of by name. John Rea wondered whether this anonymity "denotes a degree of discretion," necessary in times unsafe to mark oneself as Christian.[58] In view of other pre-Constantinian letters with an even stronger Christian character, which do contain names, I consider this explanation less likely.[59] Even in a letter written during the Diocletianic persecution, a man describes to his wife how he evaded sacrifice and mentions his own name (Copres) and those of other family members.[60] This letter on lending books seems to

[55] So Kraus, "Bücherleihe," 290, 295.

[56] Epp, adopting Rea's suggestion that the petitioner on the front could have been the writer of the back also, concludes that the correspondents of this letter were female leaders in the Oxyrhynchite church ("Oxyrhynchus NT Papyri," 31–35). Although I would like this to be true, unfortunately, the evidence does not support his hypothesis. The sender may be a woman, but could just as likely be a man; the handwriting is not in the same hand as that on the recto. Epp's "web of speculation" that these women may have been church leaders based on their literacy and reading noncanonical texts has to remain just that. Although literacy is considered an important asset for church leaders, not every literate member of a congregation would be a leader. In addition, there is no evidence that suggests that church leaders would have a preference for reading certain materials.

[57] "nec solum viris, sed et feminis" Jerome, *Apology against Rufinus* 1.9 (ed. and trans. Lardet) 26. See discussion in Kraus, "Bücherleihe," 292–93. For women possessing books, Gamble refers to the Martyrdom of Saints Agape, Irene, and Chione (*Books and Readers*, 148).

[58] P.Oxy. 63.4365, 44. Hagedorn concurs: Rea "hat . . . mit Zurückhaltung, aber sehr einleuchtend geschlossen," etc. ("Die 'Kleine Genesis'," 147).

[59] For instance, Christian letters of recommendation, discussed in ch. 4.

[60] P.Oxy. 31.2601, see full discussion in ch. 7. As Wipszycka puts it more generally: "Écartons tout de suite une hypothèse . . . selon laquelle les chrétiens, avant l'époque de Constantin, auraient généralement évité de manifester leur foi dans leurs lettres, de peur que celles-ci ne tombent entre les mains des païens, les exposant ainsi aux persécutions. Cette explication est certainement fausse. Étant donné le caractère du culte traditionnel, ceux qui s'abstenaient d'y participer étaient tout de suite repérés. En outre, il faut tenir compte du fait qu'en Égypte, pour des raisons géographiques, le tissu de l'habitat était extrêmement serré, si bien que personne ne pouvait s'échapper aux regards des voisins. On n'avait pas besoin de contrôler le contenu des lettres pour savoir si quelqu'un était ou non chrétien" ("Christianisation de l'Égypte," 65). I think here also of Dionysius of Alexandria's description of the mob violence preceding the Decian persecution. When Dionysius writes that the

omit names simply because it was a short informal note, written hurriedly, and delivered at a relatively close distance by a familiar person.[61] The writer sounds a little impatient to obtain the book, but perhaps the brevity of the letter produces that impression.

Thus this short note shows how people familiar with reading literary manuscripts use *nomina sacra* even in moments of informality. In addition, it confirms the diverse reading interests of the Oxyrhynchites, which we know already from the material record. It also makes clear that women had these specialized religious texts in their possession and were studying and/or copying them. This brings us to a letter sent by another woman.

A Christian Scribe from Oxyrhynchus (P.Oxy. 12.1592)[62]

A small papyrus fragment introduces us to a Christian scribe who not only wrote this letter, but also—I argue—could copy Christian literary manuscripts.[63] The scrap of papyrus, measuring 10.3 x 5 cm preserves eight lines of text. Grenfell and Hunt devoted just one short paragraph to this papyrus, but I find it worthy of a fuller discussion. The text dates to the end of the third/beginning of the fourth century according to palaeography and

crowd plundered houses of Christians, one can read between the lines that those involved knew which houses belonged to their Christian neighbors: "Then with one accord they all rushed to the houses of the godly, and, falling each upon those whom they recognized as neighbors" (Dionysius *apud* Eusebius, *Hist. eccl.* 6.41.5 [trans. Oulton] 2:101). Bagnall, however, cautions that "the presence of fairly high apartment buildings (a 7-story house is mentioned in XXXIV 2719) may also have contributed to a more anonymous and less cohesive urban texture than we might like to suppose" ("Family and Society," in *Oxyrhynchus: A City and Its Texts*, 185).

[61] Following Epp: "Obviously a quick communication between close acquaintances, doubtless delivered locally by a personally connected messenger, rendering names superfluous" ("Oxyrhynchus NT Papyri," 28). Epp points to party invitations as parallels of letters without names (ibid., 27).

[62] Ed. princ. Grenfell and Hunt, P.Oxy. 12.1592 (1916) 285. See also, e.g., Ghedini, 131–33 (no. 14) Naldini, *Cristianesimo* 159–60 (no. 31). For the reconstruction of lines 7–8, see Tibiletti, "Proposte di lettura," *Aeg.* 57 (1977) 164.

[63] I use the word "scribe" as a synonym for "copyist" and "book-transcriber," and do not mean "a professional member of a sacred calling" (see Parsons, "Copyists of Oxyrhynchus," in *Oxyrhynchus: A City and Its Texts* [ed. Bowman et al.], 262). For scribes and copyists of literary manuscripts at Oxyrhynchus, see Johnson, *Bookrolls and Scribes in Oxyrhynchus* (esp. ch. 2: "Scribes in Oxyrhynchus: Scribal Habits, Paradosis, and the Uniformity of the Literary Roll," 15–84) and Parsons, "Copyists of Oxyrhynchus."

is written along the fibers. The back contains illegible traces of ink. The letter reads as follows:

> χαί]ρειν. αἰδε-
> ξά[μ]ην σου τὰ γράμμα-
> τα, κ(ύρι)έ μου π(άτε)ρ, καὶ πάνυ ἐ-
> μεγαλύνθην καὶ ἠγαλλεία-
> σα ὅτει τοιοῦτός μου π(ατ)ήρ
> τὴν μνήμην ποιεῖται. αὐτὰ
> γὰρ δεξαμένη τὸ ϊερόν σου
> [πρόσωπον (?) προσεκ]ύνησα

1–2. *l.* ἐδεξάμην, 3. $\overline{\kappa\varepsilon}$ μου $\overline{\pi\rho}$, 5. $\overline{\pi\eta\rho}$, 7. ἱερόν

Translation

> . . . greetings. I received your letter, my Lord Father, and I was very much exalted and I rejoiced, that such a person as my Father remembers me. For when I received it, I [worshipped?] your holy [face?].

Although the parts containing the names of sender and recipient are broken off, we still can gain some information about the correspondents. The feminine form of the participle in line 7 identifies the sender as a woman. She addresses the recipient in line 3 as "my lord father," κ(ύρι)έ μου π(άτε)ρ, in the vocative, and in line 5 as "such a father of mine," τοιοῦτός μου π(ατ)ήρ. Strikingly, she uses the scribal practice normally reserved for divine names and writes the words for "lord" and "father" as *nomina sacra.* We know of only a few other instances of this use of a *nomen sacrum* for human beings.[64] By writing the *nomina sacra*, the sender visually expresses

[64] Examples of other occurrences: SB 14.11532 (see note above); SB 12.10773, "Brief des Tatianos an Chairemon," first half of fifth cent. (= Naldini, "Papiri della raccolta fiorentina," *Atene e Roma* n.s. 12 [1967] 167–68). The *nomen sacrum* is used in address of Chairemon: Τῷ δεσπότῃ μου τῷ τιμιωτάτῳ Χερήμονι τῷ π(ατ)ρὶ Τατιανω (reads perhaps Τατιανὸς) ἐν κυρίῳ χαίρειν (lines 1–3). This seems like a deliberate use of the *nomen sacrum* for πατήρ in the address, parallel to the use in P.Oxy. 12.1592. The latter is therefore not an isolated case. Naldini's remark on this use of a *nomen sacrum* for an address: "π(ατ)ρί: più frequentemente abbreviato come *nomen sacrum*, è titolo rivolto a religosi, spesso a monaci rivestiti di autorità" ("Papiri della raccolta fiorentina," 168). Additional references are: P.Genova 1.26 (fourth cent.), P.Stras. 1.35 (fourth/fifth cent.) and a Coptic letter, P.KellisCopt. 11 (ca. 350–380). See Choat, *Belief and Cult*, 121.

her great reverence for this addressee. The title "Father" in combination with the *nomina sacra* implies that he had the status of a bishop or some other high-positioned clergyman.[65]

The woman articulates her gratitude for receiving a letter. (The receipt of a letter, or lack thereof, occurs frequently as a topos in papyrus letters.) She does not use the common verb for thanking (εὐχαριστέω), but expresses her joy with the rare verbs "exalt" and "rejoice exceedingly" (μεγαλύνω and ἀγαλλιάω).[66] She thus alludes to the Magnificat (Luke 1:46b–47).[67] Only a small number of papyrus letters quote or allude to Christian literary writings.[68] This anonymous woman therefore represents one of the few letter writers who reveal an active command of biblical or liturgical language.

To sum up, this woman exchanges correspondence with a high church official, who has just written her a letter. The allusion to the Magnificat functions not only to articulate her gladness but also to demonstrate her biblical or liturgical knowledge to the recipient. In addition, she visually

[65] See Kramer, who calls this a title "der nur für Bischöfe, Äbte und höhergestellte Geistliche verwendet wurde" (P.Neph. Einleitung, 7). Cf. Wipszycka in her review of Naldini's *Cristianesimo*: "Le «père» est ici certainement une personne pieuse pour laquelle l'auteur de la lettre a un profond respect. Mais de cela il ne s'ensuit pas nécessairement qu'il est «un vescovo o un monaco di singolare dignità». En tout cas, si M. Naldini veut supposer qu'il s'agit d'un moine, il devrait placer la lettre au IVe siècle, et non pas au IIIe/IVe" (Wipszycka, "Remarques," 213).

[66] In documentary papyri these verbs occur only in this letter, as a DDBDP search shows.

[67] The passage reads: μεγαλύνει ἡ ψυχή μου τὸν κύριον καὶ ἠγαλλίασεν τὸ πνεῦμά μου ἐπὶ τῷ θεῷ τῷ σωτῆρί μου (My soul praises the Lord and my spirit rejoices in God my savior). The question is whether this is biblical or liturgical. For Epp, "the Magnificat verbs are without context and doubtless came from liturgy" ("Oxyrhynchus NT Papyri," 23 n. 57). Later on he comments: "I would grant, however, that two verbs in P.Oxy 1592 . . . may well be an 'echo' of Luke 1:46–47, even though there is no further context, because (a) their collocation in the Magnificat and (b) the context of the papyrus makes an allusion likely" (ibid., 27 n. 69). Harris categorizes this letter under "verbal echoes" ("Biblical Echoes and Reminiscences," in *Proceedings of the XIV International Congress of Papyrologists*, 155–60, at 156). Tibiletti writes: "Quanto alla fonte di tali reminiscenze scritturistiche [in P.Oxy. 8.1161 and 12.1592], non c'è dubbio che sia l'omiletica e la liturgia. Il che è più verosimile quando il testo è scorretto: ché, in caso contrario, potremmo sempre pensare a scribi di professione cristiani" (*Lettere cristiane*, 116).

[68] See Harris, "Biblical Echoes,"156–58; Epp, "Oxyrhynchus NT Papyri," 26–27, 35–49; Horsley, *NewDocs* 2:157: "there are less than two dozen Biblical citations and verbal echoes among that number of texts [i.e., the 97 letters collected by Naldini in his *Cristianesimo*]." Horsley gives a list of papyri with biblical quotations, verbal echoes, and reminiscences, based on Harris, "Biblical Echoes," *NewDocs* 2:157–58; Tibiletti, *Lettere private*, 115–16.

shows her respect for him by writing the *nomina sacra* in addressing him. In doing so, she expects him to know their meaning and thus the degree of her reverence for him, while also displaying her own expertise and Christian education.[69] As we will observe next, the style of handwriting used in this letter provides further insights into the sender's milieu.

Written in a literary, uncial hand, this documentary letter has a professional layout.[70] The handwriting supports my argument that *nomina sacra* form a connection between literary and documentary texts. The literary hand, of course, facilitates reading because cursive script can present difficulties to decipher. But I see more to it. As Cribiore noted, experienced scribes in antiquity used a type of handwriting appropriate for the occasion.[71] In this letter the writer probably used the literary handwriting as a polite way to address the important church official given the fact that the *nomina sacra* in addressing him also had that function. We have other papyrus letters from Oxyrhynchus written in a literary hand,[72] and such writing may represent the practice of the social circle to which these people belonged.

Considered together, the literary hand, the use of *nomina sacra*, and the scriptural allusions suggest that the writer of this papyrus letter had experience with copying Christian literary texts. Did our woman do the writing herself in

[69] Naldini and Ghedini commented on the female sender's allusion to the Magnificat in pejorative terms, describing her as a "naïve, simple woman" (Naldini, *Cristianesimo*, 159), with an exalted female mind (Ghedini, *Lettere cristiane*, 131). It is clear that neither is correct. Naldini's characterization of the letter was: "Con animo devoto una donna esprime la sua profonda riconoscenza al 'padre'—un vescovo o un monaco di singolare dignità—che l'ha ricordata con premura, scrivendole; e con religiosa commozione fa sue le esultanti parole della Madonna . . . Ingenuità di mente semplice o «esaltazione cosciente di animo femminile»?" (*Cristianesimo*, 159, referring to Ghedini in the quote).

[70] In the online edition of their *Women's Letters,* Bagnall and Cribiore classify this as professional hand, "written in an uncial script more reminiscent of literary manuscripts than of letters" (Letter 90, A14.13).

[71] "Accomplished writers knew a variety of writing styles and knew when and where each was appropriate" (Cribiore, *Writing, Teachers*, 7). An example from a later time is Dioscoros (ca. 520–585), who uses an uncial/bookhand for his own literary creations, and a fast, cursive hand for correspondence, see Verbeeck, "Dioskoros," in *Familiearchieven* (ed. Pestman) 139–62, at 148.

[72] For our time period, another Christian letter found at Oxyrhynchus penned in a literary hand is P.Oxy. 56.3858, "Barys to Diogenes" ("The letter is written in a careful and practiced hand based on a good literary type, a large sloping severe style," P.Oxy. 56.3858, 117). Outside Oxyrhynchus, one may think, for example, of the circle of Theophanes (P.Herm. Rees 4 and 5).

this bookhand or did she dictate her letter to a scribe?[73] Given the fragmentary nature of this piece, we cannot decide for certain the identity of its writer. I imagine that the unknown woman penned this professional-looking letter herself. We know of other female scribes in antiquity. Eusebius, for instance, in his *Life of Origen* mentions that the great theologian employed female calligraphers to copy his writings.[74] I therefore picture the anonymous writer of this letter as a woman belonging to a scholarly milieu.

In this section we have met people, who used *nomina sacra* in their letters; in the following chapters we shall meet others, who employed these visual markers of Christian identity. I have argued that these letter writers learned the system of *nomina sacra* in a school or church setting. In the two instances that I discussed in more detail, the use of *nomina sacra* introduced us into a bookish milieu.

Having encountered so far only tantalizing glimpses of several inhabitants of Oxyrhynchus, we will now meet a more rounded figure.

[73] With high levels of illiteracy in antiquity, many people had to rely upon others to write their letters. On (il)literacy in antiquity, see, e.g., Hanson, "Ancient Illiteracy," in *Literacy in the Roman World* (ed. Beard) 159–98, and Harris, *Ancient Literacy*.

[74] Eusebius, *Hist. eccl.* 6.23.2. See especially Haines-Eitzen's work on female scribes, "'Girls Trained for Beautiful Writing'," in *Guardians of Letters*, 41–52.

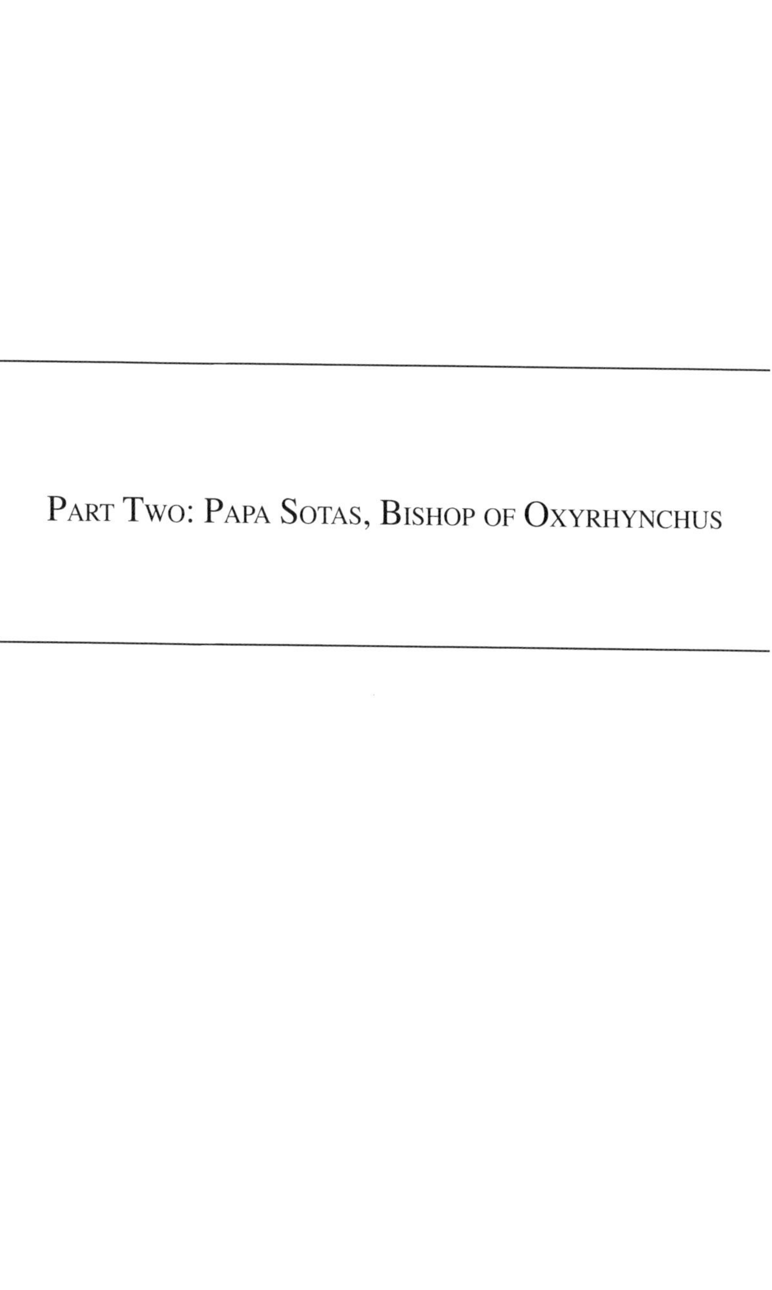

Part Two: Papa Sotas, Bishop of Oxyrhynchus

CHAPTER 4

"Beloved Papa Sotas": Recommendation, Networking, and Christian Education

In the first part of this book, I asked whether and how we could discern Christians in documentary texts using the image of recognizing people in the Oxyrhynchite agora. I framed this question as part of a debate about markers of Christian identity. In the next two chapters, we meet at a church in Oxyrhynchus and make our acquaintance with a third-century clergyman by the name of Sotas. In the papyrological record from Oxyrhynchus, Sotas stands out as Christian in many ways: his title as papa, the use of *nomina sacra* in his letters, his circle of correspondents, the content of his letters, and his nickname "the Christian." In these chapters, Sotas, a high-profile Christian, serves as a means to discuss social and Christian practices such as letters of recommendation, group formation, clergy, stewardship, scribal habits, and book production.

I consider five letters as referring to the same person Sotas:[1]

1) Sotas to Paul (PSI 9.1041)

[1] Rea proposed that PSI 4.311, a letter to Theodosius, bishop of Laodicea (died 341 C.E.) referred to the same Sotas (P.Oxy. 36.2785 [1970] 84, note to line 2). This identification rests on the letters σω preserved in the address of this papyrus letter (line 27). The ed. princ. of the letter suggested "pensare a qualche forma del verbo σῴζειν" (PSI 4.311, note to line 27), but in address formulas, ἀπόδος normally is followed by a personal name. Of course, this lacuna can be reconstructed as ἀπόδος Σώ[τα̣], but the argument is fragile, since many names start with Σω, e.g., Σωκράτης, Σωσθένης, Σωσίβιος, etc. For this letter, see, e.g., Leclercq, "Lettres chrétiennes," *DACL* 8.2 (1929) no. 34, 2790; Naldini, *Cristianesimo*, no. 39, 184–87; idem, *Documenti dell'antichità cristiana,* 36 (plus plate); Winter, *Life and Letters*, 170–71.

2) Sotas to Peter (PSI 3.208)
3) The Presbyters of Heracleopolis to Sotas (P.Oxy. 36.2785)
4) Sotas to Demetrianus (P.Oxy. 12.1492)
5) Sarapammon to his mother and Didyme (SB 12.10772)

A sixth letter, addressed to Maximus (P.Alex. 29), may also belong to Sotas's correspondence, but because the name of the sender has not been fully preserved, this remains undecided.

The first three letters in the list, and the sixth, belong to the same genre: they are letters of recommendation and form the topic of this chapter. Letters four and five, which I shall discuss in the next chapter, deal with other church business.

The treatment of the texts in this chapter differs slightly from that in the others due to the fact that all four letters of recommendation have nearly identical wording. At this point, I need to establish in more detail the coherence of the correspondence of Sotas and his role in the church. I shall therefore begin by presenting the letters of recommendation sent by and to Sotas. Then, instead of my usual method of commenting on each individual letter right after the text and translation, I shall step back to examine the whole correspondence of Sotas and establish his position in the church hierarchy. In the last part of this chapter I shall study the contents of the letters of recommendation.

Sotas to Paul (PSI 9.1041)[2]

In this letter, penned on a narrow piece of parchment (6.3 x 15 cm), Sotas introduced a group of six men to "his beloved brother Paul." The writer used the hair side of the parchment; on the flesh side, we see illegible remnants of writing.[3] Striving for legibility, he formed uncial letters combined with faster cursive forms. He abbreviated two words "I greet," προσαγορ(εύω),

[2] See Plate 1. Ed. princ. Coppola, PSI 9.1041 (1929) 74–75. As customary in the PSI series, Coppola did not give a papyrological description of the text. The letter (Pap.Vat.gr. 14) is part of the papyrus collection of the *Bibliotheca Apostolica Vaticana* in Rome, Italy. The provenance of PSI 9.1041 is attributed to Oxyrhynchus by association with PSI 3.208 and P.Oxy. 12.1492: "Da Oxyrhynchos provengono 208 e PO 1492; della stessa provenienza è, dunque, anche questa lettera" (Coppola, PSI 9.1041, 74). There is good reason to accept this, since many of the PSI texts came from the Italian excavations at Oxyrhynchus.

[3] Coppola did not mention the writing on the other side in his edition of the letter. The writing is very faint, and in a different hand than the writing on the flesh side. It is not an address. The language appears to be Greek.

in line 3, and "brother," ἄδελ(φε), in line 16, due in both instances to lack of space at the end of the line, a common practice in ancient manuscripts. In lines 1 and 16, he wrote the *nomen sacrum* for "Lord" (κύριος) with the supralinear stroke (ἐν κ̅ω̅). In order to aid the reader, the writer gave the letter a distinct layout. As is common in papyrus letters—at least those from more experienced writers—the writer left a small blank space in the prescript before the name of the sender and a large indentation in the postscript at the end of the letter. In addition to these features, the writer marked the body of the letter visually with a capital letter *tau* in the margin (so-called *ekthesis*), adding also an extra stroke to the letter's upright line. The same hand wrote the body of the letter and the final greeting. A part of the sheet remains empty at the bottom.

The letter writer displays a good command of the Greek language—no iotacisms, for instance—yet one may attribute this more to the formulaic nature of the short letter than to the scribe's literary capabilities. Noticeably, he spelled the word "catechumen" (κατηχούμενος) with a *theta* (καθηχούμενον, line 10).[4] The same spelling occurs in a letter to Sotas, which we shall see below.[5] The letter reads as follows:

χαῖρε ἐν κ(υρί)ῳ, ἀγαπητὲ
ἄδελφε Παῦλε,
Σώτας σε προσαγορ(εύω).
Τοὺς ἀδελφοὺς ἡμῶν
Ἥρωνα καὶ Ὡρίωνα
καὶ Φιλάδελφον καὶ Πε-
κῦσιν καὶ Ναρωοῦν
καθηχουμένους τῶν
συναγομένων καὶ
Λέωνα καθηχούμενον
ἐν ἀρχῇ τοῦ εὐαγ'γελίου
πρόσδεξαι ὡς καθήκε̣[ι]·

[4] See Gignac, *Grammar of the Greek Papyri* 1:92, for the change of *tau* to *theta*. He mentions, e.g., καθαχρηματίζιν for καταχρηματίζειν, in P.Oxy. 34.2722, line 36 (154 C.E.); see also ibid. 1:136–38, "false aspiration."

[5] P.Oxy. 36.2785, lines 7–8: καθηχούμενον. P.Oxy. 31.2603 (see ch. 1), a Manichaean letter of recommendation with "literary pretensions" written in a book hand has the correct spelling κατηχούμενοι (line 26). That was to be expected from the apparent level of education of its writer. See Harrop, "Christian Letter," *JEA* 48 (1962) 137 n. 8.

δι' ὧν σὲ καὶ τοὺς σὺν σοὶ
ἐγὼ καὶ οἱ σὺν ἐμ̣οὶ προσαγορεύω. ἐρρῶσθαί σε εὔ-
χομαι ἐν κ(υρί)ῳ
ἀγαπητὲ ἄδελ(φε).

8. and 10. *l.* κατηχουμένους and κατηχούμενον, 11. *l.* εὐαγγελίου.

Translation

Greetings in the Lord, beloved brother Paul, I, Sotas, greet you. Receive as is proper our brothers Heron and Horion and Philadelphus and Pekusis and Naarous, catechumens of the congregation and Leo, a catechumen in the beginning of the gospel, through whom I and those with me greet you and those with you. I pray that you are well in the Lord, beloved brother.

Sotas to Peter (PSI 3.208)[6]

Around the same time as the letter to Paul, Sotas also sent a similar letter to his "beloved brother Peter," in which he introduced one person, "our brother Heracles." Just like the letter from Sotas to Paul, the letter is written on a small sheet of parchment (5.3 x 11.8 cm) but this time on the flesh side.[7] The left side of the piece is slightly broken, resulting in the loss of the left margin, but nowhere so badly that the text cannot be reconstructed. Despite the damage, this letter probably had an outline similar to the one discussed above, with customary indentations in opening and closing greetings, setting off the body with the initial letter in the margin. The writer employed here the *nomen sacrum* for God (θεός), not Lord (κύριος) as in the previous one, writing the postscript greeting very hastily.[8] The handwriting of this letter appears different from that of the letter to Paul (PSI 9.1041). The letters, more angular and pointy, lack the elegance of the hand that wrote the letter to Paul.

[6] See Plate 2. Ed. princ. Todi, PSI 3.208 (1914) 69. The piece is part of the collection of the *Bibliotheca Medicea Laurenziana* in Florence, Italy.

[7] The editor does not mention writing on the back in the edition, but then, neither did Coppola for PSI 9.1041.

[8] P.Oxy. 63.4365 also has once $\overline{θω}$ and once $\overline{κω}$; see ch. 3.

The letter contains twelve lines, which read as follows:

χ̣αῖρε ἐν κ(υρί)ω̣, ἀγαπητὲ
ἄδ]ελφε Πέτρε, Σώτ̣[ας]
σ]ε προσαγορεύω.
τ̣ὸν ἀδελφὸν ἡμῶν
Ἡ]ρακλῆν παράδεξαι
κ]ατὰ τὸ ἔθος, δι' οὗ σὲ
κ̣αὶ τοὺς σὺν σοὶ πάν-
τ̣ας ἀδελφοὺς ἐγὼ
κ̣αὶ οἱ σὺν ἐμοὶ
προσαγορεύομε(ν).

ἐρρῶσθαί σε
ἐν θ(ε)ῷ̣ εὔχομαι.

Translation

Greetings in the Lord, beloved brother Peter, I, Sot[as], greet you. Receive our brother Heracles according to custom, through whom I and those with me greet you and all the sisters and brothers with you. I pray that you are well in God.

The Presbyters of Heracleopolis to Sotas (P.Oxy. 36.2785)[9]

A third letter, this time addressed to Sotas, originated from the presbyters of Heracleopolis, asking Sotas to receive a female church member named Taion and a male catechumen named Anos. The small sheet of papyrus (8 x 13.5 cm), preserved in its entirety, contains a letter of fifteen lines written in an experienced albeit not very elegant hand. In line 1, the writer formed the horizontal stroke above the *nomen sacrum* for Lord quickly, starting over the *omega*. A diaeresis appears above the *iota* in Taion's name. As mentioned above, the scribe wrote "cathechumen" (καθηχούμενον with *theta*) as in Sotas's letter to Paul (PSI 9.1041).

The back of the document is blank—it has no address. The letter reads as follows:

[9] See Plate 3. Ed. princ. Rea, P.Oxy. 36.2785 (1970) 83–84. The papyrus is housed in the Sackler Library at Oxford University.

χαῖρε ἐν κ(υρί)ῳ̣ ἀγαπητὲ πάπα
Σώτα πρεσβ(ύτεροι) Ἡρακλέους
πολλά σε προσαγορεύομεν·
τὴν ἀδελφὴν ἡμῶν
Ταΐωνα παραγινομένην
πρὸς σὲ παράδεξε ἐν εἰρή-
νῃ, καὶ Ἄνου̣ καθηχού-
μενον ἐν τῇ̣ Γενέσει,
εἰς οἰκοδομὴν παράδε-
ξε, δι' ὧν σε καὶ τοὺς παρὰ σοὶ
ἀδελφοὺς ἡμεῖς καὶ οἱ σὺν
ἡμεῖν προσαγορεύομεν.
ἐρρῶσθαί σε ἐν κ(υρί)ῳ̣
εὐχόμεθα, ἀγαπη-
τὲ πάπα σ̅δ̅

---

1. and 13. κ̅ω̅ pap, 2. πρεσβ' pap, 6. and 9. παράδεξε *l.* παράδεξαι, 7. καθηχούμενον, *l.* κατηχούμενον

Translation

Greetings in the Lord, beloved papa Sotas, we, presbyters of Heracleopolis, greet you much. Receive in peace our sister Taion, who is coming to you, and receive for edification Anos,[10] a catechumen in Genesis, through whom (plural) we and the ones with us greet you and the sisters and brothers[11] with you. We pray that you are well in the Lord, beloved papa. 204[12]

[10] The scribe left a little space before and after the name Anos, leading Rea to interpret it as the *nomen sacrum* for ἄνθρωπος. There is, however, no supralinear stroke. Moreover, one of the essential elements in these introductory letters is the mention of the name of the introduced person. Annos spelled with double *nu* is a known name, as Rea himself also acknowledged. The most logical interpretation therefore is that the scribe spelled the name with single *nu*.

[11] I interpret ἀδελφούς in line 11 inclusively, as brothers and sisters.

[12] The number 204 at the end of the letter is a so-called isopsephism. Isopsephy entails the numerical value of words, as the characters of the Greek alphabet serve both as letters and as numbers. Therefore, numbers can have special, cryptic meaning. See also Leclercq, "Isopséphie," *DACL* 7.2 (1927) 1603. According to Llewelyn, the number 204 in this letter to Sotas stands for the sum of the word εἰρηνικά, and is "not an encoded salutation but an esoteric legitimization

(Sot)as to Maximus (P.Alex. 29)[13]

It has been suggested that P.Alex. 29 also came from Sotas,[14] and for that reason I list it here. The provenance of this papyrus letter is unknown. Other papyri, however, from the collection at the Graeco-Roman Museum at Alexandria to which the fragment belongs, come from Oxyrhynchus,[15] which renders it possible that the papyrus came from that city. The papyrus sheet (6.5 x 15.5 cm) contains a letter addressed to the "beloved brother Maximus" and appears almost identical in wording to Sotas's letters to Peter (PSI 3.208) and Paul (PSI 9.1041) and also to the letter from the Heracleopolite presbyters (P.Oxy. 36.2785).[16] Rea suggested rendering the name of the sender in line 4 as [Sot]as ([Σώτ]ας). However the ending -ας is a normal ending for male names, so that names such as Thomas (Θωμᾶς, P.Col. 11.298) or Theonas (Θεονᾶς, SB 10.10255), just to mention names from other Christian letters of recommendation, would fit equally well. From a paleographic point of view, the handwriting of P.Alex. 29 perhaps indicates an earlier date than that in the other letters of the Sotas correspondence. Thus the identification of this papyrus as a letter from the Sotas correspondence remains uncertain.

The letter reads as follows:

[χ]α̣ίρε ἐ̣[ν κ(υρί)ω̣]
[ἀγα]πητὲ ἄδελφε
[ ] Μάξιμε,
[Σώτ(?)]ας σὲ προσαγορεύωι
[τ]ὸ̣ν ἀδελφὸν ἡμῶ̣[ν]
Δ̣[ίφ]ιλον ἐρχό̣μ̣ε̣ν̣ο̣ν
π̣[ρό]ς σὲ προσδ̣έξ]α̣ι̣

characterizing the class of letter." See Llewelyn, "Christian Letters of Recommendation," *NewDocs* 8:172; and idem, "ΣΔ, a Christian Isopsephism?" *ZPE* 109 (1995) 125–27.

[13] See Plate 4. Ed. princ. Świderek and Vandoni, "Lettre chrétienne de recommendation," P.Alex. 29 (1964) 73–74, with image (planche XVII). The papyrus is housed in the Graeco-Roman Museum in Alexandria.

[14] Rea in P.Oxy. 36.2785, note to line 2.

[15] E.g., P.Alex. 30.

[16] Nine Christian letters of recommendation from the papyrus record are very similar. Of these, the three from the Sotas correspondence given above and P.Alex. 29 begin with χαῖρε ἐν κ̅ω̅. The other five standard letters open differently. This could be an indication that P.Alex. 29 belongs to the Sotas correspondence, but it is not conclusive evidence. I shall discuss Christian letters of recommendation below.

ἐν̣ [ε]ἰρήνῃ δι᾽ [οὗ] σὲ
κ[αὶ] τοὺς σὺν σοὶ
ἐγ[ὼ] καὶ οἱ σὺν ἐμο̣ὶ̣
προσαγορεύομ̣ε̣ν.

ἐ̣ρρῶσθαί σε
εὔχομαι,
ἀγαπητὲ
ἄδελφε ἐν κ(υρί)ῳ̣

Translation

> Greetings in the Lord, beloved brother Maximus, I, (Sot?)as greet you. Receive our brother Diphilus who is coming to you in peace, through whom I and those with me greet you and those with you. I pray that you are well, beloved brother in the Lord.

Establishing Sotas

I have chosen to focus on Sotas for the simple but significant reason that he is a Christian who figures in more than one text, which allows for a more detailed picture of this person and his position. Even though scholars have recognized that several Oxyrhynchus papyri probably refer to this same person Sotas, no one so far has analyzed these texts together. By focusing on the Sotas documents, we have the special opportunity to study one Christian from Oxyrhynchus in more depth. Before we can get to know him, we must establish first that these texts indeed refer to the same person.

John R. Rea, in a note to his edition of P.Oxy. 36.2785, suggested that the Sotas of that text was "possibly the writer of [P.Oxy. 12.]1492, who may also have written P.S.I. 208 and 1041."[17] Earlier, G. Coppola had already concluded that the Sotas of the letter to Paul (PSI 9.1041) was identical with the Sotas in the letter to Peter (PSI 208) and to Demetrianus (P.Oxy.

[17] Rea, P.Oxy. 36.2785, 84, note to line 2. Martin agrees: "ces trois lettres de recommandation, provenant d'Oxyrhynchos, se rapportent, selon toute vraisemblance, au même personage" (*Athanase d'Alexandrie,* 786–87 n. 2). Rea also mentioned PSI 4.311, which I do not consider part of the Sotas correspondence (see footnote 1).

12.1492).[18] If these papyri indeed refer to one and the same man, how do they fit together? Did they form part of an archive or is it sheer serendipity that several letters from the same person have been preserved? Alain Martin defines archives as collections of texts that had been deliberately organized in antiquity by their users.[19] Did Sotas store these letters in such an archive? The little that we know about the background of these letters indicates that archaeologists did not discover them either in a jar or storage room or found them tied up together on the garbage dump. Instead, they came to light during various excavations at different times.[20] Based on the archaeology, we cannot

[18] Coppola writes, "identico indubbiamente al Sotas di 208 e probabilmente anche a quello di PO 1492" (PSI 9.1041, 74). Naldini expressed his wonder at the serendipity of finding two letters from the same person on different occasions, writing: "Accade non di rado che antichi documenti usciti dallo stesso ambiente e talvolta dalla stessa mano, dopo aver preso vie diverse, una volta pubblicati, ci presentino, l'uno accanto all'altro, quasi membra ricomposte, la suggestiva testimonianza di una voce molteplice e insieme concorde" (*Cristianesimo*, no. 28, 151).

[19] Martin writes, "ensembles pour lesquels nous avons de bonnes raisons de penser qu'ils ont été délibérément constitués et organisés par leurs utilisateurs anciens" ("Archives privées," in *Proceedings of the 20th International Congress* [ed. Bülow-Jacobsen] 572). According to Martin, "les pièces constituant un ensemble archivistique ne peuvent en aucune manière être le fruit d'un conglomérat fortuit, fût-il ancien, ni d'une récolte menée de nos jours à travers des lots distincts; elles doivent, dès l'Antiquité, avoir fait l'objet d'une accumulation et d'un classement délibérés. Si cette double condition n'est pas remplie, on préférera *dossier* à *archives*" ("Archives privées," 570). For collections of archives, see the "Leuven Homepage of Papyrus Archives" (http://www.trismegistos.org/arch.php). The following definition of an archive is maintained, I quote at length: "Most papyri are not found as individual items, but in groups, which are called 'archives' by the papyrologists. Ideally such an archive is discovered by an archaeologist, who then describes in detail the order in which the texts were put down in antiquity (often in a jar and bundled in cloth). In fact, most papyri are found in clandestine excavations . . . , and archives have to be reconstructed on the basis of the contents of the papyri and indications of a common purchase (museum archaeology). A common find is not enough to make an archive, and therefore a rubbish heap, a dump of papyri, papyri found in the same house or temple or reused for the same mummy cartonnage do not constitute by themselves archives. An archive is a group of texts which were collected in antiquity with a specific purpose . . . . The purpose may even be to discard some items from a larger archive and then throw them away. Usually such archives will have been arranged in some kind of order, but for papyrus archives this order can only be painfully reconstructed" (http://www.trismegistos.org/arch/about.php, with reference to Pestman, *New Papyrological Primer*, 51; and Martin, "Archives privées," 569–77). See also the bibliography at http://www.trismegistos.org/arch/biblio.php.

[20] Parts of the same literary manuscripts, however, have been found at different occasions, e.g., P.Oxy. 4.657 and PSI 12.1292 form parts of an opistograph scroll preserving sections of Hebrews, found separately at Oxyrhynchus by British and Italian expeditions. 14 folia of

determine whether these texts constitute the remains of Sotas's deliberately organized documents in the strict sense of the word "archive."[21]

Yet these five (possibly six) texts belong together for the obvious reason that they mention a Sotas,[22] whether as the sender,[23] the recipient,[24] or even as deliverer of money.[25] The name Sotas alone, however, cannot constitute the sole consideration because it occurred as a common name in antiquity.[26]

a Philo codex were also found by different expeditions and published as PSI 9.1207, P.Oxy. 9.1173, P.Oxy. 11.1356, P.Oxy. 18.2158 and P.Haun. 1.8 (= van Haelst 696, LDAB 3540).

[21] Sotas may have kept an archive, or at least the church he served at Oxyrhynchus probably had one. Gamble suggests that churches kept archives in their libraries: "Congregational libraries, that is, collections of texts accumulated and retained in local Christian communities for liturgical and archival purposes, were the earliest, most numerous, and most characteristic of Christian libraries" (*Books and Readers*, 145). If the letters had belonged to such an archive, the fact that four of the letters come from Sotas himself, whereas only one is addressed to him is not a real obstacle, for it is not uncommon that travelers bring home the letters they receive on the road. The papyrological record shows that when travelers received correspondence from family members, friends, or business partners, they often held on to these letters and took them back home. This practice of saving letters is especially understandable in light of letters of recommendation or introduction where one asks for hospitality—these are documents one wants to have available during the whole journey, until arriving home safely. This is the case, for instance, with Theophanes, a *scholasticus* from Hermopolis, who traveled to Antioch in Syria in the first quarter of the fourth century (322 or 323, according to Bagnall, *Egypt in Late Antiquity*, 271 n. 76). Among his papers found at Hermopolis is the letter of recommendation that Theophanes (presumably) took along on his journey. It is a Latin letter of introduction from a *rationalis* by the name of Vitalis, addressed to Delphinius. See: "Letter of recommendation on behalf of Theophanes of Hermopolis from Vitalis, rationalis, to Delphinius," ChLA 4.253 (also published in P.Ryl. 4.623). Whether Theophanes was a Christian or not is up for debate; among his correspondents are "pagans worshipping Hermes Trismegistus" (Rees, P.Herm., 2) and Christians (see again Bagnall, *Egypt in Late Antiquity*, 271–72 and notes). In the archive was also a list of expenditures for the trip to Antioch, noting money spent on food and lodging. See Matthews's recent study on this archive: *Journey of Theophanes*.

[22] There are lacunae in PSI 3.208, 2 (Σώτ̣[ας]) and P.Alex. 29, 4 (Σώτ(?)]ας). In the first instance "Sotas" is reconstructed with relative certainty; the second, as mentioned above, is less clear.

[23] Sotas to Peter, PSI 3.208; Sotas to Paul, PSI 9.1041, and Sotas to Demetrianus, P.Oxy. 12.1492 (see ch. 5).

[24] Presbyters of Heracleopolis to Sotas, P.Oxy. 36.2785.

[25] Sarapammon to his mother and Didyme, SB 12.10772 (see ch. 5).

[26] Koskenniemi writes: "Σώτας, Σώτης sind in den Papyri gut belegt, auch aus Oxyrhynchus und aus dieser Zeit" ("Fünf griechische Papyrusbriefe," *Aeg*. 33 [1953] 324, note to line 10). See also Preisigke, *Namenbuch*, 401; Foraboschi, *Onomasticon*, 302; and Hagedorn, *WörterListen*, http://www.zaw.uni-heidelberg.de/hps/pap/WL/WL.pdf (accessed September 19, 2008) 109. Eusebius mentions a "blessed Sotas" (*Hist. eccl.* 5.19.2), this is not the

Therefore we consider next the content-based reasons for taking these letters as referring to one and the same person. First, as we have just read, Sotas sent two almost identically worded letters of recommendation: the letters to Peter (PSI 3.208) and to Paul (PSI 9.1041).[27] In addition to sender and wording, writing material links these letters together: both letters are written on parchment. Because parchment occurs very rarely as writing material for letters in Egypt, this material aspect confirms that the two letters originated with the same Sotas. We will investigate the remarkable use of parchment below in more detail.[28] Furthermore, the content of all three letters indicates that the recipient of the letter from the Heracleopolite presbyters is the same Sotas of the two parchment letters: All three letters request hospitality for church members and catechumens in very similar phraseology. Judging from the handwriting, all three were written at roughly the same time. We will consider letters four and five in the following chapter as their content differs significantly from those considered here. A letter from Sotas to his "holy son Demetrianus" (P.Oxy. 12.1492) deals with the donation of a plot of land, and shows Sotas engaged in church finances. Lastly, a man writing a letter to his family describes Sotas as "the Christian" (SB 12.10772). In the course of our investigation of these documents, Sotas will emerge as leader of a Christian community, active in maintaining contacts with other churches, negotiating hospitality for people from his circle, teaching persons from other congregations, conducting business for the church, and even traveling to Antioch in Syria.

If these texts all mention the same person Sotas, as I claim they do, our next investigation must concentrate on his domicile—a relevant matter for a study on Christians at Oxyrhynchus. This raises an important issue because scholars have thought that Sotas did not hail from Oxyrhynchus but rather from Heracleopolis, a city some sixty-seven kilometers to the north of Oxyrhynchus.[29] Yet, as the reader may suspect, if Sotas had lived in Heracleopolis, I would not have introduced him here let alone dedicated two chapters of the book to him. I have convincing proof that Sotas did not reside in Heracleopolis but that we should locate him in Oxyrhynchus.

Oxyrhynchite Sotas. Given our interest in onomastics as potential marker of Christian identity, I should note that Sotas is not a Christian name. Perhaps, however, Christians would have thought of it as a derivation from σωτηρία.

[27] The letter to Maximus (P.Alex. 29) is left out here, again, due to uncertain authorship.

[28] Ch. 5.

[29] See Bagnall, "Appendix 3: The Nomes," in *Egypt in Late Antiquity*, 335.

According to the custom in papyrus letters, Sotas does not mention the location from which he writes. In order to situate him, the address section of one of the letters (P.Oxy. 36.2785), if read correctly, provides insight into his place of residency and also to his position in the Christian community. Rea, the editor of P.Oxy. 36.2785, read the opening section of that letter as follows:

Χαῖρε ἐν κ(υρί)ῳ ἀγαπητὲ πάπα
Σώτα πρεσβ(ύτερε) Ἡρακλέους
πολλά σε προσαγορεύομεν.

Greetings in the Lord, beloved papa
Sotas, presbyter of Heracleopolis,
we greet you much.

Rea interpreted the abbreviation "presb/" (πρεσβʼ) in line 2 as the vocative "presbyter," πρεσβ(ύτερε), yet another title for beloved papa Sotas, and concluded:

> This letter is written to a priest of Heracleopolis and may therefore be the sender's copy for reference in Oxyrhynchus. The inference is perhaps supported by the lack of an address on the back, but the letter may have been brought back to Oxyrhynchus even after it had served its purpose.[30]

As is often the case in papyrology, the devil is in the details. According to Rea's reading, Sotas did not live in Oxyrhynchus but rather as a presbyter at Heracleopolis. In that interpretation, this letter came from some persons without specific indication about the senders' identities. Rea's reconstruction is grammatically possible, since the verb "we greet" (προσαγορεύομεν) in line 3 suffices as greeting and does not require an explicit subject.

Kurt Treu, however, convincingly challenged Rea's interpretation in an article on formulaic Christian letters of recommendation.[31] Based on his analysis of the standard phraseology of Christian letters of introduction, Treu resolved the abbreviation in line 2 differently and thereby completely changed the situation. Treu observed that the letters of recommendation

[30] Rea, P.Oxy. 36.2785, 83.

[31] Treu, "Christliche Empfehlungs-Schemabriefe auf Papyrus," in *Zetesis*, 629–36, esp. 634–35.

follow a strict pattern, so much so that one can read them synoptically.[32] In all the other letters, the senders identify themselves explicitly. The formulaic nature of these letters then, clearly decides this case: The abbreviation in our letter must indicate the senders, not Sotas. It makes good sense that in letters of recommendation—ancient or modern—the identity of the recommender plays just as important a role as that of the person introduced[33] because the recommenders appeal to their relationship with the recipient for a favor. This reading renders the "presb(yters)," πρεσβ(ύτεροι), the explicit subject of the verb and Heracleopolis the place *from* which the letter came *to* Sotas.[34] The translation then becomes:

> Greetings in the Lord, beloved papa
> Sotas, we, presbyters of Heracleopolis,
> greet you much.

Sotas therefore likely lived in Oxyrhynchus[35] since the letter was found there.[36] As I shall argue shortly, this reconstruction has important ramifications for the interpretation of Sotas's role in the Christian community at Oxyrhynchus.

[32] Treu wrote: "Aus dem Formular ergibt sich, daß die Abkürzung πρεσβ. in der Einleitung von D [P.Oxy. 36.2785] als πρεσβ(ύτεροι) aufzulösen ist" (ibid., 634). In a note Treu stated that Rea agreed, writing to Treu that he thought this was "a very good idea" (ibid., 635 n. 7).

[33] In this respect, a comment by Cyprian, a contemporary and colleague of Sotas, deserves mention. The bishop of Carthage mistrusted letters that did not explicitly state recipients and addressees, writing in a letter: "I have also read a letter in which it was not specifically stated who were the persons who wrote it or who were the persons to whom it was written" (Letter 9.2.1, trans. Clarke, *Letters of St. Cyprian* 1:71). Cyprian mentions that he is sending back the other letter without recipients and addressees, expressing suspicion also about its handwriting (ibid.).

[34] Treu writes, "der Brief kommt von Herakleopolis nach Oxyrhynchos, nicht umgekehrt" ("Christliche Empfehlungs-Schemabriefe," 635.)

[35] Llewelyn also notes that Sotas is "presumably resident at Oxyrhynchus" ("ΣΔ, A Christian Isopsephism?" 125). Not all scholars, however, have adopted this insight. Tibiletti follows Rea's edition without changes or reference to Treu's article and his emendations (*Lettere private*, no. 31, 191). Timm, in his discussion of Heracleopolis Magna, remarks that the presbyter Sotas must have occupied an important place in that city: "Im 4. Jahrhundert muß der presbyter Sotas eine bedeutende Funktion für die Stadt gehabt haben. Er ist in Papyri mehrfach erwähnt." Although Timm refers to Treu here, apparently he has not taken into account the implications of the latter's observations ("Ihnas[iya al-Madina]" in *Das christlich-koptische Ägypten* 3:1169 n. 5).

[36] We have here an example of a case when the travelers did not take their letter of introduction back home. This makes sense given the content of this letter. As we shall see, Anos came to study with Sotas at Oxyrhynchus. Oxyrhynchus for him was not a transit, but he must have stayed in the city for a longer period of time.

Whereas Treu agreed that Sotas wrote the two letters to Paul and Peter (PSI 3.208 and 9.1041), he hesitated to identify him as the Sotas addressed in the letter from the Heracleopolite presbyters (P.Oxy. 36.2785)[37] based on his assessment of its date. In order to establish their relevance, I will begin with a close examination of the date of these letters. To start with, none of these Sotas letters contains an explicit date. Like most papyrus letters, they are dated by paleography. For instance, their respective editors assigned Sotas's letter to Peter (PSI 3.208) a date in the fourth century and the letter to Paul (PSI 9.1041) a date at the end of the third/beginning of the fourth century.[38] Sotas's correspondence with Demetrianus (P.Oxy. 12.1492) received a "late third or early fourth century" date, whereas Rea assigned the letter from the presbyters of Heracleopolis (P.Oxy. 36.2785) to the fourth century. Given the content of the letters, however, I would hesitate to ascribe the letters to different Christian authority figures and to assume that they all had the name Sotas. Moreover, my re-examination of the handwriting and comparison of the letters places these documents in the mid- to latter-half of the third century.[39] Therefore Sotas becomes the earliest Christian Oxyrhynchite for whom we have more than just one text.[40]

[37] "Sotas als Empfänger von D [P.Oxy. 36.2785] mag der Schreiber von A + B [PSI 3.208 and 9.1041] sein, doch spricht die Datierung nicht dafür. Auch in C [P.Alex. 29] wird man vorsichtshalber nicht (So)tas ergänzen" (Treu, "Christliche Empfehlungs-Schemabriefe," 633).

[38] I suspect that Coppola dated the second PSI fragment more specifically to "Sec. III ex./IV in." because of Grenfell's dating of P.Oxy. 12.1492 to that same period. This makes the whole question of dating these Sotas documents circular.

[39] The handwriting of PSI 9.1041 and P.Oxy. 12.1492 is similar in style to letters in the Heroninus archive, e.g., P.Flor. 2.120, 133, 148, 189 (all third quarter of the third cent.) or P.Oxy. 47.3367 (272 C.E.). I thank Adam Bülow-Jacobsen, Raffaella Cribiore, Hélène Cuvigny, and Roger Bagnall for lending me their expert eyes. They suggested independently that the handwriting should be placed in the third century but differed in opinion as to whether or not it was Sotas's own handwriting. My discussion of a letter that mentions Sotas (SB 12.10772) confirms this dating; see ch. 5.

[40] Of course, many literary and documentary Christian texts from Oxyrhynchus predate these letters. My point here is that those are individual pieces. The Archive of Aurelia Ptolemais dates to the late-third century and thus overlaps in time with Sotas's archive. See Bagnall, "An Owner of Literary Papyri," *CP* 87 (1992) 137–40. However, as Bagnall also points out, it is not certain whether Aurelia Ptolemais or her family were Christians. The only indication is that they possessed the *Kestoi* by the Christian writer Julius Africanus, but that is not necessarily a Christian book. The verso of the *Kestoi* contains a will (P.Oxy. 6.907, dated 276 C.E.). Judge and Pickering comment on its wording: "Will of Aurelius Hermogenes, praising his wife for 'fitting conduct in married life.' . . . One may ask whether

Habemus papam

Who was Sotas and what role did he occupy in the Christian community at Oxyrhynchus? I submit that he represents the earliest known bishop from Oxyrhynchus.[41] Sotas in his letters mentions only his name—Σώτας—without titles, patronymic, or other epithets.[42] Fortunately, the letter addressed to him by the presbyters of Heracleopolis (P.Oxy. 36.2785) provides additional information on his role in the Christian community. In their prescript the presbyters address him as "beloved papa Sotas" (ἀγαπητέ πάπα Σώτα)[43] in the vocative.[44] Πάπας, a "child's word for *father*,"[45] indicates that again we encounter here family language to identify a person in a Christian community. Occurring in the writings of such different ancient authors as Homer and

---

the . . . unusual compliments to wives may not . . . reflect the presence of believers" ("Papyrus Documentation," *JAC* 20 [1977] no. 32, 65).

[41] Based on the two papyri from the Sotas correspondence available in 1923, Ghedini already recognized that Sotas was the head of a Christian community but did not identify him as bishop. Ghedini knew the letters from Sotas to Peter, PSI 3.208, and from Sotas to Demetrianus, P.Oxy. 12.1492 (to be discussed in the next chapter). He described Sotas as "una persona di una certa superiorità" and as "capo di una comunità cristiana, sia esso sacerdote o abbate laico" (Ghedini, *Lettere cristiane*, 123). L. Michael White observed regarding P.Oxy. 12.1492: "[T]he fatherly tone of Sotas may be due to his ecclesiastical rank. Two other papyri from Oxyrhynchus . . . bear the name of the bishop Sotas as the writer" (*Social Origins* 2:162). White does not say why he concluded that Sotas is a bishop. He does not mention the letter of the priests of Heracleopolis to Sotas (P.Oxy. 36.2785).

[42] Apparently, the addressees knew him well, or at least well enough to trust the information in the letter. Addressing Paul and Peter (and perhaps Maximus, if the letter to him, P.Alex. 29, belongs to the Sotas correspondence) with "beloved brother" indicates that Sotas considered himself to be on equal footing with these correspondents. Demetrianus (from P.Oxy. 12.1492, discussed below in ch. 5) is a younger or lower ranking person. Other correspondents that are possibly bishops also do not address each other by title, e.g., SB 10.10255 from Theonas to Mensurius. In this instance, the names of the correspondents suggest that they are high level church officials: Theonas and Mensurius possibly bishops respectively of Alexandria and Carthage.

[43] P.Oxy. 36.2785, lines 1–2. In the postscript it simply reads ἀγαπητὲ πάπα, without Sotas (lines 14–15).

[44] The word πάππας/πάπας occurs most frequently in the vocative, see LSJ, 1301–2.

[45] Πάππας, also spelled πάπας, Latin *papa* (LSJ, 1301). Papas (Παπᾶς) appears also to be a personal name (Foraboschi, *Onomasticon*, 233) and Papa is the name of a village in the Herakleopolite nome (see *SB* 14.11615). Personal and geographical names are not relevant here.

Juvenal,[46] this term communicates a combination of affection and reverence.[47] From the third century on, the word papa (πάπας/*papa*) has come to be a title of respect for Christian clerics.[48]

Until now, scholars perceived Sotas not as bishop but as a priest. In her *magnum opus* on Athanasius and the Egyptian church in the fourth century, Annick Martin makes the Heracleopolite letter (P.Oxy. 36.2785) the *crux interpretationis* for other documentary uses of the word "papa." Reading the address according to the first edition of the papyrus, to "papa Sotas, presbyter of Heracleopolis,"[49] Martin argues that this title makes Sotas a priest and that the title "papa" in two other documents therefore also refers to priests.[50] The same argument—also based on the reading of that same letter—appears

[46] See, e.g., Leclercq, "Papa" in *DACL* 13.1 (1937) 1097–99; and De Labriolle, "Une esquisse de l'histoire du mot 'Papa'," in *BALAC* 1 (1911) 215–20.

[47] Leclercq describes it as "une expression où le respect s'associe à l'affection" ("Papa," 1104; with reference to J. B. De Rossi). As such, the term can also be used to flatter someone. Dickey discusses a passage in Menander's *Dyskolos*, where the advice is given to address older men as "father" or "dad" when one needs to achieve something: πρεσβύτερός τις τ[ῇ] θύρᾳ ὑπακήκο' εὐθὺς πατέρα καὶ πάππα[ν καλῶ] ("Suppose an old man answers the door [I call him] 'Father' straight away, or 'Dad'"). Menander, *Dyskolos* 494–95 (trans. Arnott, LCL); see also Dickey, "Literal and Extended Use," *Mnemosyne* 57 (2004) 138.

[48] Both Leclercq and De Labriolle discuss this development. This same word is still in use today as title for Christian clergymen both in Western and Eastern Christianity. In the Latin speaking West, eventually the word *papa* became the exclusive title for the pope in Rome. In Modern Greek usage the word means priest (παπᾶς) or pope (πάπας), depending on the emphasis. The word "papa" was probably also the form of address for teachers, as Van den Hoek points out: "Clement hardly ever calls himself a διδάσκαλος. It may well be that their title of address was πάπας rather than πατήρ, since in classical Latin 'papas' was the title by which children addressed their 'paedagogus'" ("The 'Catechetical' School," *HTR* 90 [1997] 64, see also footnote 24).

[49] In his edition of P.Oxy. 36.2785, Rea did not entertain the possibility that papa Sotas could be a bishop because—as we have seen—he read the papyrus as addressed to "our beloved brother, papas Sotas, priest of Heracleopolis." For him Sotas was a presbyter. For forms of address for a "father," see also P.Oxy. 12.1592 (discussed in ch. 3), where *nomina sacra* were used.

[50] Martin wrote: "Reste à dire un mot du titre de *papa* ou *papas*, que certains historiens ont estimé réservé aux évêques et plus spécialement à l'évêque d'Alexandrie du IVe siècle, et qui, pourtant, dans trois de nos documents, au moins, désigne le prêtre de l'église locale. Le dernier publié, le *P.Oxy.* 36, 2785 . . . au 'bien aimé *papa* Sôtas, prêtre d'Hérakléopolis', ne permet plus de douter de l'interprétation proposée par leurs éditeurs pour les deux autres. Ainsi, Kaor, 'papas d'Hermoupolis', était bien le prêtre de ce village d'Arsinoïte, . . . tout comme Aurélios Ammônios, le *papas* qui signe un contrat de marriage entre deux paysans illettrés" (*Athanase d'Alexandrie*, 652–53).

in the most recent treatment of the meaning of the word papa, by Tomasz Derda and Ewa Wipszycka.[51] After discussing several cases where the papa clearly refers to a bishop, they state that the title also applies to presbyters.[52] At this point they bring up the Heracleopolis letter (P.Oxy. 36.2785). Their understanding of the address as to "papa Sotas, presbyter" leads again to an incorrect interpretation. The reconstruction of the abbreviation in the Oxyrhynchus papyrus turns out to have great importance, because—as we have seen—one has no ground for assuming that the senders of that letter did not identify themselves and that Sotas had the double title *papas* and *presbyteros*. With this information, I will conduct a new investigation into the meaning of the word "papa."

Although one may perceive some fluidity in the use of the term "papa"[53] in general, in the third century, it designated Christian bishops, whether they

[51] Derda and Wipszycka comment: "Chaque éditeur ou lecteur de papyrus de l'époque byzantine doit se poser la question de savoir comment il faut entendre les titres *abba* et *apa*, qui apparaissent très fréquemment . . . ainsi que le titre *papas* (plus rare)" ("L'emploi des titres *Abba, Apa* et *Papas*," *JJP* 24 [1994] 23). Most pages of this article concern the meaning of the first two terms, *abba* and *apa*. The papa arrives only at the very end (ibid., 54–56). Derda and Wipszycka note that this title "est employé beaucoup plus rarement et s'applique exclusivement aux members du clergé" (ibid., 54). Sixth- and seventh-century Greek texts tend to identify or designate bishops as "papa." For Coptic texts, the situation is different; in several eighth-century Coptic texts, the word papa seems to serve as title for presbyters (ibid., 55).

[52] "Les presbytres aussi ont droit à ce titre" (ibid., 54).

[53] Only in a few instances it remains unclear whether papa refers to a bishop or a priest—for instance, in two papyri from the fourth century: 1) Kaor, a clergyman from the village Hermoupolis in the Fayum, sends a letter to an official describing himself as papa (P.Abbin. 32, ca. 346 C.E.), but did that village have a bishop? The address reads: "to my master and beloved brother Abinneus, *praepositus*, Kaor, papa of Hermoupolis, greetings" (τῷ δεσπότῃ μου καὶ ἀγαπητῷ | ἀδελφῷ Ἀβιννέῳ πραιπ(οσίτῳ) |Κάορ πάπας Ἑρμοῦ πόλεως χαίρειν; P.Abinn. 32, lines 1–3). The letter urges Abinnaeus to have clemency on a certain Paul, a soldier, because of his desertion (φυγή). This Paul must be a Christian because of his name and because Kaor intercedes for him to Abinnaeus. The Hermoupolis in this and other letters from the Abinnaeus archive is a village in the southwestern part of the Fayum Oasis, not the city Hermoupolis, therefore Deissmann concluded: "nun erschien es mir als das Nächstliegende, auch in dem Hermupolis unseres Papyrus das Dorf und in dem Papas nicht einen Bischof, sondern einen einfachen Priester zu sehen. Das Wort *Papas* kommt in alter Zeit von christlichen Dorfpriestern vor, also besteht keine Schwierigkeit, es auch hier so zu fassen. . . . in unserem Kaor, der sich *Papst* nennt, aber kein Papst ist, begrüßen wir gern einen Vertreter des Dorfchristentums und stellen ihn zu dem um eine Generation älteren Oasenpresbyter Psenosiris" (*Licht vom Osten*, 186–87). I do not know to which ancient example of village priests Deissmann refers here. 2) Another papa, Aurelius Ammonius,

presided over churches in metropolitan cities such as Alexandria or Rome or served in smaller cities.[54] Third-century writers more frequently used the official title, ἐπίσκοπος/*episcopus*, for bishop. In comparison to this official form of address, the word papa "covers the concept of spiritual fatherhood" and carries "a nuance of loving respect."[55] We find the word papa (πάπας/*papa*) in a variety of early Christian texts in Greek and Latin from the third century. The *Passion of Perpetua and Felicitas* refers to a bishop, Optatus, as "our papa" (*papa noster*, πάπας ἡμέτερος).[56] Ecclesiastical writers also employed the word papa to indicate a bishop. In her monograph on *Titles of Address in Christian Greek Epistolography to 527 A.D.*, Lucilla Dinneen examined literarily transmitted Christian letters with respect to titles and found that in these letters, the title papa was "addressed exclusively to bishops."[57]

---

signs a document on behalf of illiterate people: "I, Aurelius Ammonius, papa, have written on their behalf because they are illiterate" (Αὐρήλιος Ἀμμώνιος παπᾶς ἔγραψα ὑπὲρ αὐτῶν παρό(ν)των ἀγραμμάτων; P.Ross.Georg. 3.28, dated 343/358 C.E.). According to Wipszycka, the fact that Ammonius wrote for these newly wed peasants indicates that he cannot have been a bishop. As she stated: "On conçoit mal qu'un évêque . . . ait pu servir de scribe à des paysans" ("Remarques," *JJP* 18 [1974] 217). In both instances one can advance objections against identifying these two as bishops: in the case of Kaor, the small size of the community; in the case of Ammonius, the activity seemingly not fitting for a bishop.

[54] De Labriolle already argued this. He asked: "Les évêques des métropoles comme Rome, Carthage, Alexandrie, étaient-ils les seuls que l'on honorât de ce nom? On le dit quelquefois, mais à tort" ("Esquisse de l'histoire," 216).

[55] De Labriolle writes, "enveloppe le concept de paternité spirituelle et implique . . . chez ceux qui l'emploient une nuance d'affectueux respect" (ibid., 217).

[56] Saturus relates his vision in which he sees the bishop Optatus and the priest Aspasium sadly standing on the right and left of the entrance to heaven. The martyrs address the bishop as *papa noster*. The passage reads in the Latin: "Et exiuimus et uidimus ante fores Optatum episcopum ad dexteram, et Aspasium presbyterum doctorem ad sinistram, separatos et tristes. et miserunt se ad pedes nobis, et dixerunt «Componite inter nos quia existis, et sic nos reliquistis.» Et diximus illis: «Non tu es papa noster, et tu presbyter? Ut uos ad pedes nobis mittatis?»" *Passion of Perpetua and Felicitas* 13.1–3 (ed. Musurillo, 120, 122). Cyprian, bishop of Carthage, is also addressed as and identifies himself as papa (Leclercq, "Papa," 1100–1).

[57] Dinneen, *Titles of Address*, 108. She notes: "In the literature which we have examined, most of the examples of the title πάπας are addressed to the bishop of Alexandria. It is found once for Pope Julius. . . . We have noted three instances of its use where the identification of the persons addressed is uncertain or unknown" (ibid., 12). In one of those instances, where Origen mentions a papa Apollinarius, the papa is most likely also a bishop (ibid., 12). A TLG search corroborates Dinneen's conclusions made in 1929, also when expanded beyond epistolary literature. Indeed, Athanasius, bishop of Alexandria, heads the list of these

In Egypt, Bishop Dionysius of Alexandria (247–264) calls his predecessor Heraclas (231–247) "our blessed papa."[58] A tantalizingly interesting and fragmentary Christian papyrus letter sent from Rome and found in the Fayum oasis in Egypt mentions Dionysius's successor Maximus (264–282) several times as "papa Maximus."[59] This form of address does not appear restricted to the bishop of Alexandria, at least not in the third century. In a papyrus letter addressed to "the beloved brothers who share in the local

bishops. In the *Martyrdom of Polycarp*, one finds the first mention of a Christian bishop as father (with the word πατήρ, not πάπας), when the hostile crowds cry out: "This one is the teacher of Asia, the father of the Christians" (Οὗτός ἐστιν ὁ τῆς Ἀσίας διδάσκαλος—ὁ πατὴρ τῶν Χριστιανῶν; *Martyrdom of Polycarp* 12.2, 224). Uses of the term "papa" in Greek texts begin with Origen. In the *Dialogue with Heraclides*, Origen calls Heraclides and Demetrius "papa" (*Dial.* 1.20 and 24.21, respectively). Both men are explicitly described as bishops in the text. In a homily on 1 Samuel, Origen, preaching in Jerusalem, refers to Alexander, the local bishop, as papa (preserved in the Latin; quod in papa habetis Alexandro; *Homily on Samuel* 1, 1.22–26, in Pierre and Marie-Thérèse Nautin, *Origène,* 61–62, and locus on 96–97). The closing greetings of his *Epistle to Africanus* refer to "our good papa Apollinarius" (τὸν καλὸν ἡμῶν πάπαν Ἀπολλινάριον), who is furthermore unknown. See de Lange in *Origène, Philocalie*, 573 n. 3. He was probably a bishop.

Gregory Thaumaturgus (ca. 213–270), bishop of Caesarea in Pontus and student of Origen, addressed his so-called *Canonical epistle* to a "holy papa" (ἱερὲ πάπα). For the adjective "holy" as form of address see ch. 5. The scholarly consensus is that this otherwise unknown man was a bishop; for Fox, the addressee was a person with "authority over a country district . . . evidently a bishop, perhaps the bishop of Trapezus itself" (*Pagans and Christians*, 539). According to Leclercq, that "holy papa" must have been a bishop in Pontus: "l'expression ἱερὲ πάπα, adressée à ce correspondant anonyme qui, certainement, occupait un siege episcopal du Pont" ("Papa," 1102). Salmond observed: "This expression leads me to think that this epistle is addressed to the Bishop of Antioch or of some other Apostolic See. It must not be taken as a prescribed formula, however, as when we say 'Most Revered' in our days. . . . Rather, it is an expression of personal reverence" ("Gregory Thaumaturgus," *ANF* 6:20).

The "blessed papa Anencletus" (τῷ μακαρίῳ πάπᾳ Ἀνεγκλήτῳ), bishop of Rome, appears in a letter to Mary of Cassobola, purportedly from Ignatius of Antioch, but belonging to the spurious letters dating probably to the fourth century ("Ad Mariam" 4, in *Patres apostolici*, 2.56–59). For brief discussions of the recensions of the letters of Ignatius and the date of the spurious letters, see Schoedel, *Commentary on the Letters of Ignatius,* 3–5; and "Letters of Ignatius," in *Apostolic Fathers* 1.209–13. Furthermore, "les attestations des papyrus plus tardifs (SB XII 10767 [VIe]; P. Giss. 55 [VIe]; SB VI 9464 [VIIe]) concernent des évêques," as Derda and Wipszycka note ("L'emploi des titres," 55). If, therefore, in later times *papas* still constitutes a title of address for a bishop, it is clear that this was already the case in the third century.

58 παρὰ τοῦ μακαρίου πάπα ἡμῶν Ἡρακλᾶ (Eusebius, *Hist. eccl.* 7.7.4).

59 E.g., column 3, line 5: Μάξιμον τὸν πάπα[ν]), also line 9 (in the dative). Grenfell and Hunt, eds. P.Amh. 1.3 (1900) = Naldini, *Cristianesimo*, no. 6, see further literature mentioned there.

service,"[60] sender Heraclites, a bishop, identifies himself as a papa (written in abbreviated form as ππ).[61] Neither does this form of address appear limited to the orthodox bishops. A letter from Callistus to Paieous and Patabeit mentions a papa Heraiscus.[62] In a detailed study on this papyrus, Hans Hauben identified papa Heraiscus as, in fact, the Melitian anti-bishop to Athanasius at Alexandria.[63]

By calling Sotas "papa" instead of "brother"—the expression for persons of equal status—the presbyters, literally "the elders," of Heracleopolis, indicate Sotas's seniority in rank. So we can conclude with confidence: *habemus papam.* Our further investigations of Sotas and his activities will serve to confirm my conclusion that Sotas was a bishop.

Just as we do not know when exactly Christians and Christianity reached Oxyrhynchus, so also we do not know when the city gained a bishop. Several texts composed at a later period mention Oxyrhynchite bishops at the beginning of the fourth century. For various reasons we cannot consider these sources historically reliable, although they claim to narrate events that took place in the early-fourth century. I nevertheless mention them here, not only for the sake of completeness, but also because I find them interesting in and of themselves. The Arabic synaxarium treats Oxyrhynchus as a bishopric at the beginning of the fourth century in a case involving the succession of

60 SB 16.12304 (Panopolis, third/fourth cent.), lines 1–3: τοῖς κατὰ τόπον συνλιτουργοῖς ἀγα<πη>τοῖς ἀδελφοῖς.

61 SB 16.12304, line 1. The editio princeps of this papyrus is Treu, "P. Berol. 8508," 53–54. See also discussion by Llewelyn, "Christian Letters of Recommendation," *NewDocs* 8:169–72. According to Derda and Wipszycka, the sender is undoubtedly a bishop: "Puisque l'expression τοῖς συνλιτουργοῖς est employée dans les textes chrétiens exclusivement pour designer des évêques qui exercent leurs fonctions en même temps que celui qui écrit, nous n'avons pas de doutes sur la signification de *papas* dans ce cas" ("L'emploi des titres," 54). For a much later non-Alexandrian bishop addressed as papa, see P.Giss. 2.55, "Schreiben eines Bischofs an einen Amtsbruder." This is a sixth-century letter from Heron to Sarapion. Both men are indicated as ππ (line 2). Meyer, its editor, commented: "Schreiber und Adressat des Briefes werden als π(ά)π(ας) bezeichnet. . . . Das Wort ("Papst") bedeutet hier zweifellos 'Bischof.' . . . Der Schreiber ist dann der Bischof des Bezirks von Aphrodito, d.h. also wohl des Antaiopolites" (P.Giss. 2.55, 92–93).

62 πρὸς τ̣[ὸν] πάπαν Ἡραείσκον, 2, 25 in P.Lond. 6.1914 (written after the year 335).

63 Hauben observed that Heraiscus's name is mentioned in proximity to the title bishop and concludes that "*papas* Heraiscus was indeed the Melitian bishop of Alexandria" ("On the Melitians in P.London VI [P.Jews] 1914," in *Proceedings of the Sixteenth International Congress of Papyrologists,* 453).

bishop Theodosius.[64] The *Acta Sanctorum* for 27 August commemorate a group of seventeen martyrs from Oxyrhynchus, among them bishop Miletius (*Miletius episcopus*), who died during the Diocletianic persecution.[65]

A mediaeval Coptic manuscript preserves the most interesting of these texts referring to a bishop in the early-fourth century. This manuscript presents an appealing—but disappointingly fragmentary—account about the selection of a new Oxyrhynchite bishop situated in the beginning of the fourth century.[66] According to the narrative, bishop Peter of Alexandria (in office ca. 300–311) fled to Oxyrhynchus during the Diocletianic persecutions.[67] Upon his arrival the Oxyrhynchites informed him that their bishop had died recently.[68] Of course Peter, "the father of faith,"[69] became involved in the search for a new bishop. Just when the story gets exciting, with a virgin alone in the church with one of the presbyters, the manuscript unfortunately breaks off. Our concern here lies, of course, not with the virgin and the presbyter but rather with the bishopric of Oxyrhynchus, which this text presupposes at the beginning of the fourth century.[70]

[64] "Nach dem arabischen Synaxar (zum 25. Kihak) war der Ort schon seit Anfang des 4. Jahrhunderts ein Bistum. Damals habe Bischof Theodosius von al-Bahnasa . . . den verschleppten Amtsbruder Herakion von Abu-l-Hayyib zu seinem Nachfolger in al-Bahnasa gemacht" (Timm, "al-Bahnasa" in *Das christlich-koptische Ägypten* 1:284).

[65] *Acta Sanctorum* 1, Acta auctore Juliano presbytero ex Ms. Trevirensi collato cum Cluniacensi, BHL 5240, from *Acta Sanctorum* online (http://acta.chadwyck.com/, 2007).

[66] See Schmidt, *Fragmente einer Schrift des Märtyrerbischofs Petrus von Alexandrien*. According to Schmidt, the manuscript belonged to a tenth–eleventh century parchment codex from the Shenoute monastery near Sohag. Only two folia (numbered ⲡⲑ–ϥⲃ [89–92]) are preserved. Its inventory number is: Cod. copt. 130^5 fol. 123f. in the Bibliothèque Nationale in Paris (ibid., 3).

[67] Schmidt, *Petrus von Alexandrien*, 6 (folio 90, 5–16): ⲧⲉⲧⲛⲥⲟⲟⲩⲛ ϫⲉ ⲉⲓⲥ ⲟⲩⲛⲟϭ ⲉⲛⲟⲩⲟⲉⲓϣ ⲉⲓ̈ⲡⲏⲧ ⲕⲁⲧⲁⲙⲁ ⲉⲧⲃⲉ ⲑⲟ ⲧⲉ ⲛⲇⲓⲟⲕⲗⲏⲧⲓⲁⲛⲟⲥ ⲙⲛ ⲡⲉϥⲇⲓⲱⲅⲙⲟⲥ ⲉⲧϩⲓϫⲱⲛ ⲧⲉⲛⲟⲩ: ⲁⲓ̈ⲃⲱⲕ ⲉⲡⲙⲁⲣⲏⲥ ⲛⲕⲏⲙⲉ ϣⲁⲛϯⲃⲱⲕ ⲉⲧⲡⲟⲗⲓⲥ ⲉⲝⲱⲣⲓ̈ⲭⲟⲥ ⲉⲧⲉ ⲡⲉⲙϫⲉ ⲡⲉ. ("You know that for a long time I was fleeing from place to place because of fear for Diocletian and his persecution which is (still) now upon us. I went to the South of Egypt, until I came to the city Oxyrhynchus, which is Pemdje"). In the text, Peter reports the kind welcome he received at Oxyrhynchus from the clerics and the other faithful there (ibid., 90, 1.16–22). The hospitality of the Oxyrhynchites is a recurring topos; see also our discussion of the *Historia monachorum in Aegypto* in ch. 1.

[68] "Our father the bishop" (ⲡⲉⲛⲉⲓⲱⲧ ⲉⲛⲉⲡⲓⲥⲕⲟⲡⲟⲥ) (ibid., 90, 1.30–31).

[69] ⲡⲉⲓⲱⲧ ⲛⲧⲡⲓⲥⲧⲓⲥ (ibid., 90, 1.34–35).

[70] Schmidt concluded: "Die ganze Erzählung setzt voraus, dass in der Stadt [Oxyrhynchus] eine grössere Gemeinde vorhanden, die schon längere Zeit von Bestand war, einen Bischof und mehrere Presbyter und eine eigene ἐκκλησία besass" (*Petrus von Alexandrien*,

Apart from Sotas, the first historically reliable mention of a bishop at Oxyrhynchus occurs in the writings of Athanasius, bishop of Alexandria (328–373). Athanasius refers to an Oxyrhynchite bishop named Pelagius in 325 C.E. listed among the Melitian bishops.[71] We next encounter the Oxyrhynchite bishop known as Dionysius, "bishop of the catholic church," in ca. 351–352 (P.Oxy. 22.2344).[72] Another bishop, Theodorus, Dionysius's successor or rival, features in a papyrus letter from Dioscurides to Aquilas (P.Oxy. 34.2729, "ca. 352–359") as well as in a letter from Athanasius.[73]

This overview has shown that our papa Sotas, the earliest bishop of Oxyrhynchus so far known, occupied the episcopal see of Oxyrhynchus in the second half of the third century. We should now become further acquainted with him and take the opportunity to observe the work of a third-century Christian bishop in an Egyptian city.

Letters of Recommendation

Of the five letters that make up the correspondence of Sotas, three comprise letters of recommendation.[74] Such letters appeal to the hospitality of the

---

44). Schmidt's general assertion about the ecclesiastical situation at Oxyrhynchus at this time is probably correct. However, since these fragments do not constitute authentic writings of Peter of Alexandria, contrary to what Schmidt thought, they do not provide contemporary information about the Oxyrhynchite bishop.

[71] Πελάγιος ἐν Ὀξυρύγχῳ (Athanasius, *Apologia contra Arianos* 71.6.12). About the reliability of this account: the context is, of course, polemical, but I see no grounds why Athanasius would have made up this list of Melitian bishops.

[72] The ed. princ. dated the papyrus to 336 C.E. However, the publication of P.Oxy. 60.4089, which features the same official Flavius Paeanius, *strategus*, pushed that date some fifteen years later, to ca. 351–352 "with consequent effects for the study of the early Church, since a Christian bishop features in 2344" (Coles, P.Oxy. 60.4089, 221). See also Gonis, "Dionysius, Bishop of Oxyrhynchus, and His Date," *JJP* 36 (2006) 63–65, and Benaissa, "New Light on the Episcopal Church of Oxyrhynchus," *ZPE* 161 (2007) 199–200.

[73] Bagnall, *Egypt in Late Antiquity*, 37 n. 156. Bagnall also points out with reference to Klaas Worp that this Theodorus is mentioned in Athanasius's letter for the year 347. It is interesting to note that in the papyrus he occurs as boat-owner. At present, it is unclear how to interpret the relation between Dionysius and Theodorus, as their time in office seems to overlap, see also Benaissa, "Episcopal Church of Oxyrhynchus," 200. The two may have been rivals, suggests Gonis, "Dionysius, Bishop of Oxyrhynchus," 64–65. For later bishops, see also Timm, "al-Bahnasa," 284–86; Worp, "Checklist of Bishops," *ZPE* 100 (1994) 303–4; and Martin, *Athanase d'Alexandrie*, 780.

[74] Including "[Sot?]as to Maximus," P.Alex. 29, the numbers are six, respectively, four. Literature on letters of recommendation: Keyes, "Greek Letter of Introduction," *AJP* 56

addressees. The practice of hospitality formed a part of regular life and custom in antiquity.[75] The absence of international law and of hotel chains, so to speak, contributed to the need for hospitality.[76] The duties of friendship entailed recommending friends to influential relations in order to help them to advance their lives.[77] Just like their neighbors, early Christians valued hospitality highly:[78] in extending hospitality one may even unwittingly entertain angels.[79] In Christian circles the bishops[80] normally had the

(1935); Leclercq, "Litterae commendatitiae et formatae," *DACL* 9.2 (1930); Kim, *Form and Structure*; Llewelyn, "Christian Letters of Recommendation"; P.Berl. Sarisch. 11, "Christliches Empfehlungsschreiben," 94–101; Stowers, "11: Letters of Mediation" in idem., *Letter Writing,* 153–65; Teeter, "Christian Letters of Recommendation," *PBR* 9 (1990); idem, "Letters of Recommendation," *APF Beiheft* 3 (1997); and Treu, "Christliche Empfehlungs-Schemabriefe."

[75] For studies on hospitality in antiquity, see Hiltbrunner et al., "Gastfreundschaft," *RAC* 8; Hiltbrunner, *Gastfreundschaft in der Antike*; and Arterbury, *Entertaining Angels*. See also Horn, "The Importance of Practising Hospitality," in her *Asceticism and Christological Controversy*, 273–99.

[76] So Treu: "Die alten Griechen reisten viel, sei es als Händler, als Söldner oder als neugierige Gelehrte und Touristen wie Herodot. Da es kein internationales Recht und nur ein unvollkommenes Beherbergungswesen gab, taten sie gut daran, sich durch persönliche Beziehungen die Wege zu ebenen. So ist die große Rolle der Gastfreundschaft verständlich. Sie ist . . . nicht Sache der Emotionen, sondern fest geregelte Verbindung" ("Christliche Empfehlungs-Schemabriefe," 629).

[77] As Treu puts it: "Es gehört zu den Freundespflichten, dem Freund beim Fortkommen behilflich zu sein, z.B. indem man ihn einem einflußreichen Bekannten empfiehlt" (ibid., 630).

[78] The *Didache* states: "Everyone who comes in the name of the Lord should be welcomed" (πᾶς δὲ ὁ ἐρχομενος ἐν ὀνόματι κυρίου δεχθήτω; *Did.* 12). Christians continue the strong Hebrew Bible and Jewish tradition of hospitality.

[79] Heb 13:1–2 (NRSV): "Let mutual love continue. Do not neglect to show hospitality to strangers, for by doing that some have entertained angels without knowing it." The author alludes to Abraham and Sarah's hospitality to the three visitors at Mamre (Gen 18). Many early Christian writers referred to Abraham's exemplary hospitality, for instance 1 Clem 10.7 (see Hiltbrunner et al., "Gastfreundschaft," 1071 [section written by Gorce]. Horn lists multiple examples in her *Asceticism and Christological Controversy*, 276 n. 261). The story also inspired artists (see Hiltbrunner, "Gastfreundschaft," 1071 [section written by Gorce] and Horn, *Asceticism and Christological Controversy*, 276 n. 263).

[80] Being hospitable (φιλόξενος) constitutes one of the qualifications for bishops in the pastoral epistles (1 Tim 3:2 and Titus 1:8). A letter from Dionysius, bishop of Corinth, addressed to the Roman bishop Soter (ca. 170), also provides insight into the role of the bishop in receiving strangers. Dionysius praises Soter's hospitality, because the Roman bishop encourages those who visit Rome as a tenderly loving father does his children (λόγοις δὲ μακαρίοις τοὺς ἀνιόντας ἀδελφούς, ὡς τέκνα πατὴρ φιλόστοργος, παρακαλῶν) (Eusebius, *Hist. eccl.* 4.23.10). In Hermas, hospitality features among a catalogue of good deeds: "being

responsibility for welcoming strangers, though not exclusively.[81] Bishops were expected to extend hospitality to strangers and poor people and it seems they supported them from their own means.[82]

Since letters of recommendation occupy the central place in this chapter, I shall first look at letters of recommendation in antiquity in general. The letters from the Sotas correspondence belong to a distinct epistolary genre.[83] Scholars sometimes refer to them as letters of recommendation or introduction; Stanley Stowers calls them "letters of mediation."[84] In an article on the subject published in 1935, Clinton W. Keyes collected forty-four examples of Greek and Latin letters of recommendation transmitted both literarily and in papyri (the latter he referred to as "Letters from Actual Life").[85] Since Keyes's article appeared, a steady stream of papyrological publications has raised the number of documentary letters from thirty to nearly one hundred.[86]

---

hospitable, for doing good is sometimes found in hospitality" (φιλόξενον εἶναι, ἐν γὰρ φιλοξενίᾳ εὑρίσκεται ἀγαθοποίησίς ποτε, *Commandments* 38 [8.10]). In the *Parables*, "bishops and those who are hospitable" (ἐπίσκοποι καὶ φιλόξενοι) constitute the believers from the tenth mountain; namely those "who always gladly welcomed the slaves of God into their homes without hypocrisy. And through their ministry, the bishops always provided constant shelter for those in need and for the widows" (*Parables* 104 [9.27.2]).

[81] Widows also took on an important role in extending hospitality, as 1 Tim 5:10, for instance, makes clear (εἰ ἐξενοδόχησεν). On this topic, see Osiek and Balch, *Families in the New Testament World*, esp. ch. 8: "Family Life, Meals and Hospitality," 193–214.

[82] Cyprian makes this very clear in an epistle that he sent from his exile to the presbyters and deacons who stayed home: "I urge that you be scrupulous in your care for the widows, the sick, and all the poor, and further, that you meet the financial needs of any strangers who are in want out of my own personal funds which I have left in the care of our fellow presbyter Rogatianus. In case these funds have already been completely expended, I am sending to Rogatianus . . . a further sum" (Letter 7.2, trans. Clarke, *Letters of St. Cyprian* 1:67).

[83] Keyes calls it "perhaps the most distinctive in purpose and character" of all private letters ("Greek Letter of Introduction," 31–32).

[84] Stowers, "Letters of Mediation," 153.

[85] Keyes, "Greek Letter of Introduction," 32. The general overview that Keyes gives is still relevant. He counted thirty documentary letters (among which he mentions Rom 16:1–2) but does not list any documentary Christian letters of recommendation, despite the fact that several of them had already been published by this time. The language of the letters is not restricted to Latin and Greek. However, it is beyond the scope of this chapter to collect letters in other languages. One of the Hebrew papyri from Oxyrhynchus may also have been such a letter; see Cowley, "Notes on Hebrew Papyrus Fragments," *JEA* 2 (1915).

[86] This number is based on an HGV search for Inhalt = "Empfehlung Brief," resulting in ninety-eight hits (1 December 2007).

Epistolary handbooks from antiquity discuss these letters of recommendation as one of twenty-one types of private letters.[87] The *Epistolary Types*, a book on letter-writing attributed to Demetrius of Phaleron (Pseudo-Demetrius), described the letter of introduction as follows:

> The introductory type (συστατικός), which we write to one person for the sake of another, inserting (words of) praise, and speaking of those previously unacquainted as if they were acquainted (or, making acquainted those previously unacquainted). Such as the following: X, who is conveying the letter to you, is a man who has been well tested by us, and who is loved on account of his trustworthiness. Kindly grant him hospitality both for my sake and for his, and indeed also for your own. For you will not be sorry if you entrust to him, in any matter you wish, either words or deeds of a confidential nature. Indeed you yourself will praise him to others when you have learned how useful he can be in everything.[88]

In these kinds of letters, a person commends a stranger to one's relations and expects them to treat this person favorably.

Letters of recommendation differ from other private letters, in my opinion, in that the people who deliver the letter form also the main subject of the letter. I imagine the tired travelers, in need of a place to spend the night or of help to find a job,[89] arriving at their destination. They hand over the letter that they have carefully held onto during their journey and, ready to supply more information orally, anxiously wait for the host to read it. At that moment, the letter—as Pseudo-Demetrius observed—functions as the medium, which allows its writer to introduce his acquaintances, as if he stood there in person.[90]

[87] This is in Pseudo-Demetrius of Phaleron; see Keyes, "Greek Letter of Introduction," 28. Malherbe comments that this work is "falsely attributed to Demetrius of Phalerum." Dating this text is difficult; Malherbe concludes that "we must be content with broader limits, between 200 B.C. and A.D. 300, for the text in its present form" (*Ancient Epistolary Theorists*, 4).

[88] Keyes, "Greek Letter of Introduction," 38. The Greek title is Τύποι ἐπιστολικοί.

[89] Among the examples Keyes mentions are letters requesting both general ("Help him in whatever he needs from you," ibid., 40) and long term hospitality for the recommended people.

[90] I use the masculine pronoun here because I do not know of any letters of recommendation written by women (there are none in Bagnall and Cribiore, *Women's Letters*). Canon 81 of the council of Elvira suggests that women were involved in such correspondence, because it forbids them to send letters to lay-people and to accept letters of recommendation. It reads: "Let no women, who are faithful, dare to write on their own without their husbands'

Pseudo-Demetrius emphasized the reciprocity of granting hospitality: The person who welcomes the recommended traveler does a favor to the bearer of the letter and to his friend, and even to himself; this aspect appears in many of the letters. Some write that they will return the favor.[91]

Much shorter, and thus more like the Sotas's letters, the sample letter of another writing coach from antiquity, generally referred to as Pseudo-Libanius, appears in a work called *Epistolary Forms*.[92] This epistle reads:

> The letter of recommendation. Receive this highly honored and much sought-after man, and do not hesitate to treat him hospitably, thus doing what behooves you and what pleases me.[93]

Pseudo-Libanius makes explicit that granting hospitality does not constitute merely doing a friend a favor; it means "doing what is appropriate."[94] This theme recurs in many letters of recommendation whether literary or documentary. Welcoming a friend's friend means doing "what is proper."[95] This we also find in the Christian letters from Sotas's correspondence: Sotas

names to lay-persons, or accept letters of peace from anyone written to their name only" (ne foeminae suo potius absque maritorum nominibus laicis scribere audeant, quae fideles sunt, vel literas alicuius pacificas ad suum solum nomen scriptas accipiant, ed. Lauchert, *Kanones der wichtigsten altkirchlichen Concilien*, 26). See also Teeter, "Letters of Recommendation," 954–55. The council was held ca. 306 C.E. Some scholars have argued that only canons 1–21 stem from that time and that a local church added the other canons at a later time in the fourth century, so Meigne, "Concile ou collection d'Elvire," *RHE* 70 (1975) 361–87, see especially 364, 374.

[91] Keyes, "Greek Letter of Introduction," 41.

[92] This work (Ἐπιστολιμαῖοι χαρακτῆρες) is also transmitted under the name of Proclus the Neoplatonist. Malherbe notes that "there are two manuscript traditions of the work, one attributing it to Libanius, the other to Proclus. They do not depend on each other, but derive from a common archetype which was produced by neither author. That ascribed to Libanius is more widely attested and better transmitted, and has been considered by editors of the work to have been the more original" (*Ancient Epistolary Theorists*, 5). See also White, *Light from Ancient Letters*, 189–90.

[93] Συστατική. Τὸν τιμιώτατον καὶ περισπούδαστον ἄνδρα τόνδε δεξάμενος ξενίσαι μὴ κατοκνήσῃς σεαυτῷ πρέποντα πράττων κἀμοὶ κεχαρισμένα. Greek text and translation come from Malherbe, *Ancient Epistolary Theorists*, 74–75.

[94] Keyes, "Greek Letter of Introduction," 38–39.

[95] So, e.g., in P.Flor. 2.173, from Appianus to Heroninus (dated 256 C.E.). The letter reads in translation "Let my respected son, the most honorable Primus, have every assistance and supplies of wine . . . and everything else, so that he may bear witness (of it) to me; and let him receive hospitality and whatever else is proper" (καὶ τὴν ξενίαν ἐχέτω καὶ εἴ τι ἄλλο ἐνδέχεται, lines 8–10). Translation Keyes, "Greek Letter of Introduction," 36 n. 30.

asked Paul to receive catechumens "as is proper" (ὡς καθήκει) and Peter to welcome Heracles "according to custom" (κατὰ τὸ ἔθος). In this sense, the letters from and to Sotas form part of the general cultural milieu.

Christian letters of introduction, however, have certain features that make them a subgroup within the genre.[96] Most of the Christian letters contain strong markers of Christian identity, such as *nomina sacra* or isopsephisms[97] and the mention of position within the group (such as presbyter, papa, or catechumen). Some are even nearly word-for-word identical.[98]

Given the importance of hospitality, epistolary recommendation is a familiar practice in early Christian writings. For instance, in Rom 16:1–2, the apostle Paul introduces Phoebe, a deacon of the church at Cenchreae. The apostle appealed to the Corinthians that they honor his letter of recommendation (συστατικῶν ἐπιστολῶν, 2 Cor 3:1–3).[99] Yet the writers of the documentary letters of introduction from Egypt do not express themselves in language borrowed from the Pauline letters or from other New Testament passages. As Timothy M. Teeter has pointed out, scriptural passages do

[96] Świderek comments on one such Christian letter, P.Alex. 29, that "la forme de la lettre n'est pas specifiquement chrétienne, puisque nous connaissons aussi une lettre analogue paienne, P.Oxy 1664 de III s., mais elle est caractéristique pour le début du IV s. et la fin du III s." (P.Alex. 29, 73). I would say that the *genre* is not specifically Christian, but that *qua* wording and form, the Alexandrian papyrus fits neatly in a series of Christian letters of recommendation.

[97] See above footnote 12 and fuller discussion in ch. 7.

[98] The nine Christian stereotypical letters of recommendation that are nearly identical are: P.Alex. 29; P.Oxy. 8.1162; P.Oxy. 36.2785; P.Oxy. 56.3857; PSI 3.208; PSI 9.1041; SB 3.7269; SB 10.10255; SB 16.12304 (see Treu, "Christliche Empfehlungs-Schemabriefe," and most recently P.Oxy. 56.3857). Other Christian letters of introduction in the papyrological record (until ca. 400 C.E.): P.Abinn. 31; P.Berl. Sar. 11; P.Col. 11.298; P.Got. 11; P.Gron. 17; P.Gron. 18; and P.NagHamm. 78. Examples of Christian letters of recommendation later than the fourth century are: P.Köln 2.112 (=SB 12.10965); P.Oxy. 43.3149; and P.Princ. 2.105. However, Van Haelst dates eleven letters of recommendation to the end of the third century, not the fourth "en raison de considérations paléographiques et stylistiques," namely: P.Alex. 29; P.Got. 11; P.Gron. 17; P.Gron. 18; P.Iand. 6.101; P.Oxy. 8.1162; P.Oxy. 12.1492; P.Oxy. 31.2603 (this one, however, as discussed, is a Manichaean letter, see above, 18 n. 77), PSI 3.208 and PSI 9.1041; and SB 3.7269 ("Sources papyrologiques," in *Proceedings of the Twelfth International Congress,* 498).

[99] See also Llewelyn, "Christian Letters of Recommendation," 171, for other New Testament parallels and a brief overview of where the verb προσδέχομαι occurs in the New Testament. Christian letters written on behalf of others are known also from literary sources, but they fall beyond the scope and (mostly) time frame of the book.

indeed *not* shape the immediate context for the papyrological letters.[100] He showed that Christian letters of introduction functioned as a common means of exchange between Christian communities throughout the empire and not just limited to Egypt.

Letters of recommendation came under discussion at church councils in the fourth and fifth centuries held at places as far removed as Elvira in Spain (306 C.E.) and Antioch in Syria (314 C.E.).[101] I present Canon 11 of the Council of Chalcedon (451 C.E.) as especially relevant:

> We have decreed that all paupers and persons in need of help, subject to examination, must travel with ecclesiastical letters of peace only, and not of commendation, since it is fitting only for persons held in high esteem to be provided with letters of recommendation.[102]

This fifth-century canon, as Teeter pointed out, distinguishes between two kinds of Christian letters, each intended for a distinct class of travelers. The first one, for clergy and people of higher class, was called a "letter of recommendation" (ἐπιστολὴ συστατική). This epistle, issued by a bishop, preferably addressed another bishop. It constituted a request to provide access to the Eucharist and lodging. The other type of letter, for lay people, was called a "letter of peace" (ἐπιστολὴ εἰρηνική). Not necessarily from a bishop's hand, this letter asked only for material support.[103] The bishops at Chalcedon composed this canon because they received too many requests for letters of recommendation. Finding the writing of these letters too time consuming (or perhaps too unimportant), they therefore delegated the less important letters to lower clergy.[104] In conclusion, Teeter remarked that "the

[100] "Both Kim and Treu read these letters in the light of the New Testament, citing Philemon and a passage from St. Paul, 2 Cor 3:1" (Teeter, "Letters of Recommendation," 956).

[101] Teeter, "Letters of Recommendation," 954–60.

[102] Πάντας τοὺς πένητας καὶ δεομένους ἐπικουρίας μετὰ δοκιμασίας ἐπιστολίοις ἤγουν εἰρηνικοῖς ἐκκλησιαστικοῖς μόνοις ὁδεύειν ὡρίσαμεν καὶ μὴ συστατικοῖς, διὰ τὸ τὰς συστατικὰς ἐπιστολὰς προσήκειν τοῖς οὖσιν ἐν ὑπολήψει μόνοις παρέχεσθαι προσώποις (ibid., 959).

[103] "There was the ἐπιστολὴ συστατική, also known as the *commendatio* or *littera formata* or *canonica* or *commendaticia* or *communicatoria*, and also the ἐπιστολὴ εἰρηνική or *littera pacifica*. The former was concerned with both material support and admission to communion, and was limited to clergy and to laity of distinction; it required episcopal approval, preferably at both ends. The latter was intended only for laity, only for physical support, and required no bishop, though a bishop might write one" (ibid., 956).

[104] Later in the chapter I shall come back to this canon.

efforts of the bishops at Chalcedon to enforce a distinction between the two classes of letters imply that such distinctions were not always observed."[105] Indeed, two centuries earlier, in the time of Sotas, there still circulated only one type of letter of recommendation.

The letters that Sotas wrote appear so similar not only because they have the same author but also because they use formulaic language. Scholars have noted the similarity of these and other letters not only in general topic but also in their phrasing. In fact, nine Christian letters of recommendation have such formulaic language that one can print them synoptically, as Treu did in his article on the subject.[106] These nine letters contain the same five components:[107]

1) Name of recipient and sender or *vice versa* and greeting (beloved brother, ἀγαπητὲ ἄδελφε; greetings in the Lord, χαῖρε ἐν κ̅ω̅);[108]
2) Position and name[109] of the letter bearer(s) (sister, ἀδελφή; brother, ἀδελφός; daughter, θυγάτηρ; catechumen, κατηχούμενος);

[105] Teeter, "Letters of Recommendation," 958.

[106] At the time Treu wrote his article, seven formulaic Christian letters of recommendation were known. Treu later published number eight: SB 16.12304 in "P.Berol. 8508," 53–54; M. G. Sirivianou added a ninth: P.Oxy. 56.3857, "Christian Letter of Recommendation." Almost all letters with a sure provenance were found at Oxyrhynchus: PSI 3.208; PSI 9.1041; P.Oxy. 8.1162; P.Oxy. 36.2785; and P.Oxy. 56.3857. The Berlin papyrus (SB 16.12304) is the only exception; it came perhaps from Panopolis, since it was found in the cartonnage of the Codex Berol. 8502. P.Alex. 29 and SB 10.10255 have no known provenance (but, as we have seen, P.Alex. 29 may have been found at Oxyrhynchus, see above). P.Oxy. 43.3149 is a letter of recommendation found at Oxyrhynchus, but not of the standard type. This predominance of Oxyrhynchus papyri is to be expected, for it is true for most papyrus documents. Given the size of the papyrus find at Oxyrhynchus, its papyri always form a large percentage of all (especially provenanced) papyri. However, the large number of Christian letters of introduction found at the site is also indicative of the level of Christianization of Oxyrhynchus.

[107] Treu, "Christliche Empfehlungs-Schemabriefe," 634. See also Sirivianou, P.Oxy. 56.3857, 111; Llewelyn, "Christian Letters of Recommendation," 170; Teeter, "Christian Letters of Recommendation," 62 ("simple model").

[108] As Llewelyn remarks, four letters have χαῖρε ἐν κ̅ω̅, the others have ἐν κ̅ω̅ χαίρειν (P.Oxy. 56.3857 lacks a similar formula due to damage of the top part of the papyrus). Three of the four letters with χαῖρε ἐν κ̅ω̅ are from the Sotas correspondence, and the fourth one is perhaps from that same dossier (P.Alex. 29).

[109] Treu rightly recognized that explicitly mentioning the name of the traveler was a key point in the letters: "Unumgänglich ist die namentliche Nennung der Überbringer" ("Christliche Empfehlungs-Schemabriefe," 633).

3) Request for hospitality with specific directions (in peace, ἐν εἰρήνῃ; as is proper, ὡς καθήκει; according to custom, κατὰ τὸ ἔθος);
4) Exchange of greetings between the two communities (I and those with me, we greet you and those with you, σε καὶ τοὺς παρὰ σοὶ ἐγὼ καὶ οἱ σὺν ἐμοὶ προσαγορεύομεν);
5) Final greeting with Christian markers of identity (*nomina sacra*, isopsephism).

Some scholars have suggested that the writers of these letters had a handbook of Christian epistolography at their disposal, a Christian counterpart to those of Pseudo-Demetrius and Pseudo-Libanius discussed above.[110] For Treu, the fact that one can list these letters in a synopsis sufficiently proved that they followed a pattern,[111] yet he cautioned against a perception of the letters' model that is either too rigid or too modern.[112] Most letter writers in antiquity, Christian or not, did not bother to copy sample letters directly from epistolary handbooks but composed their own introductory letters.[113] Among the general (non-Christian) letters of recommendation, we can perceive no such standardization as in these nine formulaic Christian letters.

In order to explain the formulaic quality of these nine Christian letters, we have to look in another direction. Instead of imagining that these letter-writers consulted a Christian epistolary handbook for their correspondence, I suggest that they copied from each other and imitated each other's letters. The networking between the communities, to which the letters themselves give evidence, makes this a plausible explanation.[114] The standardization of

[110] Kim writes, "we wonder if the writers of these letters had a manual of their own" (*Form and Structure*, 99).

[111] "Die Tatsache, daß wir die Texte parallelisiert wiedergeben können, beweist an sich schon, daß ein Schema zugrundeliegt" (Treu, "Christliche Empfehlungs-Schemabriefe," 632).

[112] "Immerhin zeigen die Umstellungen, daß wir uns den Begriff des Formulars nicht mit der Starre eines heutigen Vordrucks vorzustellen haben" (Treu, "Christliche Empfehlungs-Schemabriefe," 633).

[113] Keyes suggested that they consulted books that have since disappeared (Keyes, "Greek Letter of Introduction," 42 and 44). I side with Teeter, who also disagrees with the explanation of a Christian epistolary manual, stating: "A manual . . . implies a number of models, and I know of no other type of letter between Christians or Christian congregations that is stereotyped to this degree" ("Christian Letters of Recommendation," 61).

[114] Perhaps copying or imitation also accounts for the spelling of the word κατηχούμενος with a *theta* in two of the letters. See above PSI 9.1041 and P.Oxy. 36.2785.

the letters had benefits for both addressees and writers: On the one hand, the *nomina sacra* and cryptic isopsephisms—markers of Christian identity—in combination with formulaic language rendered the letters both trustworthy and easily recognizable for the recipients. On the other hand, the brevity and strict patterns indicate that the senders could write the letters in a straightforward manner because they had to write them frequently.

Writing letters of recommendation indeed seems to have busily occupied certain Christians. This practice even formed a topic of conversation at various Church Councils held throughout the empire. Apparently, Christian networking through these letters of recommendation became so widespread and successful that—as church historian Sozomen relates—the emperor Julian ("the Apostate") in the fourth century admired this practice and its benefits. For Julian

> the point of ecclesiastical discipline which he chiefly admired, and desired to establish among the pagans, was the custom among the bishops to give letters of recommendation to those who traveled to foreign lands, wherein they commended them to the hospitality and kindness of other bishops, in all places, and under all contingencies. In this way did Julian strive to ingraft the customs of Christianity upon paganism.[115]

According to Sozomen, even the emperor Julian, not particularly known for his positive attitude towards Christianity, wanted to implement the effective system of Christian recommendation. Despite Sozomen's rhetorical stance against the pagan ruler, this remains an interesting account that confirms the popularity and effectiveness of the letters of recommendation even into the fifth century.

A detail in one of the papyrus letters prompts us to picture a bishop with many recommendations to write. In one of the formulaic Christian letters of recommendation, a letter from Theonas to Mensurius, the scribe left a line open, in which later the name of the traveler—Serenus—was inserted.[116] This suggests that the church of Theonas had ready-made letters into which they only needed to fill in the name of the traveler. If, as Naldini cautiously proposed in the editio princeps of this letter, Theonas the bishop of Alexandria

[115] Sozomen, *Hist. eccl.* 5.16.3 (trans. Hartrant, *NPNF*^{2} 2:338).

[116] Treu: "In E [SB 10.10255] ist der Name in eine freigelassene Stelle eingesetzt, das Formular was also schon vorbereitet" ("Christliche Empfehlungs-Schemabriefe," 633).

(282–300) himself sent the letter,[117] then it makes all the more sense that, as bishop of a large community, he would have letters at hand that only needed the traveler's name, in other words: a fill-in form.

Forming a Picture of a Christian Community

In most letters of recommendation, the correspondents represent not just the individuals mentioned as sender and recipient in the pre- and postscript. On the contrary, the sender and recipient both represent their whole community, as they acknowledge in the greetings: "through whom I and the ones with me greet you and the ones with you."[118] Extending hospitality to strangers constituted a matter that involved the whole congregation, as Treu aptly observed.[119] These letters indicated not just formalities between two individuals but exchanges between Christian communities.

Sotas sent letters to a Peter, a Paul,[120] and perhaps a Maximus, and addressed them with the common Christian title "beloved brother" (ἀγαπητὸς ἀδελφός).[121] We cannot identify these men given the lack of any further information in the letters themselves.[122] Canon 11 of the Chalcedon Council

[117] Naldini wrote: "C'è dunque qualche probabilità—ci chiediamo—che i corrispondenti del nostro biglietto siano per l'appunto quei due dignitari ecclesiastici che abbiamo ora menzionati, e cioè il Theonas e il Mensurio divenuti vescovi rispettivamente di Alessandria e Cartagine? Certo, la prudenza non è mai eccessiva in siffatte identificazioni; è però da notare che la personalità e la posizione gerarchica dei due corrispondenti del nostro biglietto . . . e in particolare—la rarità del nome Mensurio e il ministero del vescovo omonimo di Cartagine all'inizio del secolo IV, costituiscono tanti indizî positivi, che ci sollecitano a porre il quesito di quella identificazione e ce la fanno apparire verosimile" ("Acta Vetera," *Atene e Roma* n.s. 11 [1966] 28). In the papyri (based on a DDBDP search), this is the sole occurrence of the name Mensurius.

[118] For example: δι' ὧν σὲ καὶ τοὺς σὺν σοὶ ἐγὼ καὶ οἱ σὺν ἐμοὶ προσαγορεύομεν, PSI 9.1041, lines 13–15.

[119] "Deutlich ist, daß diese Gastfreiheit durchweg eine Pflicht der Gesamtgemeinde ist. Die Briefe gehen von Gemeinde an Gemeinde und wenn sie auch jeweils von Vorsteher an Vorsteher geschrieben werden, so treten Absender wie Empfänger doch stets in Verbindung mit ihrer Gemeinschaft auf" (Treu, "Christliche Empfehlungs-Schemabriefe," 635–36).

[120] Peter and Paul are both probably named after an apostle. See the section on Dionysius of Alexandria in ch. 2.

[121] See Naldini, *Cristianesimo*, 15–21, and discussion in Part 1.

[122] Drawing an analogy between Sotas, who received and sent letters, Martin suggested that the Paul, whom Sotas addressed in this letter, was perhaps the sender of P.Oxy. 31.2603, another letter of recommendation. "Paul est le destinataire de la première et auteur de la seconde (lettre de recommendation) et toutes deux proviennent d'Oxyrhynchos; la situation

(quoted above) implies that bishops found themselves too busy to write for common people, and thus only gave letters to important persons. One hundred fifty or two hundred years prior, however, it seems to me that bishops still wrote these letters for everyone.[123] Not all senders or recipients of letters of recommendation, however, had the rank of bishops. In some cases, senders and addressees have different ranks. We have already seen this in the letter of the Heracleopolite presbyters[124] to papa Sotas (P.Oxy. 36.2785). In the third quarter of the third century—the time of our letter—Heracleopolis[125] conceivably

est comparable à celle de Sôtas" (*Athanase d'Alexandrie*, 787 n. 3). With the identification of this letter from Paul (P.Oxy. 31.2603) as a Manichaean letter (see Introduction, 18 n. 77), this argument does not hold any more.

[123] Sotas, Paul, Peter, and Maximus were probably all bishops. The name Maximus in P.Alex. 29 caused Naldini to muse that this could have been the bishop of Alexandria: "È il caso di ricordare l'omonimo vescovo di Alessandria . . . ma sarà una semplice coincidenza" (Naldini, *Cristianesimo*, no. 19 [= P.Alex. 29] 127 n. 1). This Maximus was bishop of Alexandria from 264–282, chronologically possible with the date of the Sotas papyri. Peter and Paul are familiar names of Christians and their clerics. I already mentioned that the Theonas and Mensurius in SB 10.10255 may also have been bishops.

[124] Who are these presbyters writing to Sotas? In the papyrological and epigraphic record from Egypt and elsewhere the abbreviation πρεσβ´ is not uncommon. See, e.g., Eisen, *Amtsträgerinnen*, 126 n. 63. The same abbreviated form πρεσβ´, for instance, occurs on a Christian mummy label from Egypt that is slightly earlier than our letter. It is an inscription for a Christian woman called Artemidora, reading: Ἀρτεμιδώρας | Μικκάλου μη`τ´(ρὸς) Πα|νισκιαίνης πρεσ`β´(υτέρας) | ἐκοιμήθη ἐν κ(υρί)ῳ: "Of Artemidora, daughter of Miccalus, and of her mother Panisciaena—*presbytera*. She fell asleep in the Lord" (second–third cent. C.E.; Baratte and Boyaval, *T.Mom.Louvre* 1115, 264). In this mummy label, the πρεσβ´ unambiguously refers to a woman, whether to the daughter or to the mother. Thus this brief inscription serves as a reminder that there is another way of resolving the abbreviation in the Sotas papyrus: not just the male πρεσβ(ύτεροι), also the female πρεσβ(υτέραι). Eisen discusses other literary and documentary texts for female presbyters from Egypt, e.g., the *Testamentum Domini* et al. (*Amtsträgerinnen*, 125–28). However, caution is required here because the designation "elder" in documentary papyri refers normally to just the older of two persons (often in the case when two siblings have the same name). The papyrus itself contains, however, no additional information that provides an argument for either solution. Yet that women were active in the Heracleopolite community is clear in the letter: The first person it mentions is Taion, a female member of the congregation (ἀδελφή).

[125] These presbyters resided in Heracleopolis Magna, a major city in middle Egypt. In the Byzantine period, this was an important Christian center, figuring prominently in Coptic-Arabic martyrdoms of the Diocletianic persecution (so Timm, "Ihnas[iya al-Madina]," 1161, with examples). Evidence of Christianity at Heracleopolis has surfaced in the papyrological record. A papyrus from the beginning of the fourth cent., slightly later than our collection of Sotas letters, mentions an inheritance from a presbyter (P.Neph. 48 [15 September 323], ed. Kramer and Shelton): a contract between two monks for the sale of a house the seller had inherited from a presbyter Dioscorus (Δ]ιοσκόρου πρεσβυ[τέρου], lines 8–9). Christian

did not yet have a bishop, and therefore the presbyters of that city wrote the recommendation for Taion and Anos to bishop Sotas in Oxyrhynchus.[126] I present the following other examples where someone other than a bishop sent or received a letter of recommendation: a presbyter by the name of Leon addressed presbyters and deacons in every locality (P.Oxy. 8.1162, fourth cent.), and, in another case, someone (the name is broken off) wrote to beloved brothers and fellow-ministers in every locality (P.Oxy. 56.3857, fourth cent.). In this period, one did not have to have the rank of a bishop to have the authority to introduce people.

So far, we have focused on the beginning and ending (pre- and postscript) of the letters. Having explored the general context and correspondents of the letters, we may now take time to become acquainted with the travelers mentioned in the body of the letters. Both the lack of an address on the back of the letters, and the content, make clear that the people introduced in these letters carried the documents along with them on their travels.[127] All these letters report the travelers' names, for, as noted in the beginning of this chapter, letters of recommendation require the names of both the sender and the traveler.[128] Thus Sotas introduced us to "our brother Heracles" (to Peter, PSI 3.208), to a group of six men, "our brothers Heron and Horion and Philadelphus and Pekusis and Naarous, catechumens of the congregation, and

manuscripts from Heracleopolis are, for instance, a fragment of an apocryphal gospel (P.Vind. G.2325, third cent.) and a magic charm (*PGM* XVIIIa, third–fourth cent.).

[126] The earliest known bishop from the city is a certain Peter at the time of the Nicaean council (325) (Timm, "Ihnas[iya al-Madina]," 1162). According to Timm, this Peter appears only in the Coptic list of that council, not in the Greek list. He also refers to a Peter, bishop of Heracleopolis in Meletius's list of bishops, wondering whether this was the same person as the one from the council of Nicaea.

[127] See Llewelyn, "Christian Letters of Recommendation," 170–71: "one must assume that the letters were carried by the persons whom they recommended or introduced." Llewelyn related this to the lack of address on these letters (ibid., 171). See also Keyes, "Greek Letter of Introduction," 32 and 39–40. Treu speaks of "Überbringer" ("Christliche Empfehlungs-Schemabriefe," 633).

[128] Treu was absolutely right when he remarked: "Bei D (*P.Oxy.* 36.2785) vermutet Rea, daß der Name des Katechumenen bei der Ausfertigung nicht bekannt war und daß man daher nur 'Mensch' in der üblichen sakralen Abkürzung einsetzte. Dagegen spricht nicht nur das Fehlen des normalen Abkürzungsstriches, sondern vor allem, daß der Name einfach dazugehörte. Anos is nicht belegt, aber Annos hält auch Rea für möglich" ("Christliche Empfehlungs-Schemabriefe," 633).

Leo, a catechumen in the beginning of the gospel" (to Paul, PSI 9.1041),[129] and perhaps to "our brother D[iph]ilus" (to Maximus, P.Alex. 29).[130] The Heracleopolite presbyters in turn addressed papa Sotas to receive "our sister Taion" and "Anos, a catechumen in Genesis" (P.Oxy. 36.2785).[131] In these four short letters, we thus meet a sister, several brothers, catechumens of the congregation, a catechumen in the beginning of the gospel, and a catechumen in Genesis. The other five stereotypical letters of recommendation (from the group of nine), which are not part of the Sotas correspondence, introduce more brothers, another catechumen, and a daughter. I find these letters striking because they identify the travelers not only by name but also in terms of their relationship to the Christian community. At the heart of these letters, then, we see Christian identity framed in community terms. Community leaders (Sotas, presbyters) assessed and certified this Christian identity.

The terms "sister" and "brother" indicate baptized members.[132] These Christian letters express implicitly the rhetoric of Christian identity as a family.[133] Although males make up the majority of persons recommended in these letters, members include not only men but also women. Taion, called a "sister," comes recommended to Sotas by the presbyter of Heracleopolis (P.Oxy. 36.2785).

The letters of recommendation give us a glimpse of community organization and the process of the catechumenate. I have already noted a strict distinction between members (sisters and brothers) and catechumens in our papyrus letters, but the letter writers also distinguish between different levels or types of catechumens.[134] We encountered "Anos, a catechumen in Genesis,"

[129] We see here that Sotas mentions six catechumens in one letter and two brothers in the other letters. Can the number of people traveling provide an indication about the size of the Christian congregation? "Not very small," is my only possible conclusion, but beyond that it is impossible to move from the numbers of travelers or catechumens to a speculation about the actual size of the Christian community at Oxyrhynchus. The proportions between baptized members and catechumens are not known.

[130] That is, if Sotas was the sender of this letter.

[131] It is noteworthy that this letter introduces us to a woman and man traveling together, and that their relationship is not marked in terms of a sexual or familial relationship but by their relationship to the church.

[132] Treu noted: " 'Bruder' hat bereits den prägnanten Sinn des getauften Vollmitgliedes der Kirche" ("Christliche Empfehlungs-Schemabriefe," 633). The same holds true, of course, for "sister."

[133] See Buell, *Making Christians*.

[134] Manichaeans also distinguished between members and catechumens, therefore we find this distinction in the Manichaean letter of recommendation from Oxyrhynchus (from Paul,

traveling to Oxyrhynchus. At Oxyrhynchus itself, Sotas carefully differentiates between "a catechumen in the beginning of the gospel," and "catechumens of the congregation," as his correspondence shows.[135] Literary texts lack exact parallels to these expressions in papyrus letters. Yet the specificity of the designations for catechumens testifies to their importance in the eyes of the writers and their communities.

The presbyters of Heracleopolis recommend to Sotas a certain Anos as a "catechumen in Genesis" (καθηχούμενον ἐν τῇ Γενέσει, P.Oxy. 36.2785). It appears that Anos studied the book of Genesis. Looking ahead to the end of the fourth century, Egeria, the famous traveler, reports that at Jerusalem the bishop started with Genesis and studied the whole Bible with the catechumens in preparation for baptism.[136] Ambrose, bishop of Milan in the second half of the fourth century, valued the stories of the patriarchs in Genesis for their moral examples.[137] Therefore the book of Genesis may have featured on the reading list for catechumens in the early church because of its ethical lessons.

Another catechumen, this one from the church at Oxyrhynchus, also studied a biblical book. In his letter to Paul, Sotas described Leon as "a catechumen in the beginning of the gospel" (καθηχούμενον ἐν ἀρχῇ τοῦ εὐαγγελίου, PSI 9.1041). Initially, this makes one think of the *incipit* of

P.Oxy. 31.2603). This letter even states in the negative that the travelers are not to be confused with catechumens: "Therefore receive them in love, as friends, for they are not catechumens" προσδέξαι οὖν ἐν ἀγάπῃ ὡς φίλους, οὐ γὰρ κατηχούμενοί εἰσιν (lines 25–26). Paul, the author of this letter, thus underlines the significance of the distinction between baptized members and catechumens, even implying differences in welcoming them.

[135] These examples of different levels occur in the Sotas correspondence only (PSI 9.1041 and P.Oxy. 36.2785). SB 10.10255 (Theonas to Mensurius) mentions the "catechumen Serenus" without further ado. The other six of the nine formulaic letters are written on behalf of a sister, brothers, and a daughter.

[136] "During the forty days [the bishop] goes through the whole Bible, beginning with Genesis, and first relating the literal meaning of each passage, then interpreting its spiritual meaning. . . . And this is called 'catechesis,'" in Wilkinson, *Egeria's Travels*, 162. See also Bradshaw, "Gospel and the Catechumenate," *JTS* 50 (1999) 145.

[137] Bradshaw noted that "the biblical readings prescribed for Lenten catechetical assemblies even in the fourth century tend not only to be drawn from the Old Testament rather than the New but also to give considerable emphasis to those books from which moral lessons might be drawn." He mentions that Ambrose, "in the introduction to his *De Ioseph* . . . indicates the virtues that could be derived from the stories of the patriarchs." He concludes: "It is not without significance that the book of Genesis also featured prominently in Lenten assemblies at this period in both Jerusalem and Antioch" ("Gospel and the Catechumenate," 151–52).

the gospel of Mark: "beginning of the gospel of Jesus Christ" (ἀρχὴ τοῦ εὐαγγελίου Ἰησοῦ Χριστοῦ, Mark 1:1). Did Leon work on the gospel of Mark? I would find that remarkable, given that this gospel lacked popularity in antiquity.[138] Perhaps he studied another specific gospel book, such as Matthew's gospel or even the *Gospel of Thomas*.[139] Just as Leon, the other catechumen, worked on the first book in the Septuagint, Anos had begun to study the gospels.[140]

One letter names a particular group of travelers as "catechumens of the congregation" at Oxyrhynchus (καθηχούμενοι τῶν συναγομένων). Our epistolographers described the catechumenate of Leon and Anos in terms of their scriptural studies, but Sotas characterizes this group in their relation to the Christian community. Origen's portrayal of these different stages of catechumenate in his *Against Celsus* proves insightful in this matter. I consider Origen a good person to consult, not only because of his Egyptian roots,[141] but also since he started his professional life as a catechete.[142] Origen distinguished between two groups of catechumens: beginners and those more

[138] Only one fifth/sixth cent. fragment from this gospel has been published from Oxyrhynchus thus far (P.Oxy. 1.3). On the attestation of the gospel of Mark, see also Koester, *Ancient Christian Gospels*, 273–74.

[139] The archaeological record shows that both gospels were read at Oxyrhynchus in the third century. The earliest known Matthean fragment is from Oxyrhynchus (P.Oxy. 64.4404, second cent.). The fragments of the *Gospel of Thomas*, P.Oxy. 1.1, 4.654, and 4.655, are all three dated to the third century. Or does εὐαγγέλιον in the singular refer to the oral transmission of Jesus' message à la the apostle Paul in 1 Cor 15:1 "the gospel which I preached to you" (τὸ εὐαγγέλιον ὃ εὐαγγελισάμην ὑμῖν)? The same question whether gospel stands for one book or for the general Christian message comes up in the study of other texts, e.g., Didache 8.2: "Also do not pray like the hypocrites, but as the Lord has commanded in his gospel, pray thus" (μηδὲ προσεύχεσθε ὡς οἱ ὑποκριταί, ἀλλ' ὡς ἐκέλευσεν ὁ κύριος ἐν τῷ εὐαγγελίῳ αὐτοῦ, οὕτω προσεύχεσθε). Immediately after this sentence, the Didache presents the Lord's Prayer. Georg Schöllgen remarks: "Umstritten ist, ob 'Evangelium' sich hier und an drei weiteren Stellen in der Didache (11, 3; 15, 3.4) auf ein bestimmtes schriftliches Evangelium oder im allgemeinen Sinne auf die Frohbotschaft Jesu Christi bezieht." With reference to Wengst and Massaux, he concludes that "die Didache Mt gekannt und benutzt hat" (Schöllgen, *Didache. Zwölf Apostel-Lehre*, 118–19 n. 96).

[140] Pachomius (ca. 290–346), founder of monastic communities, also placed high emphasis on scriptural study. He required monks to be literate and to memorize parts of the psalter and New Testament (Rousseau, *Pachomius,* 81 and 70).

[141] Origen, however, wrote *Contra Celsum* not in Alexandria but in Caesarea.

[142] Auf der Maur and Waldram, "Illuminatio Verbi Divini," in *Fides Sacramenti*, 43.

advanced.[143] In the first stage of initiation, the catechumen should lead a life without sin, while the second phase Origen reserved for those fully committed to becoming Christians.[144] It seems to me that we may compare what Origen calls the "beginners' group" to the catechumens "in the beginning of the gospel" and "in Genesis." The catechumens "of the congregation" fit with the more advanced level catechumens in Origen's description.

The correspondents provide intricate detail to indicate exactly where the travelers stand in the process of the Christian identity formation. Why such specificity? On the basis of the Chalcedon canons, Teeter argued that a "letter of peace," such as these documentary letters, only asked for practical assistance as food and lodging, whereas a "letter of commendation" concerned also admission to the communion for clergy and important persons. Yet why would one describe the travelers so specifically if the only matter concerned lodging? Would Leon, a "catechumen in the beginning of the Gospel," receive less food or a less comfortable bed than sister Taion or brother Diphilus? The level of detail makes sense only if it entails full participation in the community life. This includes attendance at communal services and above all, participation (or not) in the eucharist. Furthermore, in the pre-Constantinian period, an era of (potential) persecution of admitted Christians, these letters provided an indication of the level of trust that a Christian community could place in total strangers.

[143] "But as far as they can, Christians previously examine the souls of those who want to hear them, and test them individually beforehand; when before entering the community (πρὶν εἰς τὸ κοινὸν εἰσελθεῖν) the hearers seem to have devoted themselves sufficiently to the desire to live a good life, then they introduce them. They privately appoint one class consisting of recent beginners who are receiving elementary instruction and have not yet received the sign that they have been purified (ἰδίᾳ μὲν ποιήσαντες τάγμα τῶν ἄρτι ἀρχομένων καὶ εἰσαγομένων καὶ οὐδέπω τὸ σύμβολον τοῦ ἀποκεκαθάρθαι ἀνειληφότων), and another class of those who, as far as they are able, make it their set purpose to desire nothing other than those things of which Christians approve (ἕτερον δὲ τὸ τῶν κατὰ τὸ δυνατὸν παραστησάντων ἑαυτῶν τὴν προαίρεσιν οὐκ ἄλλο τι βούλεσθαι ἢ τὰ Χριστιανοῖς δοκοῦντα)" (Origen, *Contra Celsum* 3.51 [trans. Chadwick] 163). Greek text from Origenes, *Contra Celsum libri VIII*, 193. See Auf der Maur and Waldram, "Illuminatio Verbi Divini" (especially 46–50), for discussion of the two phases.

[144] Auf der Maur and Waldram describe this stage as follows. It entailed "vor allem Glaubensunterweisung . . ., die einführt in die 'mehr göttlichen Dingen,' in die 'Weisheit,' in die 'Mysterien der von Jesus gelehrten Gottesverehrung,' in all das, 'was Jesus seinen wahren Jüngern besonders gelehrt hat'" ("Illuminatio Verbi Divini," 49).

Why did Philadelphus and Taion go on the road? For what reason did these Christians travel?[145] The letters provide evidence for Christian networking[146] but unfortunately, reveal only the slightest information about why these people went on their journeys. Christians wrote them, of course, not to establish the ground for travel but rather to ascertain Christian identity and to provide access to a different congregation. The travelers could themselves elaborate their specific situation upon arrival. Nevertheless, two letters provide a glimpse into reasons for travel: The first letter writes about a woman, and the second one about a man. The first, a letter from an unknown person to "beloved brothers and fellow ministers in every locality" (P.Oxy. 56.3857) and not a part of the Sotas correspondence, concerns a certain Germania. I find it interesting to come across a female traveler.[147] In their book, *Women's Letters from Ancient Egypt*, Bagnall and Cribiore observe that private letters from women "provide evidence for women's ability to travel in a fashion unparalleled in other sources."[148] Our letter exhorts the recipients to "receive in peace our daughter Germania, who is coming to you, needing help."[149] As we shall see later, the instructions to receive her "in peace"—that is, with the kiss of peace—shows that she ranked as a baptized member.[150] The

[145] On travel in Roman Egypt generally, see Adams, " 'There and Back Again,' " in *Travel and Geography,* 138–66.

[146] On the importance of networking in the growth of the Christian movement, see Stark, *Rise of Christianity,* 73–94; White, *Social Networks,* 3–22 and 23–36.

[147] Another traveling Christian woman is Phoebe, whose letter of recommendation the apostle Paul wrote: "I commend to you our sister Phoebe, a deacon of the church at Cenchreae, so that you may welcome her in the Lord as is fitting for the saints, and help her in whatever she may require from you, for she has been a benefactor of many and of myself as well" (Rom 16:1–2). In a passage on hospitality, the *Didascalia apostolorum* provides the first specific information on how to receive women; subsequent paragraphs discuss the welcoming of presbyters and bishops. "However, if some brother or sister comes from another congregation, let the deacon inquire (and learn) from her if she currently has a husband, (or) if she is a widow, whether she is a believer and if she belongs to the church and not to the heresy." The Latin version reads: Si quis autem de parrocia frater aut soror venerit, diaconus requirat ab ea, si adhuc virum habet, si vidua est aut fidelis et si de ecclesia est et non de heresi. Et sic iam perducens eam faciat in decreto loco sedere (*Didascalia apostolorum* 29.3–6, ed. Tidner, 47).

[148] Bagnall and Cribiore, *Women's Letters*, 81. The authors note that "there are approximately forty letters [from women] that refer in some way to women traveling. Half of these do not supply a reason for the journey" (ibid., 81).

[149] Τὴν θυγ̣α̣τέρα ἡμῶν Γερμανίαν, ἐπικουρίας δεομένην, π[αραγι]νομένην πρὸς ὑμᾶς προσδέξασθε ἐν εἰρήνῃ (P.Oxy. 56.3857, lines 4–9).

[150] See below, 123–24.

letter specifies that Germania needed help (ἐπικουρίας δεομένη, 5–6).[151] Teeter pointed out that canon 11 of the Council of Chalcedon used the same expression in the context of letters of recommendation and mentioned "all paupers and persons in need of help" (πάντας τοὺς πένητας καὶ δεομένους ἐπικουρίας).[152] The letter does not specify what sort of help Germania should receive.[153] Germania does not appear necessarily poor and destitute. If poor, why would she travel? Given the dangers associated with staying in inns when on the road, perhaps the letter meant safe lodging.[154] She may have traveled for business, for health reasons,[155] or, as we shall see in the next example, for education.

The writer describes Germania as "our daughter" (P.Oxy. 56.3857). The use of kinship terminology in this context should not prompt us to think of Germania as the writer's biological daughter but rather as a younger person,[156]

[151] The top part of the papyrus is damaged and the name of the sender(s) broken off.

[152] Teeter, "Letters of Recommendation," 957.

[153] The letter concerning Germania does not indicate that she needed financial assistance, but that is a possibility. The passage in the *Historia monachorum* referred to providing welcome for a poor stranger at the city gate (ξένος που πενόμενος, *Historia monachorum* 5.5, see ch. 1). Caring for the poor was a Christian virtue. On the development of the role of the bishop as "lover of the poor," see Brown, *Poverty and Leadership*.

[154] Constable points out that the *pandocheion*, the inn, was associated with murder and prostitution and considered not a safe place to stay, especially not for women (*Housing the Stranger in the Mediterranean World*, 18–20).

[155] See Bagnall and Cribiore, *Women's Letters*, 81–83. They mention women traveling in relation to business, childbirth, and family visits.

[156] So Sirivianou in her edition of the papyrus: "In private life 'brother' and 'sister' were used to persons of about the same age, 'father' and 'mother' to older friends, 'son' and 'daughter' to younger ones. This affectionate use may differ from the spiritual one, by which persons of all ages may be 'sons' or 'daughters' of the priest or teacher (just as all people are the sons and daughters of God . . .). . . . So 'daughter' here could have a Christian meaning, but since these terms of relationship are so common it is more likely that the word indicates that Germania was a person whom most people would describe as young, or at least younger than the sender and the likely recipients" (Sirivianou, P.Oxy. 56.3857, 116, note to line l4). Dickey in her treatment of kinship terminology provides the following summary on the use of the term daughter (θυγάτηρ) in documentary papyri: "θυγάτηρ can be used for a daughter in any context, but for other younger females only when indicating a connection to the writer . . ., and then only when accompanied by a name or in the vocative. Its extended usage [i.e., for non-family members] is restricted to people with a close connection to the writer" ("Literal and Extended Use," 165, sub F). For this letter, that would mean that the writer and the writer's community knew Germania very well, expressing to the recipients that they considered her as their own daughter (for this rhetorical function of kinship language, see ibid., 139). Dickey, however, also remarks, that kinship terms are used differently in

apparently independent enough to travel by herself.[157] If she did indeed travel alone, I would consider that remarkable. In the letter from the Heracleopolite presbyters, we read that the "sister Taion" journeyed in the company of catechumen Anos (P.Oxy. 36.2785), and evidence from other sources also indicates that women hardly ever traveled alone.[158] Possibly Germania had to go on this trip by herself, because she could not find people going in the same direction, or she traveled in the company of non-Christians, who therefore did not appear in her letter of recommendation.[159] Finally, I wonder about her destination. The fact that Germania's letter ended up in Oxyrhynchus may mean that she applied for help to the Christian community there. Or perhaps as an Oxyrhynchite traveling somewhere else, she brought her letter back home to Oxyrhynchus at the end of her trip.[160] In any case, this papyrus provides a fascinating glimpse of a Christian woman traveling.

A second letter, that the presbyters of Heracleopolis addressed to Sotas (P.Oxy. 36.2785), provides more insight into one person's reason for travel: Anos, affiliated with the Heracleopolite congregation as a "catechumen in Genesis," traveled to Sotas at Oxyrhynchus "for building up" (εἰς οἰκοδομήν). Should we interpret this as active or passive; did he go to build or to be built up? The word οἰκοδομή describes the construction of buildings, so one could wonder if Anos had become involved in erecting a church building

---

Christian circles. In P.Oxy. 12.1492, discussed below, Sotas addresses Demetrianus as his "holy son," probably also a younger, lower ranking person.

157 A woman called Valeria wrote a letter to a Christian monk, Apa Paphnouthis, requesting his prayers (P.Lond. 6.1926, mid-fourth cent.). In the address on the back she identifies herself as "daughter" (παρὰ τῆς θυγατρὸς Οὐαλερίας). However, we learn from the letter that she has two daughters, a husband and a household, so she is hardly a very young person.

158 See Bagnall and Cribiore, *Women's Letters*, 82–83.

159 She may have been a widow, see the passage from the *Didascalia apostolorum* quoted above in note 147. According to that passage, a deacon asked women who sought to receive hospitality whether they were married or widowed (*Didascalia apostolorum* 29.3–5).

160 Besides its occurrence in this papyrus, the name Germania occurs in three (not two, as ed. princ. Sirivianou wrote in her note) other papyri: P.Gen. 2.116 (Oxyrhynchus, 247 C.E.), P.Oxy. 10.1349 (Oxyrhynchus, fourth cent.), and PSI 14.1418 (Oxyrhynchus, third cent.). Since they all came from Oxyrhynchus, perhaps we should, but not necessarily, situate our Germania there. P.Oxy. 10.1349, from Sarapion to his mother Germania, is perhaps Christian, since it mentions a "holy sister" (or a sister called Hagia); see also below, P.Oxy. 12.1492, for the discussion on Sotas's "holy son Demetrianus." I see no indication, however, of a link to the Germania recommended in P.Oxy. 56.3857. Men called Germanus occur more often in the papyri. See also Dionysius of Alexandria's correspondence against Germanus (Eusebius, *Hist. eccl.* 6.40 and 7.11.1 and 19).

at Oxyrhynchus? Figuratively the word "building up" (οἰκοδομή) has both educational and moral connotations.[161] The expression "for building up" (εἰς οἰκοδομήν) occurs in a range of early Christian texts.[162] In his second letter to the Corinthians, the apostle Paul uses it twice (2 Cor 10:8 and 13:10) in speaking of the authority that he received from the Lord for building up the community.[163] Exhorting the addressees to unity among their ranks, the author of Ephesians uses the expression twice in chapter 4: The Ephesians have received gifts "for the building up of the body of Christ" (εἰς οἰκοδομὴν τοῦ σώματος τοῦ Χριστοῦ, Eph 4:12) and every member of the body works towards "the body's growth in building up itself in love" (τὴν αὔξησιν τοῦ σώματος ποιεῖται εἰς οἰκοδομὴν ἑαυτοῦ ἐν ἀγάπῃ, Eph 4:16). In these New Testament passages, the word indicates the building up of the local Christian community. Would Anos, a catechumen, visit Sotas to assist him in striving for unity or in building up the Oxyrhynchite community? This hardly seems a likely task for a catechumen, and one would expect more information in the letter itself. The best interpretation seems to be that Anos expected "edification" in the sense of scriptural and (thus) moral education from Sotas.[164] In his *Procatechesis*, Cyril of Jerusalem (315–386) compared catechesis to a building (οἰκοδομὴν εἶναι τὴν κατήχεσιν) in which all the blocks have to be in place.[165] As a "catechumen in Genesis," Anos probably studied the book of Genesis—known for its moral lessons—and memorized passages. Thus Anos made his journey to Sotas and the Christian community at Oxyrhynchus in order to receive further catechetical instruction.[166] This

[161] Lampe, 939 (building, edifice, edification, also figuratively).

[162] E.g., Ignatius, *Eph.* 9.1: ὡς ὄντες λίθοι ναοῦ πατρός, ἡτοιμασμένοι εἰς οἰκοδομὴν θεοῦ πατρός (The context is people from outside sowing different opinions among the Ephesians); Justin Martyr, *Dial.* 86.6: πορευμένοι ἦσαν οἱ υἱοὶ τῶν προφητῶν κόψαι ξύλα εἰς οἰκοδομὴν τοῦ οἴκου, ἐν ᾧ τὸν νόμον καὶ τὰ προστάγματα τοῦ θεοῦ λέγειν καὶ μελετᾶν ἐβούλοντο (Justin talks about the prefiguration of Christ's cross in the Old Testament).

[163] 2 Cor 10:8: ἐάν τε γὰρ περισσότερόν τι καυχήσωμαι περὶ τῆς ἐξουσίας ἡμῶν ἧς ἔδωκεν ὁ κύριος εἰς οἰκοδομὴν καὶ οὐκ εἰς καθαίρεσιν ὑμῶν, οὐκ αἰσχυνθήσομαι. At the end of the letter, in 2 Cor 13:10, Paul writes: διὰ τοῦτο ταῦτα ἀπὼν γράφω, ἵνα . . . χρήσωμαι κατὰ τὴν ἐξουσίαν ἣν ὁ κύριος ἔδωκέν μοι, εἰς οἰκοδομὴν καὶ οὐκ εἰς καθαίρεσιν.

[164] Auf der Maur and Waldram, "Illuminatio Verbi Divini," 50, 54.

[165] Cyril of Jerusalem, *Procatechesis* 2 (ed. Reischl).

[166] See also Naldini, *Cristianesimo*, 422. Naldini's interpretation of SB 10.10255 is that Serenus perhaps traveled to complete his baptismal instruction (cf. Wipszycka, "Remarques," 212). Students traveling to study under specific teachers was common practice in antiquity (and still today). See, e.g., Cribiore, *Writing, Teachers, and Students*, 20; eadem, *Gymnastics of the Mind*, 102–23; Watts, "Student Travel," in *Travel, Communication and Geography*, 13–23.

suggests that Sotas's church at Oxyrhynchus functioned as a center of Christian education.

Coming to the end of our journey into the Christian practice of recommendation, I wonder what happened when the travelers reached their destination. These letters all lack address instructions. If these travelers indeed arrived as strangers to the community they visited—for which reason they carried these introductory letters—one would expect specifications as to where they could locate Sotas, Paul, or Peter. These Christian letters share this absence of such directions with most papyrological letters.[167] The Christian visitors must have received oral instructions from the home front or found the Christian host community by asking around (or both).

When the travelers finally reached their destination and presented their travel documents to their host, what sort of welcome did they receive?[168] The letters merely ask the recipient to receive the people "in peace," "according to custom," or "according to what is proper." The other "non-Christian" letters of recommendation also expected a proper reception according to custom. Thus, travelers—and the letter writers recommending them—expected a reception in a general, culturally appropriate manner in the way that one ought to welcome visitors. Five of the Christian formulaic letters of introduction, however, request that the recipient receive their people "in peace" (ἐν εἰρήνῃ).[169] This expression presents not an ordinary greeting or an exhortation not to quarrel with the visitors but a specific meaning. These words signify that the hosts should welcome the guests with the kiss of peace,[170] which refers to the Christian practice of exchanging kisses among members as part of worship, namely the celebration of the eucharist. In the papyri, this expression, as Teeter noted, occurs only in Christian letters of recommendation,[171] so here

[167] PSI 4.311 contains (confused and confusing) instructions for the delivery of the letter to the bishop of Laodicea via the bishop of Antioch. Only a few papyrus letters contain directions; for examples, see Epp, "New Testament Papyrus Manuscripts," in *The Future of Early Christianity*, 49.

[168] For a summary of examples of welcoming, see Arterbury, *Entertaining Angels*, 129–31. Based on his examination of canonical and noncanonical early Christian texts, Arterbury concludes that guests receive food and lodging (a guestroom), and also necessities for the continuation of their travel. Christian guests and hosts also may have prayed together (ibid., 130).

[169] P.Alex. 29; P.Oxy. 8.1162; P.Oxy. 36.2785; P.Oxy. 56.3857; and SB 16.12304. See Sirivianou, P.Oxy. 56.3857, 116, note to line 9; Llewelyn, "Christian Letters of Recommendation," 171.

[170] For "in peace" indicating the "kiss of peace," see Penn, *Kissing Christians*," 44.

[171] Teeter, "Letters of Recommendation," 957.

the Christians have a distinctive trait. This ritual kissing represents also a form of community building within the congregation in terms of the Christian family. In the course of our investigations, we have encountered several Christians described in terms of family language: a papa, brothers, a sister, and a daughter. This kinship language functions rhetorically to construct the image of a Christian community as a family. The kissing ritual among early Christians gave concrete expression to the claim that a Christian congregation formed a kin, as Michael Penn has analyzed in his book *Kissing Christians: Ritual and Community in the Late Ancient Church*.[172] This short phrase in these papyrus letters of recommendation, to "receive in peace," evokes thus a lively image of a Christian ritual taking place in the local church, with visitors—strangers, really—being embraced as family members.

In this chapter I have shown that five (perhaps six) letters form the correspondence of Sotas. This Sotas, I argued, held the position of bishop of Oxyrhynchus in the third quarter of the third century. In fact, he is the first bishop we know of at Oxyrhynchus. The majority of the preserved correspondence of this bishop concerned the extension of hospitality to travelers. Some of these travelers, both male and female, and members of other congregations came into the eucharistic community with the kiss of peace. Persons still in the process of becoming Christians, however, could also count on a hospitable welcome. The designations of levels of catechumenate in these letters of recommendation highlight the importance of scriptural education. One of those catechumens traveled to the Oxyrhynchite community for further study and thereby indicated the central role that that community played in Christian education.

Next, we turn to two other letters from the correspondence of Sotas and get to know the bishop in a different manner.

[172] "Early Christians constructed the ritual kiss not only as a means to 'talk' about being a family, but also as a way to act it out. The adoption and modification of a typical familial gesture into a decidedly Christian ritual helped early Christians redefine the concept of family. With the kiss's assistance, Christian communities became families united by faith" (Penn, *Kissing Christians*, 31).

CHAPTER 5

The Business of the Bishop: Fundraising, Travel, and Book Production

In the previous chapter, we encountered papa Sotas, bishop of the church at Oxyrhynchus exchanging the kiss of peace with members of his congregation and visiting students during worship. We shall now investigate papa Sotas's other occupations and observe him engaged in such activities—diverse, yet central to the operation of a local church—as fundraising and book production. We shall also follow the bishop as he travels far outside the boundaries of his own diocese to Antioch in Syria.

An Ancient Fundraising Letter (P.Oxy. 12.1492)[1]

The next piece of evidence for Sotas and Christians at Oxyrhynchus allows us to witness Sotas, the local bishop, soliciting financial support for the church in the form of a plot of land. The letter, addressed to a certain Demetrianus, is written on a sheet of papyrus measuring 10.3 x 22.6 cm of which the top part and right margin have been damaged. Penned in an experienced and easily readable handwriting, the document appears very similar to that of Sotas's

[1] See Plate 5. Ed. princ. Grenfell and Hunt, "Christian Letter," P.Oxy. 12.1492 (1916) 249–50. The papyrus is housed in the British Library, London (Pap 2462). Other discussions of this papyrus: Ghedini, "XII: Sotas al figlio," in *Lettere cristiane*, 123–28; Leclercq, "Lettres chrétiennes," *DACL* 8.2 (1929) 84–85; idem, "Papyrus," *DACL* 13.1 (1937) 1423; White, "Private Letter," no. 44, in *Social Origins* 2:162–64; Naldini, *Cristianesimo*, 156–58, 436–37 (no. 30, "Sotas al 'figlio' Demetriano").

letter to Paul (PSI 9.1041)[2] and was perhaps written by the same person. The writer consequently placed a diaeresis over the initial *iota* and initial *upsilon* (lines 1, 13, 21: ϊ; line 18: ϋ). He made some minor orthographic mistakes, such as common vowel exchanges like ω for ο and ει for ι. On the whole one gets the impression from the letter, both from handwriting and vocabulary, that its writer is an educated person.

The letter reads as follows:

Χα[ῖ]ρε, ἱερ[ὲ υἱὲ
Δημητρι[ανέ. Σώτας
σε πρ[οσαγορεύω.
τὸ κοινὸν . . [
ε̣ὔ̣δηλον καὶ τὸ κο̣ι̣[νὸν
σωτήριον ἡ̣μῶν [. . .,
ταῦτα γάρ ἐστιν τὰ̣ ἐ[ν τῇ
θείᾳ προνοίᾳ. εἰ οὖν ἔ-
κρεινας κατὰ τὸ π̣α̣λ̣[αιὸν
ἔθος δοῦναι τὴν ἄ̣ρ[ο]υ̣-
ραν τῷ τόπῳ, ποίησον
αὐτὴν ἀφωρισθῆναι
ἵνα χρήσωνται, κ[α]ὶ ὡς
ἐὰν κρείνῃς περὶ τοῦ ἔ̣[ρ]γ̣[ου
θάρρει. πάντας τ[ο]ὺ̣[ς
ἐν τῷ οἴκῳ σου ἅπα̣ν̣τ̣[ας
προσαγόρευε. ἐρρῶ-
σθαι ὑμᾶς εὔχομαι
τῷ θεῷ διὰ παντὸς
καὶ ἐν παντί
(On the verso)
τῷ ἱερῷ υ[ἱ]ῷ μου Δημητριανῷ π(αρὰ) Σώ̣του.

1. ϊερ[ε, 8–9. *l.* ἔκρινας, 12. *l.* ἀφορισθῆναι, 13. ϊνα, 14. *l.* κρίνῃς, του inserted above the line, 18. ϋμας, 21. ϊερω.

[2] The letter forms in that papyrus are more "flamboyant, decorated," according to Raffaella Cribiore (email correspondence), and the *delta*s and *kappa*s have more ornate little loops.

Translation

Greetings, holy son Demetrianus. I, Sotas, greet you (sgl.). Our common . . . is abundantly manifest, and our common salvation . . .; for these are the (gifts) of the Divine providence.[3] If, therefore, you (sgl.) have decided according to the ancient custom to give the field to the place, make sure that it is marked off by boundaries so that they may use it, and whatever[4] you decide about the work, have courage.
Greet all those who are in your house, all of them. I pray to God that you (pl.) are well in every respect.

On the verso:
(Addressed) To my holy son Demetrianus from Sotas.

In this ancient fundraising letter, we get to know another side of Sotas and his position in the church at Oxyrhynchus. While in the letters of recommendation (discussed in chapter 4) we observed him extending and requesting hospitality to travelers and involved in education, here we see him building the church in a different way. He secures a donation in the form of an *aroura*, a plot of farmland about the size of half a soccer field (ca. 2756 m^2).[5] Indeed, as Wipszycka reminds us, "one should never forget that the overwhelming majority of ecclesiastical goods . . . comes from donations made by the faithful."[6]

One of those faithful is a certain Demetrianus. It is impossible from a prosopographical point of view to know whether or not the same Demetrianus figures in other papyri since he bears a common name, and Sotas—as usual in private letters—omits his patronymic. Yet Sotas adds to the address formula two other modifiers that help to contextualize the letter. Twice Sotas refers to

[3] Grenfell and Hunt translate "objects of the Divine Providence" for τὰ̣ ἐ[ν τῇ] θείᾳ̣ προνοίᾳ.

[4] Ghedini takes the ὡς ἐάν in lines 13–14 as temporal (*Lettere cristiane*, 128). I understand it as conditional.

[5] Pestman, *New Papyrological Primer*, 49. Naldini describes this as "un campo normale o un orto un po' grande" (*Cristianesimo*, 436). Pestman remarks that "a person could live on the net produce of 2 arouras" (*New Papyrological Primer*, 49).

[6] "Il ne faut jamais perdre de vue le fait que la majorité écrasante des biens ecclésiastiques . . . provient de DONATIONS FAITES PAR LES FIDÈLES" (author's emphasis, Wipszycka, *Ressources*, 29). She mentions P.Oxy. 12.1492 as example.

him—in the opening and in the address—as "(my) holy son Demetrianus."[7] Should we conclude that Sotas had a son, Demetrianus? Sotas as a bishop probably had married and had children—celibacy for clergy developed later in certain churches, and sources frequently mention children of bishops.[8] Nevertheless, given the context of this papyrus, I doubt that Demetrianus was Sotas's biological son. For no matter how dear they find their offspring, probably very few parents consider their children "holy."[9] As occurs so often in Christian letters, members of the church family use kinship language—as between papa Sotas and Demetrianus his "holy son."[10] Sotas's use of the term "son" in this letter indicates that Demetrianus was his junior and suggests a close relationship between the two men.[11]

Demetrianus was apparently not any ordinary younger person for Sotas but a "*holy* son" (*ἱερὸς* υἱός). According to Ghedini, Sotas addressed Demetrianus as a beloved member of his community,[12] and for Leclercq the address indicates

[7] τῷ ἱερῷ υ[ἱ]ῷ μου Δημητριανῷ, verso. The address on the verso forms the basis for the reconstruction of the first two lines: ἱερ[ὲ υἱὲ] Δημητρι[ανέ] (lines 1–2).

[8] See, for instance, the discussion in Hübner, *Der Klerus in der Gesellschaft*, 71–80; and Rapp, *Holy Bishops*, 213–14.

[9] Commonly used adjectives describing the feelings of parents for children are "most beloved" (φίλτατος) and "beloved" (ἀγαπητός). "Beloved brother/sister" is used in Christian and other letters as form of address for unrelated people (see ch. 2).

[10] See White: "The tone of the letter . . . lacks the intimacy that one would expect between a natural father and son, even in the case of a business letter" (*Social Origins* 2:162).

[11] In ancient letters one finds many children or younger friends addressed as son or, less frequently, daughter. Germania was called "daughter" (P.Oxy. 56.3857, see discussion in ch. 4). A certain Chaeremon, for instance, wrote to "my lord son Dorotheus" (κυρίῳ μου υἱῷ Δωροθέῳ, P.Oxy. 48.3408, lines 1–2, see also the address, 31). Yet Chaeremon is not Dorotheus's father; we know from other papyri that his father was named Aphynchis (P.Oxy. 48.3396). Dickey summarizes this use of the word "son" in papyri thus: "υἱός can be used for a son in any context, but for other males only when indicating a connection to the writer . . . and then only when accompanied by a name or in the vocative case. Its extended usage . . . is probably restricted to younger men with a close connection to the writer" ("Literal and Extended Use," *Mnemosyne* 57 [2004] 164). She lists the usages of familial forms of address with the *caveat* that they apply "only to letters written in the third century AD or earlier. From the fourth century one finds an increasing quantity of Christian letters using extended kinship terms in a peculiarly Christian way" (ibid., 165). For literarily transmitted Christian letters Dinneen describes the use of the word "son" as follows: "As a title, υἱός is addressed to juniors in age, in ecclesiastical rank, or to lay persons. The term is one of familiar address." Since Sotas was a bishop, I add her observation that "bishops use υἱός in referring to priests" but also for deacons and laypeople (Dinneen, *Titles of Address*, 75).

[12] Ghedini writes, "Demetriano deve essere un membro della comunità retta da Sotas, che lo chiama infatti « figlio » nel prescritto, e nel saluto finale; questo . . . dimostra una

that Sotas considered him his spiritual son.[13] I suggest, however, that this peculiar form of address has also other overtones. Documentary papyri[14] and biblical texts[15] do not provide insights into Sotas's remarkable use of the word "holy" in addressing Demetrianus.[16] Yet in the writings of Origen, the Alexandrian scholar and clergyman a generation before Sotas, we find helpful parallels for this form of address.[17] Origen employs this word for the authors of the Old and New Testament; he addresses the apostles, and certain poets and philosophers as "holy."[18] He also must have counted his sponsor Ambrose among this group of exceptional persons, for strikingly—and significant for understanding Sotas's use—Origen addresses Ambrose multiple times with this epithet and calls him alternately "holy Ambrose" (ἱερὲ Ἀμβρόσιε) and

maggiore intimità ed un più vivo affetto" (*Lettere cristiane*, 123).

[13] Leclercq, "Papyrus," 1423 ("fils spirituel").

[14] The form of address "holy son" (ἱερὸς υἱός) occurs only in this papyrus. In the letter from the unknown woman to her Lord Father (P.Oxy. 12.1592, line 7, discussed in ch. 2), the adjective ἱερόν appears in the neuter, but the accompanying noun—if there was one—is missing; Grenfell and Hunt proposed to read: "your holy countenance" (τὸ ἱερόν σου [πρόσωπον]). Despite the lacuna it is clear that the holiness applies to the "Lord Father" whom the woman addressed in that letter. The adjective ἅγιος is used more frequently in forms of address. A letter from Sarapion to his mother Germania (P.Oxy. 10.1349) mentions τὴν ἀδελφήν μου ἁγίαν. But did he address her as his "sister Hagia" or as his "holy sister"? Grenfell and Hunt interpreted this as a name, Hagia, writing Ἁγία, with capital letter. See also examples that Ghedini mentions (*Lettere cristiane*, 125, note to lines 1–2).

[15] Sotas did not acquire this word from church readings, whether from the Septuagint or early Christian writings: the word occurs only rarely in the Septuagint and in the New Testament (ἱερὰ γράμματα, 2 Tim 3:15, for the holy scriptures). Its lack of popularity among the translators of the Hebrew Bible and early Christian authors alike is due to its associations with pagan cult (Schrenk, "ἱερός," in Kittel, *TWNT* 3:221–84, at 3:226 and 3:229). Hellenistic Jewish writers employ this "holy" frequently. Schrenk mentions Philo, Josephus and the authors of 1, 2, and 3 Ezra and 1, 2, and 4 Macc (ibid., 226–29). The apostolic fathers, apart from 1 Clemens, do not use the predicate (ibid., 229).

[16] The Greek language possesses several words that translate into English as holy. The word "holy" (ἱερός) that Sotas employed has connotations of cultic sanctity. For many Jewish and Early Christian writers, this word holy (ἱερός) was too closely associated with pagan cult (ibid., 226 and 229).

[17] In contrast to other ancient Christian writers, the word "holy" (ἱερός) belongs to Origen's regular vocabulary (ibid., 229). Origen's use of the word is influenced by Philo's use. The scriptures for him are "holy" (ἱεραὶ βίβλοι). Hellenistic Jewish authors also describe scripture in this way (ibid., 227).

[18] Ibid., 229–30.

"holy brother Ambrose" (ἱερὲ ἀδελφὲ Ἀμβρόσιε).[19] According to Gottlob Schrenk, the epithet means that Ambrose had dedicated himself to sacred studies.[20] In my opinion it also expresses Origen's appreciation for the support that he received from his "holy brother."[21] The comparison with Sotas's letter clearly shows that just as the holy brother Ambrose supported Origen financially, so the holy son Demetrianus sponsored Sotas and the church at Oxyrhynchus, or at least, Sotas exhorted him to do so. The bishop of our papyrus letter not only encouraged "his holy son" to furnish the church with assets but also appealed to—or better, flattered—Demetrianus as a studious Christian.[22] Yet no matter how pious and educated Ambrose and Demetrianus were, one could characterize their relationship with Origen and Sotas—more or less—as that of financial dependency from the latter. The complimentary address for Demetrianus certainly forms part of Sotas's rhetorical strategy to exhort Demetrianus to make a donation. Therefore, Origen and Sotas

[19] Throughout his writings, Origen addresses his sponsor Ambrose thirteen times with the word ἱερός. At the beginning of book 4 of *Contra Celsum*, he addresses Ambrose, his sponsor and the one who urged him to write the book (see Preface, *Cels.*), as "holy Ambrose" (ἱερὲ Ἀμβρόσιε) (*Cels.* 4.1; also in 5.1; 6.1, 8.76; *Comm. Jo.* 6.2.6; *Mart.* 14 and 36; *Philoc.* 15.1; and *Hom. Ps.* 12). Four times he references him as "holy brother Ambrose" (ἱερὲ ἀδελφὲ Ἀμβρόσιε), adding "brother" (*Cels.* 7.1; *Comm. Jo.* 2.1.1, 28.1.6, 32.1.2). Origen's frequent employment of the epithet for Ambrose causes Nicholas de Lange to muse that it functions almost as a surname: "Ἱερός devient presque un surnom d'Ambrose" (*Origène, Philocalie 1–20,* 573 n. 3). Origen not only calls his sponsor "holy," but also addresses him, e.g., as "God-loving Ambrose" (φιλόθεε Ἀμβρόσιε; *Cels.* Preface 1.1). On Ambrose, see, for instance, Preuschen, *Johanneskommentar*, lxxvi–lccvii; *Origène, Contre Celse* I, 19–20 and n. 4; and de Lange, *La lettre à Africanus,* 477–78.

[20] "Das wird kaum nur 'fromm' bedeuten, sondern dem Heiligen, den heiligen Studien zugewandt" (Schrenk, "ἱερός," 230). Schrenk referred to our papyrus in a footnote (ibid., 230 n. 26). Origen portrays Ambrose indeed as a learned man. Ambrose in certain instances wrote at Origen's dictation. He wrote the *Epistula ad Africanum* on dictation and then, according to the letter, corrected it in the closing greetings: "My lord and dear brother Ambrosius, who has written this at my dictation, and has, in looking over it, corrected as he pleased, salutes you. His faithful spouse, Marcella, and her children, also salute you" (Origen, *Epistula ad Africanum* 24, ed. de Lange, 573). In this letter Ambrose thus acted as both the scribe and the learned corrector.

[21] Dionysius, bishop of Alexandria, in a letter preserved in Eusebius's *Ecclesiastical History*, refers to Christians as "holy men" (ἱεροὺς ἄνδρας, *Hist. eccl.* 7.1.1). Eusebius addresses Paulinus, bishop of Tyre and later of Antioch, to whom he dedicated his *Ecclesiastical History* and his *Onomasticon* as "my most holy Paulinus" (ἱερώτατέ μου Παυλῖνε, *Hist. eccl.* 10.1.2). In the opening of his *Demonstratio evangelica*, Eusebius calls Theodotus Θεόδοτε, ἱερὲ θεοῦ ἄνθρωπε (*Dem. ev.* 1.1). This expression also became common in later writings.

[22] The study of scripture is a recurring theme in Sotas's correspondence (see also ch. 4).

profitably applied the epithet "holy" as an expression of reverence and importance to their Christian sponsors.

The next section of the letter gives us an insight into early Christian self-understanding. Sotas uses religious language and appeals to ancient custom. In most private letters from antiquity, a fairly standard formula for the health of the recipient follows after the prescript, but Sotas does not provide such a prayer here. Instead, he writes about salvation and divine providence[23] and repeats the adjective "common" twice (lines 4–5).[24] Gregory Thaumaturgus (213–270), bishop of Neocaesarea in Pontus, also connected salvation and providence: "None of the things given to us for salvation happen outside of his [God's] providence."[25] Sotas refers to divine providence, I argue, because he believes that God gives earthly possessions through divine providence, and so one should return them to God. This concept appears in Jewish donor

[23] Reference to the divine providence by itself does not make a letter Christian. The concept of divine providence can be found in Stoic, Jewish, and Christian writers. After an investigation of papyrological occurrences of the expression, Horsley concludes: "Given its Stoic pedigree, the most we can say at present about the phrase ἡ θεία πρόνοια is that by late III [cent.] Christians were comfortable in their use of it in private correspondence" (*NewDocs* [1983] 3:141–48, at 144). In this case, the bishop's writing points to a Christian use of it. For an in-depth treatment of the concept of divine providence in antiquity and in the early church, see Bergjan, *Der fürsorgende Gott*.

[24] This expression cannot be matched with a similar one in other literary or documentary texts. Scholars have offered several reconstructions for the lacunae. In their translation Grenfell and Hunt tentatively supplemented "our common salvation (is secure?)" (P.Oxy. 12.1492, 249). White summarized the possibilities as follows: "The editors of P.Oxy. 12 suggest as a possibility for filling the lacuna at the end of line 6 something like ἀσφαλέν ('sure, secure') to balance the adjective ending of the parallel phrase in line 5; similarly, we should expect the missing noun in the first clause to be something like πιστόν (with the sense of 'faith') to match the usage of σωτήριον in the second" (*Social Origins* 2:164 n. 62). Earlier, Ghedini proposed "our common (need?) is evident" in his translation: "Il commune (bisogno?) nostro è evidente" (*Lettere cristiane*, 124). In his note to these lines, he goes a little further, writing: "è il nostro comune evidente dovere ed il mezzo comune della nostra salvezza" (ibid., 125). Taking more reconstructive liberty, Leclercq suggested reading this sentence as "the clear light of us all and our salvation is in Jesus-Christ" ("La claire lumière de nous tous et notre salut est en Jésus-Christ," in "Papyrus" 13:1423). This reading is highly unlikely for two reasons. First, this reconstruction would not fit in the space available in the line, especially since the writer did not write contracted forms of *nomina sacra* in this letter. Second, the expression "Jesus Christ" does not occur in private letters until much later (see ch. 3); ἐν $\overline{\text{κω}}$ would be a possibility (but then the scribe would have used a *nomen sacrum*).

[25] Thaumaturgus: οὐδὲν τῶν πρὸς σωτηρίαν ἡμῖν δεδομένων ἔξω τῆς αὐτοῦ ὑπάρχει προνοίας (*Metaphrase on Ecclesiastes*, ed. Migne, 993D).

inscriptions, where giving to the synagogue means giving back to God what belongs to God.[26]

Having appealed to common salvation and divine providence, Sotas brings up an "ancient custom." In this letter he inquires about Demetrianus's decision concerning the donation of a piece of land "according to the ancient custom." Although Sotas does not refer specifically to a biblical passage, the Septuagint and early Christian writings contain many passages about tithing and giving to God.[27] The letters of Sotas resonate with insistence on custom; in the letters of recommendation, he requested that the recipient welcome the travelers "according to custom" and "as is proper."[28] These references to ancient custom expose the historical consciousness of the early church and form part of the effort of this young organization to envision itself as part of a venerable tradition.

The piece of land that concerned the donation of Demetrianus went for agricultural use.[29] The terminology used makes this clear, as the word

[26] Several donor inscriptions in the late antique Jewish synagogue in Sardis contain a reference to providence, phrased as "from the gifts of the providence" (ἐκ τῶν δομάτων [τ]ῆς προνοίης), see Ameling (*Inscriptiones Judaicae Orientis*, vol. 2, no. 84) and his comments ad hoc; see also no. 124. A shorter formula, namely, with omission of δομάτων, occurs in nos. 71, 78, 80–83, 85, 132 (ibid.). According to Tessa Rajak, this phrase indicates the modesty of the giver ("Jews, Pagans and Christians," in eadem, *The Jewish Dialogue with Greece and Rome*, 457). On the providence inscriptions, see ibid., 456–61.

[27] Exod 35:5; Num 7:2, etc. See Ghedini, *Lettere cristiane*, 127, note to line 9. For White this indicates that Sotas "alludes to the idealized picture of Acts 4:34–37" (*Social Origins* 2:164 n. 63). The difference between those passages and Sotas's letter is that in Acts the money from selling the field goes to the church. Naldini refers also to this passage, concluding: "Il biglietto . . . costituisce una nuova testimonianza circa la sensibilità comunitaria diffusa nel Cristianesimo antico e già viva nella Chiesa apostolica" (*Cristianesimo*, 156).

[28] κατὰ τὸ ἔθος: Sotas to Peter, PSI 3.208, line 6 and ὡς καθήκει: Sotas to Paul, PSI 9.1041, line 12.

[29] Grenfell and Hunt wondered whether it was given for "religious purposes?" (P.Oxy. 12.1492, 249). Ghedini proposed that the plot was to serve as a cemetery ("Ο ΤΟΠΟΣ nel POXY. 1492"; and idem, *Lettere cristiane*, 123, 127). He summarizes his argument as follows: "A quale uso fosse destinata l'arura non è detto; ma viene spontaneo di pensare che la comunità ne abbisognasse o per costituire o per allargare quei fondi destinati alle riunioni liturgiche e qui—più specialmente forse—per la sepoltura" (*Lettere cristiane*, 123, see also 127–28). Naldini initially followed Ghedini (*Cristianesimo*, 156), but attempted to nuance this in the second edition, arguing that the cemeteries remained relatively close to the valley (ibid., 436). He refers to the necropoleis of Antinoe and Thebes. Lampe lists "burial place" as one of the meanings of τόπος (1397 sub A7).

aroura indicates an Egyptian measurement for agricultural land.[30] Members of the congregation could cultivate this field or rent it out to a third party. Sotas exhorts Demetrianus to donate the field to "the place" (τόπος). In this context, it makes sense to take "the place" as indicating the church.[31] The same terminology—Greek τόποι, Latin *loca*—occurs in imperial documents reinstating property rights to Christian congregations after the Great Persecution, in the year 313.[32]

[30] LSJ, 245 ἄρουρα: "tilled or arable land," also "generally, earth, ground," or "land." Wipszycka challenged Ghedini's cemetery hypothesis cited in the previous footnote, mentioning that in Egypt arable land needed to be used as such, and that the dead were buried in the desert: "L'aroure . . . est probablement une aroure de terre destinée à la culture. Il ne faut pas oublier qu'on se trouve en Égypte, où même de petites parcelles de terre cultivable sont précieuses. L'hypothèse . . . selon laquelle l'aroure en question aurait pu servir à élargir le cimetière, est certainement fausse, car on n'enterrait pas les morts dans la vallée, mais hors de la zone cultivée, dans le désert" ("Remarques," 212–13). Earlier, Wipszycka had already expressed her disagreement with Ghedini's and Naldini's interpretation of this passage along the same lines: "Je ne suis pas d'accord avec l'interprétation . . . Pourquoi penser que l'aroure en question est une aroure de terrain pour le cimetière ou pour bâtir? Il est bien plus naturel de penser que c'est une aroure de terre à cultiver. Une aroure, en Égypte, c'est beaucoup" (eadem, *Ressources*, 29 n. 1). See also Bagnall: "Egyptian cemeteries for thousands of years had regularly used nearby deserts, a practice that not only spared usable land but ensured better preservation of the bodies" (*Egypt in Late Antiquity*, 144). White also opts for farming (*Social Origins* 2:163).

[31] See also ibid., 163. Speaking about the fourth to eighth centuries, Wipszycka notes that a "place" can designate either a church or a monastery, yet that its intended meaning often remains unspecified (*Ressources*, 13). See also Naldini, *Cristianesimo*, 69, note to line 11 (No. 2. "Ireneo ad Apollinario") on τόπος. In this letter, BGU 1.27, the sender uses the verbs παρα- and προσδέχομαι; he expects to be received by a topos. P.Oxy. 8.1162 and other letters of recommendation are addressed to *topoi*.

[32] Lactantius refers to the *loca* of the Christians, the places where they met, i.e., churches, in *Mort.* 48. 7–9 (ed. Moreau, 133–34): Atque hoc insuper in persona christianorum statuendum esse censuimus, quod, si *eadem loca*, ad quae antea conuenire consuerant, de quibus etiam datis ad officium tuum litteris certa antehac forma fuerat comprehensa, priore tempore aliqui uel a fisco nostro uel ab alio quocumque uidentur esse mercati, eadem christianis sine pecunia et sine ulla pretii petitione, postposita omni frustratione atque ambiguitate restituant; qui etiam dono fuerunt consecuti, eadem similiter isdem christianis quantocius reddant . . . Quae omnia corpori christianorum protinus per intercessionem tuam ac sine mora tradi oportebit. Et quoniam idem christiani non [in] ea *loca* tantum ad quae conuenire consuerunt, sed alia etiam habuisse noscuntur ad ius corporis eorum id est ecclesiarum, non hominum singulorum, pertinentia, ea omnia lege quam superius comprehendimus, citra ullam prorsus ambiguitatem uel controuersiam isdem christianis, id est corpori et conuenticulis eorum reddi iubebis, supra dicta scilicet ratione seruata [emphasis mine]. In his translation of this rescript, Eusebius rendered the Latin *loca* with the Greek word τόποι (*Hist. eccl.* 10.5.9–11).

Sotas encourages Demetrianus to donate his field not directly to a needy individual or family but to the church. This suggests the centrally controlled finances and a professional clergy in the church at Oxyrhynchus. In an organization with a professional clergy, the laymembers need to give to the poor through the church, because the clergy have to subtract salaries from the payroll before supporting the needy. In this letter we therefore witness the development of what Georg Schöllgen described as the professionalization of the clergy.[33] Just as the church members had the responsibility to donate to the church, so the bishop had the responsibility to obtain those donations.[34]

This one *aroura* of land that Demetrianus may have donated to Sotas's church does not allow for any further conclusions about the landownership of the Oxyrhynchite church in this period.[35] In the following centuries, Christian religious institutions in Egypt as elsewhere became large landowners, yet as Bagnall states "there is no sign of substantial land ownership by the church before mid-[fourth] century."[36] Peter Brown aptly noted:

> Both before and long after 312, the Christian churches continued to draw on the sheer will to give of each local community. In the fourth and fifth centuries, quite as much as in the third century, we should not imagine that the 'wealth of the church' consisted in secure endowments

[33] Schöllgen, *Anfänge der Professionalisierung des Klerus.*

[34] Wipszycka summarizes the tasks of an Egyptian bishop as follows: "En Égypte, l'évêque était libre de conférer les ordres aux personnes de son choix; il pouvait consulter, au sujet des ordinations, ses collaborateurs ecclésiastiques ou laïcs, mais il n'était pas obligé de le faire. Il était le juge des clercs de son diocèse, même dans les affaires non ecclésiastiques. Il décidait la répartition des tâches entre les clercs. C'est lui, enfin, qui était responsable de l'ensemble des finances ecclésiastiques; s'il y avait des limitations de son pouvoir économique, elles étaient, dans la plupart des cas, imposées par la coutume, et non par les lois écrites, et elles n'étaient pas très efficaces" ("καθολικη et les autres épithètes," in eadem, *Études sur le Christianisme* 158–59).

[35] A papyrus dated to the early-fifth century reveals that the Oxyrhynchite episcopal church possessed a vineyard comprising two *arouras* that it leased out. Benaissa, the editor, remarked that this may be "the earliest papyrus published to date relating to the agricultural property of the Oxyrhynchite church" ("New Light on the Episcopal Church of Oxyrhynchus," *ZPE* 161 [2007] 203). The land register from Hermopolis, dating to the mid-fourth century, has one entry for the church for 29 ¾ arouras (P.Landlisten Hermopolis 1, lines 534–35). See also Bagnall, *Egypt in Late Antiquity*, 290 n. 168.

[36] Ibid., 290. A declaration of church property from the Diocletianic persecution (304 C.E.) lists that the church in the village of Chysis possessed no lands (P.Oxy. 33.2673). Still, I find it significant that the document mentions land, for this indicates that churches were expected to own lands. For a full discussion of this papyrus, see ch. 7.

> of land. The landed wealth of the churches accumulated only gradually, in a piecemeal manner.[37]

Sotas's letter is evidence of this trend that local churches accrued land, *aroura* by *aroura*, through small private donations.

Throughout our investigation so far, the *nomina sacra* drew our attention as markers of Christian identity. This letter differs from the other letters that we have read from Sotas not only in genre but also in scribal practices. Unlike the practice in his other letters, the *nomina sacra* in this letter to Demetrianus are not contracted. In the final greeting in line 19, "I pray to God," he writes God (τῷ θεῷ) in full.[38] This invites the question of why the *nomina sacra* were contracted in Sotas's other letters, but not in this one. The simplest explanation suggests that a different person with different scribal habits wrote this letter. But I suspect something more than this. The other letters from Sotas belong to the specific genre of letters of recommendation. As we have seen, these constituted important instruments of ecclesiastical networking and attested to the church affiliation of the persons carrying them. In a time when one could not always safely proclaim Christian identity, the people whom one asked to receive strangers had a lot at stake. The cryptic Christian scribal practice of *nomina sacra* functioned in those letters as a powerful marker of the Christian identity and thus of the reliability of the sender. In writing this fundraising letter for Demetrianus, Sotas did not need that identity booster. He wanted to obtain an in-kind donation to grow the assets of his church community.

With Sotas inquiring if Demetrianus has made up his mind about the donation, the letter assumes a previous contact between the two men on this issue.[39] We do not know Demetrianus's motivations for considering the

[37] Brown, *Poverty and Leadership*, 54.

[38] The other place where a *nomen sacrum* commonly occurs in letters is in the opening. However, in the lacuna at the end of line three, there is no space left for even a short *nomen sacrum* (as τῷ θ̅ω̅ or τῷ κ̅ω̅). Grenfell and Hunt already considered προσαγορεύω to be "rather long for the available space" (P.Oxy. 12.1492, 250, note to line 3). I assume that it was abbreviated to προσαγορ(εύω); the same way as in Sotas's letter to Paul (PSI 9.1041.3), but even then there is no room for additional words.

[39] Ghedini has a slightly different understanding, namely that Demetrianus already had informed Sotas about his decision: "pare che Demetriano abbia comunicato a Sotas la sua decisione di cedere un' arura di terreno a favore della comunità cristiane" (*Lettere cristiane*, 125). I nuance this position by suggesting that they had indeed discussed this matter (whether

donation—we only have Sotas's theological perspective.[40] Sotas's "pious reflections" of common salvation,[41] divine providence, and ancient custom relate to the generosity that the bishop expects from his holy son Demetrianus. Perhaps through these words we can hear, ever so faintly, snippets of Sotas's preaching.

Sotas the Christian at Antioch (SB 12.10772)[42]

Our next encounter with bishop Sotas takes place far away from Oxyrhynchus. We meet him about to depart from Antioch in Syria to travel back home to Egypt. Our informant, a certain Sarapammon, writes to his mother and sister, among other things, that "Sotas the Christian" will bring them a sum of money.

Sarapammon, or perhaps his scribe, has a practiced handwriting.[43] The letters, pointy and written out separately, slope slightly to the right.

in writing or in person), but that Sotas now presses Demetrianus to come forward with his donation.

[40] Wipszycka, after listing donations ranging from houses and fields to boats and even infants concludes (again, this is for the period covering the fourth through eighth centuries, and most of the evidence is later): "Les mobiles de ces donations étaient tout aussi variés. On pouvait étre mu tout simplement par la piété, par la volonté de secourir matériellement l'oeuvre de Dieu sur la terre, ou bien par l'ambition, par le désir de faire étalage de ses richesses ou de gagner de la popularité. Dans certains cas on apportait des dons pour demander sa guérison ou celle de ses proches, ou pour obtenir l'absolution de graves péchés. Très souvent, on instituait une offrande dans le testament ou sur le lit de mort, afin d'assurer le salut de son âme dans l'au-delà" (*Ressources*, 29–30).

[41] Grenfell and Hunt, P.Oxy. 12.1492, 249. Ghedini comments on these lines: "pare . . . che Sotas in questa lettera lo conforti ad attuare il proposito" (*Lettere cristiane*, 125). Ghedini even suspects that Demetrianus is in spiritual distress, which Sotas tries to alleviate through this letter: "Demetriano era forse in angustie di spirito: Sotas lo conforta: « poichè sei venuto a questa decisione, che è opera di carità, e la carità è il mezzo provvidenziale di salute . . . sta di buon animo »" (ibid., 128). Yet instead of comforting Demetrianus, I see more subtle pressure from Sotas to come forward with the donation.

[42] See Plate 6. Previously published as PSI 14.1412 and SB 6.9451. Ed. princ. Koskenniemi, "Fünf griechische Papyrusbriefe," *Aeg*. 33 (1953) 322–24 ("III. Sarapammon an seine Familie"); idem, "Epistula Sarapammonis," *Arctos* n.s. 5 (1967) 79–84. The papyrus belongs to the Istituto Papirologico "G. Vitelli," Università degli Studi di Firenze. See discussion in Moretti, "Note egittologiche," *Aeg*. 38 (1958) 199–203 ("1. Nota a P. S. I. 1412").

[43] Koskenniemi describes this as a letter, "der mit deutlicher, geläufiger Kursive von einer geübten Hand geschrieben ist" ("Sarapammon an seine Familie," 322).

Palaeography and content situate this piece in the second half of the third century.[44]

The papyrus measures 13 x 12 cm[45] and reads as follows:

[Σαρα]πάμμ̣ων Ὀλυμπιο̣[ν(ίκης) τῆ̣ ἰ]δία̣
[μου μ]ητρὶ καὶ Διδύμη̣ καλ̣[. . .]. πλῖ-
σ̣τα̣ χαίρειν. γινώσκιν ὑμ̣[ᾶς θέλω] ὅτι
μέχρι τούτου ὁλόκληρό[ς εἰμι. ἔ]λα-
βον δὲ ἀπὸ Ἴωνος τοῦ ἀδελφ[οῦ γ]ράμ-
ματα καὶ ἔγνων τὰ περὶ ὑμ̣[ῶν. μ]ὴ οὖν
ἀγωνιᾶτε. μέχρι γὰρ τούτ[ου οὔπ]ω ἤλ-
θαμεν διὰ τὸν ἀγῶνα τὸν [ἐν Ἀ]ντι-
οχεία̣, μεθ' ὃν ἐλευσόμεθα. [διεπ]εμψά-
μην σοι δι‹ὰ› Σώτου τοῦ χρησια[νοῦ] τ̣άλαν-
τα δύο καὶ διὰ Ἴωνος πεντήκ[οντα] χρυσᾶ.
ἐ̣ὰν̣ ο̣ὖ̣ν̣ θέλη̣ς {ἐὰν οὖν θέλη̣ς} [ἔστ]ιν παρ'
α̣ὐτοῦ ἢ ἐν σίτῳ̣ ἢ ἐν οἴνῳ̣ λα[βεῖν. π]αρὰ γὰρ
τ̣ὴ̣ν̣ παρά συ τιμήν συ διδι· κα̣[ὶ γὰ]ρ οὕτως
αὐτῷ̣ συνεθέμην. διεπεμψάμην δέ σοι
[διά . . .]υ δέκα χρ̣υ̣σ̣ᾶ. ταῦτα γὰρ
[ἔδωκα α]ὐτῷ̣. εἰ γὰρ ἔτι εἶχον ἐπεμ̣-
[ψάμην . . .] .ε. ὁ πατήρ μου ἔγνω περὶ
[. . . διὰ τῶν πεμ]φθ̣έ̣ν̣των γραμ-
[μάτων. . . . .]. περὶ τῆς Σύρας καὶ
[πρότερον ἔγρα]ψα καὶ νῦν δὲ γράφω[

44 Koskeniemmi compares the handwriting to hands in the Heroninos archive, mentioning as close parallel ("sehr ähnlich") in handwriting P.Flor. 2.176 (dated 253 or 256 C.E.). He then, nevertheless, goes on to date the papyrus much earlier, to the second/third century: "Da der betreffende Typus der Schrift im 2. Jahrh. auftritt, können wir unseren Papyrus ins 2. bzw. 3. Jahrh. verlegen" ("Sarapammon an seine Famile," 322). Montevecchi also dates the papyrus to the third century, preferably the first part ("Nomen christianum," in *Paradoxos politeia* [ed. Cantalamessa and Pizzolato] 485). Moretti identified Sarapammon with an Olympic athlete known from two other Oxyrhynchus papyri: PSI 5.456, dated 276 or 282 C.E. and P.Oxy. 14.1643, dated 298 C.E., therefore narrowing down the date to the latter part of the third century ("Nota a P. S. I. 1412," 199–200).

45 Originally published in the PSI series, this fragmentary letter has an interesting editing history. After publishing a papyrus containing sixteen lines, Koskenniemi discovered another fragment belonging to this same letter in the Florence collection. This expanded the text from the sixteen lines in the editio princeps to twenty-three lines. Koskenniemi republished the letter as "Epistula Sarapammonis P.S.I. 1412 particula aucta."

[ὅτι . . . . αὐ]τῆ̣ς ἀ̣νέξασθ̣.
[ ]σ̣ε̣η̣π̣
(On the verso: Traces of address.)

1. ολυμπιά̣[δι also possible, 2–3. *l.* πλεῖστα, 3. *l.* γινώσκειν, 10. *l.* χριστια[νοῦ], 14. σοι, σοι, διδοῖ or δίδει.

Translation

Sarapammon, Olympian victor, to his very mother and Didyme . . . very many greetings. I want you (pl.) to know that until now I am healthy. And I received from my brother Ion (your) letter and learned how you are doing. Therefore, do not be anxious, for until now we have not yet come because of the contest in Antioch after which we will come (home). We send to you (sgl.) via Sotas the Christian two talents and via Ion 50 *aurei* (gold coins). Therefore, if you want, it can be received from him either in grain or in wine. For he will give it to you for your local price. For thus I have also agreed with him. And I send to you via . . . ten *aurei*. For these I have given to him. For if I still have, I send . . . My father knows about . . . because of the letter sent . . . about Syra also I have written before and now I write that . . .

The sender, Sarapammon, sends home word that he is "whole, healthy" (ὁλόκληρο[ς]) and informs his mother[46] and Didyme of amounts of money they will receive.[47] The money will be brought by three different people:

[46] Because of a lacuna in line 1 (ολυμπι.[. . .]), it is a matter of debate whether Sarapammon's mother was called Olympias (Ὀλυμπιά̣[δι, so Koskenniemi) or whether Sarapammon describes himself as an Olympian athlete (ὀλυμπιο̣[ν(ικης), so Moretti). If, as Moretti argues, this Sarapammon is indeed an athlete known from other papyri, then his full name is Αὐρήλιος Σαραπάμμων ὁ καὶ Δίδυμος, and his mother's name is Theonis (Θεωνίς), not Olympias. According to Moretti, Sarapammon using the title matches the self-image of athletes from antiquity: "che poi Sarapammon usi il proprio titolo di olympionikes scrivendo alla madre non sembrerà strano a chi conosca la vanagloria di questi atleti della declinante antichità, vanagloria che evidentemente non si arrestava neppure alla soglie della propria casa" (ibid., 200). Koskenniemi replied that it is very unusual that people identify themselves by profession in private letters ("Epistula Sarapammonis," 81).

[47] Sotas is traveling home with the two talents for Sarapammon's family. This is a large sum (one talent = 6,000 drachmas). The others have amounts in gold. Gold coins did not circulate in Egypt, or at least not widely. The term *aureus/chrysous* was used in Egypt, as Cuvigny argues, only as a way of indicating amounts of money ("Les avatars du *chrysous*," *BIFAO* 103 [2003] 111–31). Cuvigny concludes: "Il se pourrait donc qu'en Égypte . . . le *chrysous* . . . ait eu une existence seulement théorique et . . . n'ait

Sotas, Ion, and a third person whose name is lost.[48] Sarapammon notifies his family that he remains still in Antioch—this must mean Antioch in Syria.[49] The letter turned up in Oxyrhynchus, so I assume that his family resided there.[50] The reference to the upcoming "contest in Antioch" may mean that Sarapammon competed as an athlete.[51] If so, we may assume as well that he belonged to the upper class of the population, for only rich people

jamais été qu'une monnaie de compte, une façon de dire « vingt drachmes » d'abord, « cent drachmes » ensuite" (ibid., 127). Rathbone, on the contrary, argues that there must have been some gold money circulating in Egypt: "there was no provincial gold coinage, and since I find it quite incredible that Roman Egypt could have functioned without gold coins (how otherwise, for example, could the surplus from cash taxes have been exported to Rome?), I believe that mainstream aurei must have circulated in quantities much larger than the known hoards might suggest" ("Monetisation," in *Coin Finds and Coin Use* [ed. King and Wigg] 326). Christiansen mentions 3,686 Egyptian gold coins found in "seven+" hoards (*Coinage in Roman Egypt*, 51). Given the amount of gold coins discovered in Egypt, the few mentions of gold coins in papyrus documents is surprising (ibid., 47; with reference to West and Johnson, *Currency in Roman and Byzantine Egypt*, 70). Christiansen notes that "the Romans may have made use of gold coins for paying or storing high amounts of money" (ibid., 46). He concludes that as of yet the role of gold coins in the economy of Roman Egypt remains "unclear" (ibid., 47).

[48] Sarapammon apparently trusted these people with his money. The writer of a roughly contemporary papyrus letter, P.Oxy. 31.2598 (late-third cent.) explicitly asks his correspondent for a reliable person to send cash along to pay for certain goods, urging: "and write back to me the price of these through (a) trusty person (δι' ἀσφαλοῦς ἀνθρώπου, 6–7), so that I may pay him thus the cash."

[49] Several other papyri that were sent from Syria have been found in Egypt. See also Cotton, Cockle, and Millar, "Papyrology of the Roman Near East," *JRS* 85 (1995), esp. 219–20.

[50] Also Koskenniemi: "Mater Sarapammonis Oxyrhynchi habitat una cum Didyma" ("Epistula Sarapammonis," 79–80).

[51] Koskenniemi suggested that Sarapammon's ἀγών (line 8) could identify him as an athlete: "Ich glaube also, dass wir uns nicht viel irren, wenn wir in unserem Sarapammon einen Athleten, Wagenlenker oder dgl. sehen, der auf einer ausländischen Tournée herumreist" ("Sarapammon an seine Familie," 322). Moretti took this further, and argued that this Sarapammon was the same as an Olympic victor known from two other Oxyrhynchus papyri—see note 46 above. On Olympic victors from Egypt, see Decker, "Olympiasieger aus Ägypten," in *Religion und Philosophie* (ed. Verhoeven and Graefe), esp. 95 n. 9 and 105; and Perpillou-Thomas, "Artistes et athlètes," *ZPE* 108 (1995) 225–51, esp. 250. Antioch hosted Olympic games, as the chronographer John Malalas records in his *Chronographia* 12.3–10 (ed. Thurn, 214–18); English translation in Jeffreys, *The Chronicle of John Malalas*. On the Olympian games at Antioch, see Schenk von Stauffenberg, "Die antiochenischen Olympien," in idem, *Die römische Kaisergeschichte bei Malalas*, 412–43; and Downey, "Olympic Games at Antioch in the Fourth Century A.D.," *TAPA* 70 (1939) 428–38.

could afford the lifestyle of an athlete, as Bagnall has remarked.[52] Athletes competed in international contests, which necessitated travel and its expenses. Sarapammon went to Antioch not only to compete in games but probably also conducted some business on the side.[53] Yet regardless of his identity and occupation in Antioch, he mentions to his family the subject of our current investigation—Sotas.

Sarapammon's letter reveals that our bishop—if indeed the Sotas mentioned in line 10 refers to him—not only accommodated other travelers by writing letters of recommendation for his parishioners and extending hospitality to foreigners, but that he himself made a long journey to Syria. There we find him in the company of an athlete. The identification hinges on the reconstruction of the epithet for Sotas. The crux of our inquiry lies in how we fill in the gap in line 10: "through Sotas the Chresia. . . (δι‹ὰ› Σώτου τοῦ χρησια[. . .). It could be a patronymic or a profession, but none of the editors of the papyrus came up with a solution. Koskenniemi noted that he clearly read χρησια[. . ., but that he could not find a "meaningful reconstruction." He wondered whether it would represent part of an as yet unknown personal name.[54] Collaboration between Rea and Parsons led to a reconstruction of this line. Working on the Sotas of the Heracleopolis letter (P.Oxy. 36.2785), Rea suggested that line 10 should read "via Sotas the Christian."[55] This indeed makes sense. The spelling of the word Christian with an *eta* instead of *iota* (χρηστιανός) should not surprise us; it actually occurs as the more common spelling for the word in papyri.[56] Yet this way of

[52] "Participation in such diversions was . . . mainly the prerogative of the wealthy" (Bagnall, *Egypt in Late Antiquity*, 106). "The world of the athlete was by nature international because excellence was defined . . . by victories in major contests throughout the Empire, not only within Egypt." (ibid., 105).

[53] As Koskenniemi also noted: "Imaginari possumus Sarapammonem non solum certamina sed etiam alias res in Syria gessisse" ("Epistula Sarapammonis," 83).

[54] "χρησια[steht in dem Papyrus möglichst deutlich geschrieben, aber bisher habe ich keine sinnvolle Ergänzung erfunden. Vielleicht steckt darin ein bisher unbekannter Eigenname" (Koskenniemi, "Sarapammon an seine Familie," 324, note to line 10).

[55] δι‹ὰ› Σώτου τοῦ χρησ‹τ›ια[νοῦ] (Rea, P.Oxy. 36.2785, note to line 2). In that line Rea actually refers to Parsons's at that time still unpublished work on P.Oxy. 42.3035, whereas Parsons refers in the publication to Rea.

[56] See Tibiletti: "la grafia con la η è la più comune" (*Le lettere private*, 118 n. 31). Examples of this spelling are χρησ<τ>ιανον (P.Oxy. 42.3035, discussed in ch. 6), χρηστιανῶν (P.Oxy 43.3119, discussed in ch. 6), χρηστιανοί (P.Lond. 6.1919, lines 16–17), χρηστοφόρος (P.Heid. 1.6; P.Lond. 6.1926); and συγχρηστός (P.Lond. 6.1919, lines 32–33). See also P.Dubl 31.10 χρηστιανῶν (Panopolis, 355); P.Oxy. 43.3149, 3–4: χρητιανός (fifth cent.?). P.Lips. 43.13

writing "Christian" (χρηστιανός) does not appear solely in papyrus letters or other documentary texts alone. The letter writer has good company, as even the scribe of the Codex Sinaiticus, for instance, wrote the word with *eta* in the three New Testament passages where this word occurs.[57]

What about the missing *tau*? Parsons argued that "Petosorapis, son of Horus, 'Chresian'"[58] meant "Petosorapis, son of Horus, Christian(?)."[59] Parsons's observations hold true in this instance as well. Thus the reconstruction of this line as reading "via Sotas the Christian" (δι‹ὰ› Σώτου τοῦ χρησ‹τ›ια[νοῦ]) is convincing.

As a marker of identity, the epithet indicates that one stands out as "Christian." So when Sarapammon described Sotas to his family as "the Christian," it must mean that they recognized him as such.[60] How did Sotas stand out distinctively as a Christian? In her article on naming practices, Hobson observes that writers mention the profession more commonly than the name of the father when distinguishing a person in private letters:

> Where specification is required, the letters far more often refer to a person by occupation than by patronymic; thus we find references to Valerius the goldsmith ... Didymus the notary ... Metellus the soldier ... Alexander the builder ... Lampon the mousecatcher ... Pindarus the field guard at Dionysias.[61]

(Hermoupolis Magna? fourth cent.) reads χρειστιανικῶν. For this spelling see also P.Laur. 2.42 about "Atheas the Christian" (see above, 39 n. 57). (*Le lettere private*, 197 n. 2). See also Montevecchi, "Nomen christianum"; Horsley, *NewDocs* 1:119 (epigraphical examples of different spellings); and idem, "Orthography," *NewDocs* 3:129–30.

[57] Acts 11:26; 26:28; and 1 Pet 4:16; see Wilkins, "Christian," *ABD* 1:926.

[58] Πετοσορᾶπιν ῾Ωρου χρησιανόν in P.Oxy. 42.3035.

[59] Parsons writes, "I can only interpret this as χρησ‹τ›ιανόν, Christian. . . . The spelling without *tau* recurs in PSI 1412, 10. . . . This is probably a phonetic spelling. . . . Dr. Gignac was able to cite eight third-century examples of this sort of assimilation. A parallel phenomenon is the variation between -σσ- and -στ-, . . . hence perhaps *crissana* and *cressiani* in Latin inscriptions" (P.Oxy. 42.3035, note to lines 4–5). An other example of a misspelling of the word is P.Oxy. 43.3149, lines 3–4: χρητιανός, where—for a change—the sigma is absent.

[60] In ch. 2 I noted that the word "Christian" is used by others, and not as term of self-definition. It can be used in a pejorative sense. However, Sarapammon would probably not have trusted Sotas with his money had he had a very negative opinion about this Christian.

[61] Hobson, "Naming Practices," 173.

In light of this, it makes sense to interpret the identification "Sotas the Christian" as a "Christian by profession," which matches papa Sotas the cleric.[62]

What was Sotas doing in Antioch?[63] I offer two hypotheses. If in Antioch for ecclesiastical matters, Sotas may have participated in the excommunication of Paul of Samosata as bishop of Antioch. Twice an ecumenical delegation of bishops met to debate their Antiochean colleague's christology. The first meeting occurred in 264 with a broad array of bishops from far away locations.[64] In the winter of 268/269,[65] a second synod "of an exceedingly large number of bishops" gathered again at Antioch to oust the bishop "from the Catholic Church under heaven."[66] Present at one of those Antiochean

[62] According to Koskenniemi, the Sotas in this letter was a banker or money changer ("trapezitam fingimus"; "Epistula Sarapammonis," 83). For Judge and Pickering, he is perhaps "an overseas trader, akin to the *entrepreneur* whose network involves the church in Alexandria" (referring to P.Amh. 1.3a; "Papyrus Documentation," 69). In light of the evidence that I have presented, these interpretations are incorrect.

[63] The travelogue of an affluent fellow countryman, Theophanes, from Hermopolis in Egypt to Antioch in Syria, enables us to picture in part Sotas's journey. Theophanes's papers detail the expenditures for him and his companions, such as food items and bathing. See Matthews, *Journey of Theophanes*, for a thorough analysis.

[64] Eusebius reports: "Among those who were the most distinguished were Firmilian, bishop of Caesarea; the brothers Gregory [Thaumaturgus] and Athenodore, pastors of the community in Pontus; and in addition to these, Helenus (bishop) of the community at Tarsus, and Nicomas, of the community at Iconium; nor must we omit Hymenaeus, of the church at Jerusalem, and Theotecnus, of this neighbouring church of Caesarea; and moreover there was Maximus also, who was ruling with distinction the brethren at Bostra; and one would not be at a loss to reckon up countless others, together with presbyters and decons, who were gathered together in the above-mentioned city for the same cause. But these were the most famous among them" (*Hist. eccl.* 7.28.1, trans. Oulton, LCL).

[65] For the date, see Millar, "Paul of Samosata, Zenobia and Aurelian," 11. It is unknown in which Olympiad Sarapammon, the writer of our letter, triumphed: "Unsicher ist die Datierung des Periodoniken Aurelius Sarapammon aus Oxyrhynchos" (Decker, "Olympiasieger aus Ägypten," 95 n. 9). Following Moretti, Decker suggested the 264th Olympiad of 277 C.E. (ibid. and 104 no. 40,). Perhaps he participated in the 261st Olympiad from 265 C.E. Olympic games were held at Antioch in 264 and 268 C.E., the same years that ecclesiastical synods met (namely 264 and 268/9) to discuss Paul of Samosata.

[66] Eusebius, *Hist. eccl.* 7.29.1 (trans. Oulton 2:213). A letter from a group of bishops, preserved by Eusebius, states that "we wrote inviting many even of the bishops at a distance to come and heal this deadly doctrine, as for example, both Dionysius at Alexandria and Firmilian of Cappadocia" (ibid., 7.30.3, trans. Oulton 2:215).

synods, among bishops from Egypt and other far away locations, we may imagine Sotas from Oxyrhynchus.[67]

Yet Sotas may not have visited Antioch for church matters. His contemporary colleague Cyprian, bishop of Carthage, in his book *De lapsis*, scolds his fellow bishops for going on prolonged business travel in other provinces and leaving behind their flocks:

> Too many bishops, instead of giving encouragement and example to others, made no account of the ministration which God had entrusted to them, and took up the administration of secular business; they left their sees, abandoned their people, and toured the markets in other territories on the look-out for profitable deals. While their brethren in the Church went hungry, they wanted to have money in abundance, they acquired landed estates by fraud, and made profits by loans at compound interest.[68]

Other sources argue as well against bishops leaving their province.[69] We cannot exclude the possibility that Sotas had gone to Antioch on business, although his participation in the excommunication of Paul of Samosata is also a plausible reason for his visit to Antioch.

[67] For the text of the acta, see Riedmatten, *Actes du procès de Paul de Samosate,* esp. 135–58. Recent discussions on the content of the debates in Lang, "Christological Controversy," *JTS* 51 (2000); and Fischer, "Die antiochenischen Synoden," *Annuarium historiae conciliorum* 18 (1986).

[68] *Laps.* 6, trans. Bénevot, *Cyprian. De Lapsis*, 9, 11. The Latin reads: Episcopi plurimi, quos et hortamento esse oportet ceteris et exemplo, diuina procuratione contempta procuratores rerum saecularium fieri; derelicta cathedra, plebe deserta, per alienas prouincias oberrantes negotiationis quaestuosae nundinas aucupari; esurientibus in ecclesia fratribus, habere argentum largiter uelle, fundos insidiosis fraudibus rapere, usuris multiplicantibus faenus augere (ed. Weber and Bévenot, *Sancti Cypriani episcopi opera* 3.1, 223–24). See also Eck, "Handelstätigkeit," *Memorias de historia antigua* 4 (1980) 127 and 132 n. 2, and Barzanò, "La questione dell'arricchimento," *Revista di storia della chiesa in Italia* 47 (1993) 360–61.

[69] See, for example, canon 19 of the Council of Elvira (ca. 306 C.E.): Episcopi, presbyteres et diacones de locis suis negotiandi causa non discedant, nec circumeuntes provincias quaestuosas nundinas sectentur: sane ad victum sibi conquirendum aut filium aut libertum aut mercenarium aut amicum aut quemlibet mittant, et si voluerint negotiari, intra provinciam negotientur (ed. Lauchert, *Kanones der wichtigsten altkirchlichen Concilien*, 16). Canon 12 of the council of Sardica (343 C.E.) allows bishops with out-of-town estates to oversee the harvest there and be absent in their diocese for no more than three weeks (ibid., 65–66). See also Eck, "Handelstätigkeit," 129–30 and Barzanò, "La questione dell'arricchimento," 360–61.

This letter featuring "Sotas the Christian" has several intriguing ramifications. First, it suggests that Sotas stood out as Christian in Oxyrhynchus, where both Sarapammon and Sotas had their domicile. Identifiable and identified as Christian in his community, the description of Sotas fits well with his position as bishop. Moreover, the letter situates Sotas at Antioch in Syria, where possibly he had attended one of the synods about the beliefs of his colleague, bishop Paul of Samosata.[70] The letter which mentions Sotas again shows the importance of Christian networking and this involved the exchange of ideas, doctrines, and advice. This networking also had a material aspect to it. We learn of Sotas's presence at Antioch only because he had brought back money from an affluent and athletic townsman. Lastly, we observe Sotas, "the Christian," in contact with people not necessarily identified as Christians. At least, we cannot discern them as such,[71] for if Christians, they would have addressed Sotas by the title by which he was known in Christian circles—*papa*.

Book Production at Oxyrhynchus

The writing material of two of Sotas's letters provides an unexpected glimpse into different activities of the Christian congregation at Oxyrhynchus. As noted above, Sotas's letters to Peter (PSI 3.208) and to Paul (PSI 9.1041) are each penned on a piece of parchment.[72] Using parchment stationery is exceptional, as papyrus formed the common writing material in classical antiquity. This holds true both for every day documentary letters found in Egypt and for what we know of the great epistolographers, such as Cicero and Pliny, and the ecclesiastical writers, such as Jerome and Augustine.[73] In their

[70] Contacts between Christians in Egypt and Syria are documented elsewhere as well, e.g., Dionysius of Alexandria's letter to Fabius, bishop of Antioch in the mid-third century (as preserved in Eusebius, *Hist. eccl.* 6.41, 42). See also Müller, "La position de l'Égypte chrétienne," *Mus* 92 (1979) 112–13 for discussion of Syrian-Egyptian exchange.

[71] Montevecchi also concludes this: "I corrospondenti non sembrano essere cristiani, certamente non lo è il mittente, perché, se lo fosse, qualificherebbe Sotas come 'il fratello,' ὁ ἀδελφός, secondo l'uso diffusissimo anche tra i pagani . . . e più tra i cristiani" ("Nomen christianum," 485–86).

[72] Naldini commented briefly in a footnote to PSI 9.1041 (= Naldini, no. 29) on the use of parchment on both letters, writing: "Si può soltanto notare che i due foglietti pergamenacei . . . presentano le stesse qualità materiali" (*Cristianesimo*, 153 n. 2).

[73] "Der Brief der eigentlichen klassischen Zeit war natürlich auf Papyrus geschrieben" (Gardthausen, *Das Buchwesen im Altertum*, 162). Further on: "Ebensowenig benutzte man

letters, Jerome and Augustine bring up the issue of writing on parchment.[74] Jerome in particular—disappointed that he received only a brief letter from his friends—complains that lack of papyrus does not constitute a valid reason:

> Why is it that, when we are separated by so great an interval of land and sea, you have sent me so short a letter? Is it that I have deserved no better treatment, not having first written to you? I cannot believe that paper can have failed you while Egypt continues to supply its wares. Even if a Ptolemy had closed the seas, King Attalus would still have sent you parchments from Pergamum, and so by his skins you could have made up for the want of paper.[75]

Faced with a shortage of papyrus, Augustine apparently sent a letter penned on parchment, a matter for which he apologizes in some detail:

> Does this letter not show that, if we are short of papyrus, we have at least abundance of parchment? The ivory tablets [i.e., wax tablets for writing] I possess I have sent to your uncle with a letter; you will the more easily forgive this bit of skin, since my message to him could not be postponed, and I considered it very impolite not to write to you.[76]

These excerpts from two great Christian letter writers confirm that they considered papyrus the common material for writing letters. Yet in case of a shortage of papyrus, they would find animal skin suitable for writing letters.

Pergament. In den großen lateinischen Briefsammlungen von Cicero, Plinius usw. hat man bis jetzt wenigstens noch keine sichere Spur gefunden, daß für diese Korrespondenz jemals Pergament Verwendung gefunden hatte" (ibid., 166).

[74] I found these examples in Hulley, "Light Cast by St. Jerome on Palaeographical Points," 83–86.

[75] Cur tot interiacentibus spatiis maris et terrarum tam parvam epistulam miseritis, nisi quod ita merui, qui vobis, ut scribitis, ante non scripsi. Chartam defuisse non puto Aegypto ministrante commercia. Et si aliqui Ptolemaeus maria clausisset, tamen rex Attalus membranas e Pergamo miserat, ut penuria chartae pellibus pensaretur (Jerome, Epist. 7.2, ed. and trans. Wright, LCL, 8–9). See also Hulley, "Light Cast by St. Jerome," 84. The letter dates from 374 C.E.

[76] Non haec epistula sic inopiam chartae indicat, ut membranas saltem abundare testetur. Tabellas eburneas, quas habeo, avunculo tuo cum litteris misi. Tu enim huic pelliculae facilius ignosces, quia differri non potuit, quod ei scripsi, et tibi non scribere etiam ineptissimum existimavi (Augustine, *Epistula* 15.1, to Romanianus, from the year 390 C.E. Text and translation by Baxter in Augustine, *Select Letters*, 12–14). Later in the letter Augustine again refers to a possible lack of papyrus ("si charta interim non desit").

However, the fact that Augustine apologized for his use of parchment in itself proves how seldom this occurred as writing material for letters.[77]

Turning to documentary letters, Adolf Deissmann already noted the rarity of the use of parchment for letter writing and commented: "Letters on parchment from antiquity are, however, very rare; I only know the letter of Soëris in Papyri Iandanae II."[78] The wealth of documents published since Deissmann wrote his *Licht vom Osten*, has not changed the basic validity of his observation. In fact, out of a total of 56,188 published documents from antiquity listed on the HGV,[79] almost two thirds (36,526 or 65 percent) are penned on papyrus.[80] The HGV lists only 353 parchment documents or less than one percent of the total number of published documents to date (0.63 percent). The earlier parchment texts (before the fourth cent.) have a provenance in the Middle East (Syria, Mesopotamia, Palestine). Not until after the late-third century do we see parchment documents from Egypt, which originate predominantly from the Arsinoites. Most of these texts on parchment date to the seventh and eighth centuries. For Oxyrhynchus alone, out of the 5,476 published documents from that nome, only four are parchment documents;[81] two of these four, as we have seen, stem from Sotas. Limiting the search to all published private letters, we find, in addition to the two letters from Sotas, only two other letters written on parchment from

[77] See also Baxter in Augustine, *Select Letters*, xxxvi; Hulley, "Light Cast By St. Jerome," *HSCP* 54 (1943) 84.

[78] Deissmann: "Pergamentbriefe aus der Antike sind allerdings sehr selten; ich kenne nur den Brief des Soëris in den Papyri Iandanae II" (*Licht vom Osten*, 118 n. 1). Private letters on parchment are so uncommon that White in his book on private letters from antiquity overlooked them when he remarked that "parchment and vellum (skins), like stone, were also used for more important correspondence and documents but *not for ordinary letters*. In Egypt, they were seldom used even for more important texts prior to the second century C.E." ([emphasis mine] *Light from Ancient Letters*, 213).

[79] Search as of August 2008. *Nota bene*: this applies to documents, as distinct from literary texts.

[80] The majority of the remaining 19,662 documents are *ostraca*, potsherds used for writing (16,098 or 28.7 percent of the total listed documents). Other texts are composed, e.g., on wood (2,524), cloth (eighty-four) or stone (sixty-seven), even fewer on metal or clay (six bronze inscriptions, one clay tablet). Provenance and climate are crucial for writing material to survive the ages—the percentage of papyri is so high, because it was the writing material of Egypt, where climate conditions preserved many. The writing tablets from the Roman military unit stationed at Vindolanda in England are made of thin pieces of local wood and equivalent in function with papyrus.

[81] P.Oxy. 6.958 (80 C.E.); P.Oxy. 6.987 (fifth–sixth cent.); and the two Sotas letters, PSI 3.208 and PSI 9.1041 (second half of third cent.).

Egypt in this time frame.[82] With this overview I have made clear that the two parchment letters from Sotas stand out sharply from the writing material used for the large majority of ancient documents, which includes especially private letters.

Sotas did not write exclusively on parchment; for his letter to Demetrianus (P.Oxy. 12.1492), he used the common writing material papyrus. Taking a lead from Jerome and Augustine, perhaps Sotas did not have papyrus at hand at the time that he wrote the two other letters. That then invites the question of how he obtained parchment, since it occurs rarely as writing material in Egypt. I think that Sotas had access to leftover pieces of parchment from Christian manuscript production in his house and put them to good use for his correspondence.

Broadening our investigation to include literary texts, the picture of the use of parchment for writing changes somewhat.[83] Other texts written on parchment found in Egypt are codices with literary texts; their number rises steadily in the first centuries of the common era.[84] As Eric Turner observed:

> It is not till the fourth century that the parchment codex begins to be at all common in Egypt. It may be observed that parchment codices are not to be expected among finds preserved in Egypt, and that no generalizations should be based on the argument from silence.[85]

[82] A search in HGV on "Material = Pergament; Inhalt = Brief" results in five parchment letters: one of them, a "Private Letter from a Soldier," was found at Dura-Europos (P.Dura 46, early-third cent. C.E.) and sent from Antioch. The ones from Egypt are: P.Iand. 2.12; PSI 3.208; PSI 9.1041; and SB 3.7269. A general search on "Material = Pergament" is also interesting, for it shows that many of the parchment documents have a provenance outside of Egypt, and that sometimes contracts were written on parchment. See also Johnson, "Role of Parchment."

[83] The number of published literary fragments from Oxyrhynchus to date (for all antiquity) is 2,935 (August 2008). Out of these, 2,840 (or 96.8 percent) are papyrus manuscripts, whereas only 84 (2.9 percent) are parchment manuscripts (also, e.g., four wax tablets and five ostraca). These numbers are based on searches on the LDAB. However, almost half of these 84 parchment manuscripts (37 manuscripts or 44 percent) are Christian. This number includes Septuagint manuscripts.

[84] The earliest parchment manuscript from Oxyrhynchus is dated first–second cent. C.E.; there is one second-cent. C.E. manuscript and one second–third cent., but most are dated to the fourth and fifth cent. and later (Based on same LDAB search).

[85] Turner, *Typology*, 37–38.

One could argue that these parchment codices excavated in Egypt came from other parts of the empire. Roberts suggested that possibility for Latin manuscripts.[86] But given the rise in numbers of literary texts on parchment, we may inevitably conclude that even in Egypt, the land of the papyri, animal skin became a vehicle for literary texts.[87] As a matter of fact, the oldest extant catalogue of a Christian library, found in Egypt, lists exclusively parchment books. The text, which Roberts dated to the first half of the fourth century, describes them as "skin."[88] Parchment was available in Egypt for writing; some private letters from Egypt mention it as writing material.[89]

The cutting and fitting of an animal skin into square and rectangular sheets for the production of parchment codices must naturally have resulted in leftover pieces. No matter how skillfully and economically one might have done this preparation, there must have been odds and ends of leftover skin. Turner alludes to this when he compares the sizes of parchment and papyrus codices.[90] Two letters from the Pachomian monastery also appear written on

[86] Roberts, *Manuscript, Society and Belief*, 6.

[87] Turner suspects that experiments with parchment as writing material for codices took place outside of Egypt (*Typology*, 38).

[88] In Greek: δέρμα. Among the books in the library were *The Shepherd* (of Hermas), such Septuagint books as *Leviticus, Song of Songs, Exodus, Job*, a four-gospel book, Acts, and two works from Origen. See Roberts, "Two Oxford Papyri," *ZNTW* 37 (1938) 184–88. Comparing the handwriting to a manuscript dated 312, Roberts remarks that the Ashmolean text is "somewhat later and in a finer hand" (ibid., 185). He writes, "All the works whose titles are preserved on this fragment were written on parchment and were therefore, we may presume, codices" (ibid., 186). See also, e.g., Harrauer, "Bücher in Papyri," in *Flores litterarum* (ed. Lang) 67. Another library inventory of Christian manuscripts from the fifth/sixth century refers to parchment and papyrus manuscripts: P.Grenf. 2.111 mentions twenty-one parchment and only three papyrus books (βιβλία δερμάτι(να) κα´ ὁμοί(ως) χαρτία γ´, lines 27–28). Harrauer rightly comments: "Man möge hier nicht übersehen, daß bereits im späten 5. Jh. n. Chr. Pergament für dauerhafte Bücher dem Papyrus den Rang abgelaufen hat" ("Bücher," 68). Another fifth/sixth century document, a Greek letter, reports the purchase of parchment for the production of a book: SB 14.11372; Koenen, "Ein Mönch als Berufsschreiber," in *Festschrift zum 150jährigen Bestehen des Berliner ägyptischen Museums*, 347–54.

[89] For instance, P.Pet. 30 (late-second cent.) mentions viewing parchment books (μεμβράνας) for sale; P. NagHamm. 71 (fourth cent.) asks for two skins (δύο δερμά̣[των]), and P. Neph. 4 (fourth cent.) requests three or four sheep skins (δέρματα προβάτων).

[90] "One obvious reason why codices of parchment do not seem to occur in sizes that match codices of papyrus is a physical one. There are clearly several ways in which an animal skin can be cut up to form sheets (double leaves) for a parchment book. The size of the skin itself limits the maximum size of a sheet. The actual dimensions of smaller sizes are no doubt governed by the most economical way of folding and cutting a skin: the manufacturer asks what size of sheets can be obtained without wastage" (Turner, *Typology*, 42).

such cuttings.[91] I argue that Sotas used these pieces of "scrap parchment" for his letters. Given the rarity of parchment as writing material for documents and the rise of its use for manuscript production in this period, I suggest that the parchment stationery from papa Sotas indicates that he and his circle were involved in manufacturing manuscripts[92] and composed these letters on the leftovers.[93] A much later Coptic letter (fifth–sixth cent.), also written on parchment, serves as a good comparison. Peshot writes to Kolouthus and Timotheus about the illumination of a manuscript that he sent them.[94] This letter provides an interesting insight into book production and illustration in that period. Relevant to my argument, we again find a letter written on parchment in a milieu where books were produced.

The use of specific Christian scribal practices such as *nomina sacra* and isopsephisms provide other evidence that Sotas and the ones with him produced books. Here I find inspiration in Kim Haines-Eitzen's book on early Christian scribes and how she shows what she calls their "multifunctionality." By this she means that "scribes who were normally involved with preparing nonliterary documents could also write or copy literary texts and apparently did so; additionally, those who usually copied literary texts could produce

[91] Robinson mentions two letters from the Pachomian archive, one "written on a long thin irregular skin, obviously the leg of an animal that could not be used to produce leaves for a codex." This is about "an archival copy of a Coptic letter from the Pachomian Abbot Theodore . . . Fifth or Sixth century" (Chester Beatty Library ac. 1486). Another manuscript (Chester Beatty Ms. W. 145 =P.Köln 174) "makes a similar impression. It is a fourth-century copy of a letter of Pachomius" ("Pachomian Monastic Library," *Manuscripts of the Middle East* 4 [1989] 27). Robinson argues from the presence of such "primitive" documents that "the usual standards of a scriptorium were lacking" (ibid.). He concludes that "the presence of relatively unskilled products alongside of relatively professional codices may indicate a plurality of places of origin, and perhaps a contrast between what was produced within the Order and what came from outside" (ibid.). For me the presence of these letters indicates that leather preparation for codex production was going on at the site.

[92] A *caveat* here from Skeat: "Few subjects are more obscure than the methods of ancient book production. . . . of practical procedure we know nothing for certain" ("Early Christian Book Production," in *Cambridge History of the Bible*: *The West from the Fathers to the Reformation* [ed. Lampe] 2:57).

[93] Unless, of course, Sotas tore a page from a codex in his library to use as stationery for his letters. This explanation, although not impossible, seems at least improbable to me.

[94] Weber, "Zur Ausschmückung koptischer Bücher," *Enchoria* 3 (1973) 53–62. Kotsifou takes this letter as point of departure for larger observations on book production in her article "Books and Book Production in the Monastic Communities of Byzantine Egypt," in *The Early Christian Book* (ed. Klingshirn and Safran) 48–66.

and copy documents."[95] I envision Sotas in a similar milieu, as the head of a Christian community, where Christian manuscripts played an important role in both worship and study.[96] As we have seen earlier, Sotas sent a letter for a catechumen in the beginning of the gospel (PSI 9.1041), and the presbyters of Heracleopolis requested papa Sotas to educate a man by the name of Anos (P.Oxy. 36.2785). I concluded that Sotas also had an educational role in the Christian community at Oxyrhynchus. The study of scripture lies at the heart of Christian education; this of necessity involves manuscripts and thus book production.

Since such a large quantity of literary fragments has been recovered from the Oxyrhynchite garbage heaps, scholars have asked where the scribes copied these manuscripts. In a detailed study, Turner has demonstrated that Oxyrhynchus had a scriptorium where "classical" manuscripts were transcribed.[97] Taking Turner's lead, other scholars have wondered whether Oxyrhynchus also had a scriptorium that specialized in copying Christian texts, or at least if they had evidence for scholarly and editorial activities associated with a scriptorium.[98] Behind a material detail—these two

[95] Haines-Eitzen, *Guardians of Letters*, 32.

[96] For a later period, with examples from the fourth/fifth to seventh/eighth centuries, Schmelz notes: "Die Produktion von Büchern war eine Arbeit, die v.a. von Mönchen ausgeführt wurde: sowohl koinobitische Klöster, zu denen ein Scriptorium gehörte, als auch Anachoreten schrieben für den Eigenbedarf und für den Verkauf christliche Bücher ab" (*Kirchliche Amtsträger*, 164). A later example of a cleric involved in book production is a document by presbyter Herakleius (P. Yale Inv. 1318 = SB 14.11858; ed. George M. Parássoglou, fourth/fifth cent.): "I, Herakleios the presbyter, acknowledge that I have received from you the book for adornment on condition that I again within a month restore (it) to you without argument" (Llewelyn, "The Development of the Codex," in *New Docs* 7:249).

[97] Turner, "Scribes and Scholars of Oxyrhynchus," in *Akten des VIII. internationalen Kongresses für Papyrologie*, 141–46.

[98] An autographed manuscript from Oxyrhynchus caused Roberts to comment: "That Oxyrhynchus in the third century may have been something of a Christian intellectual centre is suggested by the presence there of an autograph manuscript of an anti-Jewish dialogue" (*Manuscript, Society and Belief*, 24 n. 5; re: P.Oxy. 17.2070; late-third cent.). Epp looked for signs of scholarly editing in Oxyrhynchus New Testament manuscript (from the second to the beginning of the fourth cent.) but concluded that there is no evidence: "We are not concerned with *scribal activity* per se, that is, normal or routine manuscript corrections or lection marks, including punctuation . . . our search is for editing marks—beyond the copying process—that reveal primarily a *reader*'s use and critical reaction to or interaction with the text" ("New Testament Papyri at Oxyrhynchus," in *Sayings of Jesus* [ed. Petersen et al.] 63). Epp found that "critical signs indicating scholarly editing . . . rarely if ever occur in the NT papyri at Oxyrhynchus or in other Christian literature there from the early period" (ibid.,

seemingly insignificant parchment scraps—I behold the contours of a Christian scriptorium at Oxyrhynchus.

Through these short and fragmentary letters, we have observed Sotas, a third-century Egyptian bishop from Oxyrhynchus, and his activities inside and outside of the church. In this chapter we witnessed his fundraising efforts and proximity to manuscript production. We also encountered him in Antioch, Syria, where he may have attended an ecclesiastical synod leading to the excommunication of Paul of Samosata.

So far we have searched for Christians on the Oxyrhynchite marketplace and in church. In the next chapters, we examine relations between Oxyrhynchite Christians and the Roman government.

67). This can be explained from the way these texts were used: "early Christian books were essentially *practical* and produced for use in the life of the Christian community" (ibid.).

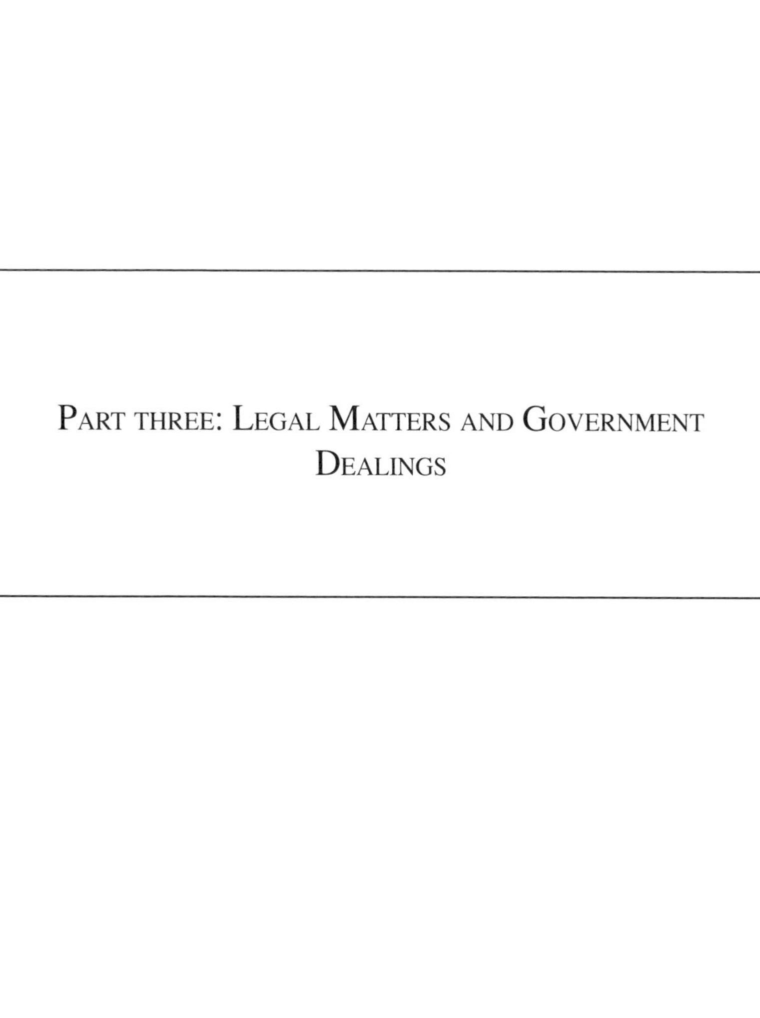

Part three: Legal Matters and Government Dealings

CHAPTER 6

Searching for Christians in Official Papers: Certificates of Sacrifice, Summons, and Property Confiscation

Having said farewell to papa Sotas and the church in Oxyrhynchus, we now enter the courthouse. I have chosen the image of the courthouse because several papyri relating to early Christians in Oxyrhynchus come to us in the form of legal documents from the middle of the third and early-fourth centuries. These represent the often difficult relations between Christians and the imperial government. The Roman state aimed to protect core Roman values exemplified through the acknowledgement of the traditional Roman deities. Christian sources, on the other hand, characterize this period as one of persecution.[1] Christians throughout the Roman Empire created epic narratives for their self-definition through stories of martyrs related in Christian hagiography. The documentary sources that we will examine in the next two chapters provide a different perspective and show a complex Roman bureaucracy, in which officials explicitly identify people as Christians, and their forms of both compliance and subtle resistance to edicts.

[1] When I use the word persecution, I am aware of its perspectival character, as Pohlsander also notes: "It is . . . good to bear in mind certain problems which may arise from the use of the word 'persecution.' 1. The term is an exclusively negative one, obscuring the fact that anti-Christian measures could serve positive ends. 2. The term is a decidedly one-sided one, viewing events from the Christian perspective only. . . . 3. The term covers a large variety of different measures. The anti-Christian measures of Nero have little in common with the anti-Christian measures of Decius" ("Religious Policy of Decius," *ANRW* 2.16.3 [1986] 1831).

In his classic treatment of the topic, Geoffrey E. M. De Ste. Croix distinguished three phases of the persecution.[2] The first phase ended before the fire in Rome in 64 C.E. The second phase, from the fire in 64 until 250 C.E., consisted of "only isolated, local persecutions." The third one, which will occupy us here, began with the Decian persecution in 250–251 and ended in 313 C.E.[3] De Ste. Croix does not discuss the first phase,[4] and neither shall I. Egypt simply does not appear "on the map," so to speak, in this earliest period.[5] Only from the end of the second phase, namely from the time of Septimius Severus, do we start to have evidence for persecution of Christians in Egypt,[6] and for the third phase in De Ste. Croix's reckoning do we have contemporary papyri from Oxyrhynchus.

The main sources for the history of the persecution in Egypt come from the writings of Eusebius and Christian martyr acts—Eusebius's *Ecclesiastical History* constituting the more important one.[7] Since these sources have

[2] De Ste. Croix pointed to the complexity of studying this period and the different approaches needed: "The persecution of the Christians in the Roman Empire has attracted the attention of scholars of many different kinds. The enormous volume of literature on the subject is partly due to the fact that it can be approached from many different directions: it offers a challenge to historians of the Roman empire . . . , to Roman lawyers, to ecclesiastical historians, to Christian theologians, and to students of Roman religion and Greek religion. In fact all these approaches are relevant and they must all be used together" ("Why Were the Early Christians Persecuted?," *Past and Present* 26 [1963] 6–38, at 6; repr., idem, *Christian Persecution, Martyrdom, and Orthodoxy* [ed. Whitby and Streeter] 105–52).

[3] De Ste. Croix, "Why Were the Early Christians Persecuted?," 7.

[4] Ibid., 7. This notion is contested, see, e.g., Lieu, "Accusations of Jewish Persecution," in *Tolerance and Intolerance* (ed. Stanton and Stroumsa) 279–98 (= eadem, *Neither Jew Nor Greek?* 135–50).

[5] As Harnack observed: "Die empfindlichste Lücke in unserem Wissen von der ältesten Kirchengeschichte ist unsere fast vollständige Unkenntnis der Geschichte des Christentums in Alexandrien und Ägypten" (*Mission und Ausbreitung* 2:706).

[6] A fourth-century Coptic text preserves a tradition of the Severan persecution at Oxyrhynchus (P.Oxy. inv. 4 1B 74/K[a]). Mistakes in chronology and a confusion of bishops make clear that this is not a contemporary text, unlike the papyri discussed in these chapters. Edition by Alcock, "Persecution under Septimius Severus," *Enchoria* 11 (1982) 1–5. Prior to the edition, Reymond and Barns had translated the text in their *Four Martyrdoms from the Pierpont Morgan Coptic Codices,* 16. Schenke gives the Coptic in a standardized spelling of Middle Egyptian in "Bemerkungen zum P.Hamb. Bil. 1 und zum altfayumischen Dialekt der koptischen Sprache," *Enchoria* 18 (1991) 69–93, at 86–88 (transcription on 87).

[7] On the persecutions in Egypt, see Delehaye, "Les Martyrs d'Égypte," *AnBoll* 40 (1922) 5–154 and 299–364. Clarysse has supplemented his work with the evidence from newly discovered texts in "The Coptic Martyr Cult," in *Martyrium in Multidisciplinary Perspective* (ed. Lamberigts and van Deun) 377–95.

Christian authors, they evidently have a bias toward reporting the heroic confessions of faith and martyrdom of Christians. As De Ste. Croix remarked, "The great majority of the trials of Christians we know about in detail end in conviction and a death sentence."[8] The persecutions of Christians in the mid-third and early-fourth century dealt blows to the church, but the number of Christians actually killed remains unknown.[9] Additionally canons of church councils dealing with the aftermath of the persecution concede that not all Christians brought before the Roman officials ended in death.[10]

The traces of the persecutions that appear in the papyrological record allow us to catch a glimpse of the impact that the persecutions had on the whole population of Egypt, both Christians and others. These papyri preserve contemporaneous evidence. Several papyrus fragments add another point of view and depict not only the Christian angle of looking at martyrdom through persecution but also a Roman perspective.[11]

Emperor Decius and the *Libelli*[12]

When Decius became emperor in late 249 C.E., the empire was in dire straits. As part of his reform program aimed at the restoration of Roman values,[13]

[8] De Ste. Croix, "Why Were the Early Christians Persecuted?," 13.

[9] For the Decian times, Frend wonders: "How many victims were there? Porphyry believed that 'thousands' had died in the persecution of Decius and Valerian. The writers of the Ancient World, however, had only their personal experiences and rumors to rely on. Accurate statistics are the product of the needs of modern government. Dionysius of Alexandria states that 'very many' were killed in Egyptian towns and villages, but he only names seventeen victims. . . . Deaths over the whole Empire may probably be numbered in hundreds rather than thousands, but they were enough to vindicate the martyrspirit at the moment when it was in danger of foundering amid the outward prosperity of the Church" (*Martyrdom and Persecution,* 413).

[10] E.g., the canons of Peter of Alexandria, and of the Councils of Elvira and Ancyra. In the end, the attitude toward the persecution led to splits in the churches (Donatists).

[11] Clarysse: "Some new contemporary papyri allow us a view of events from the side of the Roman administration" ("Coptic Martyr Cult," 377).

[12] For discussions, see Knipfing, "Libelli of the Decian Persecution," *HTR* 16 (1923) 345–90; Clarke, "Some Observations," *Antichthon* 3 (1969) 63–76; Keresztes, "The Decian *libelli*," *Latomus* 34 (1975) 761–81; Pohlsander, "Religious Policy of Decius," 1826–42; Rives, "The Decree of Decius and the Religion of Empire," *JRS* 89 (1999) 135–54; Selinger, *Die Religionspolitik des Kaisers Decius*; and idem, *Mid-Third Century Persecutions*.

[13] Frend, *Martyrdom and Persecution*, 405. See. e.g., also Pohlsander, who points to Decius's political conservatism ("Religious Policy of Decius," 1829–31) and Sordi, "I rapporti

he first released an edict that ordered all subjects in the empire to perform a sacrifice. Christian authors, ancient and modern, have often interpreted this edict as a tool specifically designed to eliminate Christians.[14] Yet rather than simply wanting to eradicate Christians, Decius wanted to get the traditional gods of the empire on his side.[15] This edict marked the beginning of a shift in Roman-Christian relations.[16]

We have rich contemporary sources dealing with the consequences of the Decian edict for Christians.[17] The correspondence and treatises (especially *De lapsis*) of Cyprian of Carthage paint a vivid picture of the impact that this edict had on the Christians in North Africa. The main spokesperson for

fra il Cristianesimo," *ANRW* 2.23.1 (1980) 340–74 (esp. "V. La persecuzione di Decio," 359–64). According to Eusebius (*Hist. eccl.* 6.49.1), Decius waged a persecution against the Christians out of hatred for his predecessor Philip, a Christian himself (Χριστιανὸν ὄντα), or so Eusebius claims earlier (*Hist. eccl.* 6.34.1). Rives remarks that the tradition that "Philip himself was a Christian and that Decius was personally hostile to him" does not "seem particularly well founded, the story is a more reliable guide to Christian perceptions than to Decius's motivations." However, "it is possible that Philip's apparent interest in the Church may have led some Christians to interpret Decius's perceived hostility as a reaction to his predecessor" ("Decree of Decius," 140).

[14] The question remains whether Decius issued the general sacrifice because of Christians or whether he had a larger agenda. I believe the latter is the case, although Cyprian reports the emperor as saying after the death of Fabian, bishop of Rome: "that he would hear much more patiently and tolerantly that a rival prince had been raised up against him than that a priest of God had been appointed at Rome" (Cyprian, *Ep.* 55.9). See Frend, *Martyrdom and Persecution*, 433 n. 105. To me this "quote" seems more anecdotal than historical.

[15] "In dieser Notlage kam es zum Ausbruch einer wahren religiösen Angst und zu unerhörten staatlichen Maßnahmen, um die Gnade der Götter zurückzugewinnen. . . . Die Form, in der Decius im Jahr 250 alle Reichsangehörigen an das Opfer heranführte, entsprach dem Zug der um sich greifenden Militarisierung des Lebens und der zunehmenden Dienstverpflichtung aller Bürger" (Vogt, *Religiösität der Christenverfolger*, 21). Pohlsander expresses his agreement with Vogt on this issue ("Religious Policy of Decius," 1837–39). See also Frend, *Martyrdom and Persecution*, 405–6.

[16] Previously, Christians had been put to death but these persecutions had been local and incidental (Barnes, "Legislation," *JRS* 58 [1968] 48; De Ste. Croix, "Why Were the Early Christians Persecuted?," 7). As Barnes concluded, our sources do not contain evidence of imperial legislation directed against Christians until the Decian edict ("Legislation," 44, 48, 50).

[17] Selinger cautions that these sources are biased: "The letters of contemporary Christians are crucial for the understanding of the effects of Decius's and Valerian's laws on the Church. These letters were carefully selected for the discourse within the Church. . . . Most of the letters were written in self-defense or for the pastoral guidance of others" (*Mid-Third Century Persecutions*, 18).

Egypt, Dionysius, bishop of Alexandria (in office 247/8–264/5),[18] in a letter to his Antiochean counterpart Fabian, relates the events in Alexandria. The troubles for the Christians started in 249, a year before Decius's edict, with mob violence in Alexandria.[19] At the issuance of the edict, Dionysius (*apud* Eusebius) described the situation as follows:

> The edict arrived, and it was almost like that which was predicted by our Lord, well-nigh the most terrible of all, so as, if possible, to cause to stumble even the elect. Howsoever that be, all cowered with fear. And of many of the more eminent persons, some came forward immediately through fear, others in public positions were compelled to do so by their business, and others were dragged by those around them. Called by name (ὀνομαστί τε καλούμενοι) they approached the impure and holy sacrifices, some pale and trembling, as if they were not for sacrificing but rather to be themselves the sacrifices and victims to the idols, so that the large crowd that stood around heaped mockery upon them, and it was evident that they were by nature cowards in everything, cowards both to die and to sacrifice. But others ran eagerly towards the altars, affirming by their forwardness that they had not been Christians even formerly; concerning whom the Lord very truly predicted that they shall hardly be saved. Of the rest, some followed one or other of these, others fled; some were captured, and of these some went as far as bonds and imprisonment, and certain, when they had been shut up for many days, then forswore themselves even before coming into court, while others, who remained firm for a certain time under tortures, subsequently gave in.[20]

According to Dionysius, many Christians observed Decius's edict and sacrificed. After this account, he detailed martyrdoms of Alexandrine Christians, who had refused to comply.

[18] Delehaye characterizes Dionysius as "le témoin le plus autorisé des souffrances de l'église d'Égypte durant la persécution de Dèce" ("Martyrs d'Égypte," 11). Unfortunately, unlike the large corpus of letters and theological treatises of his contemporary, the Latin speaking bishop Cyprian in Carthage, Dionysius's works have not been preserved in toto. It is only thanks to Eusebius that we have fragments of Dionysius's writings, mainly letters. For his works and an introduction to his life and importance, see Bienert, *Dionysius von Alexandrien*. Bienert called Dionysius "einer der bedeutendsten Bischöfe der frühen christlichen Kirche. . . . Dionysius hat beide Verfolgungen [i.e., under Decius and Valerian] miterlebt und sich in dieser schwierigen Zeit als kluger, besonnener und tatkräftiger Kirchenpolitiker und als philosophisch gebildeter Theologe erwiesen" (ibid., 1).

[19] Eusebius, *Hist. eccl.* 6.41.1–9.

[20] Ibid., 6.41.10–13 (trans. Oulton, 2:103, 105).

Proofs of compliance with the edict have been found in Egypt. Since 1893 a steady stream of papyrus documents from Egypt has added documentary evidence to Cyprian's and Dionysius's literary accounts of the Decian period.[21] These papyri provide important insight into the workings of Decius's edict.[22] The Egyptian soil has now yielded a total of forty-six *libelli*.[23] Knipfing describes these documents as follows:

> The libellus was both private request and official attestation, or more specifically it was a petition (βιβλίδιον) of an inhabitant of the empire addressed to local authorities requesting that these countersign his [or her][24] declaration of the pagan religious loyalty, and give written testimony of the pagan sacrifice performed by him [or her] in their presence, by adding their official attestation of loyalty and sacrifice.[25]

[21] In his enumeration of sources Rives also included the *Passio Pionii* (narrating the events at Smyrna in Asia Minor), although he admits that its historicity is disputed ("Decree of Decius," 136). With these sources, it should be remembered that the persecution in the Greek speaking East differed from that in the Latin West, and thus that we have to be cautious in applying the sources from Latin speaking North Africa to the situation in Egypt, the Greek speaking part of North Africa.

[22] Pohlsander puts it even more strongly: "For our understanding of the nature of Decius' decree the libelli are of far greater value than the numerous references in Christian sources" ("Religious Policy of Decius," 182).

[23] Knipfing collected 41 of these *libelli*; most of them had previously been published elsewhere. To his list should be added P.Oxy. 41.2990; P.Oxy. 58.3929; PSI 7.779; SB 6.9048; and P.Lips. 2.152. See also Reinhold Scholl in P.Lips. 2, "Liste der bisher publizierten *Libelli*," 226–32; and the "Konkordanz der bisher publizierten *Libelli*," 240–41. In editions of these *libelli*, one frequently finds them referred to as "certificate of sacrifice" (e.g., P.Oxy. 4.658; P.Oxy. 41.2990; and P.Oxy. 58.3929). This description is not quite correct according to Leadbetter: "the *libellus* is not a certificate of sacrifice, meaning a document issued by the state upon the completion of a prescribed act, but rather a request from the sacrificer asking for confirmation of an act publicly performed" ("*Libellus* of the Decian Persecution," *NewDocs* 2:181). See, e.g., also Delehaye, who typifies them as "attestations, délivrées à ceux qui avaient satisfait aux prescriptions de l'édit" ("Martyrs d'Égypte," 13). Henri Leclercq refers to them as "certificats d'apostasie" ("Libelli," 80).

[24] The majority of *libelli* found was issued to women, a fact that Knipfing himself states: "our forty-one libelli transmit thirty petitioners' names intact. The names of women predominate over those of men in the proportion of seventeen to thirteen. For the single village of Theadelphia the proportion is two to one (fourteen to seven)" (Knipfing, "Libelli of the Decian Persecution," 356). See Scholl, "Auswertung der Liste der *Libelli*," in P.Lips. 2, 234.

[25] Knipfing, "Libelli of the Decian Persecution," 345.

Some people wrote these proofs of sacrifice themselves, but in most cases professional scribes penned the petitions.[26] Having given a preliminary sketch of the situation, we now turn to Oxyrhynchus and ask what we can learn about the impact of the Decian edict there.

Libelli from Oxyrhynchus

At Oxyrhynchus four *libelli* stating observance of the Decian edict have been found: P.Oxy. 4.658; P.Oxy. 12.1464; P.Oxy. 41.2990; and P.Oxy. 58.3929.[27] In the next sections, I provide first the text and translation of these *libelli* and then a discussion.

Libellus *for Aurelius L . . . and Children (P.Oxy. 4.658)*[28]

The papyrus, measuring 7.2 x 15.4 cm, confirms the sacrifice performed by a man and his two children on 14 June 250.

τοῖς ἐπὶ τῶν ἱερῶν [καὶ
θυσιῶν πόλ[εως
παρ᾽ Αὐρηλίου Λ̣[.....
θίωνος Θεοδώρου μη[τρὸς
Παντωνυμίδος ἀπὸ τ̣ῆ̣[ς
αὐτῆς πόλεως. ἀεὶ μὲν
θύων καὶ σπένδων [τοῖ]ς
θεο̣ῖ̣ς [δ]ιετέλ[ουν ἐ]π̣ὶ̣ δ̣ὲ
καὶ νῦν ἐνώπιον ὑμῶν
κατὰ τὰ κελευσθ[έ]ν[τα
ἔσπεισα καὶ ἔθυσα κα[ὶ
τῶν ἱερῶν ἐγευσάμην
ἅμα τῷ̣ υἱῷ̣ μου Αὐρη-
λίῳ̣ Διοσκόρῳ̣ καὶ τῇ
θυγατρί μου Ἀυρηλίᾳ̣

[26] Leadbetter, "*Libellus* of the Decian Persecution," 181.

[27] Four out of the forty-six total come from Oxyrhynchus. The majority of the *libelli* come from the Fayum.

[28] Ed. princ. Grenfell and Hunt, P.Oxy. 4.658 (1904) 49–50. The papyrus belongs to the Beinecke Rare Book and Manuscript Library (P.CtYBR inv. 65). Grenfell and Hunt restored the lacuna in line 8 as [δ]ιετέλ[εσα ἔ]τ̣ι̣. Yet on the basis of P.Oxy. 58.3929, Rea could restore it to [δ]ιετέλ[ουν ἐ]π̣ι̣ δέ (read ἐπεὶ δέ; note to lines 6–7).

Λαΐδι, ἀξιῶ ὑμᾶς ὑπο-
σημιώσασθαί μοι.
(ἔτους) α´ Αὐτοκράτορος Καίσαρος
Γαίου Μεσσίου Κυίντου
Τραιανοῦ Δεκίου
Εὐσεβοῦ[ς Εὐ]τυχοῦς
[Σεβασ]τοῦ Παῦ]νι κ´
[.....]ν( )[
. . . .

1. and 12. ϊερων, 8. *l.* ἐπεὶ, 12. ἐγευσαμη̄, 16. λαϊδι, ο of υπο above the line, 19. γαϊου, 20. τραϊανου.

Translation

To the (commissioners) of offerings and sacrifices at the city from Aurelius L(?). . .thion son of Theodorus and Pantonymis, of the said city. Always have I continued to sacrifice and pour libations to the gods, and since now too in your presence in accordance with the orders I poured a libation and sacrificed and tasted the sacrifices together with my son Aurelius Dioscorus and my daughter Aurelia Lais, I request that you subscribe to this fact for me.
Year 1 of Imperator Caesar Gaius Messius Quintus Trajanus Decius Pius Felix Augustus, Pauni 20.

Libellus *for Aurelius Gaius, Taos, and Children (P.Oxy. 12.1464)*[29]

Thirteen days after the previous petition, on 27 June 250, a couple and their three children certified their compliance with the Decian edict. The light colored papyrus containing their proof of sacrifice measures 9.8 x 17.2 cm. The sheet was folded. The preserved part of the bottom margin contains no writing, which proves that, contrary to other *libelli*, this papyrus did not have signatures and names from officials; we only have the subscription of the person who sacrificed. The scribe, Aurelius Sarapion, alias Chaeremon, whose

[29] Ed. princ. Grenfell and Hunt, P.Oxy. 12.1464 (1916) 190–91. The papyrus is housed in the British Library in London (BM Papyrus 2457). See also, e.g., Knipfing, "Libelli of the Decian Persecution," 365–66.

name we know from the subscription, wrote the document in a professional documentary hand.[30]

The papyrus was reused afterwards, for the back, against the fibers, contains scribblings in two different hands with names and amounts of drachmae.

[τοῖς] ἐπὶ τῶν θυσιῶν αἱρεθεῖσι τῆς
[Ὀ]ξυρυγχ̣ε̣ιτῶν πόλεως
[παρ]ὰ Αὐρηλίου Γαιῶνος Ἀμμωνίου
[μη]τρὸς Ταεῦτος. ἀεὶ μὲν θύειν καὶ
[σπέ]νδειν καὶ σ̣έ̣βειν θεοῖς εἰθισμένος
[κατ]ὰ τὰ κελευσθέντα ὑπὸ τῆς θείας κρίσεως
[καὶ] νῦν ἐνώπιον ὑμῶν θύων καὶ σπέν-
[δω]ν καὶ γευ[σ]άμενος τῶν ἱερείων ἅμα
[Τα?]ῷ̣τι γυναικὶ [κ]αὶ Ἀμμωνίῳ καὶ Ἀμμω-
[νι]α̣ν̣ῷ υἱοῖς καὶ ε..α[31] θυγατρὶ δι᾽ ἐ̣μοῦ κ̣[α]ὶ̣
[ἀξι]ῶ̣ ὑποσημιώσασθαί μοι. (ἔτους) α´
[Αὐ]τοκράτορος Κ[α]ί̣[σαρο]ς Γαίου Μεσσίου
[Κυί]ντου Τ[ρ]αιανοῦ Δεκίου Εὐσεβοῦς
[Εὐ]τυχοῦς Σεβαστοῦ Ἐπεὶφ γ´. Αὐρή[λιος
[Γαι]ὼν ἐπιδέδωκα. Αὐρήλ(ιος) Σαραπίων
[ὁ κ(αὶ)] Χαιρήμων ἔγρ[αψα] ὑπὲρ αὐτοῦ μ̣ὴ̣ [εἰδό-
[τος] γράμματα.

---

3. γαϊωνος (so in 15 [γαϊ]ων), 7. ϋμων, 8. ϊερειων, 12. γαϊου.

Translation

To the commissioners of sacrifices at Oxyrhynchus from Aurelius Gaius son of Ammonius and Taeus. Always has it been my habit to sacrifice and pour libations and worship the gods in accordance with the orders of the divine decree, and now I have in your presence sacrificed and made libations and tasted the offerings together with Taos my wife, Ammonius and Ammonianus my sons, and . . . my daughter, acting through me, and I request you to certify my statement. Year 1 of the

[30] In the second line, he expanded the final sigma of the word πόλεως to the right margin, to fill out the line.

[31] Grenfell and Hunt restored the text here as Θ̣έκ̣λ̣α̣; however, the papyrus is hardly legible in this line and the reconstruction impossible (see footnote 61 below).

> Emperor Caesar Gaius Messius Quintus Trajanus Decius Pius Felix Augustus, Epeiph 3. I, Aurelius Gaion, have delivered (the petition). I Aurelius Sarapion, also called Chaeremon, wrote on his behalf as he is illiterate.

Subscriptions on a Libellus *(P.Oxy. 41.2990)*[32]

This battered piece of papyrus, barely larger than a credit card (7.5 x 10 cm), preserves the subscription of two officials, each of whom wrote presumably in their own hand. The first subscription, written in a light brown faded ink, presents more difficulty to decipher than the second one written in dark ink.

[Α]ὐρ(ήλιος) Ἡρακ̣λ̣[ε]ί̣δ̣η̣[ς]
εἶδον ὑμᾶς θύοντας
κ̣α̣ὶ̣ γευομ̣ένους.
(second hand) Μ(άρκος) Αὐ(ρήλιος) Σεσονγῶσις
καὶ ὡς χρηματίζω εἶδον
ὑμᾶς θύοντας καὶ {γε-}
γευσαμένους
τῶν ἱερείων.

---

4. μ΄αυ΄, 6–7. or γεγευσ{α}μένους, 8. ϊερειων

Translation

> I, Aurelius Heracleides, have seen you (pl.) offering and tasting. I, Marcus Aurelius Sesongosis and whoever I may be styled, have seen you (pl.) offering and tasting the sacrificial food.

Libellus *for Aurelius Amois, Taamois, and Taharpaesis (P.Oxy. 58.3929)*[33]

This small sheet of papyrus (7.5 x 12 cm) contains the fourth published *libellus* from Oxyrhynchus. Written in the Egyptian month Epeiph (25 June–24 July) 250, it lacks the day. A professional scribe has written the main text of the document in a small, cursive script that slopes upward. In contrast to this fast cursive, the subscription appears penned in an attractive uncial that would

[32] Ed. princ. Coles, P.Oxy. 41.2990 (1972) 89.
[33] Ed. princ. Rea, P.Oxy. 58.3929 (1991) 39–41.

not have looked bad in a book. The name of this scribe has disappeared in a damaged part of the papyrus.

τοῖς ἀναδοθεῖσ̣ι̣ ἐπὶ θυσιῶ(ν)
  κώμης Θῶσβεως
παρὰ Αὐρηλίου Ἀμόϊτος χρη(ματίζοντος) μη-
τρὸς Ταα̣μόϊτος ἀπὸ κώμ̣ης
Θῶσβεως. ἀεὶ μὲν θύων
καὶ σπένδων τοῖς θεοῖς διε-
τέλουν, ἐπὶ δὲ καὶ νῦν ἐνώπιον ὑμῶν κατὰ τὰ κελευσθ̣(έντα)
ἔθυσα καὶ ἔσπισα καὶ τῶν ἱερί-
ων ἐγευσάμην ἅμα τῇ μη-
τρί μου Ταμόϊτι καὶ τῇ
ἀδελφῇ μου Ταρπ̣α̣ήσ̣ι̣ο̣ς,
αὐτὸ τοῦτο ἀξιῶ ὑποσημι-
ώσασθαί μοι. (ἔτους) α´
Αὐτοκράτορος Καίσαρος
Γαίου Μεσσίου Κυΐντου
Τραϊανοῦ Δεκίου Εὐσεβοῦ[ς
Εὐ]τυχοῦς Σεβαστοῦ, Ἐπειφ . [
(second hand) Αὐρηλιος Ἀμόϊς
ἐπιδέδωκα. Αὐρήλιος
. . . . [. . .]. ίων ἔγραψα ὑπὲρ
. . . .
(On the back, along the fibers)
(first hand?) ἀπογρ(αφὴ) Ἀμοϊτᾶ μητ(ρὸς) Ταμόϊτ(ος).

1. σ̣ι̣ rewritten, θυσιω̄, 3. χρη̄, 7. *l.* ἐπεί, 8. κελευσ$^{\theta}$?, 9. *l.* ἔσπεισα, 9–10. *l.* ἱερείων, 12. *l.* Ταρπαήσει, 13–14. *l.* ὑποσημειώσασθαι, 17. πραϊανου, 21. ϋπερ, 22. απογρSαμοιταμητταμοιτ

Translation

To the commissioners of sacrifices of the village of Thosbis, from Aurelius Amois styled as the son of his mother Taamois from the village of Thosbis.
Always have I continued to sacrifice and pour libations to the gods, and since now too in your presence in accordance with the orders I

sacrificed and poured a libation and tasted the sacrificial meats together with my mother Taamois and my sister Taharpaesis, I request that (you) subscribe to this fact for me. Year 1 of Imperator Caesar Gaius Messius Quintus Traianus Decius, Pius Felix Augustus, Epeiph . . .

(second hand) I, Aurelius Amois, have delivered (the petition). I, Aurelius . . . ion, wrote on his behalf
(On the back, along the fibers)
(first hand?) Registration of Amoitas, mother Taamois.

The Commission of Sacrifices at Oxyrhynchus

These four documents make clear that Decius's edict engendered much bureaucratic effort. In the case of the papyrus that contained only the subscription (P.Oxy. 41.2990), we witnessed two officials, each with an inkwell, who penned their subscription after observing how people sacrificed and ate the sacrificial food. Given the many participants, this task must have occupied them for a good while. The *libelli* make clear that local commissions were established to oversee the sacrifices.[34] The commissioners had the status of town officials assigned by the city council (βουλή).[35] At Oxyrhynchus, Aurelius Heracleides and Marcus Aurelius Sesongosis,[36] the subscribers of

[34] The one at Oxyrhynchus, for instance, is addressed as "to the commissioners of sacrifices at Oxyrhynchus," τοῖς ἐπὶ τῶν θυσιῶν αἱρεθεῖσι τῆς Ὀξυρυγχειτῶν πόλεως (P.Oxy. 12.1464.1–2). The address varies in our papyri, but always contains the words τοῖς ἐπὶ τῶν θυσιῶν. In the thirty-four *libelli* found at the site of ancient Philadelphia in the Fayum, the witnesses are the same two men, Aurelius Serenus and Aurelius Hermas (granted that the part containing the prescription is preserved). See Leadbetter, "*Libellus* of the Decian Persecution," 182, and also the overview in Scholl, P.Lips. 2, "Auswertung der Liste der *Libelli*," 235. The existence of local commissions is also known outside of Egypt, for instance for Carthage, Smyrna, Rome, Alexandria, and Spain, see, e.g., Knipfing, "Libelli of the Decian Persecution," 352, 354.

[35] Knipfing, "Libelli of the Decian Persecution," 351–52. In another *libellus*, P.Ryl. 1.12, found at Arsinoe, the official signing the certificate identifies himself as the *prytanis* (ibid., 351 and 377).

[36] The name Σεσονγῶσις (or Σεσογγῶσις or Σεσονῶσις) occurs a few times in the papyri (most often B.C.E.), but never the *tria nomina* Marcus Aurelius Sesongosis (see Preisigke, *Namenbuch*, 381; Foraboschi, *Onomasticon*, 292; Hagedorn, *WörterListen*, http://www.zaw.uni-heidelberg.de/hps/pap/WL/WL.pdf (accessed September 19, 2008) 104; and DDBDP).

P.Oxy. 41.2990, form (part of) the local commission.[37]

The Oxyrhynchus *libelli* contain almost identical phraseology (especially 658 and 3929; 1464 has a slightly different form), which proves that they followed a standard text. They lack physical descriptions of the persons involved (such as whether or not they had scars) and any indications of their age and place of residence, although several *libelli* found in the Fayum contain this kind of information.[38] Apart from the fact that such descriptions would have provided interesting information for us, the difference between the Oxyrhynchite and Fayumic *libelli* shows that local commissions had some freedom in composing their sacrificial formulae. The general agreement in the wording of all the known *libelli*, however, indicates that the government in Alexandria or even the imperial government had passed down instructions for scripting them. The involvement of the provincial government also becomes clear from the time span in which this general sacrifice took place. All *libelli* found in Egypt date from the period 12 June to 14 July, a short span of just thirty-three days.[39] From Cyprian and other sources, we know that other regions of the empire had different dates, which indicates that administrators

[37] Neither man is known from other papyri. Also, with the text's top broken off, we do not know whether they were the only two witnesses, or whether there were more people on the committee at Oxyrhynchus. It is unknown where they were located exactly. Neither Aurelius Heracleides nor Marcus Aurelius Sesongosis mention their specific function, although Sesongosis adds "whoever I may be styled" (ὡς χρηματίζω), which signifies that he occupied official positions. This and his *tria nomina* indicates that Sesongosis belonged to the upper class. Knipfing describes the task of these commissioners as follows: "The local commissioners . . . presided over the sacrificers, certified in the libelli to their due performance, and controlled the number and identity of sacrificers and nonsacrificers by means of the census and tax rolls. These commissions were domiciliary, for their authority extended over all the inhabitants dwelling within their respective districts" ("Libelli of the Decian Persecution," 354–55).

[38] "Wir besitzen lediglich 5 explizite Altersangaben mit 4 näheren Beschreibungen der Petenten," Scholl noted (P.Lips. 2, "Auswertung der Liste der *Libelli*," 233). The range in age is 72 (Scholl no. 1), 60 (no. 4), 11 (no. 6), 32 (no. 10) and 35 (no. 34). The first four also contain a short description; three of them have scars on various places, the fourth one, Aurelius Asesis is "diseased, feeble" (ἐπισινής; Scholl translates: "etwas schwachsinnig," P.Lips. 2, "Auswertung der Liste der Libelli," 233, no. 10). About residence, Scholl remarks: "Nur bei dem Opferort Theadelphia kommt es vor, daß Personen, die dort opfern, aus einem anderen Ort stammen" (ibid., 233–34).

[39] Montevecchi, *Papirologia*, 289; Knipfing, "Libelli of the Decian Persecution," 350; Scholl, P.Lips. 2, "Auswertung der Liste der *Libelli*," 234.

at the provincial level determined the date for the sacrifice.[40]

We see here a complex and systematic bureaucratic apparatus, which stretched from the imperial level of the edict, to the provincial government, down to local officials in cities and villages, where eventually sacrifices were held and certifications filed.

Who Had to Sacrifice?

In order to reconstruct more fully the Christian life in Oxyrhynchus, we must discuss now the persons for whom the imperial edict intended the measures. Scholarly opinions range from suspected Christians only, to free citizens, to the entire population of the empire. Behind this issue lies the question whether one can detect any Christians in these papyrus documents. As in the children's rhyme, we have three answers to this question: "yes, no, maybe so."

Initially scholars—papyrologists and church historians alike[41]—thought that only suspected Christians had to come forward to sacrifice and obtain a *libellus*. They based this perception upon Dionysius's report in his letter to Fabian. For instance, Grenfell and Hunt describe P.Oxy. 4.658 as "an example of the *libelli* or declarations which suspects were compelled to make that they had sacrificed to the pagan gods."[42] As a result of this point of view, scholars interpreted all *libelli* as providing direct information about (suspected) Christians; people who either turned out not to be Christians after all or Christians who had apostatized. This made the *libelli* tremendously important documentary sources for early Christianity. They were so important, that Grenfell and Hunt published P.Oxy. 4.658 not under the heading "Documents"

[40] Rives reconstructs the procedure as follows: "Although there was no doubt some local variation, the general procedure followed in the edict's implementation is clear enough. When the officials of a particular region received it, they arranged for local magistrates to oversee the proceedings and set a date by which everyone would be required to have sacrificed. These dates, it seems, were set locally, and not by the central administration. During this time, people would perform their sacrifices before the officials and present their petitions, which the officials would duly sign" ("Decree of Decius," 149). See Knipfing for an enumeration of different dates throughout the empire ("Libelli of the Decian Persecution," 353–54).

[41] Knipfing mentions a large list of scholars ("Libelli of the Decian Persecution," 361 n. 106).

[42] P.Oxy. 4.658, 49. In defense of Grenfell and Hunt, I should note that at the time they published this papyrus only three others were available (although they mention only two of those).

but in the section called "Theological Fragments."[43]

Henri Leclercq proposed an opposite interpretation of the *libelli*.[44] According to this scholar, Decius had indeed issued his edict specifically against Christians.[45] He reconstructs the situation as follows by interpreting what Dionysius of Alexandria described in his letter to Fabian as a round of mass sacrifices held at the beginning of the persecution. Men, women and children came forward and performed the sacrifices upon hearing their names called from a government list (ὀνομαστί τε καλούμενοι). Upon doing so, Leclercq argues, their names went onto a public list, which eliminated the need for them to receive a *libellus*.[46] He considered these mass sacrifices, apart from the registration, as equivalent to the common Roman practice of *supplicatio*, a solemn procession of thanksgiving to the gods that lasted several days and ended in sacrifice.[47] The commissioners issued *libelli* only after the general sacrifices had taken place—in the extension period—to people who either had not had the opportunity to sacrifice for reasons such as illness or business obligations or to Christians.[48] Leclercq hypothesizes that many of those in need of *libelli* would have been Christians.[49] But, he wondered, would Christian apostates file the same form as the pagans, who somehow had not

[43] P.Oxy. 4.658 appears immediately after the "New Sayings of Jesus" and the "Fragment of a Lost Gospel" (P.Oxy. 4.654 and P.Oxy 4.655—now known to be both manuscripts of the *Gospel of Thomas*) and two biblical texts (Genesis and Hebrews).

[44] Leclercq, "Dèce," *DALC* 9.1 (1920) 309–39. Ten years later, under the heading "Libelli," he supplemented his earlier article by updating his list of all *libelli* published until then (from 25 in 1920 to 32 in 1930) without restating his earlier positions (idem, "Libelli," 80–85).

[45] Leclercq quotes the *Acta Maximi*: "Decretum ut omnes christiani relicta superflua superstitione cognoscant verum principem cui omnia subjacent, et ejus deos adorent." Despite the fact that this is a "passage isolé," he still holds that "il faudrait admettre que l'édit mentionnait spécialement les chrétiens, ce qui n'est pas invraisemblable" ("Dèce," 315, with quote from *Acta Maximi* 3).

[46] "Les noms de ceux qui avaient sacrifié en public furent probablement rayés sur le rôle d'appel au fur et à mesure de leur comparution, ce qui rendait superflu pour eux l'obtention d'un certificat" (ibid.; see an almost identical statement on page 335).

[47] He concludes: "Dèce n'innovait donc rien lorsqu'il prescrivait à tous les habitants . . . de se rendre aux temples à un jour fixé et d'y immoler les victimes" (ibid., 311).

[48] "Ceux qui avaient refusé d'obéir étaient jetés en prison, tenus pour chrétiens ou traités comme tels. Restaient ceux qui s'étaient soustraits à la formalité par la fuite ou qui n'avaient pu s'y conformer par suite d'un déplacement prolongé, d'une maladie ou d'une raison valable quelconque" (ibid., 335).

[49] "Les chrétiens n'étaient pas seuls dans ce cas [i.e., of those having missed the first round of sacrificing] . . . mais il n'était pas douteux que parmi ceux qui seraient dans ce cas, se trouveraient beaucoup de chrétiens" (ibid., 315).

sacrificed yet? I find this question justified, for—as Leclercq observed—all the *libelli* contain the word "always" with a form of the verb for offering (e.g., "I have always sacrificed," ἀεὶ θύων/θύουσα). Such a statement, with emphasis here on *always*, would constitute an "obvious lie"[50] for apostatizing Christians who had not sacrificed all their lives. Leclercq postulated that two forms existed: one for pagans who had missed the first round of sacrifice and one for the apostatizing Christians. Yet he had to admit that no forms of the latter type had been found. (Now we have almost double the number of *libelli* that Leclercq had and still none of that type.)[51] This he explained as follows: Christians who had obtained a *libellus* after apostatizing quickly destroyed these documents once the persecution had ended when they wanted reentry into the church.[52] Thus, Leclercq answered "no" to the question of whether the *libelli* give any information about Christians, for all known *libelli* consisted only of the kind issued to pagans.

With the discovery of still more *libelli* and additional scholarship, we see clearly that not just suspected Christians had to perform the sacrifices but all inhabitants of the empire.[53] In answer to our question, whether we can

[50] "un mensonge évident" (ibid., 336).

[51] Leclercq reaches this conclusion as follows: "A défaut d'un libellus destiné à un chrétien et mentionnant l'abandon de sa foi, nous ne sommes pas en mesure d'affirmer qu'on ait fait usage d'une formule différente de celle de nos vingt-cinq exemplaires et qu'il ait existé des libelli d'orthodoxie pour les païens retardataires, et des libelli d'apostasie pour les fidèles jusque-là réfractaires, nous pouvons toutefois admettre que cette deuxième catégorie de libelli ait existé" (ibid., 337).

[52] Leclerq: "ceux qui avaient obtenu un libellus d'apostasie avaient tout intérêt à le détruire une fois la persécution passée. Beaucoup d'apostats n'eurent rien de plus à coeur que de rentrer dans l'Église" (ibid.). This argument does not hold anymore: two identical *libelli* issued to a woman named Aurelia Charis have been found (Knipfing 11 and 26). The double production indicates that one certificate was kept on governmental file, the other kept by the party having sacrificed. In his 1930 *DACL* article on *libelli*, Leclercq mentions these documents and the interpretation of the duplicates, but does not relate how they affect his earlier argument ("Libelli," 81).

[53] A clue for this insight comes from a petition filed by Aurelia Ammonous, priestess of the god Petesouchus (W.Chr. 125). Her petition has number υλγ, i.e., the petition is number 433. This led Montevecchi to conclude that this *libellus* must have formed part of a τόμος συγκολλήσιμος, a roll of individual documents glued together in sequence. The high number of Ammonous's entry, Montevecchi observed, is in itself an indication that the entire population must have been obliged to sacrifice, and not just people suspected of being Christians. Another fact also supports the validity of this observation, namely that forty *libelli* were found in Theadelphia, a small village in the Fayum: "un numero tanto alto, sia pure in un capoluogo come Arsinoe, induce a ritenere probabile che tutti fossero obbligati a procurarsi il libello;

detect Christians in *libelli*, we conclude therefore: "maybe so." An important piece of that puzzle, the word "registration" (ἀπογραφή), appears on the back of one Oxyrhynchus *libellus* (P.Oxy. 58.3929, line 22). This term, as Rea noted, reminds one of census returns, called the "registration by house" (κατ' οἰκίαν ἀπογραφή),[54] and provides evidence for the administration of this bureaucratic effort. The word *libellus*, "petition," and its Greek equivalent βιβλίδιον, emphasizes the aspect of petitioning for official approval. The word "registration" (ἀπογραφή) on this Oxyrhynchus document points to "the copies retained in official files [that] would constitute an archive of registrations," and signifies that this, like the census, indicated a worldwide obligation.[55]

This understanding that the whole population had to sacrifice has changed the interpretation of the documentary *libelli* drastically. A plausible

---

come pure il fatto che i ritrovamenti, sempre casuali, ce ne abbiano restituito ventitré solo di Teadelfia, ch'era un piccolo villaggio" (Montevecchi, *Papirologia*, 288). The assumption being here, that the population of such a tiny village could not consist of so many suspected Christians. Montevecchi argues that the *libelli* were issued in duplicate, one to be filed in the roll and one for the petitioner to keep: "Il libello doveva essere redatto in duplice copia, di cui una rimaneva in mano ai funzionari ed era unita alle altre in un tomos, l'altra veniva rilasciata all'interessato" (ibid., 289). But see the comments of Rea about the length of the roll and reading of the number: "This roll would have been 34.64 metres long! [433 x 8 cm; i.e., not the 3 1/2 m. Wilcken calculated]. . . . The photograph of W.Chr. 125 in *BSAA* 9 (1907) 88 shows that the number is extremely doubtful, although it seems fairly certain that it had three digits" (P.Oxy. 58.3929, 41).

[54] P.Oxy. 58.3929, 39. Rea compares the number of *libelli* found, forty-six, to the ca. 270 census returns then known from Egypt and concludes: "Certificates of sacrifice were required only in AD 250; the census took place in Egypt at intervals of fourteen years from at least AD 5/6 . . . till AD 257/8. It may be a doubtful deduction from the statistics, but the comparatively large number of certificates seems to support the view that the head of every household was required to apply for one on a system very like that of the census returns" (ibid.). Rives also associates the certificates of sacrifice with the census, concluding: "Seen in the context of the Roman imperial bureaucracy, the aspects of Decius' decree which otherwise appear bizarre and nontraditional begin to look much more ordinary. It is in this context, I would argue, that we should place it" ("Decree of Decius," 149). Potter already referred to the similarity of sacrifice certificates and tax documents: "When they sacrificed they would obtain a certificate (*libellus*) recording the fact that they had complied with the order, just as they received a receipt from the tax-collectors whenever they paid their taxes: indeed, the procedure in this edict appears to parallel the process of tax collection very closely" (*Prophecy and History*, 43). Rives does not refer to P.Oxy. 58.3929.

[55] Rea concludes: "To sum up, the new title ἀπογρ(αφή), taken together with the evidence for the registration of these certificates in official archives and with the number of the surviving examples . . . implies that the requirement to sacrifice in the presence of the commissioners was universal" (P.Oxy. 58.3929, 41).

reconstruction of the Decian edict that would imply the whole population reads as follows: "That all men together with all women and members of the household (slaves) and infants[56] sacrifice and pour libations, and accurately taste the same sacrificial meats."[57] If indeed we have a universal obligation to sacrifice, then this implies that the people figuring in the *libelli* do not necessarily represent Christians, although that may apply to some of them. Again the question of how, if at all, one can recognize Christians in documentary texts confronts us. Since not all Christians refused to sacrifice and became martyrs, we can expect that Christians filed *libelli*.[58] Indeed, both Cyprian and Dionysius, our literary sources, attest that some Christians obtained *libelli*.[59] Yet attempting to sift out these Christians, who obtained a *libellus*, brings us back to the questions about markers of identity. None of these *libelli* (from Oxyrhynchus or from other places) contains the word "Christian" (χρηστιανός or χρηστιανή), so at best we could hope for

[56] This reconstructed formula mentions only infants. We know, however, from one *libellus* from an 11 year old boy, "Aurelius Aunes, son of Silvanus," that children were included in the edict as well (SB 3.6826, see also Knipfing, "Libelli of the Decian Persecution," 387–88, no. 37 [he could not read the age, however]; Leadbetter, "*Libellus* of the Decian Persecution," 180–81; and Scholl, P.Lips. 2, 227 and 233, no. 6). Leadbetter comments: "Aunes was a minor, indeed, the only explicitly attested minor in the corpus of libelli who sacrifices without the remainder of his family. . . . The libelli do confirm . . . that minors were expected to sacrifice as well as adults" ("*Libellus* of the Decian Persecution," 181).

[57] ὡς πάντας ἄνδρας ἅμα γυναιξὶ καὶ οἰκέταις καὶ αὐτοῖς ὑπομαζίοις παισὶ θύειν καὶ σπένδειν, αὐτῶν τε ἀκριβῶς τῶν θυσιῶν ἀπογεύεσθαι (Delehaye, "Martyrs d'Égypte," 13–14; based on *libelli*, Maximin's edict of 308 [*Mart. Pal.* 9.2] and Cyprian, *Laps.* 25).

[58] Knipfing noted "It is quite possible that one or more of the petitioners of our forty-one *libelli* may have been a Christian" ("*Libelli* of the Decian Persecution," 358)

[59] For many Christians, there was nothing wrong with buying a *libellus*, to some others it was "tantamount to a formal declaration of apostasy, and by acknowledging a *libellus* as his own a Christian was, technically, guilty of denying his faith. He joined the ranks of the *lapsi*, the fallen" (Clarke, "Observations," 74). This was at least the case in the West. A contemporary opinion from the East is lacking. The canons of Peter of Alexandria from Diocletian's persecution, written some fifty years later, suggest that "in the East libellatici were not condemned generally." According to Clarke, there is some room for doubt here, especially since both edicts may have been phrased differently ("Observations," 74). Dionysius of Alexandria appears to have taken a restrained approach toward so-called lapsed Christians, as Delehaye comments: "il faut rappeler son [Dionysius's] attitude pleine de modération et de prudence dans la question des *lapsi*, qui préoccupait alors les chefs de toutes les grandes églises. Il ratifie le jugement des martyrs qui ont accueilli avec miséricorde les apostats repentants" ("Martyrs d'Égypte," 18).

Christian nomenclature.[60] A closer look at the names in the Oxyrhynchite *libelli*, however, does not lead us to detect any Christians,[61] although we have to keep that possibility open.

We have one remaining question to address: Whom do the *libelli* not mention? Silence can tell just as much as words. In P.Oxy. 4.658 L(?)[. . .]thion testifies that he has performed the obligatory sacrifices to the gods together with two children, Dioscorus and Lais. Strikingly absent in this papyrus is the man's wife and the mother of the children. The imperial edict obliged all people, women and men, to sacrifice.[62] We see this in other *libelli*.[63] Yet this Oxyrhynchus papyrus mentions the daughter but not the wife/mother. So where might we find this woman? Several scenarios come to mind. Perhaps the parents had divorced.[64] Or, given the high mortality rate in antiquity, perhaps the mother had already died.[65] She might have performed the sacrifice on her own, since other *libelli* do indeed feature women alone.[66]

[60] See Knipfing on the challenge of identification of Christians through onomastics: "Our final problem, that of the possible identification of any *libellatici* on the basis of the nomenclature of the libelli, might be easier if we had a Christian prosopography for the period to 325" ("*Libelli* of the Decian Persecution," 358).

[61] None of the names in these petitions are clearly Christian. Perhaps Theodorus in P.Oxy. 4.658 was a Christian (so also Knipfing, "*Libelli* of the Decian Persecution," 360), but his name remains ambiguous (see ch. 2). Grenfell and Hunt proposed to read the Christian female name Thecla in a much damaged spot in P.Oxy. 4.658. This reconstruction is, however, impossible. See Davis, "Namesakes of Saint Thecla," *BASP* 36 (1999) 71–81, at 74 n. 11; repr. in idem, *The Cult of Saint Thecla*, 202 n. 7. When deciphering the papyrus, Grenfell and Hunt may have been influenced by their expectation of a Christian name, publishing their edition at a time when *libelli* still were considered direct evidence for Christianity.

[62] See the overview of Scholl in P.Lips. 2, "Auswertung der Liste der *Libelli*," 226–30.

[63] E.g., P.Oxy. 12.1464.

[64] See, for instance, Bagnall and Frier, *The Demography of Roman Egypt*, 123–24. The authors state that census returns show that "divorce was not rare among the general population of Egypt" (ibid., 123).

[65] "Granted the very high mortality levels in Roman Egypt, dissolution of marriage by the death of a spouse was always a real possibility" (ibid., 123). Scholl comments: "Ob es sich bei den Müttern bzw. dem Vater ohne Ehegatten um Witwen/Witwer oder Geschiedene handelt, läßt sich nicht erkennen" (P.Lips. 2, "Auswertung der Liste der *Libelli*," 234).

[66] E.g., Aurelia Ammonous, the priestess of Petesouchus in W.Chr. 125 (= Knipfing, "Libelli of the Decian Persecution," 364–5, no. 3; and Scholl, P.Lips. 2, 226, no. 3), and Aurelia Belle and her daughter Kaninis in Pap.Michigan inv. 263 (= Knipfing, "Libelli of the Decian Persecution," 386, no. 36; and Scholl, P.Lips. 2, 229, no. 22).

Lastly, as a Christian woman married to a "pagan" husband, she may have abstained from sacrificing.[67]

In view of their abhorrence of pagan sacrifice, contemporary Christian writers experienced the reign of the emperor Decius as one of persecution. The papyrus petitions that attest to sacrifice constitute important documentary evidence for a formative period in the history of early Christianity. They add significantly to our knowledge of that era by testifying to the large bureaucratic effort of an empire-wide requirement to sacrifice. The empire did not limit this obligation to Christians, and therefore the *libelli* do not belong to apostatized Christians. Consequently, the *libelli* nuance both early Christian historiography and later scholarship. Although impossible to determine whether any of the *libelli* found thus far attest the sacrifice of Christians, two Oxyrhynchus documents from the same decade explicitly mention Christians. We now turn to those.

The Emperor Valerian and the Christians[68]

After Decius's death in 251 the situation briefly took a turn for the better for Christians in the Roman Empire.[69] Valerian, who became emperor in 253,[70] at first did not continue Decius's policy of obligatory sacrifice but rather introduced a period of rest for Christians that lasted four years.[71] The

[67] A similar question can be asked for the *libellus* of Taamois with her children Amois and Taharpaesis (P.Oxy. 58.3929): where is the husband/father?

[68] See discussions in: Keresztes, "Two Edicts," *VC* 29 (1975) 81–95; Haas, "Imperial Religious Policy and Valerian's Persecution," *Church History* 52 (1983) 133–44; Schwarte, "Die Christengesetze Valerians," in *Religion und Gesellschaft* (ed. Eck) 103–63; and Selinger, *Mid-Third Century Persecutions*, 83–95.

[69] In a letter Cyprian, for instance, informs Demetrianus that not even a year after Decius's death Christianity was preached again in Carthage: in foro ipso, magistratibus et praesidibus audientibus (*Cyprian ad Demetrianum*, 13; cited in Frend, *Martyrdom and Persecution*, 413 and 435 n. 162).

[70] See Haas, "Imperial Religious Policy," 133–34.

[71] See Frend, *Martyrdom and Persecution*, 422; and Haas, "Imperial Religious Policy," 135. Dionysius of Alexandria in his letter to Hermammon *apud* Eusebius was initially positive about Valerian (*Hist. eccl.* 7.10.3). On this, Frend comments: "This is an exaggeration, for Dionysius wanted to flatter Gallienus and so attemped to put the blame for what now took place on Macrianus, Valerian's finance minister . . . rather than on the Emperor himself" (*Martyrdom and Persecution*, 422). Also Haas calls it "patently an exaggeration, designed in part to place the blame for the persecution of 257–260 on Valerian's finance minister Macrianus" ("Imperial Religious Policy," 135).

tide turned in 257, as Valerian began a persecution of higher clergy[72] and prohibited Christians from convening and visiting the cemeteries.[73] A second, much stricter phase started a year later in 258. We do not have the edict itself, but Cyprian renders the measures as follows:

> Valerian has sent a rescript to the Senate, directing that bishops, presbyters, and deacons are to be put to death at once, but that senators, high-ranking officials, and Roman knights are to lose their status as well as forfeit their property. And that if, after being so dispossessed, they should persist in remaining Christians, they are then to suffer capital punishment as well. Furthermore, that matrons are to be dispossessed of their property and dispatched into exile and that any members of Caesar's household who had either confessed earlier or should have done so now, are to have their possessions confiscated and are to be sent in chains, assigned to the imperial estates.[74]

Thus Valerian ordered property confiscation from affluent Christians and capital punishment for higher clergy and those who persevered in their Christian faith.

Haas argues that the sudden change in Valerian's religious policy indicated an effort to reinstate the *pax deorum*. The emperor tried to achieve this by ordering *supplicatio* to the traditional Roman gods.[75] Unlike his predecessor Decius, who ordered a general sacrifice for the entire population, Valerian seems to have addressed especially the upper class of the population in his edicts.[76] Indeed, no papyri attesting to mass sacrifices have been discovered,

[72] The bishops of Carthage and Alexandria were both exiled to desert villages: Cyprian to one called Curubis; Dionysius, together with several priests, to Cephro near the Libyan desert (*Acta Proconsularia* 1.4; Eusebius, *Hist. eccl.* 7.11.5, 10).

[73] "And it shall in no wise be permitted either to you or to any others either to hold assemblies or to enter the cemeteries, as they are called. If anyone be proved not to have gone to the place that I commanded, or be found at any assembly, he will bring the peril upon himself, for there shall be no lack of the necessary observation" (Eusebius, *Hist. eccl.* 7.11.10–11, trans. Oulton 2:159). See also Keresztes, "Two Edicts," 83–84.

[74] Letter 80.2; trans. Clarke, *Letters of St. Cyprian* 4:104. See also Keresztes, "Two Edicts," 84–86; Haas, "Imperial Religious Policy," 136; Schwarte, "Christengesetze Valerians," 133–36; and Selinger, *Mid-Third Century Persecutions*, 90–92.

[75] Haas, "Imperial Religious Policy," 140–43, esp. 142. See also Schwarte, "Christengesetze Valerians," 123–27.

[76] Haas, "Imperial Religious Policy," 143. According to Clarke, Valerian had learned from the mistakes of his predecessor and targeted "higher clergy, senators, matrons, knights and Caesarini" instead of ordinary Christians. "To persecute them [the ordinary Christians]

such as for the Decian edict. Haas interprets the emphasis on the upper class as arising from Valerian's own background in the senate and his understanding of the importance of the upper class in maintaining the traditional Roman religion. Healy argued that in view of the empire's financial distress, Valerian had economic reasons for focusing on affluent Christians.[77] Haas counters this position by remarking that "the sources seldom mention actual cases of the confiscation of property."[78] He concludes that "the simple fact that there were confiscations does not mean that the imperial government had its eye on the property of the church. Rather, it could indicate that Valerian wished to single out and punish members of the upper classes who had converted to Christianity."[79] The emperor used property confiscation as a means to penalize upper class Christians.

While confiscation of property belonging to churches and individual Christians would probably not make a noticeable difference in the empire's treasure chest,[80] one papyrus belonging to Valerian's persecution (P.Oxy. 43.3119) may contain evidence of confiscation of property from Christians. This fragmentary document preserves correspondence about an investigation somehow relating to Christians. Before we discuss that papyrus in more detail, we will first examine a slightly earlier text, which identifies a person as "Christian" (P.Oxy. 42.3035). The importance of these two papyri lies in the fact that they are both official documents that contain the word

systematically was . . . administratively too difficult" ("Some Observations," *Antichthon* 3 [1969] 72–73).

77 "The persecution of the Church and the confiscation of her property seemed to promise relief from the financial burden which was threatening the ruin of the Empire" (Healy, *Valerian Persecution*, 123). Frend commented: "The combination of a demand to 'acknowledge the saving deities' of the Empire, with the explicit interest in the Church's property may provide one reason for Valerian's measures" (*Martyrdom and Persecution*, 422). He also noted: "In this appalling crisis, the Church was relatively prosperous and stable, the one obvious refuge for persons and wealth in a disintegrating world. It did not need Egyptian magicians to convince a financial administrator in Egypt where help for the failing treasury might be found" (ibid., 422–23). (The mention of the Egyptian magicians refers to Dionysius's letter to Hermammon, Eusebius, *Hist. eccl.* 7.10.4).

78 Haas, "Imperial Religious Policy," 139.

79 Ibid.

80 Some individual Christians were wealthy. Also, some churches could collect large sums of money from its members. Cyprian's church in Carthage reportedly collected 100,000 sesterces to help out sister churches in Numidia. Wealthy Christian families are also known (Healy, *Valerian Persecution*, 123–29). From this we cannot conclude that churches owned lots of property.

"Christian." Thus they show for the first time in documentary sources the Roman government identifying people as Christians.

Wanted: "Petosorapis, Son of Horus, Christian" (P.Oxy. 42.3035)[81]

A small document, measuring 11.7 x 9.5 cm, contains a summons for Petosorapis. The text is written along the fibers in a fast hand with uncial and cursive forms. The back has no writing. The text contains the date Phamenoth 3 in the third year of Valerianus and Gallienus, which translates to 28 February 256 C.E. It reads:

(recto)
π(αρὰ) τοῦ πρυτάνεως
κωμάρχαις καὶ ἐπιστάταις εἰρήνης
κώμης Μερμέρθων. ἐξαυτῆς ἀνα-
πέμψατε Πετοσοράπιν Ὥρου χρησ<τ>ι-
ανόν, ἢ ὑμεῖς αὐτοὶ ἀνέλθατε.
(ἔτους) γ´´ Οὐαλεριανοῦ καὶ Γαλλιηνοῦ Σεβαστῶν
Φαμενὼθ γ̄.

---

1. π´; 2. επισταταις corr. from επιστατη

Translation

From the *prytanis*, to the *comarchs* and overseers of peace of Mermertha village. At once send up Petosorapis, son of Horus, Christian, or come up you yourselves.
Year 3 of Valerian and Gallienus Augusti.
Phamenoth 3.

The papyrus belongs to the genre of so-called "Orders to Arrest." The word "summonses," however, expresses more accurately the nature of these documents, since none of them contain the verb "to arrest"; instead, they all

[81] Ed. princ. Parsons, P.Oxy. 42.3035 (1974) 99–100. Literature: Gagos and Sijpesteijn, "So-Called 'Orders to Arrest'," *BASP* 33 (1996) 77–97, plates 3–5; Stephens, "An Epicrisis Return," *ZPE* (1993) 221–26; Bülow-Jacobsen, "Orders to Arrest," *ZPE* 66 (1986) 93–98; Hagedorn, "Das Formular der Überstellungsbefehle," *BASP* 16 (1979) 61–74; Drexhage, "Überstellungsbefehle," in Drexhage and Sünskes, *Migratio et Commutatio,* 102–18; Judge et al., "Summons for Petosorapis, *chresianos*," *Papyri from the Rise of Christianity in Egypt* at http://www.anchist.mq.edu.au/doccentre/PCE2.pdf.

use (a compound of) the verb "to send" (πέμπω).[82] So far, almost one hundred of these summonses have been published.[83]

In its phraseology this document largely resembles the other summonses.[84] Ursula Hagedorn has determined the standard formula for most documents originating from Oxyrhynchus as follows:

> Address.
> Send so-and-so.
> On the petition of so-and-so.[85]

The summons for Petosorapis (P.Oxy. 42.3035) differs from the majority of summonses in six respects:[86] 1) the writing follows *along* the fibers, whereas in most other summonses it goes *against* the fibers;[87] 2) it contains a date with year formula (as one of only two such papyri);[88] 3) with the verb "send up" (ἀναπέμπω) and addition of "at once" (ἐξαυτῆς), the text differs from the standard wording in Oxyrhynchus and agrees more with the form current in the Arsinoite nome;[89] 4) the papyrus does not specify why Petosorapis should

[82] Gagos and Sijpesteijn, "So-Called 'Orders to Arrest'," 79. Grenfell and Hunt first called this genre of papyri "Orders to Arrest" (P.Oxy 1.64 and 65, 122–23) and this has subsequently become the common terminology for them (German: *Haftbefehlen*); see Gagos and Sijpesteijn, "So-Called 'Orders to Arrest'," 77; Hagedorn, "Das Formular der Überstellungsbefehle," 61. Another fitting German word that Hagedorn suggests is "Vorführbefehl."

[83] I know of ninety-nine: Bülow-Jacobsen lists seventy-eight documents ("Orders to Arrest," 95–98); Gagos and Sijpesteijn added 16 others to his list in their "So-Called 'Orders to Arrest'," 95–96. To these should now be added: P.Oxy. 65.4485 and P.Oxy. 65.4486 (i and ii.); P.Yale inv. 1347 (Stephens, "An Epicrisis Return," 223); and P.Horak 11.

[84] For a detailed discussion of the "recht starre Regeln für die Textgestaltung" of this genre of documents, see Hagedorn, "Das Formular der Überstellungsbefehle," 61–74, quote at 62.

[85] Address—πέπψον τὸν δεῖνα ἐντυχόντος τοῦ δεῖνος (ibid., 63).

[86] Parsons mentions two differences: the date and the sender (P.Oxy. 42.3035, 99).

[87] With information about direction of the writing on 80 summonses, Gagos and Sijpesteijn counted 64 written against the fibers and 16 along the fibers. They concluded: "These figures clearly show that writing this type of document across—and not along—the fibers, was a practice deeply entrenched in the traditions of the Roman administration of Egypt" ("So-Called 'Orders to Arrest,'" 81).

[88] The other one is P.Med. inv. 71.39 (dated 20 February 6 B.C.E.), published in *Aeg* 54 (1974), 5, thus it appeared in print in the same year as our papyrus, so that Parsons, the editor, knew "no parallel at all" for this practice. Some summonses do contain a month and day (see Hagedorn, "Das Formular der Überstellungsbefehle," 61–62 nn. 2 and 3).

[89] Address, send up so-and-so, who is accused by so-and-so, immediately; ἀνάπεπψον (-πέμψατε) τὸν δεῖνα, ἐγκαλούμενον ὑπὸ τοῦ δεῖνος, ἐξαυτῆς (Hagedorn, "Das Formular

come up, but 5) contains the addition "or else come up yourselves";[90] and finally, 6) it mentions the *prytanis*—the chief local officer, who presided over the city council[91]—as its sender (as one of only two such papyri).[92] This last point of difference accounts probably for some of the other variations as well. The office of the *prytanis*, which issued this document, did not mass-produce these summonses and therefore did not have to conserve papyrus by writing against the fibers on leftovers of larger rolls. The scribe included a dating formula and used his own phraseology. We will return below to the role of the *prytanis* and the possible implications for the interpretation of this papyrus.

The summons for Petosorapis is addressed to the *comarchs* and overseers of peace of Mermertha village. In the Roman period, Egyptian villages had two *comarchs*, or village-leaders, local men who mediated between their village and the state and were personally and financially accountable for all that went on in the village.[93] The overseers of peace functioned as policemen.[94] Here we find the *comarchs* and the village police accountable to bring a certain Petosorapis from their village to Oxyrhynchus city. Who was he? And why did the *prytanis* want to see him?

der Überstellungsbefehle," 63).

[90] In other summonses, this phrase, "or you yourselves come up" (ἢ ὑμεῖς αὐτοὶ ἀνέλθατε), occurs also in P.Mich.Mchl. 6 (third/fourth cent.); in the singular in P.Mich.Mchl. 4: "you come up with your assistant" (σὺ ἄνελθε μετὰ τοῦ ὑπερέτου). Phrased as ἢ ὑμεῖς αὐτοὶ ἀνέρχεσθε in BGU 17.2701 (fourth cent.); P.Cair.Isid. 129 (308/9 C.E.); P.Oxy. 1.64 (third/fourth cent.); P.Oxy. 1.65 (third/fourth cent.); P.Oxy. 12.1507 (third cent.). See also P.Princ. 2.99 (fourth cent.).

[91] In the third century, "the prytanis of the boule was the chief administrative figure in the metropolis" (Bowman, *Town Councils*, 58–59).

[92] As a matter of fact, only thirty out of ninety-nine summonses mention a sender. The other from the *prytanis* is P.Oxy. 44.3190. Bowman, the editor of that papyrus, comments on this subject: "That the order was issued by the prytane (presumably of the bule of Oxyrhynchus) does not necessarily indicate any special area of judicial competence for this official. It is probably to be seen simply as part of his area of administrative competence and may perhaps be compared with the situation in P.Beatty Panop. 1.192–201 where the proedros of the bule of Panopolis is called upon by the central government to provide personnel to assist in a search for wanted persons" (P.Oxy. 44.3190, 153–54).

[93] For a study of this office, see Mißler, *Der Komarch*. The responsibilities of the *comarch* included representing his village, tax collection, division of liturgies, overseeing agricultural production as well as police tasks (discussed in ibid., chap. 7, 43–121.

[94] See Oertel, *Die Liturgie*, 278–81.

After combing through the *libelli* in search of apostatized Christians, we find here someone by name and patronymic who is clearly identified as a Christian (χρησ‹τ›ιανόν).[95] This "Petosorapis, son of Horus, Christian" does not appear in other papyri.[96] We could not have identified Petosorapis as a Christian through onomastics; both he and his father have pagan theophoric names. The sender of the document, the *prytanis*, however, explicitly marks Petosorapis as Christian. Parsons in his edition concluded that the additional Christian constituted "an individuating description," which suggested that Petosorapis "did not conceal his religion and indeed could be identified by it among the inhabitants of Mermertha."[97] Dionysius of Alexandria in his letter to Hermammon *apud* Eusebius mentions for this period people "who were said to have been openly Christians."[98] The crowded living conditions in Egyptian cities and villages would have made it difficult for Christians to keep their religious practices secret from their neighbors. How, then, to return to a question we asked in chapter 2 of this book, do you recognize a Christian when you see one? As Judge and Pickering rightly note, in this papyrus "the word [Christian] stands where the name of an occupation might otherwise be expected."[99] Other summonses add the patronymics[100] or professions[101] of the wanted people. In another papyrus sent to the village of Mermertha,

[95] For a discussion of the spelling, see the elaboration on "Sotas the Christian" in ch. 5.

[96] P.Lond. 3.1170, 10.351 (Arsinoite nome, ca. 144 C.E.) mentions a Petosarapis, son of Horus (Πετοσαράπεως Ὥρου), but the date is off by more than a century. Less importantly, this name is spelled with an *alpha* instead of *omicron*—our Πετοσορᾶπις has an *omicron*. As a matter of fact, the latter spelling is more common than Petosarapis (Πετοσαρᾶπις with *alpha*), based on a DDBDP search. Incidentally, the DDBDP wrongly lists P.Oxy. 42. 3035 with the spelling *alpha*. In the picture, however, it is clear that Parsons was correct in reading Petosorapis (line 4: πετοσοραπιν).

[97] Parsons, P.Oxy. 42.3035, 100. So also Drexhage: "lediglich als Bestandsteil der Personenbeschreibung" with reference to P.Vindob.G. 32016 III.50 (SB 16.12497), which features a Dioscorus, Christian, nominated for a liturgy ("Überstellungsbefehle," 116).

[98] οἱ λεχθέντες ἀναφανδὸν Χριστιανοὶ γεγονέναι (Eusebius, *Hist. eccl.* 7.10.3, trans. Oulton 2:150).

[99] Judge and Pickering, "Papyrus Documentation," *JAC* 20 (1977) 59. Similarly Martin, *Athanase d'Alexandrie*, 22 n. 29: "χρησ<τ>ιανόν, ici employé pour le distinguer, au même titre que le nom de métier."

[100] E.g., P.Oxy. 55.4485 ii.

[101] Drexhage observes: "In vielen Überstellungsbefehlen sind Angaben zu den Beklagten gemacht worden, die ein (sic) vage Einordnung der Personen ermöglichen" ("Überstellungsbefehle," 115). Other added descriptions can be found, e.g., "Cephalus the donkey-driver" in P.Oxy. 55.4485 i, or the camel-driver Stotoetis (P.Brook. 6). P.Mich. inv. 236 mentions a Pammounis, who was seller of something and farmer (the text is fragmentary).

the (unknown) sender addresses the village's head of police to send Eros the wine merchant.[102] One can imagine the Mermerthean police retrieving Eros at his booth in the marketplace. But how would the village police have proceeded in finding Petosorapis? If "Christian" had any association with a profession, and they added it to facilitate the retrieving of Petosorapis, we could conceive of him as Christian clergy—a Christian by profession[103]—just as I argued concerning "Sotas, the Christian" (SB 12.10772). Priests feature in two other summonses: Kephalon, priest (ἱερεύς) of Isis (P.Oxy. 31.2573) and Trypho, son of Melas the prophet, also a priest (SPP 22.1).[104] As a clergy person, Petosorapis would stand apart as a prominent member of a Christian congregation, and perhaps one could locate him in a church.[105]

By sending the summons the Oxyrhynchite *prytanis*, president of the city council, expected Petosorapis in the city expeditiously so that he could appear at a trial.[106] In case the village officials could not find him, they would have to come themselves; a sentence added to ensure efficiency, for *comarchs* were accountable for the villagers. We are thus faced with an intriguing question: why did the *prytanis* need Petosorapis, son of Horus, Christian, at a trial? Like most summonses, this papyrus does not list an explicit reason,[107] but it has to be "a matter within the competence of the official who issues the summons."[108] I consider several situations possible. Drexhage conjectures that flight, due to tax evasion, played a role in many of the second and third century summonses.[109] Judge hints at this scenario by providing several

[102] P.Oxy. 31.2576, lines 1–2: ἀρχεφόδῳ Μερμέρθων πέμψον Ἔρωτα οἰ[ν]έμπορον.

[103] For Judge, the word signified Petosorapis's "personal profession," but he also considers him as "an elder in the church" ("Summons for Petosorapis," 2).

[104] See Drexhage, "Überstellungsbefehle," 115.

[105] Judge suggests that Petosorapis may have owned the church building ("Summons for Petosorapis," 2).

[106] As Michael puts it: "the ultimate purpose of this type of document was to secure the presence of accused individuals for trial" (P.Mich.Mchl., 44).

[107] P.Oxy. 65.4485, another summons, concerning Hermogenes son of Paulus and Horion son of Pausirion, includes the reason for the arrest/accusation at the end: ἐντυχόντος Πλουτάρχου περὶ δημοσίας γῆς ("on the petition of Plutarchus concerning public land").

[108] Judge, "Summons for Petosorapis," 1.

[109] "So vage die Vermutung über die Delikte—mithin die Gründe für die Überstellung—auch sind, möchte ich aber darauf hinweisen, daß die meisten in diesem Abschnitt angesprochenen Texte einem Zeitraum entstammen (2./3. Jahrhundert n. Chr.), in dem der Steuerdruck zunahm und mehr und mehr Menschen danach trachteten, sich diesem Druck zu entziehen" ("Überstellungsbefehlen," 118). P. Mich.Mchl. 4 (third/fourth cent.) summons persons wanted by the tax collector of the village of Bacchias.

examples of the *prytanis's* involvement in tax matters.[110] This explanation makes good sense.

Alternatively, we should ask whether the *prytanis* summoned Petosorapis precisely as a Christian.[111] Judge and Pickering wonder if the addition of the adjective "Christian" in fact constituted the legal ground for asking Petosorapis to come to the metropolis.[112] Yet, as we shall now see, the dating imposes an interpretative challenge to this scenario.

At stake is whether this document comes from the persecution under Valerian. That persecution had two stages: one against higher Christian clergy and a more rigid phase against lower clergy and upper class Christians. Valerian issued his first edict, however, in the year 257, a year later than the date in our papyrus. Conceivably, however, the scribe of our papyrus made a mistake in the date. The dating formula contains the number "three" both in the year and in the month. Perhaps, when writing the year, the scribe had anticipated the number three in the month (Phamenoth 3) and inadvertently wrote "year three," while he should have penned year four or year five.[113] If so, the papyrus would fall in the period of the persecution under Valerian. Parsons, however, doubts that Petosorapis belonged to the upper class and therefore concludes that the papyrus bears no clear relation to Valerian's persecution.[114] We know nothing about his social status, apart from the fact that he stood out as a Christian, and Petosorapis, the Christian, may have represented one of the clergy singled out in Valerian's edicts.[115]

[110] Judge, "Summons for Petosorapis," 1.

[111] Parsons, P.Oxy. 42.3035, 99

[112] "After the recent requirement of Decius that all citizens should take out certificates of having sacrificed. . . . officialdom was now alert to the existence of those who were prepared to answer to the name 'Christian', and it was an efficient form of identification for legal purposes" (Judge and Pickering, "Papyrus Documentation," 67).

[113] This happened in other papyri, see for instance, P.Oxy 1.147, where the years of the eras appear wrong.

[114] P.Oxy. 42.3035, 100. Clarysse agrees that this document "is probably not related to the persecution, which started only a few years later" ("Coptic Martyr Cult," 379). Judge and Pickering summarizing Parsons conclude: "Since the date is a year before legal action was taken against eminent Christians by Valerian, and this is a local government arrest of a presumably unimportant person, it is safest to assume that the identification as a 'Christian' is simply a convenient way of distinguishing the particular Petosorapis to be detained, rather than indicating the reason for detention, which would not in any case be expected to be given in such an order" ("Papyrus Documentation," 59).

[115] Petosorapis might not have lived at Mermertha, he could have fled or gone into exile to the countryside from a larger city, just like Dionysius of Alexandria and Cyprian of Carthage.

The presence of the *prytanis* fits this second scenario also,[116] for as the main official of the city and contact person for the central government,[117] he had the responsibility for the implementation of the edict of his jursidiction. Indeed, a *prytanis* signed as official witness for the general sacrifices during Decius's reign.[118]

This document situates a Christian called Petosorapis at Mermertha, a village located south of metropolitan Oxyrhynchus, in the upper toparchy of the nome.[119] Some sixty years after this request for "Petosorapis the Christian," another papyrus testifies to the presence of Christianity in the village. A tax list from the second decade of the fourth century[120] registers an "Apphus, deacon of the church, and his brother" under the heading Mermertha.[121]

See, for instance, the discussion in Keresztes, "Two Edicts," 85–88. Dionysius of Alexandria relates in his letter against Germanus (apud Eusebius, *Hist. eccl.* 6.40.1–9) how the local population of the village of Mareotis rescued him from Roman captivity.

[116] Parsons found that "even the rare intervention of the prytanis does not guarantee an exceptional situation" (P.Oxy. 42.3035, 100). Drexhage remarks: "Im Zuge welcher Befugnis der πρύτανις vorliegenden Überstellungsbefehl an dörfliche Polizeiorgane schickte, entzieht sich unserer Kenntnis" ("Überstellungsbefehle," 107).

[117] Bowman, *Town Councils*, 56.

[118] As discussed in the section on the administration of the *libelli*, the local commission overseeing the sacrifices during the reign of Decius consisted of the city's magistrates. A *libellus* from Arsinoe contained the signature of a man who identified himself as *prytanis*, reading: "I, Aurelius Sabinus, the *prytanis*, saw you sacrificing" (P.Ryl. 1.12). Knipfing comments on this sentence: "This last quotation, with its reference to the prytanis, is interesting as an indication that the local town magistracy served on the commission for sacrificing" ("Libelli of the Decian Persecution," 351).

[119] Krüger conjectures that Mermertha was "vielleicht in Nachbarschaft zu Isieion Panga . . . und Nesm(e)imis" (*Oxyrhynchos in der Kaiserzeit*, 279; and his schematic rendition of the "Nachbarschaftskomplex," ibid., 51). See also Rowlandson, *Landowners and Tenants*, Map 3 "The Oxyrhynchite Nome in the Roman Period: An Approximate Reconstruction," xiv. Mermertha is located on the Canal of Apollophanes; a canal that, as Rowlandson suspects, "might possibly have provided a link between the Nile and the Bahr Yusuf" (*Landowners and Tenants*, 11–12, at 12). Two other summonses also are addressed to Mermertha: P.Oxy. 31.2576 and P.Yale inv. 1347 (= Stephens, "An Epicrisis Return," 223).

[120] For the date, see Bagnall, "Notes on Roman and Byzantine Documents," *ChrEg* 66 (1991) 293–96.

[121] Ἀπφοῦς διάκων ἐκκλησίας καὶ ὁ ἀδελφ(ός), P.Oxy. 55.3787, lines 24–25. The word Μερμέρθων was added later in the margin of line 22. This brings up the question whether Mermertha is the heading for a section, lines 22–29, or only for line 22 (so Bagnall). Either the entry under Thobsis or the entry under Mermertha is short. I took it to be referring to the larger section. If the latter is the case, then the deacon is not from Mermertha but from Thosbis (see discussion in Rea, P.Oxy.55.3787, note to line 22 and Bagnall, "Notes on Roman

Thus, in the first quarter of the fourth century, the Christian community at Mermertha had a church and church personnel. The foundation date of the congregation remains unknown, but the mention of Petosorapis the Christian at Mermertha—some sixty odd years prior—points to a Christian presence at the village.[122]

This papyrus, P.Oxy. 42.3035, introduced the first Christian from the Oxyrhynchite nome known by name and patronym in a dated text. It summons "Petosorapis, son of Horus, Christian," to appear before the president of the Oxyrhynchus city council. The fact that it describes him as Christian may indicate his profession as a clergy; in any case, it presumes that Petosorapis had a distinction as a Christian. The reason for his being wanted remains unclear. Does the involvement of the *prytanis* lead to the suspicion that Petosorapis had problems paying his taxes or that he was implicated by an imperial edict against Christians? In any case, the note constitutes important evidence for Christians at the Oxyrhynchite countryside in the mid-third century.

Official Document Mentioning Christians (P.Oxy 43.3119)[123]

A piece of papyrus (9 x 25.5 cm) from a roll, published as "Official Correspondence," preserves a fragmentary document. Starting the new entry that will occupy us here, the scribe marked the final letter of the word "from the Saite nome" with a long stroke.[124] The handwriting suggests a third century date. The text reads:[125]

ii

o[

(illegible traces of shorthand)

---

and Byzantine Documents," 293 and n. 35). What sort of church this was exactly we do not know, see the discussion in ch. 7, at P.Oxy. 33.2673.

[122] For the presence of Christianity in the countryside, see also Origen, *Cels.* 3.9. Dionysius of Alexandria relates in his letter against Germanus (Eusebius, *Hist. eccl.* 6.40.4–9), how the local population of Mareotis rescued him from Roman captivity.

[123] Ed. princ. Rea, "Official Correspondence," P.Oxy. 43.3119 (1975) 77–79; and Whitehorne, "Document of Valerian's Persecution?" *ZPE* 24 (1977) 187–96.

[124] Similarly, he closed the previous entry by drawing the sign for ἔτους across the column (line 11).

[125] In lines 12–20, I have incorporated in the text suggestions that Rea made in the notes. I could not find helpful parallels by searching the DDBDP; the text appears to be not formulaic enough to allow for such restoration.

(illegible traces of shorthand)
(illegible traces of shorthand)
μετὰ τὰ ..[
οἱ δηλωθεν[
διασημοτάτου δ[
προσ`κ´εκρίσθαι τω[
γνώριζε ἐ̣ν̣ τῷ̣ .[
ὃ̣ ἐκομισάμην γρ̣ [
(ἔτους) ζ´[
Σαΐτου· Αὐρηλί[ου Ἑρμεί(ου or νου?) ( )
π̣ε̣ρ̣ὶ ἐξετάσ̣[ε]ως [π]ό̣ρ[ων? ( )
χρηστιανῶν κ.[( )
Αὐρήλιος Ἑρμε̣ί̣[ας or νας?
...[...] π̣[ε]ρ̣ὶ̣ οἰκ̣ο̣π̣[έδων? ( )
ἐπ̣ὶ̣ τ̣ῶν ὑπογεγρ̣α̣[μμένων? ( )
χ[ρ]ηστιανῶν κελ̣ε̣υ̣[σθέντων? ( ) ὑπὸ τοῦ διασημο]τ̣άτου ἡγεμόνος .[
..].ου Αἰλίου Γορδ̣ι̣[ανοῦ

Translation of lines 12–20

From the Saite nome, Aurelius (Hermeias or Hermeinas)
about inspection (of resources?)
Christians . . .
Aurelius Herme(ias or -inas?). . .
. . . about (lands?)
underwritten . . .
Christians, ordered . . . by the most
illustrious prefect. . .
. . . Aelius Gordianus . . .[126]

I concur with Rea's words introducing this papyrus: "Incomprehensible as this fragment still remains, it has a strong claim on our attention."[127] Intriguingly, this document mentions "Christians" twice. The text, however,

[126] Neither Rea nor Whitehorne provide a translation because of the fragmentary state of the text.

[127] Rea, P.Oxy. 43.3119, 77. Whitehorne also quoted Rea's first line to open his own article ("Document of Valerian's Persecution?" 187).

offers insurmountable challenges because of its fragmentary nature with more than half of the text missing.[128]

The papyrus contains remnants of two documents entered into an official book,[129] both of which deal with legal matters.[130] The first letter ends with the date which preserves "year 7" of the reign of an emperor. Rea and Whitehorne both argue convincingly that this indicated year seven of the reign of Valerian, (i.e., 259/260).[131] Therefore this letter is contemporaneous with the summons for Petosorapis, the Christian (P.Oxy. 42.3035).

We focus on the second letter in the daybook. The original, of which this entry forms a copy, came from the Saite nome in Egypt's Western Delta. With this letter, an official in the Saite nome transmits important information to colleagues in another nome.[132] Although it (partly) preserves the names of two officials, we cannot identify these with known administrators.[133] The letter may have functioned to inform the colleagues of the Oxyrhynchite nome about measures, or perhaps it counseled them to act.[134]

[128] Whitehorne, "Document of Valerian's Persecution?" 187.

[129] So Whitehorne, who argued that the lines 5–11 are not, as Rea suggested, a cover letter for the following letter in lines 12–20 (ibid., 188–90).

[130] Ibid., 190.

[131] Rea, P.Oxy 43.3119, 77; and Whitehorne, "Document of Valerian's Persecution?" 192–95. As both scholars mention, seven emperors reigned for seven or more years in the third century, yielding seven possible dates. Whitehorne lays out the prerequisites for finding a match: "i) there is legislation against Christians; ii) that legislation is being promoted by the authorities throughout Egypt; iii) the legislation in question is directed against not only the persons but also the property of Christians" (ibid., 192). This situation exists only during the reign of Valerian.

[132] So Whitehorne, "Document of Valerian's Persecution," 192. He refers to P.Ryl. 2.78 as example of this practice. An other example of such official correspondence is P.Oxy. 60.4060 (ca. 161 C.E.), preserving letters to the strategus of the Oxyrhynchite nome from other nomes. Topics in these letters are, for instance, inquiries about runaway slaves or the sale of confiscated property.

[133] The first is Aurelius Herme(ias) or Herme(inas) of the Saite nome. The last line mentions an Aelius Gordianus. This man is not known from elsewhere, but he was probably working for the prefect. See Rea's comment that this Aelius Gordianus cannot be identified with the man named as Severus Alexander's advisor in the *HA*, *Vita Sev. Alex.* 68, because that is a corrupt passage. Aelius Gordianus in this papyrus is not the prefect; there is too much space to be filled in between the ἡγεμόνος in line 19 and his name in line 20 (see Rea, note to line 19, 79). He is perhaps, as Whitehorne suggests, "a member of [the prefect's] staff who was acting on his authority" ("Document of Valerian's Persecution?" 191). According to Whitehorne, the prefect was most likely one of the people involved (ibid., 190).

[134] Ibid., 192.

This entry twice mentions "Christians." Obviously, the plural indicates more than one Christian, but with so much text lacking, we do not know whether two or more personal names preceded the word as in the case (in the singular) of Petosorapis. Or perhaps it uses the word "Christians" abstractly for a group of people not further identified by name in the same way that Pliny refers to Christians in his letters to Trajan much earlier than this text (in the early-second century). In any case, again the marker "Christian" refers to an outsider. These Christians occupy a central place in the letter.[135]

Although fragmentary, the letter seems to indicate that possessions attracted the officials' interest. Parsons suggested reconstructing line thirteen as περὶ ἐξετάσ[ε]ως [π]όρ[ων] ("about inspection of resources"). According to Whitehorne, "the conclusion that the letter dealt with a judicial inquiry involving property held by Christians seems to be inescapable."[136] The situation that the papyrus sketches fits Cyprian's testimony about this period. In a letter Cyprian complained that "the coming of the persecution . . . pulled me down under the heavy weight of proscription, for the public notice could be read: *If anyone holds in possession any part of the goods of Caecilius Cyprianus, the bishop of the Christians*."[137] Although Cyprian does not finish the sentence, it indicates the confiscation of his possessions. Confiscation of property entailed a heavy sentence for upper class people.[138] In *De lapsis*,

[135] "The mention of Christians in this heading as well as in the main body of the text is assurance . . . that they were a central concern of the letter and not just something mentioned in passing" (Whitehorne, "Document of Valerian's Persecution," 191).

[136] Ibid., 191. See also Clarysse, "Coptic Martyr Cult," 379; and Judge and Pickering, "our earliest immediate contact . . . with official action against 'Christians' " ("Papyrus Documentation," 59).

[137] Persecutio enim ueniens te ad summam martyrii sublimitatem prouexit, me autem proscriptionis honore depressit, cum publice legeretur: si quis tenet possidet de bonis Caecili Cypriani episcopi Christianorum (Letter 66.4.1, trans. Clarke, *Letters of St. Cyprian* 1:109).

[138] Tacitus, writing much earlier, in the first century, suggests that some Roman men preferred suicide above sentence, for "if convicted, a man's property was confiscated and his burial forbidden, whereas those who settled their own fates had their bodies buried and their wills respected—a bonus for getting it over quickly" (*Annals* 6.29.1; cited in Crook, *Law and Life of Rome*, 275). Later this changed, and "if you wanted to save your property you must be still more prompt, and commit suicide before any charge had been preferred, that is, before you were even on trial" (ibid., 276).

Cyprian mentions love for their patrimony—*amor patrimonii*[139]—as a reason for Christians apostatizing.[140]

This fragmentary papyrus adds another significant voice—an official bureaucratic one—to the statements of the Cyprian. With its suggested emphasis on property confiscation, the document preserves a material aspect of Valerian's persecution. It also shows that government officials had an interest in Christians and suggests that Christians were in some ways distinctive.

The four *libelli* from Oxyrhynchus discussed in this chapter provide important documentary evidence for thc first empire-wide persecution and thus for the history of early Christianity. Two other Oxyrhynchus papyri from the mid-third century explicitly mention Christians. The Oxyrhynchite *prytanis* introduced us to Petosorapis as the first known Christian from Oxyrhynchus in a dated text. This Petosorapis may have had the professional occupation of a Christian clergyman. A fragmentary communication between nomes mentioned Christians in what appeared to represent a confiscation of property; a practice we shall witness in greater detail in the next chapter.

[139] Cyprian, *Laps*. 6, 10, 11, 12. See also Cyprian's correspondence, e.g., *Ep*. 10 and 24. In *Ep*. 24, bishop Caldonius mentions to Cyprian that Christians relinquerunt possessiones quas fiscus tenet (Frend, *Martyrdom and Persecution*, 434 n. 136); see Clarke, *Letters of St. Cyprian* 1:71. Cyprian's property was also confiscated, see *Laps*. 10 and *Ep*. 66.

[140] "A blind love for their patrimony has deceived many, and if they were not free and ready to take themselves away, it was because their property held them in chains" (Decepit multos patrimonii sui amor caecus; nec ad recedendum parati aut expediti esse potuerunt quos facultates suae velut conpedes ligaverunt; Cyprian, *Laps*. 11.1–4). Cyprian continues in 12: "But how can those who are tethered to their inheritance be following Christ? And can those who are weighed down by earthly desires be seeking heaven and aspiring to the heights above? They think of themselves as owners, whereas it is they rather who are owned; enslaved as they are to their own property, they are not the masters of their money but its slaves" (*Laps*. 12.1–6; trans. Bénerot).

CHAPTER 7

Subversion and Resistance During the Great Persecution: From Countryside Church to Alexandrian Courtroom

After the persecution under Valerian and Gallienus, a time of peace for Christians in the Roman Empire followed.[1] This lasted until the beginning of the fourth century when Diocletian instigated the so-called "Great Persecution" (303–311).[2] The main sources for this period constitute the writings of Eusebius and Lactantius, and to a lesser extent, hagiographical

[1] This roughly forty-year period started when Gallienus became the sole emperor in 260/261 and issued rescripts for the edicts against Christians (Eusebius, *Hist. eccl.* 7.13). For a discussion on the implications of the rescripts, see Keresztes, "The Peace of Gallienus," *Wiener Studien* 9 (1975) 174–85. Eusebius summarizes this period of peace and the growth of the church at the beginning of book eight of his *Ecclesiastical History*. According to Keresztes, "Eusebius' description of the freedom of the Christian Church and its recognition by local and Imperial authorities during this period up to the Great Persecution is not exaggerated" (ibid., 182).

[2] For scholarly discussions on the Great Persecution, see, e.g., Schwarte, "Diokletians Christengesetz," in *E fontibus haurire* (ed. Günther and Rebenich) 203–40; and the reaction by Löhr, "Some Observations,'" *VC* 56 (2002) 75–95. Furthermore, Davies, "Origin and Purpose," *JTS* 40 (1989) 66–94; Portmann, "Motiven der diokletianischen Christenverfolgung," *Historia* 39 (1990) 212–48; Kolb, "Chronologie und Ideologie," *Antiquité tardive* 3 (1995) 21–31; De Ste. Croix, "Aspects of the 'Great' Persecution," *HTR* 47 (1954) 75–113; repr., idem, *Christian Persecution, Martyrdom, and Orthodoxy*, 35–78. On Egypt in particular, see: Delehaye, "Les Martyrs d'Égypte," *AnBoll* 40 (1922) 5–154 and 299–364. Clarysse supplemented Delehaye's work with the evidence from newly discovered texts in "The Coptic Martyr Cult," in *Martyrium in Multidisciplinary Perspective* (ed. Lamberigts and van Deun) 377–95. See also Papaconstantinou, *Culte des saints en Égypte*.

literature.[3] In his *Ecclesiastical History*, Eusebius described the onset of Diocletian's persecution as follows:

> It was in the nineteenth year of the reign of Diocletian, and the month Dystrus, or March, as the Romans would call it, in which, as the festival of the Saviour's Passion was coming on, an imperial letter was everywhere promulgated, ordering the razing of the churches to the ground and the destruction by fire of the Scriptures, and proclaiming that those who held high positions would lose all civil rights, while those in households, if they persisted in their profession of Christianity, would be deprived of their liberty. Such was the first document against us. But not long afterwards we were further visited with other letters, and in them the order was given that the presidents of the churches should all, in every place, be first committed to prison, and then afterwards compelled by every kind of device to sacrifice.[4]

Eusebius's account of these times implies that Diocletian's persecution impacted Egypt greatly.[5]

The papyrological record from this period offers a corrective voice to histories of the persecution that rely exclusively on these Christian, literary-theological, and hagiographical accounts. In this chapter we travel from a village church in the Oxyrhynchite countryside to a courtroom in the

[3] Delehaye contrasts the accounts of Dionysius of Alexandria about "lapsing" Christians during the Decian persecution with the heroizing descriptions of Diocletian's persecution by Eusebius and Phileas. Thus he characterizes the impression left by the literary sources about Diocletian's persecution: "Eusèbe et Philéas sont tout à l'admiration. L'ardeur et la constance des martyrs est leur thème à peu près exclusif, et il est si peu question chez eux de chutes et d'apostasies, que l'on songe à peine, au milieu de cet élan général, à la possibilité d'une défaillance." However, as Delehaye observes, "on devine bien que la réalité ne fut point si glorieuse" ("Martyrs d'Égypte," 24). On the importance of martyr stories for Christian self-understanding and identity, see Castelli, *Martyrdom and Memory*, 2004.

[4] Eusebius, *Hist. eccl.* 8.2.4–5 (trans. Oulton 2:257, 259): ἔτος τοῦτο ἦν ἐννεακαιδέκατον τῆς Διοκλητιανοῦ βασιλείας, Δύστρος μήν, λέγοιτο δ' ἂν οὗτος Μάρτιος κατὰ Ῥωμαίους, ἐν ᾧ τῆς τοῦ σωτηρίου πάθους ἑορτῆς ἐπελαυνούσης ἥπλωτο πανταχόσε βασιλικὰ γράμματα, τὰς μὲν ἐκκλησίας εἰς ἔδαφος φέρειν, τὰς δὲ γραφὰς ἀφανεῖς πυρὶ γενέσθαι προστάττοντα, καὶ τοὺς μὲν τιμῆς ἐπειλημμένους ἀτίμους, τοὺς δ' ἐν οἰκετίαις, εἰ ἐπιμένοιεν τῇ τοῦ Χριστιανισμοῦ προθέσει, ἐλευθερίας στερεῖσθαι προαγορεύοντα. καὶ ἡ μὲν πρώτη καθ' ἡμῶν γραφὴ τοιαύτη τις ἦν· μετ' οὐ πολὺ δὲ ἑτέρων ἐπιφοιτησάντων γραμμάτων, προσετάττετο τοὺς τῶν ἐκκλησιῶν προέδρους πάντας τοὺς κατὰ πάντα τόπον πρῶτα μὲν δεσμοῖς παραδίδοσθαι, εἶθ' ὕστερον πάσῃ μηχανῇ θύειν ἐξαναγκάζεσθαι.

[5] Especially *Hist. eccl.* 8.8–9.

metropolis Alexandria and encounter Christians affected by and dealing with the imperial edict. The papyri considered in this chapter range in genre from official documents to a private letter and give examples of the complexities involved in negotiating different allegiances. Some documents show glimpses of the interruption of private life, and others that of a whole Christian community.

Inspecting a Church in Rural Egypt During the Great Persecution (P.Oxy. 33.2673)

An official document preserved in three copies (P.Oxy. 33.2673) introduces us to Aurelius Ammonius, son of Copreus, reader of the former church at the village of Chysis in the Oxyrhynchite countryside. The document details the confiscation of the church's property. An identically phrased but poorly preserved document (P.Harr. 2.208) has lost the most relevant parts and serves as supporting evidence only. Content and dating of these official documents suggest that we should interpret these texts in light of the persecution under Diocletian.

On 5 February 304 C.E., Ammonius filed a report with three high-ranking Oxyrhynchite officials.[6] In the declaration, he stated that the former church of the village of Chysis possessed no property apart from some bronze or copper materials.[7]

The document has survived in three copies[8]—already an indication of the level of bureaucracy involved. These were found tied together, with all

[6] Ed. princ. Rea, P.Oxy. 33.2673 (1968) 105–8, and idem, "P.Oxy. XXXIII 2673.22: ΠΥΛΗΝ to ʽΥΛΗΝ," *ZPE* 35 (1979) 128. Discussions of this papyrus by Wipszycka, "Lecteur," in *Études sur le Christianisme,* 415–20 (= *ZPE* 50 [1983] 117–21); eadem, "Encore sur le lecteur," *ZPE* 50 (1983) 421–26; Clarke, "An illiterate lector?" *ZPE* 57 (1984) 103–4; Bagnall, *Egypt in Late Antiquity*, 256–57 n. 142; Gamble, *Books and Readers*, 250 n. 31; White, "Declaration of Church Property," *Social Origins* 2:166–70; Judge and Pickering, "Papyrus Documentation," *JAC* 20 (1977) 59–60 ("Declaration on church property by an anagnostes"); Clarysse, "Inventories in Coptic Churches and Monasteries" in *Archives and Inventories in the Eastern Mediterranean* (ed. Vandorpe and Clarysse) 85–93.

[7] A more appropriate title for this papyrus would have been: "Declaration of Absence of Church Property."

[8] Another document extant in three copies and written in three different hands is P.Oxy. 1.55 (dated 283 C.E.). See also, for example P.Oxy. 49.3498, line 36: κυρία ἡ πρᾶσις καὶ παραλώρησις τρισσὴ γραφεῖσα ("The sale and cession written in three copies is authoritative").

three[9] written by different scribes in professional and competent hands.[10] On all three sheets a certain Aurelius Serenus has penned the subscription on Ammonius's behalf. The text below comes from copy A (measuring 12 x 26 cm).[11] The back has no writing.

ἐπὶ ὑπάτων τῶν κυρίων ἡμ̣[ῶν αὐτοκρατόρων
Διοκλητιανοῦ τὸ ἔνατον καὶ Μαξ[ιμιανοῦ
  τὸ η΄ Σεβαστῶν
Αὐρηλίοις Νείλῳ τῷ καὶ Ἀμμωνίῳ γυμ[( ) βουλ(ευτῇ)
ἐνάρχῳ πρυτάνει καὶ Σαρμάτῃ καὶ Ματρίνῳ ἀμφ[οτέροις
γυμ( ) βουλ(ευταῖς) συνδίκοις τοῖς πᾶσι τῆς λαμ(πρᾶς) καὶ λαμ(προτάτης)
Ὀξυρυγχιτῶν πόλεως (vac.)
Αὐρήλιος Ἀμμώνιος Κοπρέως ἀναγνωσ-
τὴς τῆς ποτε ἐκ<κ>λησίας κώμης Χύσεως
ἐπιθεμένων ὑμῶν ἐμοὶ ἀκολούθως
τοῖς γραφ<ε>ῖσι ὑπὸ Αὐρηλίου Ἀθανασίου ἐπιτρό-
που πριουάτης ὡς ἐκ κελεύσεως τοῦ δια-
σημ(οτάτου) μαγίστρου τῆς πριουάτης Νερατίου
Ἀπολλωνί<δ>ου περὶ τοῦ παραστῆσαι ἅπαντα
τὰ <ε>ἴδη τὰ [ἐ]ν τῇ αὐτῇ ποτε ἐκ<κ>λησίᾳ̣ κ̣α̣ὶ̣ ἐ̣μοῦ
προενεγ'καμένου μὴ ἔχειν τὴν <αὐτὴν> ἐκ<κ>λη-
σ{ε}ίαν μήτε χρυσὸν μήτε ἄσημον
μήτε ἀργύριον μήτε ἐσθῆτα μήτε τετρά-
ποδα μήτε ἀνδράποδα μήτε οἰκόπαιδα
μ̣ή̣τε ὑπάρχοντα μήτε ἀπὸ χαρισμάτων
μηδ' α̣ὖ ἀπὸ διαθηκῶν εἰ μὴ μ̣όνην

For official documents written in multiple copies, see Nielsen, "A Catalogue of Duplicate Papyri," *ZPE* 129 (1999) 187–214.

[9] This was perhaps the way they were sent out, as Roger Bagnall suggested to me in correspondence: "possibly they were submitted in this form and never got separated and sent their way to the various destinations (*prytanis* and the two *syndikoi*?)."

[10] All three scribes started out the document writing legibly in professional cursive hands, but, as is common in handwritten texts, their writing becomes more cramped toward the end of the page scribbling in the words to leave room for the subscription, the hand becoming fast, much smaller, and less neat.

[11] Rea, the editor, benefitted from the triple preserved document, adding readings from copy B and C when copy A was hard to read, a real luxury for a papyrologist. In line 22 Rea originally read χαλκῆν πύλην (a "bronze gate"). In a subsequent publication, he corrected the reading to χαλκῆν ὕλην, "bronze materials" ("ΠΥΛΗΝ to ῾ΥΛΗΝ," 128; see also "Additions and Corrections," in P.Oxy. 48, xvii).

τὴν ε̣ὑ̣[ρε]τ̣ῖσαν χαλκῆ̣[ν] ὕλην καὶ παραδο-τ̣ῖ̣σαν τῷ λογιστῇ πρὸς τὸ κατενεγ'χθῆναι ἐπὶ τὴν λαμ(προτάτην) Ἀλεξάνδριαν ἀκολούθως τοῖς γραφ<ε>ῖσι ὑπὸ τοῦ διασημ(οτάτου) ἡμῶν ἡγεμόνος Κλωδίου Κο<υ>λκιανοῦ καὶ ὀμνύω τὴν τῶν κυρίων ἡμῶν αὐτοκρατόρων Διοκλητιανοῦ καὶ Μαξιμιανοῦ Σεβασ̣(τῶν) καὶ Κωνσταντίου καὶ Μαξιμιανοῦ τῶν ἐπιφανεστάτων καισάρων τύχην ταῦθ' οὕτως ἔχειν καὶ μηδὲν διεψεῦσθαι ἢ ἔνοχος εἴην τῷ θείῳ ὅρκῳ

(ἔτους) κʹ καὶ ιβʹ τῶν κυρίων ἡμῶν Διοκλητιανοῦ καὶ Μαξιμιανοῦ Σεβαστῶν καὶ Κωνσταντίου καὶ Μαξιμιανοῦ τῶν ἐπιφανεστάτων καισάρων·

Μεχεὶρ [ιʹ·

(second hand) Αὐρήλιος Ἀμμώνιος ὤμοσα τὸν ὅρκον ὡς (πρόκειται)· Αὐρ(ήλιος) Σερῆνος ἔγρα(ψα) ὑ(πὲρ) αὐτοῦ μὴ ει̣(δότος) γρά(μματα)

---

19. *l.* οἰκόπεδα, 22–23. *l.* εὑρεθεῖσαν, παραδοθεῖσαν.

Translation

During the consulship of our lords the emperors Diocletian, for the ninth time, and Maximian, for the 8th time, the Augusti.
To Aurelius Neilus alias Ammonius (former-?) gymnasiarch and city-council member, *prytanis* in office, and Sarmates and Matrinus, both (former-?) gymnasiarchs, city-council members, *syndic*s, all of them of the glorious and most glorious city of the Oxyrhynchites, Aurelius Ammonius, son of Copreus, reader of the former church of the village of Chysis. Whereas you (pl.) commanded me in accordance with what was written by Aurelius Athanasius, *procurator rei privatae*, because of an order of the most eminent *magister rei privatae*, Neratius Apollonides, about the surrender of all the goods in the same former church and whereas I declared that the same former church had neither gold nor silver nor money nor clothes nor cattle nor slaves nor lands nor possessions, neither from gifts nor from bequests, apart from only the bronze matter which was found and given over to the *logistes* in order to be brought down to the most glorious Alexandria in accordance with what was written by our most eminent governor Clodius Culcianus, I also swear by the genius of our lords the emperors Diocletian and Maximian, the Augusti, and Constantius and Galerius, the most illustrious Caesars, that these things are thus, and that nothing is cheated, or I may be liable

to the divine oath.
In the 20th and 12th year of our lords the emperors Diocletian and Maximian, the Augusti, and Constantius and Galerius, the most illustrious Caesars. Mecheir 10th.
(2nd hand) I, Aurelius Ammonius, swore the oath as aforesaid. I, Aurelius Serenus, wrote for him because he does not know letters.

A similar document, P.Harr. 2.208,[12] most likely also comes from Oxyrhynchus.[13] Dated 9 February 304, it was written only four days after the "Declaration of Church Property" from the former church of Chysis (P.Oxy. 33.2673). More importantly, although fragmentary, the parts of the document preserved are identical with those of P.Oxy. 33.2673, lines 22–33,[14] which allows for a fairly certain reconstruction of the missing parts. This papyrus measures 7 x 8.7 cm. As the editor, Donatella Limongi noted, the professional, cursive handwriting[15] appears so similar to that of copy A of P.Oxy. 33.2673 that both documents came in all likelihood from the hand of the same scribe[16] and probably derived from the same office at Oxyrhynchus.[17] The papyrus reads:

] . [. .] . [
[c. 13 letters παρ]ạδοθεῖσαν τῷ̣ λ̣ογιστῇ̣
[πρὸς τὸ κατενεγχθ]ῆ̣γ̣αι ἐπὶ τὴν λαμ(προτάτην) Ἀλεξάνδρια(ν)
[ἀκολούθως τοῖς γρα]φẹῖσι ὑπὸ τοῦ διασημοτάτου
[ἡμῶν ἡγεμόνος Κλ]ῳ̣δίου Κουλ{κουλ}κιανοῦ
[καὶ ὀμνύω τὴν τῶν] κ̣υ̣[ρ]ị́ων ἡμῶν Διοκλ̣ητιανοῦ
[καὶ Μαξιμιανοῦ Σεβαστῶν] κ̣αὶ Κωνστὰν΄τίọυ̣ κ̣[α]ị Μαξιμιανọῦ̣
[τῶν ἐπιφανεστάτων Κ]ạισάρων τύχην̣ τ̣αῦ̣θ' οὕτως
[ἔχειν καὶ μηδὲν] διẹψẹῦσθαι ἢ ἔνοχος εἴην τῷ̣ θεί[ῳ̣]
[ὅρκῳ̣. (ἔτους) κ΄΄ κα]ị ιβ΄΄ τῶν κυρίων ἡμῶν Διοκλητια(νοῦ)

[12] Ed. princ. Donatella Limongi, P.Harr. 2.208 (1985) 108–10.

[13] In the Preface to the volume, the editors write: "Oxyrhynchus is the provenance of many of the texts in the present volume, and may well be the provenance of others which provide no internal indication" (P.Harr. 2, vii).

[14] The exception is that the word αὐτοκρατόρων lacks in line 6 of the Harris papyrus (compared to the P.Oxy. declarations).

[15] "Una cancelleresca con una forte concessione alla corsiva" (P.Harr. 2.208, 109).

[16] "La scrittura . . . è molto simile a quella della copia A di P. Oxy. XXXIII 2673 e non si può escludere che si tratti della stessa mano" (ibid.).

[17] As Limongi states: "E' dunque probabile che questa dichiarazione sia uscita dallo stesso ufficio ossirinchita in cui sono state stilate le tre copie del documento edito come P. Oxy. XXXIII 2673" (ibid.).

[καὶ Μαξιμιανοῦ Σεβαστ]ῶν καὶ Κωνσταντίου καὶ Μαξιμιανοῦ
[τῶν ἐπιφανεστάτων Καισ]άρ[ων], Μεχεὶρ ιδʹ

Translation

> [. . .]given over to the *logistes* in order to be brought down to the most glorious Alexandria in accordance with what was written by our most eminent governor Clodius Culcianus, I also swear by the genius of our lords Diocletian and Maximian, the Augusti, and Constantius and Galerius, the most illustrious Caesars, that these things are thus and that nothing is cheated, or I may be liable to the divine oath.
> In the 20th and 12th year of our lords the emperors Diocletian and Maximian, the Augusti, and Constantius and Galerius, the most illustrious Caesars, Mecheir 14th.

Apart from the date (14 February instead of the tenth) and the word "Augusti," the preserved text of P.Harr. 2.208 is exactly the same as that of P.Oxy. 33.2673.[18] Since the top and bottom of the Harris papyrus have broken off, two important parts have gone missing in the Harris fragment: first, the section containing the specifics, a parallel to the circumstances outlined in lines 8–22 of P.Oxy. 33.2673; and second, the subscription. Therefore the information that we find most interesting—namely, who filed it, from what village or city, and what property they reported and delivered to the *logistes*—we do not find in this papyrus.[19] Given this absence of specificity, my investigations concentrate on the triple preserved declaration about the former church at Chysis (P.Oxy. 33.2673). In the following analysis, P.Harr. 2.208 plays a supporting role.

Meeting Government Officials

The declaration attesting the property confiscation from the church at Chysis (P.Oxy. 33.2673) is addressed to the senators in the city council and (former?)

[18] The word αὐτοκρατόρων is present in P.Oxy. 33.2673, line 27.

[19] All we find out is that something is being transported to Alexandria. Whether this belonged to a church, as was the case in the parallel text (P.Oxy. 33.2673), or consisted of someone's personal property (see P.Oxy. 33.2665, discussed below) cannot be known. The occurrence of the participle παραδοθεῖσαν in both documents (P.Oxy. 33.2673, lines 22–23 and—clearly preserved in the Harris papyrus—P. Harr. 2.208, line 2) could suggest that the antecedent in the Harris papyrus is also the word ὕλη, in the sense of material, "stuff."

administrators of the gymnasium: Aurelius Neilus alias Ammonius, Aurelius Sarmates, and Aurelius Matrinus. Neilus alias Ammonius also functioned as the city's *prytanis*, the president of the city council, and Sarmates and Matrinus also performed as *syndics*, or important officers "whose chief task was to represent the town, externally in its dealings with the imperial government, and internally in its dealings with private citizens."[20] The three operated in the countryside, in the village of Chysis. The declaration is occasioned by two high financial officials at the level of the government of the province of Egypt: Aurelius Athananius and his superior Neratius Apollonides.[21] Presumably, these two officials issued orders in compliance with the imperial edict. At the time of writing, the confiscated bronze materials from the church had gone into the possession of the Oxyrhynchite *logistes*, the "imperial official in overall charge of a particular city."[22] At the top of the chain of command, occupying the highest government job in Roman Egypt, stood Clodius Culcianus, prefect of Egypt. Culcianus held this position in the early years of the fourth century,[23] hence, the persecutions of Christians under the emperor Diocletian took place during his term in office. This man figures prominently in Christian literary texts such as the *Acts of Phileas* and Eusebius's *Ecclesiastical History*. In short, the men involved in this matter all have high-ranking official positions both at the local and the provincial level.[24] This document, then, exposes the pervasive reach of Roman power in the life of an Egyptian village. The existence of three copies in nonidentical

[20] Bowman, *Town Councils*, 47; with reference to Rees, "The *Defensor Civitatis* in Egypt," *JJP* 6 (1952) 73–102.

[21] The *procurator rei privatae* was a financial officer subordinate to the *magister rei privatae*, see Lallemand, *Administration civile de l'Égypte*, 89 and 90–92. Bowman remarks that "These investigations . . . register the fact that such tasks (i.e., investigations and confiscation of property) are delegated to the syndikoi and the prytanis by officials of the central government, and that the syndikoi are associated with the prytanis of the boule." In this context he mentions MChr 196, P.Oxy. 33.2665, and P.Oxy. 33.2673; the last two, he suggests, "are connected with the persecution of Christians" (*Town Councils*, 49).

[22] Bagnall, *Egypt in Late Antiquity*, 337. The Latin term is *curator civitatis*.

[23] When precisely Culcianus was appointed as prefect is not clear. The papyri indicate that he held that office for at least five years. The earliest reference to him is dated 6 June 301 (P.Oxy. 46.3304), the latest dates from 29 May 306 (P.Oxy. 8.1104). See also Parsons in P.Oxy. 50.3529, note to line 1. Eusebius's claim (*Hist. eccl.* 9.11.4) that Culcianus was murdered after the persecution cannot be independently verified.

[24] In his description of the destruction of the Nicomedean church on 23 February 303, Lactantius mentions the presence of high officials at the scene: "the prefect came to the church with military leaders, tribunes and fiscal officers" (ad ecclesiam praefectus cum

hands, presumably one copy for each official, indicates that someone dictated the text to a group of scribes. Thus the government had allocated many people to this project, even though it had insignificant returns.

Reader of a Village Church

The declaration presents to us a Christian: Aurelius Ammonius, "reader of the former church of the village of Chysis."[25] As a lower church official, the reader had the responsibility of reciting liturgical texts in church services.[26] In

ducibus et tribunis et rationalibus venit, *Mort.* 12.2). That situation is different, for Diocletian and Galerius are also present.

[25] ἀναγνώστης τῆς ποτε ἐκκλησίας κώμης Χύσεως, P.Oxy. 33.2673, lines 8–9. Fourteen years after the declaration on church property, we again encounter Ammonius. On 10 November 318, "Aurelius Ammonius, son of Copreus" appears in an application for a lease of five arouras of land near Ision Panga (Ἀμμωνίο[υ] Κοπρέ̣[ω]ς, P.Oxy. 45.3257, line 4). In her article on *copronyms*, Pomeroy lists both papyri under one heading, thus also identifying them as one person, "Κοπρεύς f(ather) of Aur. Ammonios (lector)" ("Copronyms and the Exposure of Infants," in *Studies in Roman Law* [ed. Bagnall and Harris] 147–62, esp. 154). Gamble assumes that readers were often younger men: "Cyprian speaks of these as young men "deserving higher ranks" but not yet qualified for them by age. For the office of lector there was apparently no stipulated age, but the necessary skills and deportment meant that readers were usually at least in late adolescence, between the years of sixteen and twenty" (*Books and Readers*, 224). If that were also the case with Ammonius, then he is still young when he files the declaration. Ision Panga and Chysis were both located in the upper toparchy, see Krüger, *Oxyrhynchos in der Kaiserzeit*, 51 with a schematic drawing of the upper toparchy, and 273, no. 149; "Isieion Panga" in Timm, *Das christlich-koptische Ägypten* 3:1181; Rowlandson, *Landowners and Tenants*, 10, 18–19, and map on xiv. Christian clergy involved in business transactions are common. For examples, see Schmelz, *Kirchliche Amtsträger*, 203–54; and Wipszycka, *Ressources*, esp. 154–73 (e.g., 163), although our text is on the early side compared to their focus. Schmelz comments: "Die meisten Priester, Diakone und niederen Amtsträger in der Chora Ägyptens bestritten ihren Unterhalt aus Zuwendungen ihrer Kirche und, weil diese häufig nicht ausreichten, aus verschiedenen weltlichen Arbeiten" (*Kirchliche Amtsträger*, 203).

[26] On this office in the fourth to eighth centuries, see Wipszycka, "Ordres mineurs," in her *Études sur le Christianisme*, 225–55, 238–48, previously published in *JJP* 22 (1992) 181–215. For this period, in which our texts falls very early, she writes that "la tâche du lecteur consistait à lire, au cours des réunions liturgiques, des morceaux de la Bible et des textes de dévotion" (ibid., 239). However, they probably were not allowed to read gospel passages (ibid.). Turner described the office as follows: "We know that there was a priestly office or order in the early church held by the reader, ἀναγνώστης. It was his duty to read the sacred scriptures aloud to the congregation. . . . Persons belonging to this order proudly added the qualification ἀναγνώστης to their tombstones" (*Typology*, 84–85, with reference to Eusebius, *Hist. eccl.* 6.43). According to Haas, "The office of reader or lector (*anagnostes*)

a largely illiterate society, a reader provided the Christian congregation access to its scriptures.[27] Readers are mentioned in many literary and documentary sources.[28] The status of church readers in Egypt at the beginning of the fourth century remains unclear.[29] We know from the Apostolic Constitutions that in Syria, toward the end of the fourth century, ordination of readers happened

was one of the oldest defined offices in the early church and, by the mid-third century, was considered a clerical, rather than a lay, position. The reader stood on the bottom rung of the clerical *cursus honorum*, and patriarchal protégés were normally first appointed readers" (*Alexandria in Late Antiquity*, 223).

[27] So Gamble: "In any congregation only a small number of persons could read at all, and fewer could read publicly. In the early period, and long afterward in small communities, there may have been no more than one or two who had the ability. The task of reading inevitably fell to the literate, and because the congregation depended upon them for its access to texts, a great importance accrued to them" (*Books and Readers*, 220). According to the *Traditio apostolica*, the lector reads the scriptures and the bishop interprets them (Geerlings, *Apostolische Überlieferung*, 174). In earlier times, some readers may have also interpreted the readings. Gamble makes this suggestion based on 2 Clem 19.1: "it would seem that at least in some churches the responsibility of the reader was not only to read the scripture but also to deliver the homily that interpreted and applied the scripture he had read. This would make the reader's role prominent indeed, even if not official" (*Books and Readers*, 219).

[28] In several instances the word occurs in a non-Christian context. At Oxyrhynchus an ἀναγνώστης shows up in a papyrus dated 58 C.E.; too early to designate him as a Christian reader (P.Oxy. 49.3463, line 18). SB 4.7336, line 28, features a reader called Sarapas, mentioned in an account for a pagan religious festival; in this context, it is unlikely that he was Christian. Other such examples are SB 4.7338, P.Oxy. 24.2421, P.Ant. 2.93 and P.Gron. 9 (see also Wipszycka, "Ordres mineurs," 238–39 n. 27).Turning to Christian readers: Eusebius (*Hist. eccl.* 6.43.11) in a detailed list of clergy at the Roman church in the mid-third century, mentions a total of fifty-two exorcists, readers, and doorkeepers. The earliest certainly Christian "reader" in the papyri appears in SB 6.9557, dated during the episcopate of papa Maximus of Alexandria (in office 264–282 C.E.), who is mentioned in the papyrus. Roughly a decade later than our papyrus we meet a colleague of Ammonius, another reader from the Oxyrhynchite countryside, in a tax list: Besarion, reader, from Tampetei (Βησαρίων ἀνα[γ]ν̣ώστης) P.Oxy. 55.3787, lines 56–57 (313–320 C.E.). I take this Besarion as a Christian reader; the mention of a "deacon of the church" (Ἀπφοῦς διάκων ἐκκλησίας, 24–25) earlier in the register and the frequency of Christian names suggest that (cf. Wipszycka, who maintains that "l'ἀναγνώστης mentionné dans ce meme document n'appartient pas au clergé, car, au mot désignant la fonction, le scribe n'a pas ajouté la precision τῆς ἐκκλησίας, come il l'a fait pour le διάκων" ["Papyrus documentaires," 1309]). Another reader in a papyrus from Oxyrhynchus is Morus (P.Oxy. 41.2969, dated 323 C.E., see also below); from elsewhere, e.g., Herminus (P.Neph. 12, fourth cent.). See also Martin (*Athanase d'Alexandrie*, 784) who provides a list of lectores and also other offices.

[29] See Bagnall: "lectors (*anagnostai*), an order of lower clergy . . . whose ordained status is uncertain" (*Egypt in Late Antiquity*, 284–85).

by the laying on of hands.[30] In contrast to Syria, the bishop in Egypt handed the readers being ordained a codex.[31]

Contemporary texts suggest that readers served together with deacons and priests.[32] If, however, other clergy had served at Chysis, why then would Ammonius, the church reader, have filed the declaration?[33] Ammonius was thus most likely the responsible person for the church at Chysis, for churches in rural areas did not have an extensive clergy staff at this time.[34] In addition,

[30] See *Apostolic Constitutions* 8.22: "Ordain a reader by laying your hands upon him, and pray to God saying, 'Do now look down upon your servant, who is to be entrusted to read your holy scriptures to your people, and give him your holy spirit, the prophetic spirit. You who instructed your servant Ezra to read your Law to the people do now also at our prayers instruct your servant and grant that he may without blame perfect the work committed to him, and thereby be declared worthy of a higher degree.'" (Quoted by Gamble, *Books and Readers*, 221). Gamble comments: "Here, in contrast to Hippolytus's rule, the reader is subject to the laying on of hands, and the readership is a recognized order of the clergy" (ibid., 221).

[31] According the *Traditio apostolica*, upon their appointment lectors received a book from the bishop, but no laying on of hands: Ἀναγνώστης καθίσταται ἐπιδόντος αὐτῷ βιβλίον τοῦ ἐπισκόπου· οὐδε γὰρ χειροθετεῖται ("The reader is appointed when the bishop delivers him a book. For he is not ordained"). Greek from Geerlings, *Apostolische Überlieferung*, 242 ("11. De Lectore"). Geerlings postulates: "Die Vorschrift in TA 11, daß der Bischof dem Lektor ohne Handauflegung ein Buch überreicht, ist so lapidar, daß man davon ausgehen kann, daß der Dienst des Lektors in der christlichen Kirche voll installiert ist" (*Apostolische Überlieferung*, 173). This text exists in Coptic translation. See also Wipszycka, "Ordres mineurs," 239.

[32] The *Traditio Apostolica* and the passage from Eusebius quoted above depict churches with an extensive clerical hierarchy. Other early-fourth century texts, such as the *Acta* of Munatius Felix, preserved in the *Gesta apud Zenophilum* (from Cirta in North Africa, see below) and the *Acta Saturnini* (from Abitina in Numidia, see also below) also mention a range of clerics for their congregations besides readers. However, this may only reflect the size of their congregations, presumably larger in urban areas.

[33] Higher clergy may have fled, following the example of other, more prominent church leaders such as Peter of Alexandria, or they may have perished under the persecution already. Peter of Alexandria fled Alexandria, and before him, in the third century, such important bishops as Dionysius of Alexandria and Cyprian of Carthage had left their cities to avoid being killed.

[34] Bagnall notes: "A plethora of clergy was not in all likelihood characteristic of the earlier-fourth century. There are reports of clusters of ten or more villages in Mareotis under a single presbyter in the time of Athanasius. . . . It is perhaps closer to the mark to describe the situation as complex and fluid, with regularized structures not yet in place and the availability of clergy and churches varying from place to place" (*Egypt in Late Antiquity*, 284, with reference to Wipszycka).

the government officials responsible for confiscation of church property would certainly have wanted to deal with someone directly in control.[35]

At the foot of all three documents, Serenus wrote the oath formula for Ammonius, stating that the latter "does not know letters" (line 34). The fact that the reader of the church could not write has stimulated academic debate;[36] it is indeed rather strange that a reader cannot write,[37] although other instances have been noted.[38] There are three possible explanations for why

[35] Below we shall see, for instance, that in the contemporary *Acta* of Munatius Felix the bishop negotiates with the officials. Readers do figure prominently in other texts of that period, such as martyria from Diocletian's persecution, for example, the martyrdom of Dioscorus (a fragment of which is preserved in a fourth-century manuscript from Oxyrhynchus, P.Oxy. 50.3529): Culcianus asks Dioscorus whether he is a lector. He replies that his father was one. ([Κουλκιανὸ]ς αὐτῷ εἶπ[εν· ἀναγνώστης εἶ; Διόσκορος] [εἶπεν· οὐκ, ἀλλ᾽ ὁ πατ]ήρ μου ἀναγ[νώστης ἦν]). Apparently Culcianus expected Dioscorus to be a lector. According to the *Acta Saturnini* (12 February 304) the congregation of Abitina in Numidia met in the house of the lector, Emeritus. Interviewed by the proconsul, this Emeritus reportedly said: "I am the guardian in whose house the congregation was assembled" (ego sum auctor . . . in cuius domus collecta facta fuit). And later: "In my house we conducted the Lord's Supper" (in domo mea. . . egimus dominicum). White, *Social Origins* 2:88 (Latin) and 89 (translation).

[36] Wipszycka, "Lecteur," 415–20, and eadem, "Encore sur le lecteur," 421–26; Clarke, "Illiterate lector?" 103–4, Bagnall, *Egypt in Late Antiquity*, 256–57 n. 142; Gamble, *Books and Readers*, 250 n. 31.

[37] Wipszycka remarks: "Qu'un ἀναγνώστης, un 'lecteur', ne sache pas écrire, voilà qui est surprenant" ("Lecteur," 416). Clarysse calls it "rather astonishing for a lector: even if he was a Copt, it must have been easy for him to write down his name and a short declaration in Greek" ("Coptic Martyr Cult," 380); and White finds it "perplexing" (*Social Origins* 2:169).

[38] An interesting case is that of Morus, a reader at Oxyrhynchus some twenty years later, in the year 323. He also is unable to sign his own name, but for medical reasons: Morus, ἀναγνώστης needed Horion to sign for him because he (Morus) had hurt his eyes (Ὠ̣[ρίων] ἔγρα(ψα) ὑ(πὲρ) αὐτ(οῦ) βεβ<λ>αμμένου τὰς ὄψη̣σ̣ς (sic, with two sigmas); read ὄψεις]) (P.Oxy. 41.2993, lines 11–12). Being incapable of writing because of bad eyesight differs significantly from being illiterate. The very fact that Horion explicitly mentions this as reason why Morus did not sign himself indicates that Morus had been literate. Thus this example actually supports the view that readers are able to write. The question remains whether he was a church reader. According to J. C. Shelton in the edition, an ἀναγνώστης "may be either a pagan who earns his living by reading or a Christian lector " (P.Oxy. 41.2969, 55). Eye-related illness in Egypt is not uncommon (see also below in the letter of Copres to Sarapias, P.Oxy. 31.2601). An illiterate deacon from the early-fourth cent., is, e.g., "Aurelius Besis son of Akoris." His contract reads: "Since today I was ordained into your diaconate and made a public profession to you that I should be inseparable from your bishopric," etc. Then at the end it reads: "I, Aurelius Besis, the aforesaid, have had the aforesaid document made and agreed as aforesaid, [I] Aurelius Hierakion [wrote] on his behalf [since he is illiterate]" (Horsley, "A Deacon's Work Contract" [= CPR 11] *NewDocs* 1:122). Clarke offers several

Ammonius did not sign the declaration himself. As the first and most literal explanation for the signature formula, perhaps Ammonius indeed could not write a short statement under the declaration and relied on his memory for reciting scriptural passages in his function as church reader.[39] As a second explanation for the fact that someone else signed for Ammonius, perhaps Ammonius only knew Egyptian.[40] According to Rea, the village church in Chysis belonged to a predominantly Egyptian-speaking community, and their reader used Coptic manuscripts in the service. This would involve the underlying and incorrect assumption that Egyptian speakers are ignorant and illiterate. Moreover, as Cribiore has shown, students had to learn to write Greek before they could learn to write Coptic.[41] So whether or not we have Egyptian- or Greek-speaking villagers,[42] this still does not adequately explain why Ammonius did not sign the declaration.[43] For Ammonius needed to write only the short sentence, "I, Aurelius Ammonius, swear the oath as aforesaid" (Αὐρήλιος Ἀμμώνιος ὤμοσα τὸν ὅρκον ὡς πρόκειται). If Ammonius had known how to write in Coptic, he would not have had any difficulty copying

other examples of illiterate readers from epigraphical and literary sources. Some readers, he shows, were young children (Clarke, "Illiterate Lector," 103–4). In his article "(Il)literacy in Non-Literary Papyri from Graeco-Roman Egypt," Kraus gives the example of village scribes who are illiterate, unable to write more than their own names. He warns also that it cannot be maintained that "those we expect to be able to read and write actually are in possession of these abilities" (ibid., 334).

[39] Bagnall offers this as a possibility (*Egypt in Late Antiquity*, 256–57 n. 142).

[40] Rea, ed. princ. 105. Turner followed this interpretation: "An individual *reader* whose church suffered in the persecution of A.D. 304 is mentioned in P.Oxy. XXXIII 2673, 8, and 34 where he is further described as 'illiterate.' What this means is that he was a 'reader' of Coptic, not Greek texts" (*Typology*, 85). See also Judge and Pickering: "no doubt a poor Coptic-speaking community—Ammonius the lector did not know how to sign his name in Greek" ("Papyrus Documentation," 59).

[41] Cribiore, "Greek and Coptic Education," in *Ägypten und Nubien* (ed. Emmel) 279–86. See also eadem, *Gymnastics of the Mind*, 157. As Bagnall observes, literacy in Coptic is at this time not the domain of poor people: "One may be tempted to look to the Coptic texts for the voice of the others. Those hopes too are destined to be disappointed, for the documents of daily life do not become common in Coptic until much later, long after Chalcedon. . . . Coptic in the fourth century is still largely the instrument of one milieu, the Christian monasteries. . . . this too is not the viewpoint of the poor. The creators of Coptic were bilingually literate men, not products of the peasantry" (*Egypt in Late Antiquity*, 5).

[42] See on this and related questions Bagnall, *Egypt in Late Antiquity*, "Spoken and Written Greek in the Villages," 240–46.

[43] Wipszycka argued that "l'explication proposée par J. Rea n'est pas acceptable, faut-il penser que le 'lecteur' Aurelius Ammonios ne savait vraiment pas écrire? Cette hypothèse est manifestement tout à fait invraisemblable" (Wipszycka, "Lecteur," 416).

a short sentence in Greek, since Greek and Coptic share the same alphabet.[44] Wipszycka offered a third explanation. She proposed that Ammonius pretended illiteracy because he did not want to sign the oath[45] and to swear to the *tyche* (good fortune) of the emperors.[46] This psychological interpretation of the question of Ammonius's illiteracy provides a better explanation than the more widespread scholarly opinion that, as a Copt, Ammonius did not know Greek.[47] According to this interpretation, Ammonius would have publicly acknowledged the validity of the document and then arranged for the signing by someone else.[48] James Scott's work on forms of resistance

[44] Wipszycka wrote: "Pour une personne habituée à écrire en copte, cela ne devait pas présenter de difficulté. Il est faux de voir une analogie entre le cas du 'lecteur' Ammonios et ceux des prêtres égyptiens sachant écrire en démotique, et pas en grec. La différence entre l'écriture démotique et l'écriture grecque est totale, celle entre l'écriture copte et l'écriture grecque est minime" (ibid., 416).

[45] See De Ste. Croix's observation on the oath formula: "One often hears it said that the Christians were martyred 'for refusing to worship the emperor.' In fact, emperor worship is a factor of almost no independent importance in the persecution of the Christians. It is true that among our records of martyrdoms emperor-worship does crop up occasionally, but far more often it is a matter of sacrificing *to the gods*—as a rule, not even specifically to 'the gods of the Romans.' And when the cult act involved does concern the emperor, it is usually an oath by his Genius (or in the East by his Τύχη) or a sacrifice to the gods on his behalf." ("Why Were the Early Christians Persecuted?" *Past and Present* 26 [1963] 10).

[46] "Mon explication du P.Oxy. XXXIII 2673 va dans un autre sens. Je suppose que c'est pour des raisons religieuses que le 'lecteur' Ammonios n'a pas voulu signer le document de sa main et s'est déclaré analphabète. Notre Ammonios a dû être tiraillé entre des sentiments opposés. D'un côté, il redoutait les répressions; de l'autre côté, il sentait que son comportement, tout en n'enfreignant pas les règles admises dans l'Église, n'était pas irréprochable; il sentait que ce n'était pas une bonne action que de livrer aux autorités les objets appartenant à sa communauté, et qui étaient probablement des objets servant au culte. La pression de la part des extrémistes, qui désiraient le martyre et condamnaient sévèrement ceux qui obéissaient aux ordres des autorités impériales, était probablement très forte" (Wipszycka, "Lecteur," 417).

[47] Her analysis is followed by Clarysse, "Coptic Martyr Cult," 380.

[48] In his *De idolatria* Tertullian provides an interesting example of different attitudes among Christians to swearing oaths. Debating with a fictive Christian discussion partner, Tertullian disputes the view that a written oath differs from a spoken one, thereby implying that some Christians advocated that position. At stake is whether signing a contract of borrowing involves swearing an oath. The imaginary discussion partner claims: "I have written . . . but I have not said anything" (scripsi . . . sed nihil dixi). Tertullian disagrees, arguing that "the hand cannot write anything which the soul has not dictated" and that that also holds true even if someone else dictated, ergo: one has still sworn an oath (*Idol.* 23.1–3, ed. and trans. Waszink and Van Winden, 66–67, and remarks on 284–90). See also Wipszycka, "Lecteur," 418.

by subordinate groups helps to understand the situation better.[49] Ammonius would have played dumb to preserve his religious integrity as a small act of resistance against the imperial measures.

Ammonius functioned as the reader of the former church at Chysis (modern Schuscha), a "not unimportant" village on the Bar Yusuf canal near the southern border of the Oxyrhynchite nome[50] and one of the villages in the Oxyrhynchite nome with a granary.[51] Living along the Bar Yusuf canal on the trade route between Oxyrhynchus city and Hermopolis Magna, we can assume that the villagers had a regular exchange not only with goods but also with ideas from metropolitan areas. We can presume that they came into contact with Christians in this way. After encountering Petosorapis from Mermertha in the previous chapter, we meet here another Christian from the countryside. Eusebius asserts in his *Demonstratio evangelica* that Christianity had spread widely in Egyptian villages. Meeting rural Christians in papyrus documents thus confirms Eusebius's observation.[52]

From our papyrus declaration we learn of a church in the village of Chysis before the year 304. We do not know when Christians at Chysis began to congregate. Christians may have gathered for worship at someone's house, a so-called *domus ecclesia*, and may even have met in Ammonius's home.[53] The church in the declaration may refer also to a building specifically set aside or built as church. Both were referred to as church.[54] The description

[49] Scott notes that "the hidden transcript is not just behind-the-scenes griping and grumbling; it is enacted in a host of down-to-earth, low profile stratagems designed to minimize appropriation" (*Domination and the Arts of Resistance*, 188).

[50] Krüger characterizes it as "(eine) wahrscheinlich nicht unbedeutende Siedlung" (*Oxyrhynchos in der Kaiserzeit*, 268; see also the map on page 369). Also according to Drew-Bear, "Χύσις devait être un gros village" (*Le nome Hermopolite. Toponymes et sites*, 322–26, at 326). Judge and Pickering describe it as an "obscure . . . village" ("Papyrus Documentation," 69).

[51] Krüger, *Oxyrhynchos in der Kaiserzeit*, 62.

[52] Eusebius, *Dem. ev.* 8.5. Edition: Heikel, *Eusebius Werke, Bd.* 6: *Die Demonstratio evangelica* (GCS 23) 1913. The passage is highly rhetorical. Eusebius claims that the prophecy in Isa 19 about the altar in Egypt is fulfilled.

[53] In Abitina, the congregation met in their lector's house. At Cirta the Christians met at a house according to the *Acta* of Munatius Felix (see also Edwards, *Optatus: Against the Donatists*, 153 n. 24).

[54] As Rordorf observes: "Die . . . Tatsache, daß die Privathäuser, die in den ersten drei Jahrhunderten zu gottesdienstlichen Zwecken benützt wurden, auch einfach 'Kirchen' genannt werden konnten, macht es schwer, im einzelnen Fall zu entscheiden, ob es sich um eine Hauskirche oder um ein von den Christen eigens erbautes Kirchengebäude handelt, wenn in einem Text von einer Kirche die Rede ist" ("Die christlichen Gottesdiensträume" *ZNTW* 54

of the church as "the *former* church" (ἡ *ποτε* ἐκκλησία) implies that they no longer used the building in February of 304.[55] Eusebius and Lactantius both recount the destruction of churches during Diocletian's persecution.[56] Yet some scholars have suggested that not all churches suffered burning or complete ruin during the Great Persecution but rather only the stripping of valuables and closure.[57] Whether the case or not with other churches, the Chysis church not only had its possessions confiscated, but the description "former church" implies that the building no longer existed at the time of the document.

Church Inventory

The enumeration of assets in the declaration gives an indication of what officials expected to find in a church.[58] They defined their list rather broadly and checked for lands,[59] cattle, money and precious metals, clothing, and

[1963] 110–28, at 122). Rordorf's time frame is the pre-Constantinian period; he mentions examples from the period of the Great Persecution, thus contemporary to our text here.

[55] As mentioned in the "Introduction," by the early-fourth century there were at least two churches in Oxyrhynchus city (P.Oxy. 1.43).

[56] See Eusebius, *Hist. eccl.* 8.2.4, quoted above. Eusebius also claims that he witnessed the destruction of churches: "we saw with our very eyes the houses of prayer cast down to their foundations from top to bottom" (ibid. 8.2.1, trans. Oulton 2:257). According to Lactantius the persecution began with the destruction of the Christian church at Nicomedia and the burning of the Scriptures (*Mort.* 12). Lactantius also refers to Constantius ordering the destruction of church buildings in the West, but not the killing of people (*Mort.* 15.7). Lactantius speaks of the churches as *loca*, places. See also Rordorf, "Die christlichen Gottesdiensträume," 123.

[57] For instance, Frend mentions that a church in Heraclea, Thrace, was not destroyed but locked and sealed, with reference to a Martyrdom of Philip. It is however not clear what text he is referring to here (*Martyrdom and Persecution*, 499). White points to the Edict of Milan, quoted by Lactantius, containing a section on the reinstatement of possessions to churches. This leads White to observe that "the provisions for restoration of church properties . . . make it clear that a universal 'destruction of churches' was not the order of the day, but rather the rhetorical symbol among the Christians. It appears instead that search and seizure of the properties was more common" (*Social Origins* 2:116 n. 42).

[58] According to Judge and Pickering, "the catalogue presumably defines the range of property expected to be found in the possession of a church at this time" ("Papyrus Documentation," 59). So also Bagnall: "The list . . . at least suggests what the authorities thought a church might possibly own" (*Egypt in Late Antiquity*, 290).

[59] Sotas solicited the donation of a field from Demetrianus (P.Oxy. 12.1492). The fact that this checklist includes land signifies that churches were owning land, or at least, were expected to do so.

also, listed as inventory, slaves. They could sell all of these. The fact that P.Oxy. 33.2673 and P.Harr. 2.208 are almost exactly the same suggests to me that the officials worked from a standardized checklist.[60] This signals the government's systematic bureaucratic effort.

The *Gesta apud Zenophilum*, trial proceedings from the year 320, incorporate an earlier document, the *Acta* of Munatius Felix, dated 19 May 303, from Cirta in Numidia (present day Constantine in Algeria).[61] This earlier document, contemporaneous with our papyrus text, serves as an interesting point of comparison. It depicts the following situation: A delegation of government officials visits the church in Cirta and requests books and other church property. From the church are brought out a good amount of gold and silver objects, some clothes, and quite a number of shoes:

> Two gold chalices, six silver chalices, six silver urns, a silver cooking-pot, seven silver lamps, two wafer-holders, seven short bronze candle-sticks with their own lights, eleven bronze lamps with their own chains, 82 women's tunics, 38 capes, 16 men's tunics, 13 pairs of men's shoes, 47 pairs of women's shoes, and 19 peasant clasps.[62]

[60] Such a checklist could have been based on finds from other churches, temple inventories, or private possessions. For an overview of church inventory lists and bibliography, see Dosálová, P.Prag.Wess. 2.178 "Klosterinventar" (1995) 137–39; and eadem, "Gli inventari dei beni delle chiese e dei conventi su papiro," *Analecta Papyrologica* 6 (1994) 5–19. See also van Minnen, P.L.Bat. 25.13, with a list of inventories on page 47. All these documents, however, are much later than our papyrus. As for temple inventories: In their introduction to P.Oxy. 12.1449, Grenfell and Hunt listed the objects from temple dedication split out into gold, silver, bronze, and stone, clothing and miscellanea (P.Oxy. 12.1449, 136). Until the mid- or late-third century, Egyptian temples submitted yearly an inventory of priests, revenues, and possessions, the so-called γραφαὶ ἱερέων καὶ χειρισμοῦ. For an overview of such declarations, see P.Oxy. 49.3473, 141–42. See also Battaglia, "Dichiarazioni templari," *Aeg* 64 (1984) 79–99; and Burkhalter, "Le mobilier des sanctuaires d'Égypte" *ZPE* 59 (1985) 123–34. On private possessions: see, e.g., P.Oxy. 34.2713, "Petition to a Prefect" (297 C.E.) about a woman complaining about her uncle's taking her share of the inheritance. She refers to "slaves and lands and moveables" (ἀνδροπόδων καὶ οἰκοπέδων καὶ ἐνδομ[ενίας]); P.Oxy. 43.3119, the fragmentary preserved official document probably from the persecution under Valerian, dealt with Christians and property. A papyrus contemporary with ours, P.Oxy. 33.2665 contains an inquiry into private property of an individual Christian.

[61] Critical edition: *Gesta apud Zenophilum*, Appendix I in *S. Optati Melevitani Libri VII*, ed. Ziwsa, 185–97. See also the new study of this text by Duval: "L'église et la communauté," in her *Chrétiens d'Afrique*, 13–209 with photographic reproduction of pages of the Cormery manuscript that contains this text in the appendix, 470–85.

[62] Calices duo aurei, item calices sex argentei, urceola sex argentea, cucumellum argenteum, lucernas argenteas septem, cereofala duo, candelas breves aeneas cum lucernis suis septem, item

Upon a closer inspection, another silver lamp and a silver box appear, and then four large jars and six barrels from the dining room.[63]

It would have been so interesting to have an account as detailed as the *Acta* of Munatius Felix on the interior of a village church in Egypt in the early years of the fourth century.[64] But in our declaration, the lector Ammonius swears that the

> church had neither gold nor silver nor money nor clothes nor cattle nor slaves nor lands nor possessions, neither from gifts nor from bequests, apart from only the bronze matter which was found and given over to the *logistes* (P.Oxy. 33.2673, lines 15–23).

The document mainly states the negative; what was *not* there. They took only "bronze stuff" (χαλκῆν ὕλην, line 22). In comparison to the long list of possessions of the congregation at Cirta in North Africa, the inventory of the church at Chysis appears particularly meager;[65] it had nothing apart from that "bronze stuff."[66] These "bronze materials" from Chysis could indicate either bronze lamps, as in the Cirta inventory, or also liturgical vessels.[67] That

---

lucernas aeneas undecim cum catenis suis, tunicas muliebres LXXXII, mafortea XXXVIII, tunicas viriles XVI, caligas viriles paria XIII, caligas muliebres paria XLVII, capulas rusticanas XVIIII. *Gesta apud Zenophilum*, the Latin from Ziwsa's edition, 187.4–10; with modification from Duval (viz. in the last line of the quotation *capulas* instead of *caplas*, *Chrétiens d'Afrique*, 416). Translation by Edwards, *Optatus: Against the Donatists*, 154. The "capulas rusticanas" could also be translated as "plain cloaks." I find the enumeration of shoes and clothing striking. They may refer to either liturgical vestments or everyday pieces; Duval argues that they are for charity (ibid., 415–17). Clothing in antiquity constituted a different commodity than today; for instance, wills often list items of clothing, even worn pieces.

[63] *Gesta apud Zenophilum*, 187.16–7 and 21–22.

[64] For a later period, several inventories of churches and monasteries exist, but given the distance in time they have little relevance for the Chysis church declaration (see literature above). As Duval rightly states, "en fait l'Église de Cirta est la seule dont l'équipement liturgique en 303 est connu en détail" (*Chrétiens d'Afrique*, 408). She provides photographs of liturgical vessels such as mentioned in the text, figs. 4–8.

[65] Granted, Cirta was a city, so a richer inventory should not surprise us.

[66] Rea refers to P.Col. 7.141 lines 23–33 χαλκῆς χυτῆς ὕλης ("poured copper material," line 26, see also line 29), with the comment that "It might have been either copper or bronze. . . . The wording indicates that it was cast copper which needed further refining" ("Additions and Corrections" in P.Oxy 48, xvii). SB 14.11958.2 line 75 ("Teil einer Abrechnung über Arbeiten an einem Tempel," Oxyrhynchite, 117 C.E.) reads: εὑρεθ( ) ὕλης χαλκοῦ[?].

[67] Both are known also from the later church and monastery inventories (see footnote above), but also the "pagan" temples (e.g., P.Oxy. 12.1449 line 36 λύχ(νος) χα(λκοῦς)). Rea concluded for our papyrus: "In our context a mass of unworked bronze seems unlikely.

the officials had found bronze materials and confiscated them suggests that they had already inspected the church.

Records of immovables were kept in the city archives, so we should assume that the document has the facts correct with regard to these, but did this "bronze stuff" really represent all that the Chysis church possessed? If so, the church had modest means, to say the least. The apparent paucity of possessions of the Chysis church gives rise to an intriguing set of explanations.[68] Ammonius might have hidden some of the objects in the church or at home. Or they might have spared church property on account of bribery by Ammonius or collusion on the part of the officials.[69] We can imagine Ammonius and his fellow Christians from Chysis secretly hiding some of their church's possessions, such as a silver lamp or liturgical vessel (as their contemporaries in Cirta did), or even some clothing. Unless assuming a very modest church, we have to suppose that one of the parties involved, whether Ammonius, the church lector, or the government officials, had acted in some fraudulent way.[70]

Missing Manuscripts

A large part of the *Acta* of Munatius Felix details the search for books at the homes of church readers. Government officials knew well the importance of scriptures for Christians.[71] Indeed, in the *Acta* of Munatius Felix, the first question the Roman officials ask does not regard church gold and silver but rather manuscripts,[72] and the bishop, Paul, appears ready to hand in all

The very general term was probably chosen for the sake of brevity. The most likely guess is that the phrase refers to a quantity of bronze objects, not necessarily the sacred ones that spring to mind" ("ΠΥΛΗΝ to ῾ΥΛΗΝ," 128).

68 Rea remarks that "it is doubtful whether we should believe that this village church was extremely poor or suspect that the nil return was part of the Christian resistance" (P.Oxy. 33.2673, 106).

69 Rémondon suspects this: "Je ne doute pas que les autorités aient fermé les yeux" ("L'Église dans la société égyptienne à l'époque byzantine," *ChrEg* 47 [1972] 254–77, at 255).

70 Bagnall points out, that the declaration was "unlikely to be false in the matter of real property, which could be checked in the registers" (*Egypt in Late Antiquity*, 289–90).

71 As Gamble remarks: "At the start of the fourth century, Diocletian took it for granted that every Christian community, wherever it might be, had a collection of books and knew that those books were essential to its viability" (*Books and Readers*, 150).

72 "When they arrived at the house in which the Christians gathered, Felix, the permanent priest for life and curator, said to Paul the Bishop: 'Bring forth the writings of the Law, and

other valuables but the books.[73] However, the declaration from Oxyrhynchus does not mention manuscripts; they did not occur on the checklist. The congregation at Chysis must have possessed at least some manuscripts.[74] Why else would it have a reader, whose job it was to read Christian texts during worship? These books may have belonged either to the church or privately to some member. They did not form part of the checklist of goods transported to Alexandria, I propose, because the treasury had no interest in collecting them. Christian manuscripts had no market value, whereas the other items listed—money, clothes, slaves, and property—could go for sale by the *res privata*. The manuscripts were ritually burned[75]—on the spot or in the marketplace—in accordance with Diocletian's edict.[76] Given this scenario,

---

anything else that you have here, as is commanded, so that you may comply with the edict.' Paul the Bishop said, 'The readers have the codices [or, scriptures]; but we give what we have here.'" "cum uentum esset ad domum, in qua christiani conueniebant, Felix flamen perpetuus curator Paulo episcopo dixit: proferte scripturas legis et, si quid aliud hic habetis, ut praeceptum est, ut iussioni parere possitis. Paulus episcopus dixit: scripturas lectores habent. sed nos, quod hic habemus, damus" (*Gesta apud Zenophilum*, 186.20–24; trans. Edwards in *Optatus: Against the Donatists*, 153). See also White, *Social Origins* 2:106–8.

[73] In other literary sources discussing the persecution, the handing over or not of Christian manuscripts also figures prominently. See Gamble, *Books and Readers*, 147–51. People who had done so were called *traditores*. In fact, *traditio* (handing over manuscripts) became an important theological issue in the West resulting in the Donatist controversy.

[74] Looking ahead to church and monastery inventories from the fifth and sixth century, we find that they mention manuscripts among their various worldly possessions. P.Prag. Wess. 2.178 (fifth/sixth cent.), a monastery inventory, lists the manuscripts at the beginning of the list, after four silver cups, a silver pitcher, and a small altar: "different parchment and papyrus books: five" (βιβλία διάφορ[α] βεβρ[άινα] |καὶ χάρτινα ε̣, lines 5–6). P.Grenf. 2.111 (fifth/sixth cent.), a church inventory, has "parchment books: 21; papyrus ones: 3" (βιβλία δερμάτι(να) κα΄| ὁμοί(ως) χαρτία γ΄, lines 27–28), and P.L.Bat. 25.13 (seventh/eighth cent.) enumerates "some forty odd books," most of them in Greek, some bilingual Greek-Coptic, others Coptic.

[75] In his archaeological report on the first excavation season at Oxyrhynchus, Grenfell suggested that some of the Christian papyri found on the garbage heap were deposited there during the persecutions: "It is not improbable that they [i.e., what is now P.Oxy. 1.1 and 2] were the remains of a library belonging to some Christian who perished in the persecution during Diocletian's reign, and whose books were then thrown away" ("Oxyrhynchus and Its Papyri," 6). This cannot be maintained because numerous Christian manuscripts were deposed on those garbage heaps in later centuries also.

[76] Eusebius, *Hist. eccl.* 8.2.4 ("destruction by fire of the Scriptures," trans. Oulton 2:259). Eusebius describes witnessing the burning of Christian books in the agora: "the inspired and sacred Scriptures committed to the flames in the midst of the marketplaces" (ibid., 8.2.1, trans. Oulton 2:257). Such a public burning makes sense. On book burning in antiquity, see Sarefield, "Symbolics of Book Burning," in *The Early Christian Book* (ed. Klingshirn and

it is likely that the manuscripts' owners would try to avoid this fate for their precious books. The *Acta* of Munatius Felix suggest that clergy from the Cirta church had hidden manuscripts in their homes and I imagine that this happened at Chysis, too.

We do not know what happened to the confiscated goods that were transported from Oxyrhynchus to Alexandria. In the case of the Chysis church, the possessions did not amount to much, but from the enumeration of property at the church in Cirta, North Africa, we learn that some churches contributed valuables in gold and silver. The government might have sold or stored these objects, but at the very least, they catalogued them. This inventory therefore not only served the negative side of confiscation; it also meant that the institutions had an official document listing confiscated material. The congregation could use this legal document to appeal for restitution. Lactantius reports that after the persecution, Licinius ordered the restoration of property to Christians.[77] This restitution of property must relate to land and buildings. The congregation at Chysis would not have received their "bronze stuff" back again, but they might well have received its value eventually.

The documents discussed here make clear that Diocletian's persecution not only had personal and theological implications for Christians but indeed also had a material aspect which greatly affected the Christian community at the village of Chysis in rural Egypt. They also exemplify the government's thoroughness in implementing the imperial edict, at the provincial and local level, by its involvement in the village of Chysis through confiscation of property. Christians, however, employed subtle strategies to evade the edict's measures. This greatly nuances our understanding of the period by helping us to see that resistance occurred not only in the grand and torturous deaths

Safran) 159–73; especially 164–69 on the burning of Christian books. As Sarefield remarks: "the fury of the early fourth-century persecutors was directed specifically at Christian texts ..." (ibid., 164–65).

[77] *Mort.* 48. 7–10. See also *Mort.* 48.13: His litteris propositis etiam verbo hortatus est, ut conventicula <in> statum pristinum redderentur ("After this letter had been published, he [Licinius] even encouraged orally that the places of assembly be restored to their former state"). According to Städele, the legal term for the Christian places of assembly used in the edicts is *conventiculum* (in his *Laktanz,* 71 n. 195). In this meaning it occurs in *Mort.* 15.7; 34.4; 36.3; 48.9. Frend remarks: "detailed instructions for the complete restoration of Church property, bona fide purchasers having the right, however, to indemnity from the Imperial Treasury" (*Martyrdom and Persecution*, 519).

like those of the nameless martyrs from the Egyptian Thebaid[78] but also in the small negotiations and rebellions around writing and hiding property.

Paul of the Oxyrhynchite Nome: Martyr of the Great Persecution (P.Oxy. 33.2665)[79]

Another document from the Great Persecution, "Report of Property Registrars," dated 305–306 C.E., again confronts us with government bureaucracy in the persecution of Christians and points to an otherwise unknown martyr from Oxyrhynchus.[80] This light-colored papyrus (19 x 26 cm) has some damage in the top and bottom part, but the body is preserved reasonably well. The scribe wrote in a regular, quite elegant and legible professional hand and gave attention to layout. The text reads:

> ἐπὶ ὑπάτων τῶν κυρίων ἡμῶν αὐτοκρατόρων Κω]ν̣[σ]τ̣α̣ν̣[τίου] τ̣ὸ̣ . . . καὶ Μαξιμιανοῦ τὸ . . . Σ]εβαστ̣[ῶν· Αὐρηλίοις Ἱερακ]ί̣ωνι τῷ [κ]α̣ὶ̣ Δ̣[ιονυσ]ί̣[ῳ] γυμν̣[α]σ̣ι̣ά̣[ρ]χῳ βουλευτῇ .... πρ]υ̣τάνι τῆς λαμπρᾶς καὶ λαμπροτάτης Ὀξυρυγχιτῶν πόλεως καὶ . . .]μ̣ῳ γυμν̣α̣σιάρ̣χῳ καὶ Σαραπίωνι .... σ]υ̣ν[δ]ί̣κοις τῆς αὐτῆς πόλεως Αὐρήλιοι ..].[.]ν ὁ καὶ Ἡρακλιανὸς ἀρχιερατεύσ̣[ας] καὶ [Ἀ]γαθῖνος ἐξηγητὴς ἀμφότεροι βουλευταὶ τῆς αὐτῆς πόλεως βιβλιοφύλακες τοῦ αὐτοῦ νομοῦ τ[ο]ῖ̣[ς] φ̣[ιλτάτο]ι̣[ς] χαίρειν· ἐπεστί̣[λατε ἡμῖν κ]εκελευκέναι Αὐρήλιον Ἀθανάσιον ἐπίτροπον τῆς κατ᾽ Αἴγυπτον πριουάτης δι᾽ ὧν ἔγραψεν κατὰ θεῖον πρόσταγμα τῶν δεσποτῶν ἡμῶν βασιλέων τε καὶ Κὰ ι῾σάρων ἀκολούθως τοῖς ἐπιτετῖσι πρὸς αὐτὸν γράμμασι Νερατίου Ἀπολλωνίδου τὰ ὑ̔πάρχοντα Παύλου ἀπὸ τοῦ Ὀξυρυγχίτου ἀποφάσι ὑποβληθέντος τοῦ διασημοτάτου ἡγουμένου Θ̣η̣βαΐδος Σατρίου Ἀριανοῦ προσκρειθῆναι

[78] Eusebius claims to have been an eyewitness (*Hist. eccl.* 8.9.4).

[79] Ed. princ. Rea, P.Oxy. 33.2665 (1968) 89–91.

[80] M.Chr. 196, "Auskunftserteilung durch die βιβλιοφύλακες ἐγκτήσεων über das Vermögen eines Inquisiten" (P.Lips. Inv. Nr. 508) dated to 2 July 309, is a document very similar to P.Oxy. 33.2665. It contains also an inquiry into the property of a private person, in this case a cavalry officer and *promotus* of the third legion called Theothorus (Θεόθορος, with *theta* instead of *delta*), who is sentenced by the military dux. Based on his name, Theothorus may have been a Christian. I see no connection to the Great Persecution; the document does not mention the "divine edict" and Theothorus had to appear before the military leader, not the governor.

τοῖς τοῦ ταμίου λογισμοῖς καὶ ἐνγρ[ά]φως ἐπιδοῦναι· ὅθεν ἐξετάσαντες
διὰ τῶν κατακιμένων ἐν τοῖς βιβλιοφυλακίοις βιβλ̣[ί]ων
δηλοῦμεν τὸν Παῦλον μηδὲν κεκτῆσθαι μηδ᾽ ὅ̣λ̣ω̣ς διεστρῶσθαι διὰ τῶ(ν)
κατακιμένων ἐν τοῖ[ς] βιβλιοφυλακίοις βιβλ̣[ίω]ν̣ μηδὲ `ε᾽ ἰδέναι τὴν τού-
του γυνεκα τινα [...] τω μὴ φ̣α̣ί̣ν̣εσθαι τὸν [π]ρ̣[ο]κ̣ί̣μ̣ε̣ν̣ο̣ν̣ Παῦλον
διεστρωμέ̣[νον διὰ] τ̣[ῶ]ν̣ α̣ὐ̣τῶν κατακιμένων [ἐ]ν τοῖς δημ[ο]σίοις ἀρχίοις
βιβλίων
(second hand) ἐ̣ρ̣ρ̣ῶσθαι ὑμᾶ̣ς̣ εὔχομα̣ι̣, φί`λ´(τατοι)
(first? hand) (ἔτους) [.. καὶ .] . . τῶν κυρίων ἡμῶν Κωνσ̣τ̣[α]ν̣τίου καὶ
Μαξιμιανοῦ
Σεβαστῶν [....................]. Μαξιμίνου τῶν ἐπιφανεστάτων
Καισάρων

---

10. *l.* ἐπεστείλατε, 11. προσ᾽ταγμα pap, 13. *l.* ἐπιτετεῖσι, 14. *l.* ἀποφάσει, 15. *l.* προσκριθῆναι, 16. *l.* ταμείου, 17, 19, 21. *l.* κατακειμένων, 17, 19. *l.* βιβλιοφυλακείοις, 18. τῶ pap, 20. *l.* γυναίκα, προκείμενον, 21. *l.* ἀρχείοις

Translation

In the consulship of our lords the emperors Constantius for the . . . th time and Galenius for the . . . th time, Augusti.
To the most beloved Aurelii Hierakion, also called Dionysius, gymnasiarch, city councilor . . . *prytanis* of the glorious and most glorious city of the Oxyrhynchites, and . . . mus, gymnasiarch, and Sarapion . . . *syndikoi* of the same city, the Aurelii . . . also called Heraclianus, former chief priest, and Agathinus, *exegetes*,[81] both city councilors of the same city, keepers of the archives of the same nome, greetings.
You have written to us that Aurelius Athanasius, *procurator rei privatae* in Egypt has commanded by a letter in which he wrote according to a divine edict of our masters the emperors and Caesars in accordance with the letter dispatched to him from Neratius Apollonides that the possessions of Paul from the Oxyrhynchite nome, who has been placed under sentence by the most eminent *praeses* of the Thebaid Satrius Arrianus, be adjudged to the accounts of the treasury and that (we) deliver a written report. Whence we declare, having searched through the records stored in the archives, that Paul owns nothing, nor at all through the records stored in the archives, nor do we know of any wife of his . . . the aforementioned Paul does not appear to have been registered in the same records stored in the public records. I pray you are well, most beloved ones.

[81] "Civic official with various responsibilities including record-keeping and baths" (Bagnall, *Egypt in Late Antiquity*, Appendix 4, 336).

> In the . . . th and the . . . th year of our lords Constantius and Maximianus, the Augusti, and of (Severus and) Maximinus, the most noble Caesars.

The keepers of the archives (*bibliophylakes*)[82] of the Oxyrhynchite nome report to important local and government officials at Oxyrhynchus that they have examined the record for a certain Paul and have found no property registered under his name. The governor of the Thebaid, Satrius Arrianus, had placed Paul under sentence. Who was this Paul, and why did the governor sentence him?

The document describes Paul as "Paul from the Oxyrhynchite nome" (ἀπὸ τοῦ Ὀξυρυγχίτου scil. νομοῦ). In previous documents we encountered people identified by patronymic, profession, or both: "papa Sotas" (P.Oxy. 36.2785); "Petosorapis, the son of Horus, Christian" (P.Oxy. 42.3035); and "Aurelius Ammonius, son of Copreus, reader of the former church of Chysis" (P.Oxy. 33.2673). Yet strikingly this Paul has no other modifier than "from the Oxyrhynchite nome."[83] This broad geographical indicator locates him not just in the city, but in the Oxyrhynchite nome, a large area of 780 km^2, with tens of thousands of inhabitants.[84] Paul's name suggests a Christian identity.[85] Rea proposed already that his geographical epithet indicates that Paul was a well-known figure in the region.[86] Yet we cannot identify him in

[82] Βιβλιοφύλαξ, "keeper of archives" (LSJ 315). See also note in Mitteis, *Grundzüge und Chrestomathie der Papyruskunde,* 94

[83] Judge and Pickering touch upon the problem that it would have been hard for the archive keepers to search their files on just the name Paul: "It is curious that he should be referred to simply as »Paul from the Oxyrhynchite nome«, for it can hardly have been expected that he could have been traced by such an uninformative description" ("Papyrus Documentation," 60). The issue is more complex because this document does not contain the original request, but rather it is the reply to a request. In the request letter that these record keepers had received, we can assume that this Paul was specified with at least his patronymic and possibly his profession.

[84] Krüger came to an estimate of 300,000 inhabitants for the nome (*Oxyrhynchos in der Kaiserzeit*, 37–38), but as noted above in the "Introduction," this figure is too high. The area calculation is from Bagnall, *Egypt in Late Antiquity*, 335.

[85] See Clarysse's statement: "his name shows that he was almost certainly a Christian" ("Coptic Martyr Cult," 380). Judge and Pickering refer to this as "The New Testament association of the name" ("Papyrus Documentation," 60). This Paul thus was a second generation Christian at least. Yet Paul was not an exclusively Christian name; Manichaeans also used it (e.g., P.Oxy. 31.2603).

[86] In Rea's words: "The fact that he is described simply as 'Paul from the Oxyrhynchite nome' implies that he had attained a certain fame, perhaps mainly outside the nome" (P.Oxy. 33.2665, 89).

other sources. He may have occupied a high position in Oxyrhynchite society, which would make him easily discernable in the agora or even within the Christian community.

Other information indicates that, even if well-known, this Paul did not possess riches. Rea interpreted the document to mean that Paul did have possessions, but that they had been confiscated.[87] However, the document does not precisely say that. It states that the registrars checked whether Paul owned anything—if he did, they would confiscate it—and they report back that they did not find any property registered either under his name[88] or under that of his wife.[89]

The circumstances that this papyrus evoke seem to suggest that Paul became a Christian martyr.[90] The date of this text in 305–306 and the mention of a "divine edict" both situate it in the Great Persecution. The appearance of Satrius Arrianus, "the most notorious persecutor of all,"[91] governor of the Thebaid, and a man known from many Christian martyr stories also suggests that persecution.[92] If indeed the case, this unassuming papyrus reveals significant historical information: an additional Christian martyr called Paul, a person without significant possessions, well-known in the Oxyrhynchite area but unknown from other sources,[93] received a sentence from Satrius Arrianus as a victim of the Great Persecution.

[87] "The registrars report to the prytanis and two syndics that their records contain no entries relating to a man whose property has been confiscated" (ibid., 89).

[88] Clarysse concludes: "he was not an owner of immovables" ("Coptic Martyr Cult," 380).

[89] Line 19 can be translated as "nor does his wife know," or as "nor do we know his wife." Rea's interpretation makes most sense: "it seems better to take this sentence too as reporting the contents of the archives rather than the results of other inquiries" (P.Oxy. 33.2665, 91, note to line 20).

[90] Clarysse also suggests this ("Coptic Martyr Cult," 380).

[91] So Reymond and Barns, eds., *Four Martyrdoms*, 7. They mention our papyrus, "which shows Arianus in a characteristically grim light" (ibid.)

[92] He features, for example, in the trial proceedings from the year 305 for a priest from a village near Antinoopolis, Stephanus, preserved in a fourth-century Coptic manuscript edited by van Minnen, "The Earliest Account of a Martyrdom in Coptic," *AnBoll* 113 (1995) 13–38 and plate, esp. 21–22 and 30–31, and in the *Martyrdom of Saint Coluthus* 88*v* 2.3 and 89*v* 2.28, in Reymond and Barns, *Four Martyrdoms*, 25–26. The mention of Arrianus in our papyrus led Clarysse to conclude that Paul was sentenced for being a Christian: "No doubt, he was sentenced for his religious beliefs and his properties had to be confiscated after his death" ("Coptic Martyr Cult," 380).

[93] Papaconstantinou, *Culte des saints en Égypte*, 170–71 and 171–73, mentions several martyrs named Paul; this Paul from the Oxyrhynchite nome is not among them.

Aurelius Athanasius: A Christian in the Imperial Government

Besides Ammonius the church reader and Paul the martyr, another intriguing Christian emerges from the documents that we have examined in this chapter: Aurelius Athanasius.[94] He occupied the function of *procurator rei privatae* in Egypt, a financial officer subordinate to the *magister rei privatae*,[95] and resided in Alexandria. If this Athanasius is a Christian, it is remarkable that he appears in these papyri persecuting other Christians.

The identification hinges upon his name. All indications suggest that Athanasius (and the female Athanasia) is a Christian name.[96] In the papyri we find the earliest occurrence of this name in P.Laur. 1.20, line 10 (dated 200–250). Most texts that mention a person called Athanasius come from administrative sources and thus provide no clues as to religious affiliation. The name, however, does not occur in a clearly pagan context either. It gains popularity in Egypt at the end of the third century with several Athanasii appearing at the end of the third and beginning of the fourth century. In later centuries, the name becomes quite popular, probably due more to its famous holder (Saint) Athanasius of Alexandria than to its theological significance of immortality, although both aspects may have made it an attractive name for parents to give to their children. Thus the emergence of this name in the third century and absence of indications of a pagan context signal it as new Christian nomenclature.

The situation of a Christian government official during times of persecution is not unprecedented; we even have reports that Christians formed part of the imperial household.[97] Other historical records offer several examples for understanding Athanasius's options, which ranged from martyrdom to apostasy. Eusebius mentions another high ranking financial officer, Adauctus,[98] who functioned as "*magister rei privatae* and *rationalis*

[94] P.Oxy. 33.2673, line 11; and P.Oxy. 33.3665, line 10. Presumably he was also mentioned in P.Harr. 2.208, the document parallel to P.Oxy. 33.2673.

[95] Lallemand, *Administration civile de l'Égypte*, 89 and 90–92.

[96] Horsley concluded "that the name may be of exclusively Christian use. The theological outlook reflected by a name with such an etymology reinforces this presumption" ("Athanasios," in *NewDocs* 3:90).

[97] See, e.g., Clarke, "Notes and Observations," *HTR* 64 (1971) 121–24 (for an earlier period, namely second quarter of the third century, based on an inscription).

[98] Eusebius describes Adauctus as "a man of illustrious Italian birth who had advanced through every grade of honour under the emperors, so as to pass blamelessly through the

summarum at Diocletian's court."[99] According to Eusebius, Adauctus became a Christian martyr while still in office.[100] Athanasius, however, might have found a way to avoid the impact of the persecution by encouraging fellow Christians to renounce their faith. The ninth canon of the Synod of Ancyra, convened in 314,[101] discusses the issue of Christians, who had compelled others to commit apostasy.[102] Either way, Athanasius at Alexandria found himself in a contradictory position between his job and his religious adherence.

In these documents, we have detected not only persecuted Christians—a church reader and a martyr—but also a senior governmental servant, who as a Christian had actively implemented the imperial edict against other Christians. This analysis has revealed an important feature of these papyri: they bring to the surface such fascinating hybrids and cross-loyalties.

general administration of what they call the magistracy and ministry of finance" (*Hist. eccl.* 8.11.2, trans. Oulton 2:287).

[99] Frend, *Martyrdom and Persecution*, 447, with additional information on Christian officials. See Eusebius, *Hist. eccl.* 8.11.2.

[100] "He was adorned with the crown of martyrdom, enduring the conflict for piety while actually engaged as finance minister" (ibid.). Another Christian who was an important official in Egypt was a certain Philomorus, who, Eusebius adds, "had been entrusted with an office of no small importance in the imperial administration at Alexandria, and who, in connexion with the dignity and rank that he had from the Romans, used to conduct judicial inquiries every day, attended by a bodyguard of soldiers" (ibid., 8.9.7, trans. Oulton 2:279).

[101] For this date, see Hefele, *A History of the Councils,* 199–200, at 200: "after the Easter which followed the death of Maximin; consequently in 314."

[102] "Those who have not only apostatized, but have become the enemies (ἐπανέστησαν) of their brethren, and have compelled them (to apostasy) or have been the cause of the constraint put upon them " (Hefele, *History of the Councils*, 210). Frend claims that "Canon 3 of the Council of Ancyra shows that some Christians even became government agents and persuaded others to lapse with them" (*Martyrdom and Persecution*, 498). However, this is not the case in the third canon or any of the other canons of Ancyra. Perhaps Frend was thinking of the canons of the Council of Elvira (of the year 306). These mention officials, namely those holding the often hereditary postion of flamen, who had to sacrifice as part of that profession (canons 2–4; Hefele, *History of the Councils*, 138–40). But they do not imply that these officials encouraged others to apostatize.

Balancing Belief and Business (P.Oxy. 31.2601)[103]

Finally, a private letter brings us from the Oxyrhynchite nome and countryside into the courtroom at Alexandria. This papyrus contains the correspondence between a man called Copres and a woman Sarapias. The main interest of the letter lies in the fact that Copres informs her how he made someone else sacrifice on his behalf.

The narrow papyrus sheet measures 7 x 26.6 cm. Copres filled the recto of the sheet entirely with writing, continued in the left margin, and added three sentences on the back. He penned his letter on a damaged sheet. In the lower part of the sheet below line 19, two to three strips of the upper (horizontal) layer of the papyrus have broken off and left the vertical fibers of the back exposed. On this spot several lines are left blank. No text appears lacking, however, and even the first *rho* of ἀρουρῶν in line 19 continues on the vertical fibers.[104]

The hand is "a competent sloping semicursive assignable to the late third or to the fourth century." The document is written by one person, which suggests that the sender penned his own letter.[105] It reads:

Κοπρῆς Σαραπιάδι ἀδελ-
φῇ πλεῖστα χαίρειν·
πρὸ μὲν πάντων
εὔχομε ὑμᾶς ὁλοκλη-
ρῖν παρὰ τῷ̣ κυρί(ῳ̣) θ[(ε)ῷ̣.
γινώσκιν σε θέλω
ὅτι τῇ ι̣̅α̣̅ εἰσήλθαμεν
καὶ ἐγνώσθη ἡμ̣ῖ̣ν
ὅτι οἱ προσερχόμενοι
ἀναγκάζονται θ̣ύ-
ειν καὶ ἀποσυστα̣τ̣ι̣-
κὸν ἐποίησα τῷ̣ ἀ-

[103] Ed. princ. Parsons, P.Oxy. 31.2601 (1966) 167–71. An edition with brief notes can be found in Pestman, *New Papyrological Primer*, 255–57. Naldini basically follows Parsons's assessment and interpretation of the letter and its historical circumstance (*Cristianesimo*, 169–72). See also Judge and Pickering, "Papyrus Documentation," 53 and 69.

[104] Parsons also concluded that "presumably the papyrus was already damaged when the letter was written" (P.Oxy. 31.2601, 170, note to line 19).

[105] So also ibid., 167.

δελφῷ μου καὶ μέ-
χρι τούτου οὐδὲν
ἐπράξαμεν ἐκατη-
χ̣ή̣σ̣α̣μεν δὲ ῥήτορα
τῇ ῑ. ἵνα τῇ ῑδ̣ εἰ-
σαχθῇ τὸ πρᾶγμα
περὶ τῶν ἀρουρῶ(ν).
(fibers of the recto broken off)
εἴ τι δὲ ἐὰν πράξω-
μεν γράφω σοι· οὐ-
δὲν δέ σοι ἔπεμψα
ἐπιδὴ εὗρον αὐτὸν
Θεόδωρον ἐξερχόμε-
νον· ἀποστέλ̣λ̣ω̣ σ̣οι
δὲ αὐτὰ διὰ ἄλλου τα-
χέως· γράφε δὲ ἡμῖν
περὶ τῆς ὁλοκληρίας
ὑμῶν πάντων καὶ
πῶς ἔσχεν Μαξιμῖνα
(left margin)
καὶ Ἀσενά. καὶ εἰ δυνατόν ἐστιν ἐρχέσθω (broken off fibers) μετὰ τῆς μητρός σου
(On the verso, along the fibers)
ἵνα θεραπευθῇ τ̣ὸ̣ λ̣ε̣υ̣κ̣ωμάτιον· ἐγὼ γὰρ (space) εἶδον ἄλλους
θεραπευθέντ̣ας· ἐρρῶσθ̣α̣ί̣ σ̣ε̣ ε̣ὔχομε. ἀσπάζ̣ομαι πάντας τοὺς ἡμῶν κατ᾽ ὄνομα.
(upside down compared to previous two lines)
ἀπ(όδος) τῇ ἀδελ̣φῇ π(αρὰ) Κοπρῆτ(ος) ϙθ
(illegible traces of letters)[106]

4. ϋμας, 7. ι̣α̣: the bow of the α crosses the ι; perhaps [[ι]]α, 10. αναγ̓ κ, 13. μου: μ written over σο, 17. ϊνα. ῑδ̣: δ corrected from α? Both numeral strokes are very faint, the second perhaps delusory, 19. αρουρω̄, 29. ϋμων, 32. ϊνα, 34. απ΄, π΄. κοπρητ·

[106] According to Parsons, "the traces are too substantial to be accident or offset; the script should be Greek (it is not Latin or Coptic or Aramaic). But I have found no satisfactory reading" (P.Oxy. 31.2601, 171, note to line 35).

Translation

> Copres to Sarapias, his sister, very many greetings. Before all things I pray before the Lord God that you (pl.) are well.
> I want you to know that we arrived on the 11th and it was made known to us that those who appear in court are compelled to sacrifice and I made a power of attorney to my brother and until now we have achieved nothing but we have instructed an advocate on the 1?th, so that the matter about the *arourai* might be brought into court on the 14?th.
> But if we achieve anything, I write you. But I have sent you nothing since I found that Theodorus himself is going out. But I am sending you this (letter) through someone else quickly. But write us about the well-being of you all and how Maximina has been, and Asena. And if it is possible, let her/him come with your mother so that her/his leucoma may be healed.[107] For I have seen other people (that had been) healed. I pray for your (sgl.) health. I greet all our (friends/loved ones) by name.
> Deliver to my sister from Copres. 99.

This is the only contemporary papyrus document that gives a personal perspective on the imperial measures against Christians. As we have seen, all the other papyri relating to the persecutions were official documents.[108] Away on a trip for a court case about a piece of land, Copres gives word to Sarapias at Oxyrhynchus (where the letter has been found) about what happened to him after his arrival. Copres does not mention his whereabouts, but most likely he wrote from Alexandria. Sarapias, the woman whom he addresses as his "sister," is his wife,[109] and the two persons mentioned by name at the end, Maximina and Asena, probably indicate their children.

[107] Who is having eye problems? According to Pestman, the subject of ἐρχέσθω is Maximina (*New Papyrological Primer*, 257, note to line 31), according to Naldini, it is Asena, "Kopres . . . invita presso di sé un certo Asena (su figlio?) affetto da leucoma" (*Cristianesimo*, 169). It also may be Copres's mother-in-law.

[108] This is true for the *libelli* as well. For although they were filed per individual or family, they still cannot be considered private documents because they follow, as we have seen, a standard, prescribed outline.

[109] Sarapias cannot be Copres's sister because he refers to "your mother" in line 31; had she been his sister he would have written "our mother." It was also common parlance in Egypt (as it is still elsewhere) to address one's spouse as sister or brother. See also Dickey: "It is distinctly possible—and now tacitly assumed by many editors—that the majority of spouses for whom ἀδελφός or ἀδελφή is used are not siblings" ("Literal and Extended Use," *Mnemosyne* 57 [2004] 158). Wipszycka remarks that this was "une lettre destinée à sa mère." This is certainly a slip (*Études sur le Christianisme*, 419).

Copres had a legal case about several *arouras* of land.[110] He and his family must have been well-to-do, for Copres could afford to travel to and to stay at Alexandria (perhaps Theodorus had traveled with him). He had the means to hire a lawyer to deal with the court case about agricultural land.[111] He probably penned this letter himself. This ability to write indicates that he had received schooling and fits well with the overall impression of his social status.

This letter contains markers of Christian identity—*nomina sacra* and an isopsephism—which identify Copres as a Christian.[112] In line 5 Copres wrote παρὰ τῷ κυρι̅θ̅ ("before the Lord G[od]") apparently realizing after penning the *iota* of the word κυρίῳ that he needed or wanted to write it as *nomen sacrum*. Only the *theta* of θεός (θ[(εῷ)] remains, but the supralinear stroke continues to the right and indicates that he wrote the *nomen sacrum* for that word.[113] This shows that Copres had at least some Christian education or experience in reading Christian manuscripts.

Copres concluded his letter with the number 99.[114] This does not represent

[110] As we have seen, papa Sotas encouraged Demetrianus to donate one *aroura* to the church (P.Oxy. 12.1492; ch. 5).

[111] Bagnall remarks: "Lawyers and stays away from home were expensive, and only the urban elite could afford such direct access [i.e., to the governor]" (*Egypt in Late Antiquity*, 64). See also Judge and Pickering, "Papyrus Documentation," 69.

[112] The name Copres is not a marker of Christian identity. Based on its etymology this is, I would say, a rather "dirty" name, being derived from the Greek word cluster "dung" (κόπρος) and "dung heap" (κοπρία). See Pomeroy, "Copronyms," 149. Kajanto lists it under the "uncomplimentary cognomina"-in his "On the Problem of 'Names of Humility,'" *Arctos* 3 (1962) 45–59, esp. 48–50, at 51. Hobson has suggested that copronyms protect against the evil eye, based on a practice in a Palestinian village, "where the Arabic word for dung is found used as a name in order to protect the bearer from the evil eye, appropriate in a situation where, for instance, the parents' previous children have died at an early age" ("Towards a Broader Context," *EMC* 32 [1988] 361). Pestman accepts Hobson's interpretation: "Κοπρῆς: this name and others . . . were used in order to protect the bearer from the evil eye. Copronyms do not have the connotation of 'persons found on a rubbish heap' (οἱ ἀπὸ κοπρίας)" (*New Papyrological Primer*, 256). All in all, Copres is not a name that makes one stand out as Christian, neither is Sarapias. Theodorus, mentioned in line 24, could be Christian nomenclature. Maximina and Asena are names as rare as those of their parents, Sarapias and Copres, are common. Maximina appears only here in papyri, Asena occurs in the Septuagint (2 Esdras) and in sixth-century papyri. See also Parsons, P.Oxy. 31.2601, 170, notes to lines 30 and 31.

[113] Parsons, P.Oxy. 31.2601, 170, note to line 5. Parsons also noted there that "after the theta there is space for two letters."

[114] Parsons mentions Irenaeus, the Council of Nicaea, and gives several parallels of amen in letters, cautioning that he has "found no example before the earlier 4th cent." He typifies the use of the isopsephy as perhaps "a sign of special zeal" (P.Oxy. 31.2601, note to line 34,

just the number. Rather, in the cryptic language of isopsephy, one writes amen (ἀμήν) with this number, for in Greek the numerical value of the letters of the word "amen" adds up to the number 99: α´ (= 1) + μ´ (= 40) + η´ (= 8) + ν´ (= 50) = ϙθ´(= 99).[115] Early Christians used numbers and names as "theological tools," as François Bovon has shown.[116] Isopsephy in Christian circles became popular among church fathers and especially in so-called Gnostic groups.[117] Five other papyrus letters from the fourth century contain the isopsephism for amen (ϙθ).[118] The use of ϙθ to mean "amen" in Copres's letter, datable

171). For literature and other examples, see Bovon, "Names and Numbers," *NTS* 47 (2001) 267–88; Vidman, "Koppa Theta," *ZPE* 16 (1975) 215–16; Leclercq, "Isopséphie," *DACL* 7.2 (1927) 1603–6; Llewelyn, "ΣΔ, a Christian Isopsephism?" *ZPE* 109 (1995) 125–27; idem, "The Christian Symbol ΧΜΓ," *NewDocs* 8 (1998) 156–68; Robert, "Isopséphie de Amen," *Hellenica* 11 (1960) 310–11; and Skeat, "A Table of Isopsephisms," *ZPE* 31 (1978) 45–54.

[115] Bovon refers to another use of the number 99, related to the *flexio digitorum*: "Passing from tens to hundreds was particularly important because counting up to 99 was executed by the left hand, while counting from 100 on was done with the right hand. Remembering that the left side was considered a negative one, the passage to 100 was considered with pleasure." Bovon refers in this respect to the passage in the *Gospel of Truth*, wherein the shepherd finding the 100th sheep rejoices "for ninety-nine is a number that is in the left hand that holds it" ("Names and Numbers," 284).

[116] Bovon, "Names and Numbers," 267.

[117] Leclercq, "Isopséphie," 1603–4. In his *Adversus haereses*, Irenaeus refers to the isopsephism for "amen" when he discusses the Gnostic sect of the Marcosians: Οὕτως οὖν καὶ (ἐπὶ) τοὺς ἀριθμοὺς τοὺς καταλειφθέντας, ἐπὶ μὲν τῆς δραχμῆς τοὺς ἐννέα, ἐπὶ δὲ τοῦ προβάτου τοὺς ἕνδεκα ἐπιπλεκομένους ἀλλήλοις τὸν τῶν ἐνενηκονταεννέα τίκτειν ἀριθμόν· ἐπεὶ ἐννάκις τὰ ἕνδεκα ἐνενηκονταεννέα γίνεται. Διὸ καὶ τὸ ἀμὴν τοῦτον λέγουσιν ἔχειν τὸν ἀριθμόν (*Haer.* 1.16.1). "Accordingly, when the numbers that are left over—namely nine in refence to the coins and eleven in reference to the sheep—are multiplied by each other, the number ninety-nine is the result because nine multiplied by eleven makes ninety-nine. And for this reason, they say 'Amen' contains this same number" (trans. Unger, *St. Irenaeus of Lyons Against the Heresies*, 69). Copres's use of the isopsephy of amen does not give any indication about his theological leanings. According to Ivo of Chartres (ca. 1040–1116), the 318 fathers at the Council of Nicaea recommended the use of the isopsephy in letters: "Addat praeterea separatim in epistola etiam nonagenarium et novem numeros, qui secundum greca elementa significant αμην" (*Decretum* 6, 163); see also Leclercq, "Litterae commendititiae et formatae," 1574–75.

[118] These letters are: P.Oxy. 8.1162, line 15 (Oxyrhynchus, fourth cent.); P.Oxy. 56.3857, line 13 (Oxyrhynchus, fourth cent.); P.Oxy. 56.3862, line 1 (Oxyrhynchus, fourth/fifth cent.); PSI 13.1342, line 1 (Hermopolite, ca. 330–350); and SB 16.12304, line 13 (Panopolis?, third/fourth cent.). For other genres besides letters, see, e.g., P.Oxy. 6.925, a fifth- or sixth-century Christian oracular petition that closes with the isopsephism of amen and contains many other markers of identity, such as six *nomina sacra* and a cross. Grenfell and Hunt suppose that it had been placed in a church (P.Oxy. 6.925, 291).

to the early years of the fourth century, provides evidence of one of the earliest papyrological records of this practice. Apart from one document, PSI 13.1342, the other letters also contain *nomina sacra* besides the isopsephy.[119] The use of the isopsephy in this letter strikes me as a strong indication of the family's piety. By writing "amen" at the end of his letter, it appears as if Copres concludes a prayer or a part of a liturgy.[120] "Names and numbers," Bovon concludes, "are a gift from God that express an extralinguistic reality beyond what other words are capable of transmitting."[121] In that light we should interpret the *koppa theta* at the end of Copres's letter to his wife as a prayer, a sign of his faith, and a sign that he had arrived safe and sound.[122]

Copres brings up the issue of the sacrifice immediately after the *proemium* (the standard section in a letter with greetings).[123] He informs Sarapias that he had arrived (safely) at his destination and, upon arrival or some time thereafter, found out that he would have to make a sacrifice in order to take his case about a piece of land to court[124]—which was apparently the reason for his trip. The passive voice of "it was made known to us/it became known to us" (ἐγνώσθη ἡ̣μ̣ῖν, line 8) does not specify how Copres found out about

[119] P.Oxy. 8.1162 and P. Oxy. 56.3857 even contain rare *nomina sacra* for Emmanuel; the former also for μάρτ(υς). The PSI letter is a business letter, which may explain the absence of *nomina sacra*, although it does start with χμγ. The position of the "amen" in these early letters occurs either at the very end of the letter, as in Copres's letter, or in the first line. Last line, as final "word" of the letter: P.Oxy. 8.1162 and SB 16.12304. In P.Oxy. 56.3857 it is written at the end of body of the letter, just before the final greeting. In P.Oxy. 56.3862 and PSI 13.1342 the isopsephy stands in the first line of the letter, in both cases preceded by χμγ. Three of the five other roughly contemporary letters with this isopsephy are Christian letters of recommendation (P.Oxy. 8.1162; P.Oxy. 56.3857; and SB 16.12304), written by and addressed to clergy members. Only P.Oxy. 56.3862 does not have an explicit connection with Christian clergy (with a fourth- or fifth-cent. date, this letter is also much later than Copres's letter), although Philoxenus, the writer of that letter, clearly is a very pious person even citing scripture.

[120] As becomes clear from a TLG search, "amen" can be found at the end of many sermons; often added after prayer formulas, such as "to the ages of ages. Amen." Origen repeatedly refers to the Hebrew meaning of the word. Participants say "amen" after receiving the Eucharist.

[121] Bovon, "Names and Numbers," 288.

[122] This is assuming that Copres expected Sarapias to understand his cryptic final greeting. If not, it may have had an apotropaic function.

[123] The turn of phrase, "I want you to know" (γινώσκειν σε θέλω), is an exceedingly common one in private letters used to begin the letter body and introduce the reason for writing.

[124] εἰσάγω: LSJ 493 "II 3. as a law-term . . . *to bring* a cause *into court*."

the sacrifice. He may have read an official posting or heard it through social contacts. Yet his use of the verb "to compel, force" (ἀναγκάζω) tells Sarapias that he did not consider this a voluntary sacrifice.

The situation that Copres faced in the courtroom resembles the one that Lactantius describes in his *De mortibus persecutorum*.[125] Lactantius first refers to an edict meant to make it difficult for Christians to go to court:

> The next day an edict was published, in which it was ordered that every lawsuit against them (i.e., the Christians) should succeed, that they themselves should not be able to go to court, not about insult,[126] not about adultery, not about stolen matters, in short, that they should not have freedom nor voice.[127]

More specifically, altars were set up in courtrooms and people were forced to sacrifice there in the presence of the judges. Sacrifice constituted the test of loyalty to the Roman empire.[128] This stipulation about sacrificing in court, which probably forms the historical background of this letter, also provides a date for the papyrus in the early years of the fourth century. The edict took effect on 23 February 303,[129] thus we may suppose that Copres composed his letter not long thereafter.

Copres, however, apparently did not perform the edict's obligatory sacrifice. Instead, he found a clever way out of an undesired situation and reports that he made his "brother" the recipient of a power of attorney (ἀποσυστατικός). This brother conducted the sacrifice for Copres. Who

[125] See also Parsons, P.Oxy. 31.2601, 167–68.

[126] Städele with reference to Krause, *Gefängnisse*, explains: "[u]nter *inuria* sind Körperverletzungen und Beleidigungen zu verstehen" (*Laktanz*, 122 n. 38).

[127] With this expression Lactantius touches upon a topos that the Roman people lost their freedom and right to express themselves under the tyrants, as Städele remarks (*Laktanz*, 122 n. 38). Städele translates it as "Recht auf Meinungsäußerung" (*Laktanz*, 123). The Latin reads: Postridie propositum est edictum, quo cavebatur, ut . . . adversos eos omnis actio valeret, ipsi non de inuria, non de adulterio, non de rebus ablatis agere possent, libertatem denique ac vocem non haberent (Lactantius, *Mort*. 13.1, ed. Städele, 122).

[128] Lactantius adds as if the judges were the gods: "and lest by chance judgment should be pronounced to him (i.e., a Christian), altars were placed in the council chambers and before the judgment seat, so that the parties in a lawsuit/litigants ought to sacrifice first and in this way plead their cases, so therefore one ought to approach the judges as the gods." (et ne cui temere ius diceretur, arae in secretariis ac pro tribunali positae, ut litigatores prius sacrificarent atque ita causas suas dicerent, sic ergo ad iudices tamquam ad deos adiretur) (Lactantius, *Mort*. 13.1 [ed. Städele] 122).

[129] Judge and Pickering, "Papyrus Documentation," 53.

was this brother? Copres's sibling? A fellow Christian? Or a "pagan" friend? It was common practice in antiquity, as in certain circles today, to address friends in familial terms, and hence the "brother" did not necessarily indicate a sibling.[130] Although Christians used (and still use) sibling language to address each other, I doubt that this "brother" represented a fellow Christian. Why would he sacrifice and Copres not? The "brother" therefore must have been a "pagan" friend, who performed the sacrifice for Copres as a favor. Otherwise the lawyer (ῥήτωρ)[131] that Copres mentions hiring would have taken care of it.

Not the only Christian who resolved the enigma of sacrifice in this practical way, Copres had employed a solution that church leaders refused to accept. Peter, bishop of Alexandria, addresses this strategy and the appropriate punishment for it in his Canons from the year 306.[132] The fifth canon applies here:

> And there are those who have not nakedly written down a denial [of their faith] but rather, when in great distress, like boys who are sensible and deliberate among their foolish fellows, have mocked the schemes of their enemies: they have either passed by the altars, or have made a written declaration, or *have sent pagans [to sacrifice] in their place*. Certain ones of those who confessed the faith, as I have heard, have forgiven them since, above all, with great piety they have avoided lighting the sacrificial fire with their own hands and have avoided the smoke rising from the unclean demons, and since indeed they were unaware, because of their thoughtlessness,

[130] As Dickey notes, "Kinship terms in papyrus letters do not always refer to actual relatives and so pose many problems for modern readers." About the use of brother, she writes: "the widespread use in letters of ἀδελφός, for example, for people other than brothers does not imply that ἀδελφός no longer meant 'brother' at all, but rather that there were certain situations in which it was appropriate to call someone other than a brother 'brother'" ("Literal and Extended Use," 131, 133).

[131] The word ῥήτωρ indicates 1) a "public speaker, . . . 2) one who gives sentence, judge . . . 3) advocate (with reference to the papyri), 4) later, teacher of eloquence, rhetorician" (LSJ, 1570). Given the court situation, the advocate makes most sense here. See also Bagnall, who comments: "When legal business required more than a competent contract-writer or petition-drafter, lawyers were available. Their usual title (*rhetor*) speaks to the rhetorical education they received, but it should not be assumed that they were ignorant of the law" (*Egypt in Late Antiquity*, 91).

[132] On the date of these Canons, Vivian states: "The first canon states that 'this is now the fourth Easter under persecution.' Since the persecution under Diocletian began during Lent of 303, these canons must have been written in 306, but the text does not make clear whether they were written before or after Easter" (*St. Peter of Alexandria*, 140).

> of what they were doing. Nevertheless, six months of penance will be given to them.[133]

The bishop of Alexandria mentions that Christians, in order to avoid having to sacrifice, sent pagans (ἐθνικούς) in their place. This seems like the situation to which Copres alludes in his letter. Thus Copres, a Christian, had a pagan friend, whom he trusted enough to ask him to conduct the sacrifice for him, and who apparently agreed to do so.[134] He had a Christian family but also refers to a pagan friend without any further notice; presumably this reflects a common situation for Christians. Copres does not seem concerned about the church-related effects of his actions, at least not in his short epistle to Sarapias. He may, of course, have had no idea about repercussions, like those we read in the canon.[135]

An Easy Way Out?

Scholars have expressed surprise at Copres's easy way out.[136] His quick and apparently legal solution indicates that he knew how to react. Parsons

[133] [Emphasis mine.] καὶ μὴ γυμνῶς ἀπογραψαμένοις τὰ πρὸς ἄρνησιν, ἀλλὰ διαπαίξασι κατὰ πολλὴν στενοχωρίαν (ὡς ἄν παιδία βουλευτικὰ ἔμφρονα ἐν παιδίος ἄφροσι) τὰς τῶν ἐχθρῶν ἐπιβουλάς, ἤτοι ὡς διελθόντες βωμούς, ἤτοι ὡς χειρογραφήσαντες, ἤτοι ὡς ἀνθ' ἑαυτῶν βαλόντες ἐθνικούς· εἰ καί τισιν αὐτῶν συνεχώρησάν τινες τῶν ὁμολογησάντων, ὡς ἤκουσα, ἐπεὶ μάλιστα κατὰ πολλὴν εὐλάβειαν ἐξέφυγον αὐτόχειρες γενέσθαι τοῦ πυρός, καὶ τῆς ἀναθυμιάσεως τῶν ἀκαθάρτων δαιμόνων· ἐπεὶ τοίνυν ἔλαθεν αὐτοὺς ἀνοίᾳ τοῦτο πράξαντας. ὅμως ἑξάμηνος αὐτοῖς ἐπιτεθήσεται τῆς ἐν μετανοίᾳ ἐπιστροφῆς (Routh, *Reliquiae sacrae* 4:28). Translation modified from Vivian, *St. Peter of Alexandria*, 186–87. Peter justifies the six months with a reference to Isa 9:6, the announcement of the birth of the child, which, according to Luke, was born after six months. He also refers to the kingdom of heaven.

[134] According to De Ste. Croix, "some Christians successfully deceived the authorities by inducing pagans to impersonate them at the ceremony of sacrificing" ("Aspects," 100). The procedure Copres describes to Sarapias appears to be slightly different. The main difference lies in the fact that Sotas made his "brother" a power of attorney, he did not ask the person to impersonate him. In doing so, Copres created a legal solution to his problem.

[135] Wipszycka also comments: "Il ne semble pas que Kopres ait eu des doutes sur l'honnêté de son comportement" ("Lecteur," 419).

[136] Parsons describes how Copres "easily evaded the sacrificial test" (P.Oxy. 31.2601, 168). For Judge and Pickering, this papyrus letter "confirms the impression that people were generally not anticipating conflict, insofar as it shows the perfunctory way in which he [Copres] side-stepped Diocletian's new rule on sacrificing" ("Papyrus Documentation," 70).

commented that for Copres the sacrifice constituted "a minor nuisance."[137] Copres, however, found the obligatory sacrifice significant enough to mention at the beginning of his letter. He clearly wanted his wife Sarapias to know about the situation as soon as possible.[138] Since he announces that Theodorus will visit her soon with goods, Copres evidently wanted eagerly, sooner even than Theodorus's arrival, to tell his family about what had happened to him.

Wipszycka finds Copres's lack of emotions striking.[139] Copres indeed does not describe whether he had worried about what had happened or even whether he thought it amusing that he had evaded the sacrifice. That does not mean, however, that he did not have feelings about it. This lack of emotions reflects more the genre of ancient letters than that it does Copres's situation or personality.[140]

What can we say about Copres? Parsons portrayed him as a zealous Christian but not a smart one at that,[141] for he called into question Copres's acumen based on the aberrant spelling of the *nomen sacrum* in line 5.[142] Leaving aside the question of his intelligence—since the brevity of the letter does not give adequate information about this—Copres seems more practical than "zealous" in his Christian faith. In addressing his family, he identifies

[137] P.Oxy. 31.2601, 168.

[138] Copres explicitly says that he was in a hurry to write Sarapias (ἀποστέλλῳ ϛοι δὲ αὐτὰ διὰ ἄλλου ταχέως, lines 25–27). This may explain why he used a damaged sheet. Was it the only available piece of writing material he had at hand?

[139] "C'est sans aucune émotion qu'il en parle," Wipszycka, "Lecteur," 419.

[140] As Chapa, for instance, noticed in his study on condolence letters. These letters are worded fairly stereotypically with many common places, whereas in this genre of letters we would expect show of emotion (*Letter of Condolence*, 49). This is not to say that people in antiquity did not have strong emotions and feelings, of course they did! Sometimes they surface in the papyri, such as in the affidavit of the woman who complains about her husband and his abuse, P.Oxy. 6.903. However, private letters or business letters in antiquity were not, as they are today, vehicles for expressing strong personal emotions in an explicit fashion. Bagnall and Cribiore note that "in later centuries the ethos of letter writing starts to change, particularly in the direction of the expression of the writer's personal feelings" (*Women's Letters from Ancient Egypt*, "Late Medieval Letters as Comparative Evidence," esp. 26).

[141] "Copres writes colourless, paratactic Greek, with normal vulgarisms of spelling and syntax; he shows his Christianity by using the abnormal ϙθ, but mishandles a *nomen sacrum*. That is, he was a man of average education, a zealous but not very intelligent Christian" (P.Oxy. 31.2601, 168). The use of the isopsephy for amen indicated especially for Parsons a sign of Copres's devotion (ibid., 171, note to line 34).

[142] "Due presumably to inexperienced or unintelligent Christians" (ibid., 170, note to line 5).

himself as a Christian by his use of *nomina sacra* and isopsephy (probably this made him pious in the eyes of the readers), but in the courtroom he prefers not to stand out as such. His awareness of the dangers of admitting to being a Christian reveals itself not only from the fact that he asked a pagan friend to perform the sacrifice for him but also from the fact that he makes this incident the first, and presumably therefore most important, matter that he writes about to his wife. His urge to communicate this quickly also indicates his awareness of the danger.

This private letter alluding to measures in the Great Persecution gives an impression of how the imperial edicts affected the lives of individual Christians. When addressing a letter to his family, Copres, the sender, employs encoded signals to exhibit his piety but did not want to stand out as a Christian in the courtroom.

Although the papyri examined in this chapter contain neither the high drama nor bloody details known from hagiographical texts, these mundane documents exhibit the texture of Roman persecution as local communities and individuals experienced it. Ordinary people felt the powerful presence of the Roman government from the remote corners of the Egyptian countryside to the Alexandrian courtroom. The Christians in these papyrus documents adopted different tactics of identity. Instead of confessing the *nomen Christianum*, they wove the fabric of their everyday life with subtle yet distinct threads of resistance.

CHAPTER 8

Early Christians in the Oxyrhynchus Papyri: New Voices in Ancient History

In this book we have encountered Christians in various locations and social settings in and around the ancient Egyptian city of Oxyrhynchus. By looking at markers of Christian identity in documentary papyri, we have detected women and men who do not normally figure in histories of early Christianity. My detailed analysis of these underutilized manuscripts has offered glimpses into the lives of early Christians different from those that Christian literary writings offer. Through these documentary papyri, we have distinguished voices of individuals involved in the normal concerns of life—writing a thank you note, penning yet another letter of recommendation, and appearing in court. The documents surveyed in this study have indicated that Christians followed the customs of their contemporaries, while at the same time the complex workings of their Christian identity have come vividly into view.

Literary Polemics Versus Documentary Papyri

Early Christian polemical writings stress the moral, social, and theological differences between Christians, Jews, and pagans. They also sharply distinguish between "orthodox" Christians and "heretics"—between us and them. Thus these literary sources give the impression of clearly distinct religious groups in this period for whom doctrinal debate constituted the primary concern. The situation on the ground differed. Despite the claims to the contrary from polemical literary texts, most Christians, today and in the past, live their lives in ways often indistinguishable from their neighbors of different religions; one could not discern them at a glance in the marketplace. In our search to sift out Christians in documentary texts from Oxyrhynchus we encountered such ambivalent situations. Christians shared certain affective traits with their monotheistic and polytheistic neighbors, adopted to a large degree common naming practices, and used standard models of written communication. Similarly, although the theological diversity of early Christianity at Oxyrhynchus remains evident from the literary fragments discovered there—ranging from the *Gospel of Mary* to the gospel of Matthew—this diversity does not appear in the pre-Constantinian documents from Oxyrhynchus. In our documents, both Petosorapis and Sotas had explicit marks as "Christian," but were they orthodox or so-called Gnostic Christians? Among the people whom we have investigated, little or nothing suggests divergent theological orientations. From the standpoint of papyrological investigation, theological inner-Christian divergences remain muted and indistinct.

This difference between literary writings and papyrus documents stems from matters of genre. The polemical or apologetical character of literary texts requires different reading strategies from those suited to the genres of the documentary papyri. Letters of recommendation have a formulaic character. Material constraints sometimes influence the content of documents, for example, a narrow sheet of papyrus forces one writer to cram information about a family business. A governmental declaration follows official stipulations and imperial protocol. The rhetorical conventions and aims of the documentary papyri differ from those of our primary literary and theological sources. While literary and theological works generally function as part of a debate defining "the other" as heretic or pagan, most papyrus documents from Oxyrhynchus consist of inner-group communications or even interfamilial squabbles. Maria and her neighbors might possibly have spent long evenings on the street corners of Oxyrhynchus discussing the nature of Christ and other pressing theological issues. Yet they had equal, if not more, concern about everyday matters, such as hopes for their family's health, community relations, finances, food, and clothing.

The fact that one often cannot distinguish between "heretic" and "orthodox," or even among pagans, Jews, and Christians, matters on another level as well. From the papyrological standpoint, the similarity of these groups, one to another, helps to explain why many literary texts emphasize difference so strongly. By means of these writings, Christians, Jews, and other groups had to carve out their identity as standing out from the rest, especially because they did not always do so in their daily lives. Our investigations of documentary papyri have provided a fresh perspective on early Christians and their identity-forming practices as compared to their more explicit literary texts.

Clergy, Church, and Congregation at Oxyrhynchus

Papa Sotas gave us our closest encounter with an Oxyrhynchite Christian. A small collection of five (or six) letters concerning him enabled us to construct a relatively detailed picture of this man and his role in the Oxyrhynchite community. This set of letters made Sotas the earliest Christian from Oxyrhynchus for whom more than one text has survived. Our research constitutes the first systematic effort to delve deeply into this correspondence and to provide from these disparate documents a portrait of the man and the ecclesiastical world of the time. Most importantly, we could determine that Sotas, a bishop, occupied the episcopal see of Oxyrhynchus, probably in the third quarter of the third century. Thus he represents the earliest known bishop from that city. Our investigation of Sotas resulted in further interesting insights into the institutions of the church in Egypt in this period.

We became acquainted with Sotas through letters of recommendation for catechumens and church members. Individuals sought Sotas out to help them to present themselves in a specific social context. We should not, however, understand these texts solely on the individual level. Rather, their formulaic character and widespread use attest to the larger network and social practices of the Christian community. Moreover, these texts show an historical development of the modes of Christian self-identification that we see becoming crystallized by the time we encounter them here. Although many people shared the practice of writing letters of recommendation, Christians had distinct and specific markers of identity, such as *nomina sacra*, standardized language, and the status of their correspondents, most of whom occupied leadership positions in their local churches.

Looking over the bishop's shoulder as he penned a letter asking for the donation of a field, we witnessed an early stage of the later trend when churches tended to amass large estates. At the same time, we noticed behind this request for a contribution to the church centrally organized church finances at Oxyrhynchus. Such centrally administrated assets indicate the professionalization of the clergy and suggest that Sotas featured on the church's payroll. Quite unexpectedly we also detected Sotas's presence in Antioch, Syria, in the circle of an athlete. Unless the bishop went abroad for private business, he probably went to represent the Oxyrhynchite church at one of the gatherings to oppose or judge bishop Paul of Samosata.

By examining scribal practices, use of writing material, and characteristics particular to literary hands, we have found evidence for distinctively Christian scribes and Christian book production at Oxyrhynchus. Considering that so many Christian literary manuscripts have been found at Oxyrhynchus, it is a significant discovery to argue, as we have, that a center of book production existed there. At Oxyrhynchus, this center appears in the vicinity of the bishop; at least Sotas had access to leftover scraps of animal skin used for copying manuscripts. The likely presence of people capable of copying manuscripts among the writers of private letters adds to our understanding of the multifunctionality of Christian scribes.

Throughout our quest for Christians at Oxyrhynchus, Christian clergy—a bishop, a church reader, and another clergyman ("Lord Father")—stood out prominently in the papyri. We concluded that the epithet Christian itself, such as "Sotas, Christian" and arguably "Petosorapis, Christian," used by outsiders, signified Christian clergy. The fact that one could recognize clergy members as Christian through specific forms of address and by the inclusion of their title signals more broadly that they stood out as distinct and distinguishable in the larger community.

Education proved a vital means through which we could detect how Christians formed and expressed a distinct identity. Already at an elementary level, students received instruction on the scribal system of *nomina sacra*. These *nomina sacra* construct a visual in-group language. Compared to literary usage, the results of our investigation have caused us some surprise in that these documentary papyri notably lacked mention of the name Jesus Christ, while the *nomen sacrum* for Emmanuel occurred more prominently. Scriptural allusions in a private letter provided evidence of Christian education. More generally, the papyri show how those who wanted to become Christians had to follow the staged process of the catechumenate. These steps became so significant that letters of recommendation indicated the specific level of Christian education of travelers.

From Peace to Persecution

If the Oxyrhynchite church in the Sotas correspondence remained at peace, then reverberations of persecutions came through in other documents. Whereas hagiography and historiography often present the persecutions in simple binary terms, as involving a choice between martyrdom or apostasy, the papyri present a more complicated situation. The find from Oxyrhynchus contains a range of documents, such as *libelli*, a summons, a declaration of church property, and orders for confiscating private property, which pertain to the empire-wide persecutions in the mid-third and early-fourth century. From the Roman side, these documents concern almost solely the confiscation of property from both private persons and churches and show a wide array of mechanisms by which the Roman government attempted to effect apostasy. Moreover, these documents revealed the pervasive influence of the Roman government even in the Egyptian countryside. They testify to the large impact that the imperial measures had on the lives of all sorts of people and communities—an impact also abundantly clear in the literary accounts from Christian authors. Instead of spectacular confessions and heroic deaths, however, we witnessed violence mostly taking place through material deprivations—especially through the seizure of property from individuals and the church community. Instead of the stark moral contrasts that punctuate the martyrologies, the documentary papyri suggest moral ambiguities that beset ordinary people and indicate small acts of resistance, such as the reader who feigned illiteracy. Yet behind a request to confiscate the property may also lie the violent death of a Christian man, Paul of the Oxyrhynchus nome, who does not appear in hagiographical texts.

Investigating these documents made clear that distinctive markers of Christian identity relate to particular social contexts. In relation to the government, we observed a Christian avoiding the need to sacrifice by asking his friend to act as his power of attorney. This same man, however, in describing the situation to his family, used clear symbolic markers of Christian identity.

Voices of Women

Throughout this book we have sought out and investigated early Christian women; some of them appeared by name, others remained anonymous. Taion came to Oxyrhynchus from Heracleopolis. Unlike the man traveling with her to receive catechesis from Sotas, she already had a full membership in the church. We met another Christian woman, Germania, also a full church member, on the road and perhaps even traveling by herself. Apparently she needed help, but her letter of recommendation did not specify what sort of help. Another Christian woman, Sarapias, received a letter conveying news from her husband Copres. His attempt to write *nomina sacra* and his use of the isopsephism for "amen" indicate that Sarapias would have appreciated and understood these signs.

Through the lens of onomastics, we spotted other women, such as three different Marias, whom we could perhaps identify as Christians based on their name. We also encountered on separate occasions two anonymous, obviously educated women and members of a studious milieu. One of them participated in an exchange of apocryphal books. She possessed a copy of *4 Ezra* and had borrowed a copy of the book of *Jubilees*. The other early Christian woman maintained a correspondence with a clergy member, alluded in her letter to scripture, and creatively applied *nomina sacra*. This woman could possibly also have functioned as a scribe of literary texts; she clearly had the appropriate scribal skills and style of handwriting. Some of these women appeared in traditional roles as wives and mothers, but others worked as scribes or scholars. These women made contributions to the life of their community in the form of networking, epistolary exchange, study, and manuscript production.

Adieu to Oxyrhynchus

Fragments of Christian literary manuscripts dating to the second century feature prominently among the papyri from Oxyrhynchus. Firm evidence of the presence of Christians from documentary papyri found at the site first appears in the mid-third century. By then, Christians had emerged in an already full-fledged and distinct community. Through analysis of the earliest Christian papyrological documents, we discovered a congregation with a professional clergy (a bishop), a widespread—regional, extraregional, and "international"—network, active fundraising, an educational program that attracted out-of-town students, and book production. Letters of recommendation from the desk of the bishop introduced us by name to seven men affiliated with the Oxyrhynchite church as members or as catechumens.

Since these seven people traveled, and the church had the financial ability to support its clergy, we can propose that the church must have had a substantial congregation. Such a well-developed community in the third quarter of the third century clearly must have taken root earlier.

The Christians of Oxyrhynchus, whom we detected in the documents, came from diverse socioeconomic backgrounds. As noted, well-to-do people will more likely appear in papyrological sources, and we have seen them here among the Oxyrhynchite Christians. Notably we mention Demetrianus, likely sponsor of the Oxyrhynchite church, and Copres, a businessman in Alexandria. Not everyone, however, possessed such means. One traveler, Germania, needed help, and another, Paul from the Oxyrhynchite nome, had no property registered in the Oxyrhynchite archives. A rural Christian congregation, behaving in a manner perhaps a bit less straightforward than required, put up only few worldly possessions in a confiscation of its property.

In this study we have met Christians in various social settings, in relation to their family, to their local church, in contact with clergy, and with government officials. In these different settings, they constructed Christian identities for themselves in a variety of ways appropriate for the occasion. My historical detective work, based on the documentary evidence from Oxyrhynchus, has several important implications for the broader field of early Christian historiography. For one, we have seen that the literary sources give us a partial view and tend to overemphasize the theological at the expense of other identity-forming practices. Moreover, in the scholarship of early Christianity, we frequently have to resort to reading against the grain in order to ask of elite texts questions about those people, whom they considered theologically, socially, or politically marginal to the concerns of the text. Although interpreting documentary evidence does by no means prove hermeneutically simple, it does provide us with a fresh set of data, new rhetoric, and a larger mix of marginal and mainstream writings. The mundane quality of these papyrus documents makes them so striking and so valuable for our understanding of early Christianity.

Documentary evidence gives a complex vision of overlapping identities in the ancient world; we often have difficulty even distinguishing Christian papyri from others. Because of the brevity of these underutilized texts and the sheer amount of evidence that they give us, a better, if more complicated, picture of early Christians and their interactions with their neighbors of many religions has emerged. The resulting picture blurs the social and religious boundaries.

This way of doing history from "the underside" provides potential narratives from a variety of perspectives and creates a nuanced historiography through everyday situations. The data allow us to see historical situations from multiple viewpoints. Thus we see them both from the perspective of Romans officials and from the perspective of those who remained deeply compromised by Roman power. We see them both from the perspective of the leaders and builders of local Christian communities, through their hospitality and scriptural education, and also from that of the catechumens, scribes, and folk of the rank and file. Weaving these documentary threads into the carpet of early Christian historiography brings out the color and contrast of this fascinating and important period. 99

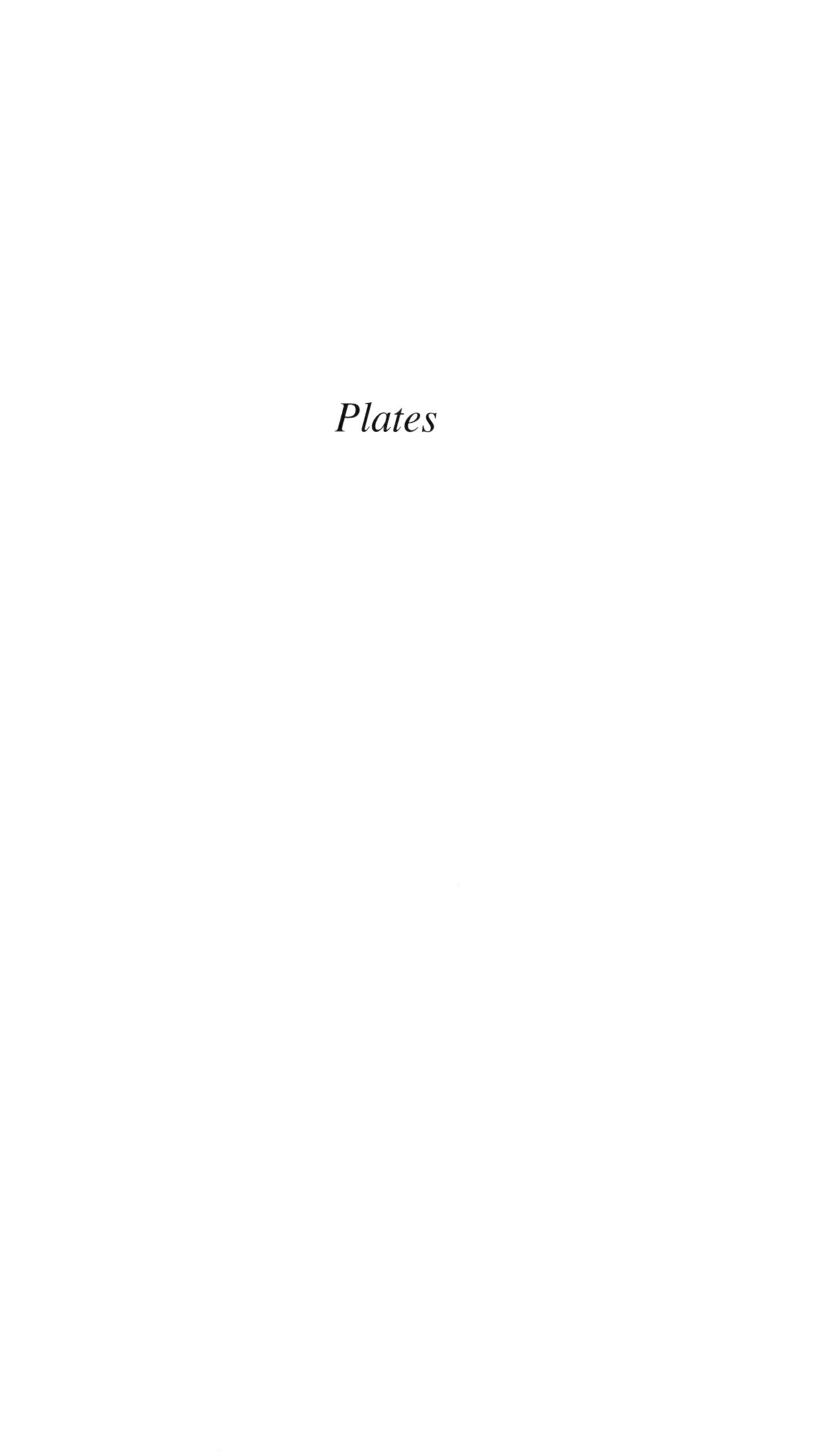

Plates

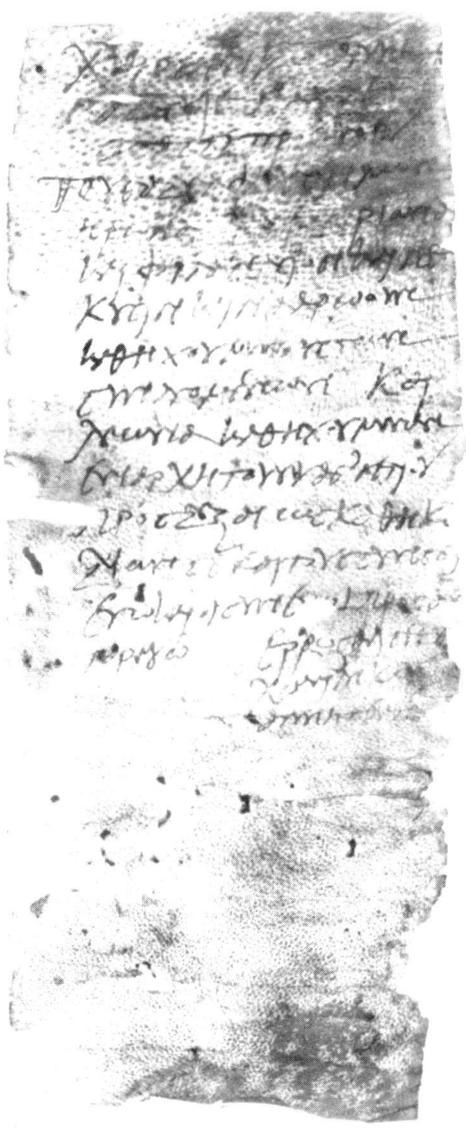

Plate 1: PSI 9.1041

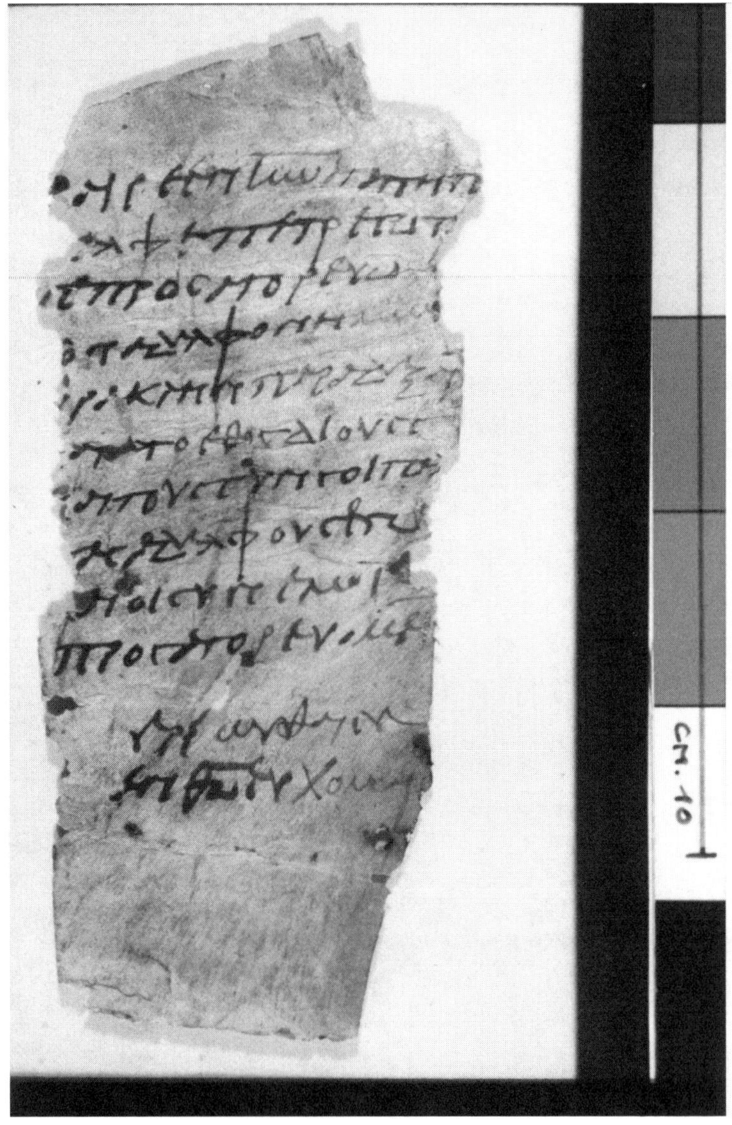

Plate 2: PSI 3.208

Florence, Biblioteca Medicea Laurenziana. By permission of the Ministero per i Beni e le Attività Culturali. Every other reproduction, by whatever means, is forbidden.

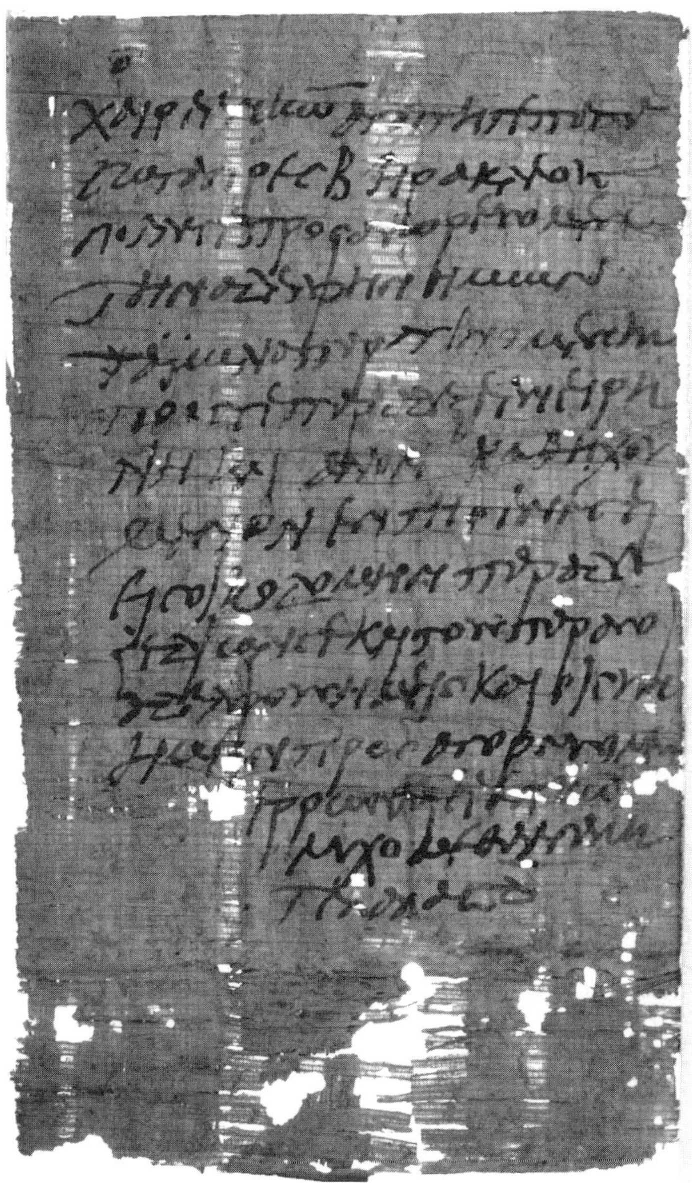

Plate 3: P.Oxy. 36.2785
Courtesy of the Egypt Exploration Society, London.

Plate 4: P.Alex. 29.
By permission of the Graeco-Roman Museum in Alexandria.
Image courtesy of Jean-Luc Fournet.

Plate 5: P.Oxy. 12.1492
 Papyrus 2462.

Plate 6: SB 12.10772 = PSI 14.1412

Bibliography

A. Papyrological Editions (selection)[1]

CPJ = *Corpus papyrorum judaicarum*. Edited by V. Tcherikover. 3 vols. Cambridge, Harvard University Press, 1957–1964.

P.Alex. = *Papyrus grecs du Musée Gréco-Romain d'Alexandrie*. Edited by Anna Świderek and Mariangela Vandoni. Travaux du Centre d'Archéologie Méditerranéenne de l'Académie Polonaise des Sciences 2. Warsaw: PWN-Éditions scientifiques de Pologne, 1964.

P.Amh. 1 = *The Amherst Papyri, Being an Account of the Greek Papyri in the Collection of the Right Hon. Lord Amherst of Hackney, F.S.A. at Didlington Hall, Norfolk*. Vol. 1 *The Ascension of Isaiah and Other Theological Fragments*. Edited by Bernard P. Grenfell and Arthur S. Hunt. London: Frowde, 1900.

P.Berl.Sarisch. = *Berliner griechische Papyri, Christliche literarische Texte und Urkunden aus dem 3. bis 8. Jh. n. Chr.* Edited by Panagiota Sarischouli. Serta Graeca 3. Wiesbaden: Reichert, 1995.

P.Harr. 2 = *The Rendel Harris Papyri of Woodbrooke College, Birmingham*. Vol. 2. Edited by R. A. Coles, M. Manfredi, P. J. Sijpesteijn, A. S. Brown et al. Studia amstelodamensia ad epigraphicam, ius antiquum et papyrologicam pertinentia. Zutphen, Holland: Terra, 1985.

P. Laur. 2 = *Dai papyri della Bibliotheca Medicea Laurenziana*. Edited by Rosario Pintaudi. Papyrologica Florentina 2. Florence Gonnelli, 1977.

P.Leid.Inst. = *Papyri, Ostraca, Parchments and Waxed Tablets in the Leiden Papyrological Institute*. Edited by Francisca A. J. Hoogendijk and Peter van Minnen. Leiden, 1991 (Pap.Lugd.Bat.XXV).

[1] For a complete list of papyrological editions, see John F. Oates, Roger S. Bagnall, Sarah J. Clackson, Alexandra A. O'Brien, Joshua D. Sosin, Terry G. Wilfong, and Klaas A. Worp, eds. *Checklist of Editions of Greek and Latin Papyri, Ostraca and Tablets*, 5th ed. BASP Suppl. 9, 2001. Online and expanded edition available at http://scriptorium.lib.duke.edu/papyrus/texts/clist.html.

P.Lips. 2 = *Griechische Urkunden der Papyrussammlung zu Leipzig* 2. Edited by Ruth Duttenhöffer with a contribution by Reinhold Scholl. Archiv für Papyrusforschung, Beiheft 10. Munich/Leipzig: Saur, 2002.

P.Mich.Mchl. = Michael, Edward Mike. A Critical Edition of Select Michigan Papyri. Ph.D. diss., University of Michigan, 1966.

P.Oxy. = *The Oxyrhynchus Papyri*. Edited by Bernard P. Grenfell and Arthur S. Hunt et al. 72 vols. Published by the Egypt Exploration Society in Graeco-Roman Memoirs. London: Egypt Exploration Fund, 1898–

PSI = *Papiri greci e latini*. Edited by Girolamo Vitelli and Medea Norsa et al. 15 vols. Pubblicazioni della Società Italiana per la ricerca dei papiri greci e latini in Egitto. Florence: Istituto papirologico "G. Vitelli," 1912–2008.

SB = *Sammelbuch griechischer Urkunden aus Aegypten*. Edited by Friedrich Preisigke, Friedrich Bilabel, Emil Kiessling, and Hans-Albert Rupprecht et al. 26 vols. 1913–2006.

B. Ancient Authors

Acta Sanctorum. Database. An electronic version of the Acta Sanctorum. 68 vols. Antwerp and Brussels: Société des Bollandistes, 1643–1940.

Apostolic Fathers. Translated by Bart Ehrman. 2 vols. LCL 24, 25. Cambridge, Mass.: Harvard University Press, 2003.

Athanasius. *Apologia conta Arianos sive Apologia secunda*. Vol. 2.1 of *Athanasius Werke*. Edited by Hans Georg Opitz. Berlin: De Gruyter, 1940.

Augustine. *Select Letters*. Translated by James Houston Baxter. LCL 239. Cambridge, Mass.: Harvard University Press, 1930.

Cyprian. *Epistularium*. Vol. 3.2 of *Sancti Cypriani episcopi opera*. Edited by Gerardus F. Diercks. Corpus Christianorum: Series latina. Turnhout: Brepols, 1996.

_____. *De lapsis*. Vol. 3.1 of *Sancti Cypriani episcopi opera*. Edited by Robert Weber and Maurice Bévenot. Corpus Christianorum: Series latina. Turnhout: Brepols, 1972.

_____. *De lapsis and De ecclesiae catholicae unitate*. Edited and translated by Maurice Bévenot. Oxford: Clarendon, 1971.

_____. *Letters*. Translated and annotated by Graeme W. Clarke. 4 vols. Ancient Christian Writers. New York: Newman, 1984-1989.

Cyril of Jerusalem. *Procatechesis*. Vol. 2 of *Cyrilli Hierosolymarum archiepiscopi opera quae supersunt omnia*. Edited by Wilhelm K. Reischl. Munich, 1860. Repr., Hildesheim: Olms, 1967.

Cyril of Jerusalem. *Procatechesis* in *Cyril of Jerusalem*. Translated by Edward Yarnold. The Early Church Fathers. London: Routledge, 2000.

Didache, Zwölf Apostel Lehre. Edited and translated by Georg Schöllgen. Fontes Christiani. Freiburg: Herder, 1991.

Dionysius of Alexandria. *Das erhaltene Werk. ΔΙΟΝΥΣΙΟΥ ΛΕΙΨΑΝΑ*. Edited by Wolfgang A. Bienert. Bibliothek der griechischen Literatur 2. Stuttgart: Anton Hiersemann, 1972.

Egeria. *Travels*. Translated by John Wilkinson. 3d ed. Warminster: Aris and Phillips, 1999.

Eusebius. *Ecclesiastical History*. 2 vols. Vol. 1 (Books 1–5) translated by Kirsopp Lake. LCL 153. Vol. 2 (Books 6–10) translated by J. E. L. Oulton. LCL 265. Cambridge, Mass.: Harvard University Press, 1926–1932. Repr., 1992–1994.

_____. *Werke*. Edited by Ivar A. Heikel. 9 vols. GCS. Leipzig: J. C. Hinrichs, 1902–1975.

Gesta apud Zenophilum. Pages 185–97 in Optatus. *S. Optati Melevitani Libri VII*. Appendix I. Edited by Karl Ziwsa. Corpus scriptorum ecclesiasticorum latinorum 26. Prague: Temsky, 1893.

Gregory Thaumaturgus. *Epistula canonica*. In vol. 2 of *Les canons des pères grecs*. Edited by P.-P. Joannou. Rome: S. Nilo, 1963.

_____. *Metaphrasis in Ecclesiasten Salamonis*. In vol. 10 of Patrologiae Graeca. Edited by Jacques-Paul Migne. Paris: 1857–1866.

_____. *Life and Works*. Translated by Michael Slusser. The Fathers of the Church. Washington, D.C. : The Catholic University of America Press, 1998.

Hippolytus. *Traditio apostolica. Apostolische Überlieferung*. Lateinisch-Griechisch-Deutsch. Translated and annotated by Wilhelm Geerlings. Fontes Christiani. Freiburg: Herder, 1991.

Ignatius of Antioch (Pseudo-). *Ad Mariam*. In vol. 2 of *Patres apostolici*. Edited by Franciscus X. Funk and Franciscus Diekamp. Tübingen: H. Laupp, 1913.

_____. *Lettres. Martyre de Polycarpe*. Edited and translated by Pierre Th. Camelot. 4th rev. ed. SC 10. Paris: Cerf, 1969.

Irenaeus. *Contre les hérésies*. Edited and translated by Louis Doutrelau, Charles A. Mercier, and Adelin Rousseau. 5 vols. Pages 152–53, 210–11, 263–64, 293–94 in SC 100. Paris: Cerf, 1952–1982.

_____. *Against the Heresies*. Translated by Dominic J. Unger. Ancient Christian Writers 55. New York: Paulist Press, 1992.

Ivo of Chartres. Decretum 6. Migne text online at http://project.knowledgeforge.net/ivo/decretum/ivodec_6_1p0.pdf.

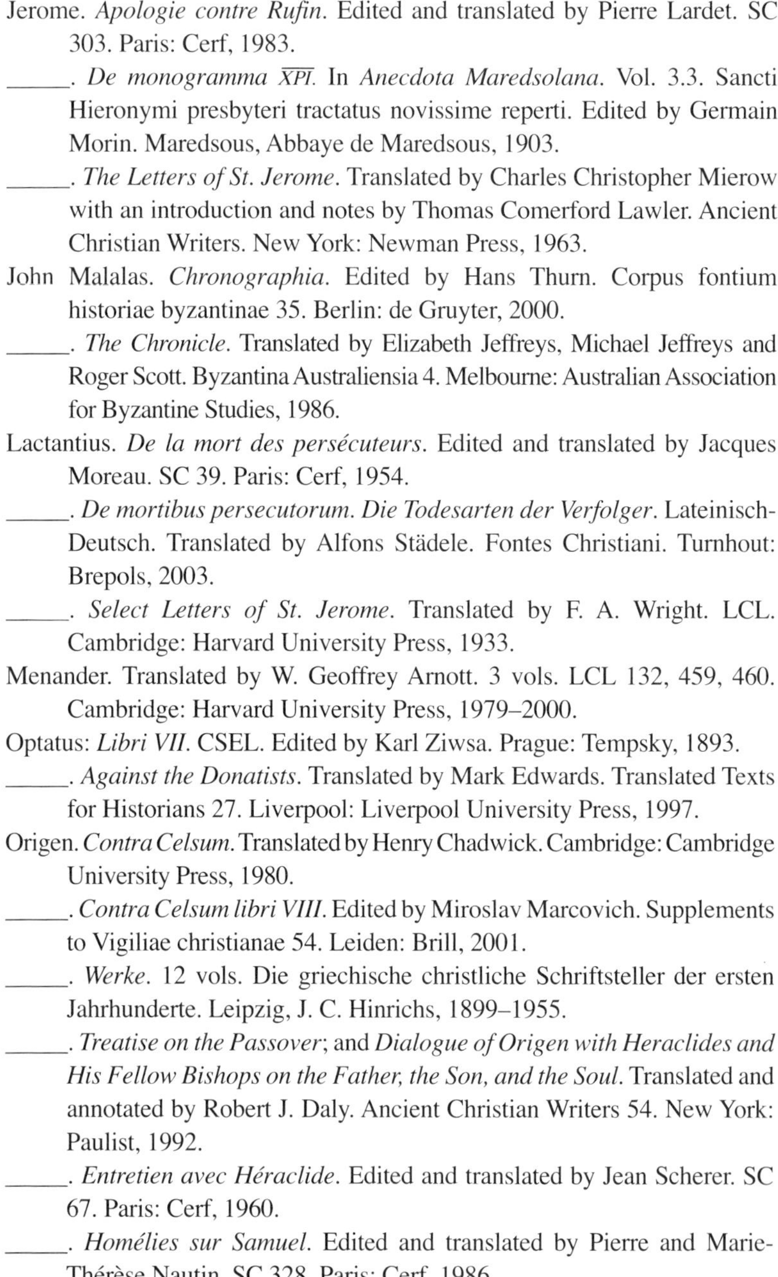

Jerome. *Apologie contre Rufin.* Edited and translated by Pierre Lardet. SC 303. Paris: Cerf, 1983.

_____. *De monogramma* $\overline{\text{XPI}}$*.* In *Anecdota Maredsolana.* Vol. 3.3. Sancti Hieronymi presbyteri tractatus novissime reperti. Edited by Germain Morin. Maredsous, Abbaye de Maredsous, 1903.

_____. *The Letters of St. Jerome.* Translated by Charles Christopher Mierow with an introduction and notes by Thomas Comerford Lawler. Ancient Christian Writers. New York: Newman Press, 1963.

John Malalas. *Chronographia.* Edited by Hans Thurn. Corpus fontium historiae byzantinae 35. Berlin: de Gruyter, 2000.

_____. *The Chronicle.* Translated by Elizabeth Jeffreys, Michael Jeffreys and Roger Scott. Byzantina Australiensia 4. Melbourne: Australian Association for Byzantine Studies, 1986.

Lactantius. *De la mort des persécuteurs.* Edited and translated by Jacques Moreau. SC 39. Paris: Cerf, 1954.

_____. *De mortibus persecutorum. Die Todesarten der Verfolger.* Lateinisch-Deutsch. Translated by Alfons Städele. Fontes Christiani. Turnhout: Brepols, 2003.

_____. *Select Letters of St. Jerome.* Translated by F. A. Wright. LCL. Cambridge: Harvard University Press, 1933.

Menander. Translated by W. Geoffrey Arnott. 3 vols. LCL 132, 459, 460. Cambridge: Harvard University Press, 1979–2000.

Optatus: *Libri VII.* CSEL. Edited by Karl Ziwsa. Prague: Tempsky, 1893.

_____. *Against the Donatists.* Translated by Mark Edwards. Translated Texts for Historians 27. Liverpool: Liverpool University Press, 1997.

Origen. *Contra Celsum.* Translated by Henry Chadwick. Cambridge: Cambridge University Press, 1980.

_____. *Contra Celsum libri VIII.* Edited by Miroslav Marcovich. Supplements to Vigiliae christianae 54. Leiden: Brill, 2001.

_____. *Werke.* 12 vols. Die griechische christliche Schriftsteller der ersten Jahrhunderte. Leipzig, J. C. Hinrichs, 1899–1955.

_____. *Treatise on the Passover*; and *Dialogue of Origen with Heraclides and His Fellow Bishops on the Father, the Son, and the Soul.* Translated and annotated by Robert J. Daly. Ancient Christian Writers 54. New York: Paulist, 1992.

_____. *Entretien avec Héraclide.* Edited and translated by Jean Scherer. SC 67. Paris: Cerf, 1960.

_____. *Homélies sur Samuel.* Edited and translated by Pierre and Marie-Thérèse Nautin. SC 328. Paris: Cerf, 1986.

Origen. *Philocalie, 1–20. Sur les écritures et La lettre à Africanus sur l'histoire de Suzanne*. Edited and translated by Nicholas de Lange in Marguerite Harl and Nicholas de Lange. SC 302. Paris: Cerf, 1983.

_____. *Contre Celse*. Edited and translated by Marcel Borret. 5 vols. SC 132, 136, 147, 150, 227. Paris: Cerf, 1967–1976.

Passion de Perpétua et de Félicité suivi des Actes. Introduction, texte critique, traduction, commentaire et index. Edited and translated by Jacqueline Amat. SC 417. Paris: Cerf, 1996.

Plutarch. *Isis and Osiris* in *Moralia*. Vol. 5. Translated by Frank C. Babbitt. LCL 306. Cambridge, Mass.: Harvard University Press, 1936. Repr., 1993.

Rufinus, Tyrannius. *Historia monachorum, sive, De vita sanctorum patrum*. Edited by Eva Schulz-Flügel. Patristische Texte und Studien 34. Berlin: de Gruyter, 1990. Sozomen. *The Ecclesiastical History of Sozomen Comprising a History of the Church from A.D. 323 to A.D. 425*. Translated by Chester D. Hartranft. In *NPNF*², 1890. Repr., Peabody, Mass.: Hendrickson, 1995.

Strabo. *Geography* 8. Book 17. Edited by Horace L. Jones. LCL 267. Cambridge, Mass.: Harvard University Press, 1932. Repr., 1982.

Tertullian. *De idolatria: Critical Text, Translation, and Commentary*. Edited and translated by J. H. Waszink and J. C. M. van Winden. Supplements to *VC* 1. Leiden: Brill, 1987.

C. Modern Authors

Adams, Colin. "'There and Back Again:' Getting Around in Roman Egypt." Pages 138–66 in *Travel and Geography in the Roman Empire*. Edited by Colin Adams and Ray Laurence. London: Routledge, 2001.

Aland, Kurt. *Biblische Papyri. Altes Testament, Neues Testament, Varia, Apokryphen*. Vol. 1 of *Repertorium der griechischen christlichen Papyri*. PTS 18. Berlin: de Gruyter, 1976.

Aland, Kurt, and Barbara Aland. *Der Text des Neuen Testaments. Einführung in die wissenschaftlichen Ausgaben und in Theorie wie Praxis der modernen Textkritik*. Stuttgart: Deutsche Bibelgesellschaft, ²1989.

Alcock, Anthony. "Persecution under Septimius Severus." *Enchoria* 11 (1982) 1–5 and plates 1–2.

Alford, Richard D. *Naming and Identity: A Cross-Cultural Study of Personal Naming Practices*. New Haven, Conn.: HRAF Press, 1988.

Ameling, Walter. *Kleinasien*. Vol. 2 of *Inscriptiones Judaicae Orientis*. TSAJ 99. Tübingen: Mohr Siebeck, 2004.

Andorlini, Isabella et al., eds. *Atti del XXII Congresso Internazionale di Papirologia. Firenze, 23–29 agosto 1998*. Firenze: Instituto Papirologico "G. Vitelli," 2001.

Arnaoutoglou, Ilias. "Marital Disputes in Greco-Roman Egypt." *JJP* 25 (1995) 11–28.

Arterbury, Andrew E. *Entertaining Angels: Early Christian Hospitality in Its Mediterranean Setting*. New Testament Monographs 8. Sheffield: Sheffield Phoenix, 2005.

Auf der Maur, Hans Jörg, and Joop Waldram. "Illuminatio Verbi Divini—Confessio Fidei—Gratia Baptismi. Wort, Glaube und Sakrament in Katechumenat und Taufliturgie bei Origenes." Pages 41–95 in *Fides Sacramenti—Sacramentum Fidei. Studies in Honour of Pieter Smulders*. Edited by Hans Jörg Auf der Mauer et al. Assen: Van Gorcum, 1981.

Bagnall, Roger S. "The Number and Term of the Dekaprotoi." *Aeg* 58 (1978) 160–67.

_____. "Religious Conversion and Onomastic Change in Early Byzantine Egypt." *BASP* 19 (1982) 105–24.

_____. *Currency and Inflation in Fourth Century Egypt*. BASPSup 5. Chico, Calif.: Scholars, 1985.

_____. "Church, State and Divorce in Late Roman Egypt." Pages 41–61 in *Florilegium Columbianum: Essays in Honor of Paul Oskar Kristeller*. New York: Italica, 1987. Repr. chapter 4 in *Later Roman Egypt: Society, Religion, Economy and Administration*. Collected Studies Series 758. Aldershot, U.K.: Ashgate, 2003.

_____. "Conversion and Onomastics: A Reply." *ZPE* 69 (1987) 243–50.

_____. "Combat ou vide. Christianisme et paganisme dans l'Égypte romaine tardive." *Ktema* 13 (1988) 285–96. Repr. chapter 10 in *Later Roman Egypt: Society, Religion, Economy and Administration*. Collected Studies Series 758. Aldershot, U.K.: Ashgate, 2003.

_____. "Notes on Roman and Byzantine Documents." *ChrEg* 66 (1991) 282–96.

_____. "An Owner of Literary Papyri." *CP* 87 (1992) 137–40.

_____. *Egypt in Late Antiquity*. Princeton, N.J.: Princeton University Press, 1993.

_____. "Charite's Christianity." *BASP* 32 (1995) 37–40.

Bagnall, Roger S. *Reading Papyri, Writing Ancient History*. Approaching the Ancient World. London: Routledge, 1995.

_____. *Later Roman Egypt: Society, Religion, Economy and Administration*. Collected Studies Series 758. Aldershot, U.K.: Ashgate, 2003.

_____. "Family and Society in Roman Oxyrhynchus." Pages 182–93 in *Oxyrhynchus: A City and Its Texts*. Edited by A. K. Bowman et al. Graeco-Roman Memoirs 93. London: Egypt Exploration Society, 2007.

Bagnall, Roger S., and Raffaella Cribiore. *Women's Letters from Ancient Egypt, 300 BC–AD 800*. Ann Arbor: University of Michigan Press, 2006.

Bagnall, Roger S., and Bruce W. Frier. *The Demography of Roman Egypt*. Cambridge Studies in Population, Economy, and Society in Past Time 23. Cambridge: Cambridge University Press, 1994.

Bagnall, Roger S., and Dominic W. Rathbone, eds. *Egypt from Alexander to the Early Christians: An Archaeological and Historical Guide*. Los Angeles: J. Paul Getty Museum, 2004.

Bammel Caroline P. "Problems of the Historia Monachorum." *JTS* 47 (1996) 92–104.

Barnes, Timothy D. "Legislation against the Christians." *JRS* 58 (1968) 32–50.

Battaglia, Emanuela. "Dichiarazioni templari. A proposito di *P.Oxy.* XLIX, 3473." *Aeg* 64 (1984) 79–99.

Bauer, Walter. *Rechtgläubigkeit und Ketzerei im ältesten Christentum*. BHT 10. Tübingen: Mohr Siebeck, 1934.

Baumeister, Theofried. "Die Historia Monachorum in Aegypto und die Entwicklung der koptischen Hagiographie." Pages 269–80 in vol. 1 of *Coptic Studies on the Threshold of a New Millennium. Proceedings of the Seventh International Congress of Coptic Studies, Leiden,...2000*. Edited by Mat Immerzeel and Jacques van der Vliet. Orientalia Lovaniensia Analecta 133. Leuven: Peeters, 2004.

Barzanò, Alberto. "La questione dell'arricchimento dei vescovi e del clero da Cipriano a Damaso. Tra polemica anticristiana, autocritica ecclesiale e legislazione imperiale." *Rivista di storia della chiesa in Italia* 47 (1993) 359–66.

Becker, Adam H., and Annette Yoshiko Reed, eds. *The Ways That Never Parted: Jews and Christians in Late Antiquity and the Early Middle Ages*. TSAJ 95. Tübingen: Mohr Siebeck, 2003.

Bell, H. Idris, ed. *The Abinnaeus Archive: Papers of a Roman Officer in the Reign of Constantius II*. Oxford: Clarendon, 1962.

Bell, H. Idris, and T. C. Skeat. *Fragment of an Unknown Gospel and Other Early Christian Papyri*. London: Trustees of the British Museum, 1935.

Benaissa, Amin. "New Light on the Episcopal Church of Oxyrhynchus." *ZPE* 161 (2007) 199–206.

Bergjan, Silke-Petra. *Der fürsorgende Gott. Der Begriff der ΠΡΟΝΟΙΑ Gottes in der apologetischen Literatur der Alten Kirche*. Arbeiten zur Kirchengeschichte 81. Berlin: de Gruyter, 2002.

Bienert, Wolfgang. *Dionysius von Alexandrien. Zur Frage des Origenismus im 3. Jahrhundert*. Berlin: de Gruyter, 1978.

Bilde, Per, ed. *Ethnicity in Hellenistic Egypt*. Studies in Hellenistic Civilization 3. Aarhus: Aarhus University Press, 1992.

Bourdieu, Pierre. *Outline of a Theory of Practice*. Translated by Richard Nice. Cambridge Studies in Social and Cultural Anthropology 16. Cambridge: Cambridge University Press, 1977.

Bovon, François. "Names and Numbers in Early Christianity." *NTS* 47 (2001) 267–88.

Bowman, Alan K. *Town Councils of Roman Egypt*. ASP 11. Toronto: Hakkert, 1971.

_____. *Egypt after the Pharaohs, 332 BC–AD 642: From Alexander to the Arab Conquest*. Berkeley: University of California Press, 1996.

Bowman, Alan K., R. A. Coles, N. Gonis, D. Obbink, and P. J. Parsons, eds. *Oxyrhynchus: A City and Its Texts*. Graeco-Roman Memoirs 93. London: Egypt Exploration Society, 2007.

Boyarin, Daniel. *Dying for God: Martyrdom and the Making of Judaism and Christianity*. Stanford: Stanford University Press, 1999.

Boyaval, B. "La tablette scolaire Pack[2] 1619." *ZPE* 14 (1974) 241–47.

_____. "Le cahier scolaire d'Aurelios Papnouthion." *ZPE* 17 (1975) 225–35.

Bradshaw, Paul F. "The Gospel and the Catechumenate in the Third Century." *JTS* 50 (1999) 143–52.

Breccia, Evaristo. "Fouilles d'Oxyrhynchos." Pages 36–45 in *Le Musée Gréco-Romain 1931–1932*. Bergamo: Instituto Italiano d'arte grafiche, 1933.

Brown, Peter. *Poverty and Leadership in the Later Roman Empire*. Menahem Stern Jerusalem Lectures. Hanover, N.H.: University Press of New Eng-land, 2002.

Brown, Schuyler. "Concerning the Origin of the Nomina Sacra." *SPap* (1971) 7–19.

Buell, Denise Kimber. *Making Christians: Clement of Alexandria and the Rhetoric of Legitimacy*. Princeton, N.J.: Princeton University Press, 1999.

Bülow-Jacobsen, Adam. "Orders to Arrest. *P.Haun*. inv. 33 and 54 and a Consolidated List." *ZPE* 66 (1986) 93–98.

Burkhalter, Fabienne. "Le mobilier des sanctuaires d'Égypte et les 'listes des prêtres et du cheirismos'." *ZPE* 59 (1985) 123–34.

Burkitt, Francis C. *The Religion of the Manichees*. Donnellan Lectures for 1924. Cambridge: Cambridge University Press, 1926.

Castelli, Elizabeth A. *Martyrdom and Memory: Early Christian Culture Making*. Gender, Theory, and Religion. New York: Columbia University Press, 2004.

Castelli, Elizabeth A., and Hal Taussig. "Introduction: Drawing Large and Startling Figures: Reimagining Christian Origins by Painting Like Picasso." Pages 3–20 in *Reimagining Christian Origins: A Colloquium Honoring Burton L. Mack*. Edited by Elizabeth A. Castelli and Hal Taussig. Valley Forge, Pa.: Trinity Press International, 1996.

Chapa, Juan. *Letters of Condolence in Greek Papyri*. Papyrologica Florentina 29. Firenze: Gonnelli, 1998.

Choat, Malcolm. *Belief and Cult in Fourth-Century Papyri*. Studia Antiqua Australiensia 1. Turnhout, Belgium: Brepolis, 2006.

Christiansen, Erik. *Coinage in Roman Egypt: The Hoard Evidence*. Aarhus: Aarhus University Press, 2004.

Clackson, Sarah J. "Coptic Oxyrhynchus." Pages 332–41 in *Oxyrhynchus: A City and Its Texts*. Edited by A. K. Bowman et al. Graeco-Roman Memoirs 93. London: Egypt Exploration Society, 2007.

Clarke, G. W. "Some Observations on the Persecution of Decius." *Antichthon* 3 (1969) 63–76.

_____. "Notes and Observations. Two Christians in the *Familia Caesaris*." *HTR* 64 (1971) 121–24.

_____. "An illiterate lector?" *ZPE* 57 (1984) 103–4.

Clarysse, Willy. "Literary Papyri in Documentary 'Archives'." Pages 43–61 in *Egypt and the Hellenistic World. Proceedings of the International Colloquium Leuven 24–26 May 1982*. Edited by E. Van 't Dack, P. Van Dessel, and W. Van Gucht. Studia Hellenistica 27. Leuven: Peeters, 1983.

_____. "The Coptic Martyr Cult." Pages 377-95 in *Martyrium in Multidisciplinary Perspective. Memorial Louis Reekmans*. Edited by M. Lamberigts and P. van Deun. BETL 117. Leuven: Leuven University Press/Peeters, 1995.

_____. "Inventories in Coptic Churches and Monasteries." Pages 85–93 in *Archives and Inventories in the Eastern Mediterranean*. Edited by Katelijn Vandorpe and Willy Clarysse. Koninklijke Vlaamse Academie van Belgie voor Wetenschappen en Kunsten, 2007.

Cohen, Shaye J. D. "'Those Who Say They Are Jews and Are Not': How Do You Know a Jew in Antiquity When You See One?" Pages 1–45 in *Diasporas in Antiquity*. Edited by Shaye J. D. Cohen and Ernest S. Frerichs. Brown Judaic Studies 288. Atlanta, Ga.: Scholars Press, 1993.

_____. *The Beginnings of Jewishness: Boundaries, Varieties, Uncertainties*. Hellenistic Culture and Society 31. Berkeley: University of California Press, 1999.

Colin, Frédérik. "Onomastique et société. Problèmes et méthodes à la lumière des documents de l'Égypte hellénistique et romaine." Pages 3–15 in *Noms, identités culturelles et romanisation sous le Haut-Empire*. Edited by Monique Dondin-Payre and Marie-Thérèse Raepsaet-Charlier. Brussels: Livre Timperman, 2001.

Constable, Olivia Remie. *Housing the Stranger in the Mediterranean World: Lodging, Trade, and Travel in Late Antiquity and the Middle Ages*. Cambridge: Cambridge University Press, 2003.

Cotton, Hannah M., Walter E. H. Cockle, and Fergus G. B. Millar. "The Papyrology of the Roman Near East: A Survey," *JRS* 85 (1995) 214–35.

Cowley, Arthur E. "Notes on Hebrew Papyrus Fragments from Oxyrhynchus." *JEA* 2 (1915) 209–13.

Cribiore, Raffaella. "Greek and Coptic Education in Late Antique Egypt." Pages 279–86 in vol. 2 of *Ägypten und Nubien in spätantiker und christlicher Zeit. Akten des 6. internationalen Koptologenkongresses, Münster, 20.–26. Juli 1996*. Edited by Stephen Emmel et al. Sprachen und Kulturen des christlichen Orients 6. Wiesbaden, Germany: Reichert, 1999.

_____. *Gymnastics of the Mind: Greek Education in Hellenistic and Roman Egypt*. Princeton: Princeton University Press, 2001.

_____. *Writing, Teachers, and Students in Graeco-Roman Egypt*. ASP 36. Atlanta, Ga.: Scholars Press, 1996.

Crook, John A. *Law and Life of Rome*. Aspects of Greek and Roman Life. Ithaca, N.Y.: Cornell University Press, 1967.

Crum, Walter E. "Fragments of a Church Calendar." *ZNTW* 37 (1938) 23–32.

Cuvigny, Hélène. "Les avatars du *chrysous* dans l'Égypte ptolémaïque et romaine." *BIFAO* 103 (2003) 111–31.

Davies, P. S. "The Origin and Purpose of the Persecution of AD 303." *JTS* 40 (1989) 66–94.

Davis, Stephen. "Namesakes of Saint Thecla," *BASP* 36 (1999) 71–81.

Davis, Stephen. *The Cult of Saint Thecla: A Tradition of Women's Piety in Late Antiquity*. Oxford Early Christian Studies. Oxford: Oxford University Press, 2001.

De Ste. Croix, G. E. M. "Aspects of the 'Great' Persecution." *HTR* 47 (1954) 75–113.

_____. "Why Were the Early Christians Persecuted?" *Past and Present* 26 (1963) 6–38.

_____. *Christian Persecution, Martyrdom, and Orthodoxy*. Edited by Michael Whitby and Joseph Streeter. Oxford: Oxford University Press, 2006.

Decker, Wolfgang. "Olympiasieger aus Ägypten." Pages 93–105 in *Religion und Philosophie im Alten Ägypten. Festgabe für Philippe Derchain zu seinem 65. Geburtstag am 24. Juli 1991*. Edited by Ursula Verhoeven and Erhart Graefe. Orientalia Lovaniensia Analecta 39. Leuven: Peeters, 1991.

Deissmann, Gustav Adolf. *Licht vom Osten. Das Neue Testament und die neuentdeckten Texte der hellenistisch-römischen Welt*. 4th ed. Tübingen: Mohr, 1923.

Delehaye, Hippolyte. "Les Martyrs d'Égypte." AnBoll 40 (1922) 5–154 and 299–364.

_____. "Le calendrier d'Oxyrhynchque pour l'année 535–536." AnBoll 42 (1924) 83–99.

Denis, Albert-Marie. "Les Fragments grecs du Livre des Jubilés." Pages 150–62 in *Introduction aux pseudépigraphes grecs d'Ancient Testament*. Studia in Veteris Testamenti Pseudepigrapha 1. Leiden: Brill, 1970.

Derda, Tomasz, and Ewa Wipszycka. "L'emploi des titres *Abba, Apa* et *Papas* dans l'Égypte Byzantine." *JJP* 24 (1994) 23–56.

Dickey, Eleanor. "Literal and Extended Use of Kinship Terms in Documentary Papyri." *Mnemosyne* 57 (2004) 131–76.

Dinneen, Lucilla. *Titles of Address in Christian Greek Epistolography to 527 A.D.* Washington, D.C.: Catholic University of America, 1929.

Dosálová, Ruzena. "Gli inventari dei beni delle chiese e dei conventi su papiro." *Analecta Papyrologica* 6 (1994) 5–19.

_____. P.Prag.Wess. 2.178 "Klosterinventar" (1995) 137–39.

Downey, Glanville. "The Olympic Games at Antioch in the Fourth Century A.D." TAPA 70 (1939) 428–38.

Drew-Bear, Marie. *Le nome Hermopolite: Toponymes et sites*. ASP 21. Missoula: Scholars Press, 1979.

Drexhage, Hans-Joachim. "Zu den Überstellungsbefehle aus dem römischen Ägypten." Pages 102–18 in *Migratio et Commutatio. Studien zur Alten Geschichte und deren Nachleben*. Edited by Hans-Joachim Drexhage and Julia Sünskes. St. Katharinen: Scripta Mercaturae, 1989.

Drioton, Etienne. "La discussion d'un moine anthropomorphite audien avec le patriarche Théophile d'Alexandrie en l'année 399." *Revue de l'Orient chrétien* 20 (1915–1917) 92–100 and 113–28.

Duval, Yvette. *Chrétiens d'Afrique à l'aube de la paix constantinienne. Les premiers échos de la grande persécution*. Collection des Études Augustiniennes, Série Antiquité 164. Paris: Institut d'Études Augustiniennes, 2000.

Eck, Werner. "Handelstätigkeit christlicher Kleriker in der Spätantike." *Memorias de historia antigua* 4 (1980) 127–37.

Eisen, Ute E. *Amtsträgerinnen im frühen Christentum. Epigraphische und literarische Studien*. Forschungen zur Kirchen- und Dogmengeschichte 61. Göttingen: Vandenhoeck & Ruprecht, 1996.

Elm, Susanna. *Virgins of God: The Making of Asceticism in Late Antiquity*. Oxford Classical Monographs. Oxford: Clarendon, 1994.

Emmett, Alanna M. "An Early Fourth-Century Female Monastic Community in Egypt?" Pages 77–83 in *Maistor: Classical, Byzantine and Renaissance Studies for Robert Browning*. Edited by Ann Moffatt. Byzantina Australiensia 5. Canberra: Australian Association for Byzantine Studies, 1984.

Epp, Eldon Jay. "New Testament Papyrus Manuscripts and Letter Carrying in Greco-Roman Times." Pages 35–56 in *The Future of Early Christianity. Essays in Honor of Helmut Koester*. Edited by Birger A. Pearson. Minneapolis: Fortress Press, 1991.

_____. "The Significance of the Papyri for Determining the Nature of the New Testament Text in the Second Century: A Dynamic View of Textual Transmission." Pages 274–97 in *Studies in the Theory and Method of New Testament Textual Criticism*. Edited by Eldon Jay Epp and Gordon D. Fee. Studies and Documents 45. Grand Rapids, Mich.: Eerdmans, 1993.

_____. "The Codex and Literacy in Early Christianity and at Oxyrhynchus: Issues Raised by Harry Y. Gamble's Books and Readers in the Early Church." *CRBR* 10 (1997) 15–37.

Epp, Eldon Jay. "The New Testament Papyri at Oxyrhynchus in Their Social and Intellectual Context." Pages 47–68 in *Sayings of Jesus: Canonical and Non-Canonical: Essays in Honour of Tjitze Baarda*. Edited by William L. Petersen, Johan S. Vos, and Henk Jan de Jonge. NovTSup 89. Leiden: Brill, 1997.

_____. "The Oxyrhynchus New Testament Papyri: 'Not Without Honor Except in Their Hometown'?" *JBL* 123 (2004) 5–55.

_____. *Perspectives on New Testament Textual Criticism: Collected Essays, 1962–2004*. Leiden: Brill, 2005.

_____. "The Jews and the Jewish Community in Oxyrhynchus: Socio-Religious Context for the New Testament Papyri." Pages 13–52 in *New Testament Manuscripts: Their Texts and Their World*. Edited by Thomas J. Kraus and Tobias Nicklas. Texts and Editions for New Testament Study 2. Leiden: Brill, 2006.

_____. "New Testament Papyri and the Transmission of the New Testament." Pages 315–331 in *Oxyrhynchus: A City and Its Texts*. Edited by A. K. Bowman et al. Graeco-Roman Memoirs 93. London: Egypt Exploration Society, 2007.

Farid, F. "The Prescript of *P. Oxy* 1680." *Anagennesis* 1 (1981) 11–18.

Fehérvári, Géza. "The Kuwaiti Excavations, 1985–7." Pages 109–28 in *Oxyrhynchus: A City and Its Texts*. Edited by A. K. Bowman et al. Graeco-Roman Memoirs 93. London: Egypt Exploration Society, 2007.

Festugière, André-Jean. *Historia monachorum in Aegypto. Édition critique du texte grec*. Subsidia hagiographica 34. Bruxelles: Société des Bollandistes, 1961.

Fichman, I. F. "Die Bevölkerungszahl von Oxyrhynchos in byzantinischer Zeit." *APF* 21 (1971) 111–20.

_____. (Itzhak F. Fikhman). "On Onomastics of Greek and Roman Egypt." Pages 403–14 in *Classical Studies in Honor of David Sohlberg*. Edited by Ranon Katzoff. Ramat Gan: Bar-Ilan University Press, 1996.

Fischer, Joseph Anton. "Die antiochenischen Synoden gegen Paul von Samosata." *Annuarium historiae conciliorum* 18 (1986) 9–30.

Foraboschi, Daniele. *Onomasticon alterum papyrologicum*. Milano: Varese Istituto Editoriale Cisalpino, 1971.

Frank, Georgia. "Miracles, Monks, and Monuments: The *Historia Monachorum in Aegypto* as Pilgrim's Tales." Pages 483–505 in *Pilgrimage and Holy Space in Late Antique Egypt*. Edited by David Frankfurter. RGRW 134. Leiden: Brill, 1998.

Frankfurter, David. *Religion in Roman Egypt: Assimilation and Resistance*. Princeton, N.J.: Princeton University Press, 1998.

Franklin, Simon. "A Note on the Pseudepigraphal Allusion in Oxyrhynchus Papyrus No. 4365" *VT* 48 (1998) 95–96.

Frend, William H. C. *Martyrdom and Persecution in the Early Church: A Study of a Conflict from the Maccabees to Donatus*. Oxford: Basil Blackwell, 1965.

Gagos, Traianos and Pieter J. Sijpesteijn. "Towards an Explanation of the Typology of the So-Called 'Orders to Arrest'." *BASP* 33 (1996) 77–97.

Gamble, Harry Y. *Books and Readers in the Early Church: A History of Early Christian Texts*. New Haven: Yale University Press, 1995.

Gardner, Iain, Alanna Nobbs and Malcolm Choat, "*P.Harr.* 107: Is This Another Greek Manichaean Letter?" *ZPE* 131 (2000) 118–24.

Gardthausen, V. *Das Buchwesen im Altertum und im Byzantinischen Mittelalter*. Vol. 1 of *Griechische Palaeographie*. 2d ed. Leipzig: Veit, 1911.

Ghedini, Giuseppe. "*Ὁ ΤΟΠΟΣ* nel POXy. 1492." *Aeg* 2 (1921) 337–38.

_____. *Lettere cristiane dai papiri greci del III e IV secolo*. Milano: Vita e Pensiero, 1923.

Gignac, Francis T. *A Grammar of the Greek Papyri of the Roman and Byzantine Periods*. Milano: Istituto editoriale cialpino. La goliardica, 1976.

Gonis, Nikolaos. "Notes on two epistolary conventions." *ZPE* 119 (1997) 148–52.

_____. "Dionysius, Bishop of Oxyrhynchus, and His Date." *JJP* 36 (2006) 63–65.

Grenfell, Bernard P. "A.– Oxyrhynchus and Its Papyri." Pages 1–12 in *Egypt Exploration Fund: Archaeological Report 1896–1897*. Edited by F. L. Griffith. London: Egypt Exploration Society, 1897.

Grenfell, Bernard P., and Arthur S. Hunt. "Excavations at Oxyrhynchus." *Archaeological Report*. London: Egypt Exploration Fund (1902–1903) 5–9; (1903–1904) 14–17; (1904–1905) 13–17; (1905–1906) 8–16; (1906–1907) 8–11.

Haas, Christopher J. "Imperial Religious Policy and Valerian's Persecution of the Church, A.D. 257–260." *Church History* 52 (1983) 133–44.

_____. *Alexandria in Late Antiquity*. Baltimore: Johns Hopkins University Press, 1997.

Haelst, Joseph van. "Les sources papyrologiques concernant l'église en Égypte à l'époque de Constantin." Pages 497–503 in *Proceedings of the Twelfth International Congress of Papyrology*. Edited by Deborah H. Samuel. ASP 7. Toronto: A. M. Hakkert, 1970.

_____. *Catalogue des papyrus littéraires juifs et chrétiens*. Papyrologie 1. Paris: Publications de la Sorbonne, 1976.

Hagedorn, Dieter. " *Ὀξυρύγχων πόλις* und *ἡ Ὀξυρυγχιτῶν πόλις*." *ZPE* 12 (1973) 277–92.

_____. "Die 'Kleine Genesis' in P.Oxy. LXIII 4365." *ZPE* 116 (1997) 147–48.

_____. "WörterListen aus den Registern von Publikationen griechischer und lateinischer dokumentarischer Papyri und Ostraka," http://www.zaw.uni-heidelberg.de/hps/pap/WL/WL.pdf.

Hagedorn, Ursula. "Das Formular der Überstellungsbefehle im römischen Ägypten." *BASP* 16 (1979) 61–74.

Haines-Eitzen, Kim. *Guardians of Letters: Literacy, Power, and the Transmitters of Early Christian Literature*. Oxford: Oxford University Press, 2000.

Hanson, Ann Ellis. "Ancient Illiteracy." Pages 159–98 in *Literacy in the Roman World*. Edited by Mary Beard. JRA, Supplement 3. Ann Arbor, Mich.: Journal of Roman Archaeology, 1991.

Harding, Mark. "A Hebrew Congregational Prayer from Egypt." *NewDocs* 8:145–47.

Harnack, Adolf von. *Die Mission und Ausbreitung des Christentums in den ersten drei Jahrhunderten*. 2 vols. Leipzig: Hinrichs, 1924.

Harrauer, Hermann. "Bücher in Papyri." Pages 59–77 in *Flores litterarum Ioanni Marte sexagenario oblati. Wissenschaft in der Bibliothek*. Edited by Helmut W. Lang. Biblos Schriften 163. Wien: Böhlau, 1995.

Harris, Bruce F. "Biblical Echoes and Reminiscences in Christian Papyri." Pages 155–60 in *Proceedings of the XIV International Congress of Papyrologists. Oxford, 24–31 July 1974*. Graeco-Roman Memoirs 61. London: Egypt Exploration Society, 1976.

Harris, William V. *Ancient Literacy*. Cambridge, Mass.: Harvard University Press, 1989.

Harrison, Tony. *The Trackers of Oxyrhynchus*. London: Faber and Faber, 1991.

Harrop, J. H. "A Christian Letter of Commendation." *JEA* 48 (1962) 132–40.

Hauben, Hans. "On the Melitians in P.London VI (P.Jews) 1914: The Problem of Papas Heraiscus." Pages 447–56 in *Proceedings of the Sixteenth International Congress of Papyrology*. Edited by Roger S. Bagnall et al. ASP 23. Chico, Calif.: Scholars Press, 1981.

Healy, Patrick J. *The Valerian Persecution*. London: Constable, 1905.

Hefele, Karl Joseph. *A History of the Christian Councils from the Original Documents to the Close of the Council of Nicaea, A.D. 325*. Translated by William R. Clark. Edinburgh: T&T Clark, 1871.

Hemer, C. J. "Ammonius to Apollonius, Greeting." *Buried History* 12 (1976) 84–91.

Hilhorst, A. "Erwähnt P.Oxy. LXIII 4365 das Jubiläenbuch?" *ZPE* 130 (2000) 192.

Hill, Charles E. "Did the scribe of P(52) use the nomina sacra? Another look." *NTS* 48 (2002) 587–92.

Hiltbrunner, Otto. *Gastfreundschaft in der Antike und im frühen Christentum*. Darmstadt: Wissenschaftliche Buchgesellschaft, 2005.

Hiltbrunner, Otto, Denys Gorce and Hans Wehr. "Gastfreundschaft." *RAC* 8 (1972) 1062–123.

Hobson, Deborah. "Towards a Broader Context of the Study of Greco-Roman Egypt." EMC 32 (1988) 353–63.

_____. "Naming Practices in Roman Egypt." *BASP* 26 (1989) 157–74.

Hoek, Annewies van den. "The 'Catechetical' School of Early Christian Alexandria and Its Philonic Heritage." *HTR* 90 (1997) 59–87.

Horn, Cornelia B. *Asceticism and Christological Controversy in Fifth-Century Palestine: The Career of Peter the Iberian*. Oxford Early Christian Studies. Oxford: Oxford University Press, 2006.

Hornblower, Simon, and Elaine Matthews, eds. *Greek Personal Names. Their Value as Evidence*. Proceedings of the British Academy 104. Oxford/British Academy: Oxford University Press, 2000.

Horsley, Greg H. R. *NewDocs*. 9 vols. The Ancient History Documentary Research Centre. North Ryde: Macquarie University, 1981–2002.

_____. "Nomina sacra in Synagogue Inscriptions." *NewDocs* 1:107–12.

_____. "Athanasios." *NewDocs* 3:90.

_____. "A Deacon's Work Contract." *NewDocs* 1:121–24.

_____. "Divine Providence in a Letter of Judas." *NewDocs* 3:141–48.

_____. ". . . a problem like Maria." *NewDocs* 4:229–30.

_____. "Name Change as an Indication of Religious Conversion in Antiquity." *Numen* 34 (1987) 1–17.

Hübner, Sabine. *Der Klerus in der Gesellschaft des spätantiken Kleinasiens.* Altertumswissenschaftliches Kolloquium 15. Stuttgart: Franz Steiner, 2005.

Hulley, Karl Kelchner. "Light Cast By St. Jerome on Palaeographical Points." *HSCP* 54 (1943) 83–92.

Hurtado, Larry W. "The Origin of the Nomina Sacra: A Proposal." *JBL* 117 (1998) 655–73.

_____. "The Earliest Evidence of an Emerging Christian Material and Visual Culture: The Codex, the Nomina Sacra and the Staurogram." Pages 271–88 in *Text and Artifact in the Religions of Mediterranean Antiquity. Essays in Honour of Peter Richardson.* Edited by Stephen G. Wilson and Michel Desjardins. Studies in Christianity and Judaism 9. Waterloo, Ont.: Canadian Corporation for Studies in Religion, 2000.

_____. *Lord Jesus Christ: Devotion to Jesus in Earliest Christianity.* Grand Rapids: Eerdmans, 2003.

_____. "P52 (P. Rylands Gk. 457) and the Nomina Sacra: Method and Probability." *Tyndale Bulletin* 54 (2003) 1–14.

_____. *The Earliest Christian Artifacts: Manuscripts and Christian Origins.* Grand Rapids, Mich.: Eerdmans, 2006.

Husson, Geneviève, and Dominique Valbelle, *L'état et les institutions en Égypte des premiers pharaons aux empereurs romains.* Paris: Armand Colin, 1992.

Ilan, Tal. "In the Footsteps of Jesus: Jewish Women in a Jewish Movement." Pages 115–36 in *Transformative Encounters: Jesus and Women Re-viewed.* Edited by Ingrid R. Kitzberger. Biblical Interpretation Series 43. Leiden: Brill, 2000.

_____. *Lexicon of Jewish Names in Late Antiquity. Part 1: Palestine 330 BCE–200 CE.* TSAJ 91. Tübingen: Mohr Siebeck, 2002.

Jankowski, Stanislaw. "I 'nomina sacra' nei papiri dei LXX (secoli II e III d. C.)." *SPap* 16 (1977) 81–116.

Johnson, Janet H., ed. *Life in a Multi-Cultural Society: Egypt from Cambyses to Constantine and Beyond.* SAOC 51. Chicago: Oriental Institute of the University of Chicago, 1992.

Johnson, Richard Ronald. "The Role of Parchment in Greco-Roman Antiquity." Ph.D. diss., University of California, Los Angeles, 1968.

Johnson, William A. *Bookrolls and Scribes in Oxyrhynchus.* Studies in Book and Print Culture. Toronto: University of Toronto Press, 2004.

Jomard, Edme François. *Description de l'Égypte.* Paris: Imprimerie impériale, 1818.

Jones, Brian W. and John E. G. Whitehorne. *Register of Oxyrhynchites, 30 B.C.–A.D. 96*. ASP 25. Chico, Calif.: Scholars Press, 1983.

Judge, Edwin A. and S. R. Pickering. "Papyrus Documentation of Church and Community in Egypt to the Mid-Fourth Century." *JAC* 20 (1977) 47–71.

Judge, Edwin et al. "Summons for Petosorapis, *chresianos*." In *Papyri from the Rise of Christianity in Egypt*. Edited by Don C. Barker, Malcolm Choat, B. F. Harris, Edwin A. Judge, and Alanna M. Nobbs. http://www.anchist.mq.edu.qu/doccentre/PCE2.pdf.

Kajanto, Iiro. "On the Problem of 'Names of Humility' in Early Christian Epigraphy." *Arctos* 3 (1962) 45–59.

Kasher, Aryeh. "The Jewish Community of Oxyrhynchus in the Roman Period." *JJS* 32 (1981) 151–57.

Kenyon, Frederic. "The Library of a Greek of Oxyrhynchus." *JEA* 8 (1922) 129–38.

Keresztes, P. "The Decian *Libelli* and Contemporary Literature." *Latomus* 34 (1975) 761–81.

_____. "The Peace of Gallienus: 260–303 A.D." *WS* 9 (1975) 174–85.

_____. "Two Edicts of the Emperor Valerian." *VC* 29 (1975) 81–95.

Kessler, Dieter. "Zwei Grabstelen mit Oxyrhynchosfischen." *WO* 14 (1983) 176–88.

Keyes, Clinton W. "The Greek Letter of Introduction." *AJP* 56 (1935) 28–44.

Kim, Chan-Hie. *Form and Structure of the Familiar Greek Letter of Recommendation*. SBLDS 4. Missoula, Mont.: Society of Biblical Literature for the Seminar on Paul, 1972.

King, Karen L. *What is Gnosticism?* Cambridge, Mass.: Harvard University Press, 2003.

Knipfing, John R. "The Libelli of the Decian Persecution." *HTR* 16 (1923) 345–90.

Koenen, Ludwig. "Ein Mönch als Berufsschreiber. Zur Buchproduktion im 5./6. Jahrhundert." Pages 347–54 in *Festschrift zum 150jährigen Bestehen des Berliner Ägyptischen Museums*. Mitteilungen aus der Ägyptischen Sammlung 8. Berlin: Academie-Verlag, 1974.

Koester, Helmut. *Ancient Christian Gospels: Their History and Development*. Philadelphia: Trinity, 1990.

Kolb, Frank. "Chronologie und Ideologie der Tetrarchie." *Antiquité tardive* 3 (1995) 21–31.

Koskenniemi, Heikki. "Fünf griechische Papyrusbriefe aus Florentiner Sammlungen." *Aeg* 33 (1953) 315–30.

Koskenniemi, Heikki. "Epistula Sarapammmonis P.S.I. 1412 particula aucta." *Arctos* n.s. 5 (1967) 79–84.

Kotsifou, Chrysi. "Books and Book Production in the Monastic Communities of Byzantine Egypt." Pages 48–66 in *The Early Christian Book*. Edited by William E. Klingshirn and Linda Safran. CUA Studies in early Christianity. Washington, D.C.: Catholic University of America Press, 2007.

Kraft, Robert A. "Continuities and Discontinuities in the Transitions from Jewish to Christian Scribal Practices. http://ccat.sas.upenn.edu/rs/rak/jewchrpap.html.

_____. "The Pseudepigrapha in Christianity." Pages 55-86 in *Tracing the Threads: Studies in the Vitality of Jewish Pseudepigrapha*. Edited by John C. Reeves. Early Judaism and Its Literature 6. Atlanta, Ga.: Scholars Press, 1994.

Kraus, Theodor. "Sarapiskopf aus Oxyrhynchos." *JdI* 75 (1960) 88–99.

Kraus, Thomas J. "(Il)literacy in Non-Literary Papyri from Graeco-Roman Egypt: Further Aspects of the Educational Ideal in Ancient Literary Sources and Modern Times." *Mnemosyne* 53 (2000) 322–42.

_____. "Bücherleihe im 4. Jh. n. Chr.: P.Oxy. LXII 4365–ein Brief auf Papyrus und die gegenseitige Leihe von apokryph gewordener Literatur." Biblos 50 (2001) 285–96.

Krüger, Julian. *Oxyrhynchos in der Kaiserzeit. Studien zur Topographie und Literaturrezeption*. Europäische Hochschulschriften 3, 441. Frankfurt am Main: Lang, 1990.

Kruijf, Theo C. de. "The Name Christians: A Label or a Challenge?" *Bijdragen* 59 (1998) 3–19.

Kutzner, Edgar. *Untersuchungen zur Stellung der Frau im römischen Oxyrhynchos*. Europäische Hochschulschriften 3, 392. Frankfurt am Main: Lang, 1989.

Labriolle, Pierre de. "Une esquisse de l'histoire du mot 'Papa'." BALAC 1 (1911) 215–20.

Lallemand, Jacqueline. *Administration civile de l'Égypte de l'avènement de Dioclétien à la création du diocèse (284–382). Contribution à l'étude des rapports entre l'Égypte et l'Empire à la fin du IIIe et au IVe siècle*. Koninklijke Academie van België, klasse der letteren 57.2. Brussel: Paleis der Academiën, 1964.

Lampe, Geoffrey W. H. *A Patristic Greek Lexicon*. Oxford: Clarendon, 1961–1968.

Lang, Uwe M. "The Christological Controversy at the Synod of Antioch in 268/9." *JTS* 51 (2000) 54–80.

Lauchert, Friedrich. *Die Kanones der wichtigsten altkirchlichen Concilien nebst den apostolischen Kanones.* Sammlung ausgewählter kirchen- und dogmengeschichtlicher Quellenschriften 12. Freiburg: Mohr, 1896.

Leadbetter, W. L. "A *libellus* of the Decian Persecution." *NewDocs* 2:180–85.

Leclercq, Henri. "Dèce." *DACL* 4.1 (1920) 309–39.

_____. "Isopséphie." *DACL* 7.2 (1927) 1603–6.

_____. "Lettres chrétiennes." *DACL* 8.2 (1929) 2683–85.

_____. "Libelli." *DACL* 9.1 (1930) 80–85.

_____. "Litterae commendatitiae et formatae." *DACL* 9.2 (1930) 1571–76.

_____. "Papa." in *DACL* 13.1 (1937) 1097–99.

_____. "Papyrus." *DACL* 13.1 (1937) 1370–1520.

Lieu, Judith M. "Accusations of Jewish Persecution in Christian Sources." Pages 279–98 in *Tolerance and Intolerance in Early Judaism and Christianity.* Edited by Graham N. Stanton and Guy G. Stroumsa. Cambridge: Cambridge University Press, 1998. Repr. pages 135–50 in *Neither Jew nor Greek? Constructing Early Christianity.* Studies of the New Testament and Its World. Edinburgh: T&T Clark, 2002.

_____. " 'I am a Christian': Martyrdom and the Beginning of 'Christian' Identity." Pages 211–31 in *Neither Jew Nor Greek? Constructing Early Christianity.* Studies of the New Testament and Its World. Edinburgh: T&T Clark, 2002.

_____. *Neither Jew nor Greek? Constructing Early Christianity.* Studies of the New Testament and Its World. Edinburgh: T&T Clark, 2002.

_____. *Christian Identity in the Jewish and Graeco-Roman World.* Oxford: Oxford University Press, 2004.

Lieu, Samuel N. C. *Manichaeism in Mesopotamia and the Roman East.* RGRW 118. Leiden: Brill, 1994.

Llewelyn, S. R. "Ammonios to Apollonios (P.Oxy. XLII 3057): The Earliest Christian Letter on Papyrus?" *NewDocs* 6:172–77.

_____. "ΣΔ, a Christian Isopsephism?" *ZPE* 109 (1995) 125–27.

_____. "The Development of the Codex'." *NewDocs* 7:249–56.

_____. "Christian Letters of Recommendation." *NewDocs* 8:169–72.

_____. "The Christian Symbol ΧΜΓ, an Acrostic or an Isopsephism?" *NewDocs* 8:156–68.

Löhr, Winrich A. "Some Observations on Karl-Heinz Schwarte's 'Diokletian's Christengesetz'." *VC* 56 (2002) 75–95.

MacLennan, Hugh. "Oxyrhynchus: An Economic and Social Study." Ph.D. diss. Princeton University, 1935.

Malherbe, Abraham J. *Ancient Epistolary Theorists*. SBLSBS 19. Atlanta, Ga.: Scholars Press, 1988.

Margoliouth, David S. "Notes on Syriac Papyrus Fragments from Oxyrhynchus." *JEA* 2 (1915) 214–16.

Martin, Alain. "Archives privées et cachettes documentaires." Pages 569–77 in *Proceedings of the 20th International Congress of Papyrologists*. Edited by Adam Bülow-Jacobsen. Copenhagen: Museum Tusculanum, 1994.

Martin, Annik. "Aux origines de l'église copte: l'implantation et le développement du christianisme en Égypte (Ier-IVe siècles)." *REA* 83 (1981) 35–56.

_____. *Athanase d'Alexandrie et l'église d'Égypte au IVe siècle (328–373)*. Collection de l'École française de Rome 216. Rome: École française de Rome, 1996

Martin, V. "Abinnaeus and His Correspondents." Pages 22–33 in *The Abinnaeus Archive: Papers of a Roman Officer in the Reign of Constantius II*. Edited by H. Idris Bell. Oxford: Clarendon, 1962.

Matthews, John. *The Journey of Theophanes. Travel, Business, and Daily Life in the Roman East*. New Haven: Yale University Press, 2006.

Meigne, Maurice. "Concile ou collection d'Elvire." *RHE* 70 (1975) 361–87.

Metzger, Bruce M. *Manuscripts of the Greek Bible: An Introduction to Greek Palaeography*. New York: Oxford University Press, 1981.

_____. "The Fourth Book of Ezra." Pages 516–24 in *Apocalyptic Literature & Testaments*. Vol. 1 of *The Old Testament Pseudepigrapha*. Edited by James Charlesworth. ABRL. New York: Doubleday, 1983.

Metzger, Hubert. "Spätantik-byzantinische Papyri aus der Sammlung Erzherzog Rainer in Wien." *Museum Helveticum* 18 (1961) 24–27.

Millar, Fergus. "Paul of Samosata, Zenobia and Aurelian: The Church, Local Culture and Political Allegiance in Third-Century Syria." *JRS* 61 (1971) 1–17.

Millard, Alan R. "Ancient Abbreviations and the nomina sacra." Pages 221–26 in The *Unbroken Reed: Studies in the Culture and Heritage of Ancient Egypt in Honour of A. F. Shore*. Edited by Christopher Eyre, Anthony Leahy and Lisa Montagno Leahy. Occasional Publications 11. London: Egypt Exploration Society, 1994.

Minnen, Peter van. "The Earliest Account of a Martyrdom in Coptic." AnBoll 113 (1995) 13–38.

Mißler, Herbert Ernst Ludwig. *Der Komarch. Ein Beitrag zur Dorfverwaltung im ptolemäischen, römischen und byzantinischen Ägypten*. Ph.D. diss., Marburg/Lahn, 1970.

Modena, Giuseppe. "Il Cristianesimo ad Ossirinco secondo i papiri. Chiese e conventi e loro condizione economica." *BSAA* 31 (=N. S. IX-2) (1927) 254–69.

_____. "Il Cristianesimo ad Ossirinco. Papiri letterari e cultura religiosa." *BSAA* 33 (= N. S. X) (1939) 293–310.

Modona, Aldo Neppi. "La vita pubblica e privata degli Ebrei in Egitto nell'età ellenistica e romana, II." *Aeg* 3 (1922) 19–43.

Modrzejewski, Joseph Mélèze. "ΙΟΥΔΑΙΟΙ ΑΦΗΙΡΗΜΕΝΟΙ. La fin de la communauté juive d'Égypte (115–117 de n.è)." Pages 337–61 in *Symposion 1985. Vorträge zur griechischen und hellenistischen Rechtsgeschichte*. Edited by Gerhard Thür. Köln: Böhlau, 1989.

Montevecchi, Orsolina. "Nomen christianum." Pages 485–500 in *Paradoxos politeia. Studi patristici in onore di Guiseppe Lazzati*. Edited by R. Cantalamessa and L. F. Pizzolato. Studia Patristica Mediolanesia 10. Milano: Vita e Pensiero, 1979.

_____. *La papirologia*. Milano: Vita e Pensiero,1988.

_____. "ΤΗΝ ΕΠΙΣΤΟΛΗΝ ΚΕΧΙΑΣΜΕΝΗΝ P.Oxy. XLII 3057." *Aeg* 80 (2000) 187–94.

Montserrat, Dominic. "News Reports: The Excavations and Their Journalistic Coverage." Page 28–39 in *Oxyrhynchus: A City and Its Texts*. Edited by A. K. Bowman et al. Graeco-Roman Memoirs 93. London: Egypt Exploration Society, 2007.

Moretti, Luigi. "Note egittologiche. 1. Nota a P. S. I. 1412." *Aeg* 38 (1958) 199–203.

Morris, Royce L. B. "Bishops in the Papyri." Pages 582–87 in *Proceedings of the 20th International Congress of Papyrologists. Copenhagen, 23–29 August, 1992*. Edited by Adam Bülow-Jacobsen. Copenhagen: Museum Tusculanum, 1994.

Müller, C. Detlef G. "La position de l'Égypte chrétienne dans l'Orient ancien: Influences et communications avec les pays voisins d'Afrique et d'Asie." *Le Muséon* 92 (1979) 105–25.

Musurillo, Herbert, ed. and transl. *The Acts of the Christian Martyrs: Introduction, Texts and Translations*. Oxford Early Christian Texts. Oxford: Clarendon Press, 1972.

Naldini, Mario, ed. *Documenti dell'antichità cristiana. Papiri e pergamene greco-egizie della Raccolta Fiorentina.* Firenze: Felice le Monnier, 1965.

_____. "Acta Vetera. Un papiro cristiano della raccolta fiorentina. Lettera di Theonas a Mensurio," *Atene e Roma* n.s. 11 (1966) 27–30.

_____. "Dai papiri della raccolta fiorentina. Lettera di Tatianos al 'padre' Chairemon." *Atene e Roma* n.s. 12 (1967) 167–68.

_____. "In margine alle 'lettere cristiane' nei papyri." *CClCr* 2 (1981) 167–76.

_____. "In margine alle 'Lettere cristiane' nei papyri." *JJP* 19 (1983) 163–168.

_____. Nuove testimonianze cristiane nelle lettere dei papyri greco-egizi (sec. II–IV)." Pages 831–46 in *Il Cristianesimo nei secoli.* Vol 2. of *Studi sul cristianesimo antico e moderno in onore di Maria Grazia Mara.* Edited by Manlio Simonetti and Paolo Siniscalco. Roma: Augustinianum, 1995.

_____. *Il cristianesimo in Egitto: lettere private nei papiri dei secoli II–IV.* Biblioteca patristica 32. 2d ed. Fiesole (Firenze): Nardini, 1998.

_____. "Nuovi contributi nelle lettere cristiane su papiro dei primi quattro secoli." Pages 1017–24 in *Atti del XXII Congresso Internazionale di Papirologia. Firenze, 23–29 agosto 1998.* Edited by Isabella Andorlini et al. Firenze: Instituto Papirologico "G. Vitelli," 2001.

Nielsen, Bruce. "A Catalogue of Duplicate Papyri." *ZPE* 129 (1999) 187–214.

Nongbri, Brent. "The Use and Abuse of $\mathfrak{P}^{52}$: Papyrological Pitfalls in the Dating of the Fourth Gospel." *HTR* 98 (2005) 23–48.

Obbink, Dirk. "Imaging Oxyrhynchus." *Egyptian Archaeology* 22 (2003) 3–6.

O'Callaghan, José. "I nomi propri nelle lettere cristiane (Papiri greci del V secolo)." *Aeg* 41 (1961) 17–25.

_____. *Nomina sacra in papyris Graecis saeculi III neotestamentariis.* AnBib 46. Rome: Biblical Institute, 1970.

Oertel, Friedrich. *Die Liturgie: Studien zur ptolemaïschen und kaiserlichen Verwaltung Ägyptens.* Leipzig: Teubner, 1917. Repr. Aalen: Scientia, 1965.

O'Leary, De Lacy. *The Saints of Egypt.* 1937. Amsterdam: Philo Press, 1974.

Osiek, Carolyn and David L. Balch. *Families in the New Testament World: Households and House Churches.* Louisville, Ky.: Westminster John Knox Press, 1997.

Otranto, Rosa. "Alia tempora, alii libri. Notizie ed elenchi di libri cristiani su papiro." *Aeg.* 77 (1997) 101–24. Repr. *Antiche liste di libri su papiro.* Roma: Storia e letteratura, 2000.

Paap, Anton H. R. E. *Nomina sacra in the Greek papyri of the first five centuries A.D.: The sources and some deductions*. Papyrologica Lugduno Batava 8. Leiden: E. J. Brill, 1959.

Padró i Parcerisa, Josep. "Excavaciones en Oxirrinco (1992–2002)." http://www.munimadrid.es/UnidadWeb/Contenidos/EspecialInformativo/TemaCulturaYOcio/Cultura/MuseosMuni/TemploDebod/Actividades/PDFsNilo/oxirrinco.pdf

_____. "Recent Archaeological Work." Pages 129–38 in *Oxyrhynchus: A City and Its Texts*. Edited by A. K. Bowman et al. Graeco-Roman Memoirs 93. London: Egypt Exploration Society, 2007.

Papaconstantinou, Arietta. "La liturgie stationnale à Oxyrhynchos dans la première moitié du 6e siècle. Réédition et commentaire du *POxy* XI 1357." *Revue des études byzantines* 54 (1996) 135–59.

_____. *Le culte des saints en Égypte des Byzantins aux Abbassides. L'apport des inscriptions et des papyrus grecs et coptes*. Le monde byzantin. Paris: CNRS, 2001.

Parlasca, Klaus. "Ein Sarapistempel in Oxyrhynchos?" *ChrEg* 81 (2006) 253–75.

Parsons, Peter. "The Earliest Christian Letter?" Page 289 in *Miscellanea Papyrologica*. Edited by R. Pintaudi. Pap. Flor. 7. Florence: Gonnelli, 1980.

_____. *City of the Sharp-Nosed Fish: Greek Lives in Roman Egypt*. London: Weidenfeld and Nicolson, 2007.

_____. "Copyists of Oxyrhynchus." Pages 262–70 in *Oxyrhynchus: A City and Its Texts*. Edited by A. K. Bowman et al. Graeco-Roman Memoirs 93. London: Egypt Exploration Society, 2007.

Penn, Michael P. *Kissing Christians: Ritual and Community in the Late Ancient Church*. Philadelphia, Pa.: University of Pennsylvania Press, 2005.

Perpillou-Thomas, Françoise. "Artistes et athlètes dans les papyrus grecs d'Égypte." *ZPE* 108 (1995) 225–51.

Pestman, Pieter W. *The New Papyrological Primer.* 2d ed. Leiden: Brill, 1994.

Petrie, W. M. Flinders. *Tombs of the Courtiers and Oxyrhynkhos*. Egyptian Research Account and British School of Archaeology in Egypt 37. London: British School of Archaeology in Egypt, 1925.

Pfeilschifter, Georg. “Oxyrhynchos. Seine Kirchen und Klöster auf Grund der Papyrusfunde.” Pages 248–64 in *Festgabe Alois Knöpfler zur Vollendung des 70. Lebensjahres*. Edited by Heinrich M. Gietl and Georg Pfeilschifter. Freiburg im Breisgau: Herder, 1917.

Pintaudi, Rosario. “The Italian Excavations.” Pages 104–8 in *Oxyrhynchus: A City and Its Texts*. Edited by A. K. Bowman et al. Graeco-Roman Memoirs 93. London: Egypt Exploration Society, 2007.

Pohlsander, Hans A. “The Religious Policy of Decius.” *ANRW* 2.16.3 (1986) 1826–42.

Pomeroy, Sarah B. “Copronyms and the Exposure of Infants in Egypt.” Pages 147–62 in *Studies in Roman Law in Memory of A. Arthur Schiller*. Edited by Roger S. Bagnall and William V. Harris. Leiden: Brill, 1986.

Portmann, Werner. “Zu den Motiven der diokletianischen Christenverfolgung.” *Historia* 39 (1990) 212–48.

Potter, David S. *Prophecy and History in the Crisis of the Roman Empire. A Historical Commentary on the Thirteenth Sibylline Oracle*. Oxford Classical Monographs. Oxford: Clarendon, 1990.

Preisigke, Friedrich. *Namenbuch, enthaltend alle griechischen, lateinischen, ägyptischen, hebräischen, arabischen und sonstigen semitischen und nichtsemitischen Menschennamen, soweit sie in griechischen Urkunden (Papyri, Ostraka, Inschriften, Mumienschildren usw.) Ägyptens sich vorfinden*. Heidelberg: Selbstverlag des Herausgebers, 1922.

Pruneti, Paola. “Papiri della Società Italiana. Lista delle riedizioni dei testi documentari.” *Papyrologica Florentina* 19.2:475–502=*Miscellanea papyrologica*. Edited by Mario Capasso, Gabriella Messeri Savorelli, Rosario Pintaudi. Florence: Gonnelli, 1990.

Rajak, Tessa. “Jews, Pagans and Christians in Late Antique Sardis: Models of Interaction.” Pages 447–62 in eadem. *The Jewish Dialogue with Greece and Rome: Studies in Cultural and Social Interaction*. Boston: Brill, 2002.

Ramelli, Ilaria. “Una delle più antiche lettere cristiane extracanoniche?” *Aeg* 80 (2000) 169–85.

Rapp, Claudia. *Holy Bishops in Late Antiquity. The Nature of Christian Leadership in an Age of Transition*. The Transformation of the Classical Heritage 37. Berkeley: University of California Press, 2005.

Rathbone, Dominic. "Monetisation, Not Price-Inflation, in Third-Century A.D. Egypt?" Pages 321–39 in *Coin Finds and Coin Use in the Roman World. The Thirteenth Oxford Symposium on Coinage and Monetary History*. Edited by Cathy E. King and David G. Wigg. SFMA 10. Berlin: Mann, 1996.

Rémondon, Roger. "L'Église dans la société égyptienne à l'époque byzantine." *ChrEg* 47 (1972) 254–77.

Reymond, Eve A. E., and John W. B. Barns, eds. *Four Martyrdoms from the Pierpont Morgan Coptic Codices*. Oxford: Clarendon, 1973.

Riedmatten, Henri de. *Les actes du procès de Paul de Samosate. Étude sur la christologie du IIIe au IVe siècle*. Paradosis 6. Fribourg en Suisse: St-Paul, 1952.

Rink, Hermann. *Straßen- und Viertelnamen von Oxyrhynchus*. Darmstadt: Winters, 1924.

Rives, James B. "The Decree of Decius and the Religion of Empire." *JRS* 99 (1999) 135–54.

Robert, Louis. "Pas de date 109, mais le chiffre 99, isopséphie de Amen." *Hellenica* 11 (1960) 310–11.

Roberts, Colin H. *An Unpublished Fragment of the Fourth Gospel in the John Rylands Library*. Manchester: Manchester University Press, 1935.

_____. "Two Oxford Papyri." *ZNTW* 37 (1938) 184–88.

_____. "Early Christianity in Egypt: Three Notes." *JEA* 40 (1954) 92–96.

_____. *Manuscript, Society, and Belief in Early Christian Egypt*. London: Oxford University Press, 1979.

Roberts, Colin H., and T. C. Skeat. *The Birth of the Codex*. London: Oxford University Press, 1983.

Robinson, James M. "The Pachomian Monastic Library." *Manuscripts of the Middle East* 4 (1989) 26–40.

Rordorf, D. Willy. "Was wissen wir über die christlichen Gottesdiensträume der vorkonstantinischen Zeit?" *ZNTW* 54 (1963) 110–28.

Rousseau, Philip. *Pachomius: The Making of a Community in Fourth-Century Egypt*. The Transformation of the Classical Heritage 6. Berkeley: University of California Press, 1985.

Routh, Martinus Josephus. *Reliquiae sacrae, sive, auctorum fere iam perditorum secundi tertiique saeculi post Christum natum ad codices mss. recensuit, notisque illustravit, quae supersunt* IV. 2d ed. Oxford 1846. Reprint Hildesheim: Georg Olms, 1974.

Rowlandson, Jane. *Landowners and Tenants in Roman Egypt: The Social Relations of Agriculture in the Oxyrhynchite Nome*. Oxford Classical Monographs. Oxford: Clarendon and Oxford University Press, 1996.

_____. "Oxyrhynchos (el-Behnesa)." Pages 158–61 in *Egypt from Alexander to the Early Christians: An Archaeological and Historical Guide*. Edited by Roger S. Bagnall and Dominic W. Rathbone. Los Angeles: J. Paul Getty Museum, 2004.

_____ et al., eds. *Women and Society in Greek and Roman Egypt*. Cambridge, U.K: Cambridge University Press, 1998.

Rudberg, Gunnar. *Neutestamentlicher Text und Nomina Sacra*. Skrifter utg. af K. Humanistika vetenskaps-samfundet 17:3. Uppsala, Akademiska Bokhandeln, 1915.

Rupprecht, Hans-Albert. *Kleine Einführung in die Papyruskunde*. Die Altertumswissenschaft. Darmstadt: Wissenschaftliche Buchgesellschaft, 1994.

Russell, Norman, and Benedicta Ward. *The Lives of the Desert Fathers. The Historia monachorum in Aegypto*. Cistercian Studies Series 34. London and Oxford: Cistercian Publications, 1981.

Sarefield, Daniel. "The Symbolics of Book Burning: The Establishment of a Christian Ritual of Persecution." Pages 159–73 in *The Early Christian Book*. Edited by William E. Klingshirn and Linda Safran. CUA Studies in Early Christianity. Washington, D.C.: Catholic University of America Press, 2007.

Sarris, Peter. *Economy and Society in the Age of Justinian*. Cambridge: Cambridge University Press, 2006.

Schenk von Stauffenberg, Alexander. "Die antiochenischen Olympien." Pages 412–43 in *Die römische Kaisergeschichte bei Malalas. Griechischer Text der Bücher IX-XII und Untersuchungen*. Stuttgart: Kohlhammer, 1931.

Schenke, Hans-Martin. "Bemerkungen zum P.Hamb. Bil. 1 und zum altfayumischen Dialekt der koptischen Sprache." *Enchoria* 18 (1991) 69–93.

Schmelz, Georg. *Kirchliche Amtsträger im spätantiken Ägypten nach den Aussagen der griechischen und koptischen Papyri und Ostraka*. APF Beiheft 13. München: K. G. Saur, 2002.

Schmidt, Carl. *Fragmente einer Schrift des Märtyrerbischofs Petrus von Alexandrien*. TU 4b. Leipzig: Hinrichs, 1901, 1–50.

Schoedel, William R. *A Commentary on the Letters of Ignatius of Antioch*. Hermeneia. Philadelphia: Fortress, 1985.

Scholl, Reinhold. "'Freilassung unter Freunden' im römischen Ägypten." Pages 159–69 in *Fünfzig Jahre Forschungen zur antiken Sklaverei an der Mainzer Akademie 1950-2000. Miscellanea zum Jubiläum*. Edited by Heinz Bellen and Heinz Heinen. Forschungen zur antiken Sklaverei 35. Mainz: Akademie der Wissenschaften und der Literatur, 2001.

_____. "Liste der bisher publizierten *Libelli*," "Auswertung der Liste der *Libelli*," and "Konkordanz der bisher publizierten *Libelli*." Pages 226–41 in P.Lips.2. 2002.

Schöllgen, Georg. *Anfänge der Professionalisierung des Klerus und das kirchliche Amt in der syrischen Didaskalie*. JAC Ergänzungsband 26. Münster: Aschendorffsche Verlagsbuchhandlung, 1998.

Schrenk, Gottlob. "*ἱερός*." Pages 221–84 in *TWNT* 3. Edited by Gerard Kittel. Stuttgart: Kohlhammer, 1938.

Schulz-Flügel, Eva. ed. *Tyrannius Rufinus, Historia monachorum sive De vita sanctorum patrum*. PTS 34. Berlin: de Gruyter, 1990.

Schwarte, Karl-Heinz. "Die Christengesetze Valerians." Pages 103–63 in *Religion und Gesellschaft in der römischen Kaiserzeit. Kolloquium zu Ehren von Friedrich Vittinghoff*. Edited by Werner Eck. Kölner historische Abhandlungen 35. Köln: Böhlau, 1989.

_____. "Diokletians Christengesetz." Pages 203–40 in *E fontibus haurire. Beiträge zur römischen Geschichte und zu ihren Hilfswissenschaften*. Edited by Rosmarie Günther and Stefan Rebenich. Studien zur Geschichte und Kultur des Altertums 8. Paderborn: Ferdinand Schöningh, 1994.

Scott, James C., *Domination and the Arts of Resistance: Hidden Transcripts*. New Haven: Yale University Press, 1990.

Selinger, Reinhard. *Die Religionspolitik des Kaisers Decius. Anatomie einer Christenverfolgung*. Europäische Hochschulschriften III, 617. Frankfurt am Main: Peter Lang, 1994.

_____. *The Mid-Third Century Persecutions of Decius and Valerian*. Frankfurt am Main: Peter Lang, 2002.

Skeat, Theodore C. "Early Christian Bookproduction: Papyri and Manuscripts." Pages 54–79 in *The West from the Fathers to the Reformation*. Edited by G. W. H. Lampe. Vol. 2 of *The Cambridge History of the Bible*. Cambridge: Cambridge University Press, 1969.

_____. "A Table of Isopsephisms (*P.Oxy*. XLV 3239)." *ZPE* 31 (1978) 45–54.

Sordi, Marta. "I rapporti fra il Cristianesimo e l'impero dai Severi a Gallieno." *ANRW* 2.23.1 (1980) 340–74.

Stanton, Greg R. "The Proposed Earliest Christian Letter on Papyrus and the Origin of the Term Philalellia." *ZPE* 54 (1984) 49–63.

Stark, Rodney. *The Rise of Christianity: A Sociologist Reconsiders History*. Princeton, N.J.: Princeton University Press, 1996.

Stephens, Susan A. "An Epicrisis Return and Other Documentary Fragments from the Yale Collection." *ZPE* 96 (1993) 221–26.

Stewart-Sykes, Alistar. "Catechumenate and Contra-Culture: The Social Process of Catechumenate in Third-Century Africa and Its Development." *St. Vladimir's Theological Quarterly* 47 (2003) 289–306.

Stowers, Stanley Kent. *Letter Writing in Greco-Roman Antiquity*. LEC 5. Philadelphia: Westminster Press, 1986.

Subías Pascual, Eva. *La corona immarcescible. Pintures de l'Antiguitat tardana de la necròpolis alta d'Oxirinc (Mínia, Egipte)*. Sèrie Documenta 1. Tarragona: Institut Català d'Arqueologia Clàssica, 2003.

Teeter, Timothy M. "Christian Letters of Recommendation in the Papyrus Record." *PBR* 9 (1990) 59–69.

_____. "Letters of Recommendation or Letters of Peace?" Pages 954–60 in *Akten des 21. internationalen Papyrologenkongresses, Berlin 1995*. APF Beiheft 3 (1997).

Thomas, Thelma K. *Late Antique Egyptian Funerary Sculpture: Images for This World and for the Next*. Princeton, N.J.: Princeton University Press, 2000.

Tibiletti, Giuseppe. "Proposte di lettura." *Aeg* 57 (1977) 164–65.

_____. *Le lettere private nei papyri greci del III e IV secolo d. C.: tra paganesimo e cristianesimo*. Milano: Vita e Pensiero, 1979.

_____. "Appunti su una lettera di Ioudas (P.Oxy. XLVI, 3314)." Pages 407–11 in *Scritti in onore di Orsolina Montevecchi*. Edited by Edda Bresciani et al. Bologna: Clueb, 1981.

Timm, Stefan. *Das christlich-koptische Ägypten in arabischer Zeit*. 6 vols. Wiesbaden: Reichert, 1984.

Tov, Emanuel. *Scribal Practices and Approaches Reflected in the Texts Found in the Judean Desert*. Studies on the Texts of the Desert of Judah 54. Leiden: Brill, 2004.

Townsend, Philippa. "Who Were the First Christians? Jews, Gentiles and the *Christianoi*." Pages 212–30 in *Heresy and Identity in Late Antiquity*. Edited by Eduard Iricinschi and Holger M. Zellentin. TSAJ 119. Tübingen: Mohr Siebeck, 2008.

Traube, Ludwig. *Nomina Sacra. Versuch einer Geschichte der christlichen Kürzung*. Quellen und Untersuchungen zur lateinischen Philologie des Mittelalters 2. München: Beck, 1907.

Treu, Kurt. "Christliche Empfehlungs-Schemabriefe auf Papyrus." Pages 629–36 in *Zetesis. Album amicorum door vrienden en collega's aangeboden aan Prof. Dr. E. de Strycker.* Antwerpen: De Nederlandsche Boekhandel, 1973.

_____. "P.Berol. 8508: Christliches Empfehlungsschreiben aus dem Einband des koptisch-gnostischen Kodex P.8502." *APF* 28 (1982) 53–54.

Tuckett, Christopher M. "P52 and nomina sacra." *NTS* 47 (2001) 544–48.

_____. "'Nomina sacra': yes and no?" Pages 431–58 in *Biblical Canons*. Edited by Jean-Marie Auwers and Henk Jan de Jonge. BETL 163. Leuven: Leuven University Press, 2003.

Turner, Eric G. "Roman Oxyrhynchus." *JEA* 38 (1952) 78–93.

_____. "Recto and Verso," *JEA* 40 (1954) 102–6.

_____. "Scribes and Scholars of Oxyrhynchus." Pages 141–46 in *Akten des VIII. internationalen Kongresses für Papyrologie, Wien 1955*. MPER N.S. 5. Wien: Roher, 1956.

_____. "Oxyrhynchus and Rome." *HSCP* 79 (1975) 1–24.

_____. *The Typology of the Early Codex*. Haney Foundation Series 18. Philadelphia: University of Pennsylvania Press, 1977.

_____. "The Graeco-Roman Branch." Pages 160–77 in *Excavating in Egypt: The Egypt Exploration Society 1882–1982*. Edited by T. G. H. James. London: British Museum, 1982.

_____. *Greek Manuscripts of the Ancient World*. 2d rev. ed. Edited by P. J. Parsons. London: University of London, Institute of Classical Studies, 1987.

Verbeeck, B. "Dioskoros: dorpshoofd, dichter en notaris." Pages 139–62 in *Familiearchieven uit het land van Pharao. Een bundel artikelen samengesteld naar aanleiding van een serie lezingen van het Papyrologisch Instituut van de Rijksuniversiteit van Leiden in het voorjaar van 1986*. Edited by P. W. Pestman. Zutphen: Terra, 1989.

Vidman, L. "Koppa Theta = Amen in Athen." *ZPE* 16 (1975) 215–16.

Vivian, Tim. *St. Peter of Alexandria, Bishop and Martyr.* Studies in Antiquity and Christianity. Philadelphia: Fortress, 1988.

Vogt, Joseph. *Zur Religiösität der Christenverfolger im Römischen Reich.* Sitzungsberichte der Heidelberger Akademie der Wissenschaften, Philosophisch-historische Klasse. Heidelberg: Carl Winter Universitätsverlag, 1962.

Watts, Edward. "Student Travel to Intellectual Centers: What Was the Attraction?" Pages 13–23 in *Travel, Communication and Geography in Late Antiquity: Sacred and Profane*. Edited by Linda Ellis and Frank L. Kidner. Hants, England: Ashgate, 2004.

Weber, Manfred. "Zur Ausschmückung koptischer Bücher." *Enchoria* 3 (1973) 53–62.

White, John L. *Light from Ancient Letters*. Philadelphia: Fortress, 1986.

White, L. Michael. "Finding the Ties that Bind: Issues from Social Description." Pages 3–22 in *Social Networks in the Early Christian Environment: Issues and Methods for Social History*. Edited by L. Michael White. Semeia 56. Atlanta: Scholars Press, 1992.

_____. "Social Networks: Theoretical Orientation and Historial Applications." Pages 23–36 in *Social Networks in the Early Christian Environment: Issues and Methods for Social History*. Edited by L. Michael White. Semeia 56. Atlanta: Scholars Press, 1992.

_____. *Social Origins of Christian Architecture*. 2 vols. Valley Forge, Pa.: Trinity, 1996–1997.

Whitehorne, John. "P.Oxy. XLIII 3119: A Document of Valerian's Persecution?" *ZPE* 24 (1977) 187–96.

_____. "The Pagan Cults of Roman Oxyrhynchus." *ANRW* 2.18.5 (1995) 3050–91.

Wilkins, Michael J. "Christian." *ABD* I (1992) 925–26.

Winter, John Garrett. *Life and Letters in the Papyri*. Ann Arbor, Mich.: University of Michigan Press, 1933.

Wipszycka, Ewa. *Les ressources et les activités économiques des églises en Égypt du IVe au VIIIe siècle*. Bruxelles: Fondation égyptologique Reine Élisabeth, 1972.

_____. "Remarques sur les lettres privées des IIe-IVe siècles. (A propos d'un livre de M. Naldini)." *JJP* 18 (1974) 203–32.

_____. "La Chiesa nell'Egitto del IV secolo: le strutture ecclesiastiche." Pages 182–201 in vol. 6 of *Miscellanea historiae ecclesiasticae*. Bibliothèque de la revue d'histoire ecclésiastique 67. Bruxelles: Nauwelaerts, 1983.

_____. "Un lecteur qui ne sait pas écrire ou un chrétien qui ne veut pas se souiller? (P.Oxy. XXXIII 2673)." *ZPE* 50 (1983) 117–21.

_____. "La valeur de l'onomastique pour l'histoire de la christianisation de l'Égypte. À propos d'une étude de R. S. Bagnall." *ZPE* 62 (1986) 173–81.

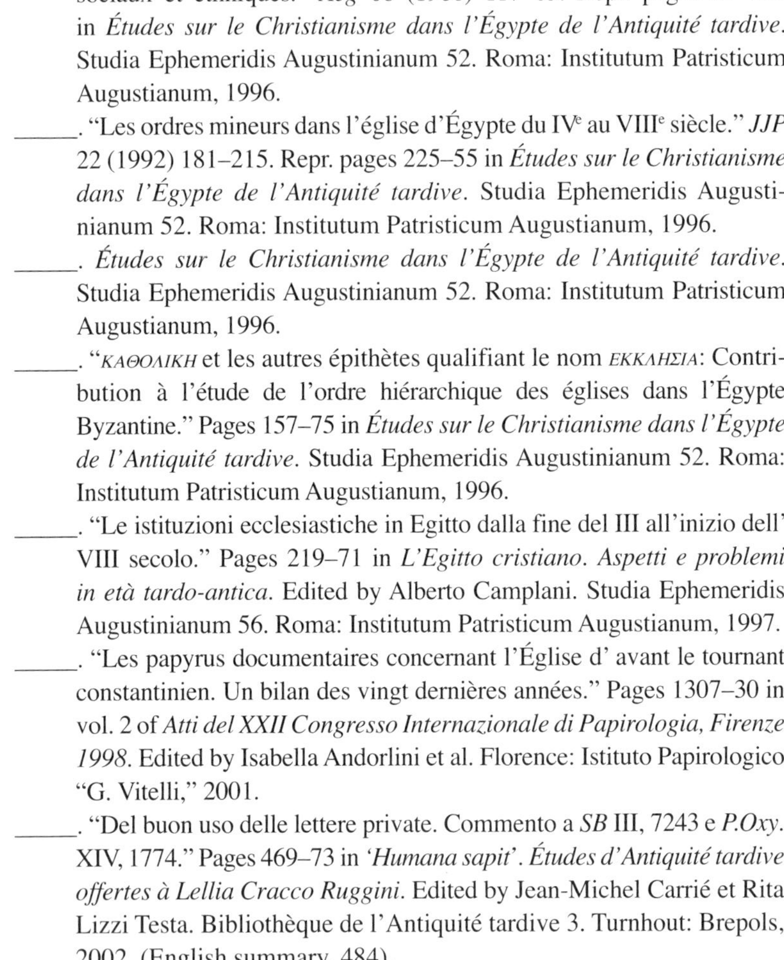

Wipszycka, Ewa. "La christianisation de l'Égypte aux IVe-VIe siècle. Aspects sociaux et ethniques." *Aeg* 68 (1988) 117–65. Repr. pages 63–105 in *Études sur le Christianisme dans l'Égypte de l'Antiquité tardive*. Studia Ephemeridis Augustinianum 52. Roma: Institutum Patristicum Augustianum, 1996.

_____. "Les ordres mineurs dans l'église d'Égypte du IVe au VIIIe siècle." *JJP* 22 (1992) 181–215. Repr. pages 225–55 in *Études sur le Christianisme dans l'Égypte de l'Antiquité tardive*. Studia Ephemeridis Augustinianum 52. Roma: Institutum Patristicum Augustianum, 1996.

_____. *Études sur le Christianisme dans l'Égypte de l'Antiquité tardive*. Studia Ephemeridis Augustinianum 52. Roma: Institutum Patristicum Augustianum, 1996.

_____. "ΚΑΘΟΛΙΚΗ et les autres épithètes qualifiant le nom ΕΚΚΛΗΣΙΑ: Contribution à l'étude de l'ordre hiérarchique des églises dans l'Égypte Byzantine." Pages 157–75 in *Études sur le Christianisme dans l'Égypte de l'Antiquité tardive*. Studia Ephemeridis Augustinianum 52. Roma: Institutum Patristicum Augustianum, 1996.

_____. "Le istituzioni ecclesiastiche in Egitto dalla fine del III all'inizio dell' VIII secolo." Pages 219–71 in *L'Egitto cristiano. Aspetti e problemi in età tardo-antica*. Edited by Alberto Camplani. Studia Ephemeridis Augustinianum 56. Roma: Institutum Patristicum Augustianum, 1997.

_____. "Les papyrus documentaires concernant l'Église d' avant le tournant constantinien. Un bilan des vingt dernières années." Pages 1307–30 in vol. 2 of *Atti del XXII Congresso Internazionale di Papirologia, Firenze 1998*. Edited by Isabella Andorlini et al. Florence: Istituto Papirologico "G. Vitelli," 2001.

_____. "Del buon uso delle lettere private. Commento a *SB* III, 7243 e *P.Oxy.* XIV, 1774." Pages 469–73 in *'Humana sapit'. Études d'Antiquité tardive offertes à Lellia Cracco Ruggini*. Edited by Jean-Michel Carrié et Rita Lizzi Testa. Bibliothèque de l'Antiquité tardive 3. Turnhout: Brepols, 2002. (English summary, 484).

Worp, Klaas A. "A Checklist of Bishops in Byzantine Egypt (A.D. 325–ca. 750)." *ZPE* 100 (1994) 283–318.

Yiftach-Firanko, Uri. *Marriage and Marital Arrangements. A History of the Greek Marriage Document in Egypt. 4th century BCE–4th century CE*. Münchener Beiträge zur Papyrusforschung und antiken Rechtsgeschichte 93. München: C. H. Beck, 2003.

Youtie, Herbert Chayyim."AGRAMMATOS: An Aspect of Greek Society in Egypt." Pages 611–27 in vol. 2 of *Scriptiunculae*. Amsterdam: Adolf M. Hakkert, 1973.

Zucker, Friedrich. "Priester und Tempel in Ägypten in den Zeiten nach der decianischen Christenverfolgung." Pages 167–74 in *Akten des VIII. internationalen Kongresses für Papyrologie, Wien 1955*. MPER N.S. 5. Wien: Roher, 1956.

Index of Primary Sources

Biblical texts

Apostolic Fathers

Ancient Authors

Papyri

Index of Authors and Subjects

Harvard Theological Studies

61. Schifferdecker, Kathryn. *Out of the Whirlwind: Creation Theology in the Book of Job*, 2008.
60. Luijendijk, AnneMarie. *Greetings in the Lord: Early Christians and the Oxyrhynchus Papyri*, 2008.
58. Pearson, Lori. *Beyond Essence: Ernst Troeltsch as Historian and Theorist of Christianity*, 2008.
57. Hills, Julian V. *Tradition and Composition in the* Epistula Apostolorum, 2008.
56. Nickelsburg, George W. E. *Resurrection, Immortality, and Eternal Life in Intertestamental Judaism and Early Christianity.* Expanded Edition, 2006.
55. Johnson-DeBaufre, Melanie. *Jesus Among Her Children: Q, Eschatology, and the Construction of Christian Origins*, 2005.
54. Hall, David D. *The Faithful Shepherd: A History of the New England Ministry in the Seventeenth Century*, 2006.
53. Schowalter, Daniel N., and Steven J. Friesen, eds. *Urban Religion in Roman Corinth: Interdisciplinary Approaches,* 2004.
52. Nasrallah, Laura. *"An Ecstasy of Folly": Prophecy and Authority in Early Christianity*, 2003.
51. Brock, Ann Graham. *Mary Magdalene, The First Apostle: The Struggle for Authority,* 2003.
50. Trost, Theodore Louis. *Douglas Horton and the Ecumenical Impulse in American Religion*, 2002.
49. Huang, Yong. *Religious Goodness and Political Rightness: Beyond the Liberal-Communitarian Debate*, 2001.
48. Rossing, Barbara R. *The Choice between Two Cities: Whore, Bride, and Empire in the Apocalypse*, 1999.
47. Skedros, James Constantine. *Saint Demetrios of Thessaloniki: Civic Patron and Divine Protector, 4th–7th Centuries* C.E., 1999.
46. Koester, Helmut, ed. *Pergamon, Citadel of the Gods: Archaeological Record, Literary Description, and Religious Development*, 1998.
45. Kittredge, Cynthia Briggs. *Community and Authority: The Rhetoric of Obedience in the Pauline Tradition*, 1998.
44. Lesses, Rebecca Macy. *Ritual Practices to Gain Power: Angels, Incantations, and Revelation in Early Jewish Mysticism*, 1998.
43. Guenther-Gleason, Patricia E. *On Schleiermacher and Gender Politics*, 1997.
42. White, L. Michael. *The Social Origins of Christian Architecture* (2 vols.), 1997.
41. Koester, Helmut, ed. *Ephesos, Metropolis of Asia: An Interdisciplinary Approach to its Archaeology, Religion, and Culture*, 1995.

40. Guider, Margaret Eletta. *Daughters of Rahab: Prostitution and the Church of Liberation in Brazil*, 1995.

39. Schenkel, Albert F. *The Rich Man and the Kingdom: John D. Rockefeller, Jr., and the Protestant Establishment*, 1995.

38. Hutchison, William R. and Hartmut Lehmann, eds. *Many Are Chosen: Divine Election and Western Nationalism*, 1994.

37. Lubieniecki, Stanislas. *History of the Polish Reformation and Nine Related Documents*. Translated and interpreted by George Huntston Williams, 1995.

– Davidovich, Adina. *Religion as a Province of Meaning: The Kantian Foundations of Modern Theology*, 1993.

36. Thiemann, Ronald F., ed. *The Legacy of H. Richard Niebuhr*, 1991.

35. Hobbs, Edward C., ed. *Bultmann, Retrospect and Prospect: The Centenary Symposium at Wellesley*, 1985.

34. Cameron, Ron. *Sayings Traditions in the Apocryphon of James*, 1984. Reprinted, 2004,

33. Blackwell, Albert L. *Schleiermacher's Early Philosophy of Life: Determinism, Freedom, and Phantasy*, 1982.

32. Gibson, Elsa. *The "Christians for Christians" Inscriptions of Phrygia: Greek Texts, Translation and Commentary*, 1978.

31. Bynum, Caroline Walker. Docere Verbo et Exemplo*: An Aspect of Twelfth-Century Spirituality*, 1979.

30. Williams, George Huntston, ed. *The Polish Brethren: Documentation of the History and Thought of Unitarianism in the Polish-Lithuanian Commonwealth and in the Diaspora 1601–1685*, 1980.

29. Attridge, Harold W. *First-Century Cynicism in the Epistles of Heraclitus*, 1976.

28. Williams, George Huntston, Norman Pettit, Winfried Herget, and Sargent Bush, Jr., eds. *Thomas Hooker: Writings in England and Holland, 1626–1633*, 1975.

27. Preus, James Samuel. *Carlstadt's* Ordinaciones *and Luther's Liberty: A Study of the Wittenberg Movement, 1521–22*, 1974.

26. Nickelsburg, George W. E. *Resurrection, Immortality, and Eternal Life in Inter-testamental Judaism*, 1972.

25. Worthley, Harold Field. *An Inventory of the Records of the Particular (Congregational) Churches of Massachusetts Gathered 1620–1805*, 1970.

24. Yamauchi, Edwin M. *Gnostic Ethics and Mandaean Origins*, 1970.

23. Yizhar, Michael. *Bibliography of Hebrew Publications on the Dead Sea Scrolls 1948–1964*, 1967.

22. Albright, William Foxwell. *The Proto-Sinaitic Inscriptions and Their Decipherment*, 1966.

21. Dow, Sterling, and Robert F. Healey. *A Sacred Calendar of Eleusis*, 1965.

20. Sundberg, Jr., Albert C. *The Old Testament of the Early Church*, 1964.
19. Cranz, Ferdinand Edward. *An Essay on the Development of Luther's Thought on Justice, Law, and Society*, 1959.
18. Williams, George Huntston, ed. *The Norman Anonymous of 1100 A.D.: Towards the Identification and Evaluation of the So-Called Anonymous of York*, 1951.
17. Lake, Kirsopp, and Silva New, eds. *Six Collations of New Testament Manuscripts*, 1932.
16. Wilbur, Earl Morse, trans. *The Two Treatises of Servetus on the Trinity: On the Errors of the Trinity, 7 Books, A.D. 1531. Dialogues on the Trinity, 2 Books. On the Righteousness of Christ's Kingdom, 4 Chapters, A.D. 1532*, 1932.
15. Casey, Robert Pierce, ed. Serapion of Thmuis's *Against the Manichees*, 1931.
14. Ropes, James Hardy. *The Singular Problem of the Epistles to the Galatians*, 1929.
13. Smith, Preserved. *A Key to the Colloquies of Erasmus*, 1927.
12. Spyridon of the Laura and Sophronios Eustratiades. *Catalogue of the Greek Manuscripts in the Library of the Laura on Mount Athos,* 1925.
11. Sophronios Eustratiades and Arcadios of Vatopedi. *Catalogue of the Greek Manuscripts in the Library of the Monastery of Vatopedi on Mt. Athos*, 1924.
10. Conybeare, Frederick C. *Russian Dissenters*, 1921.
9. Burrage, Champlin, ed. *An Answer to John Robinson of Leyden by a Puritan Friend: Now First Published from a Manuscript of A.D. 1609*, 1920.
8. Emerton, Ephraim. *The* Defensor pacis *of Marsiglio of Padua: A Critical Study*, 1920,
7. Bacon, Benjamin W. *Is Mark a Roman Gospel?* 1919.
6. Cadbury, Henry Joel. 2 vols. *The Style and Literary Method of Luke*, 1920.
5. Marriott, G. L., ed. Macarii Anecdota*: Seven Unpublished Homilies of Macarius*, 1918.
4. Edmunds, Charles Carroll and William Henry Paine Hatch. *The Gospel Manuscripts of the General Theological Seminary*, 1918.
3. Arnold, William Rosenzweig. *Ephod and Ark: A Study in the Records and Religion of the Ancient Hebrews*, 1917.
2. Hatch, William Henry Paine. *The Pauline Idea of Faith in its Relation to Jewish and Hellenistic Religion*, 1917.

1. Torrey, Charles Cutler. *The Composition and Date of Acts*, 1916.

Harvard Dissertations in Religion

In 1993, Harvard Theological Studies absorbed the Harvard Dissertations in Religion series.

31. Baker-Fletcher, Garth. *Somebodyness: Martin Luther King, Jr. and the Theory of Dignity*, 1993.
30. Soneson, Jerome Paul. *Pragmatism and Pluralism: John Dewey's Significance for Theology*, 1993.
29. Crabtree, Harriet. *The Christian Life: The Traditional Metaphors and Contemporary Theologies*, 1991.
28. Schowalter, Daniel N. *The Emperor and the Gods: Images from the Time of Trajan*, 1993.
27. Valantasis, Richard. *Spiritual Guides of the Third Century: A Semiotic Study of the Guide-Disciple Relationship in Christianity, Neoplatonism, Hermetism, and Gnosticism*, 1991.
26. Wills, Lawrence Mitchell. *The Jews in the Court of the Foreign King: Ancient Jewish Court Legends*, 1990.
25. Massa, Mark Stephen. *Charles Augustus Briggs and the Crisis of Historical Criticism*, 1990.
24. Hills, Julian Victor. *Tradition and Composition in the* Epistula apostolorum, 1990.
23. Bowe, Barbara Ellen. *A Church in Crisis: Ecclesiology and Paraenesis in Clement of Rome*, 1988.
22. Bisbee, Gary A. *Pre-Decian Acts of Martyrs and* Commentarii, 1988.
21. Ray, Stephen Alan. *The Modern Soul: Michel Foucault and the Theological Discourse of Gordon Kaufman and David Tracy*, 1987.
20. MacDonald, Dennis Ronald. *There Is No Male and Female: The Fate of a Dominical Saying in Paul and Gnosticism*, 1987.
19. Davaney, Sheila Greeve. *Divine Power: A Study of Karl Barth and Charles Hartshorne*, 1986.
18. LaFargue, J. Michael. *Language and Gnosis: The Opening Scenes of the Acts of Thomas*, 1985.
12. Layton, Bentley, ed. *The Gnostic Treatise on Resurrection from Nag Hammadi*, 1979.
11. Ryan, Patrick J. *Imale: Yoruba Participation in the Muslim Tradition: A Study of Clerical Piety*, 1977.
10. Neevel, Jr., Walter G. *Yāmuna's* Vedānta *and* Pāñcarātra*: Integrating the Classical and the Popular*, 1977.
9. Yarbro Collins, Adela. *The Combat Myth in the Book of Revelation*, 1976.

8. Veatch, Robert M. *Value-Freedom in Science and Technology: A Study of the Importance of the Religious, Ethical, and Other Socio-Cultural Factors in Selected Medical Decisions Regarding Birth Control*, 1976.
7. Attridge, Harold W. *The Interpretation of Biblical History in the* Antiquitates judaicae *of Flavius Josephus*, 1976.
6. Trakatellis, Demetrios C. *The Pre-Existence of Christ in the Writings of Justin Martyr*, 1976.
5. Green, Ronald Michael. *Population Growth and Justice: An Examination of Moral Issues Raised by Rapid Population Growth*, 1975.
4. Schrader, Robert W. *The Nature of Theological Argument: A Study of Paul Tillich*, 1976.
3. Christensen, Duane L. *Transformations of the War Oracle in Old Testament Prophecy: Studies in the Oracles Against the Nations*, 1975.
2. Williams, Sam K. *Jesus' Death as Saving Event: The Background and Origin of a Concept*, 1972.
1. Smith, Jane I. *An Historical and Semantic Study of the Term "Islām" as Seen in a Sequence of Qur'an Commentaries*, 1970.